鳥 山 明

Our dog, Mato (short for "Matroshka"), whose picture was in **Dragon Ball** Vol. 13, has died. She was 10 years old. She got kidney disease about six months ago. I devoted myself to taking her to the vet regularly for her subcutaneous fluid treatments, even when I had deadlines, even when I had a cold. Mato put up a good fight, but she just couldn't go on anymore. Our saving grace was the neighborhood vet, who showed such compassion in trying to help her. Thank you so much.
    –*Akira Toriyama, 1995*

Widely known all over the world for his playful, innovative storytelling and humorous, distinctive art style, **Dragon Ball** creator Akira Toriyama is also known in his native Japan for the wildly popular **Dr. Slump**, his previous manga series about the adventures of a mad scientist and his android "daughter." His hit series **Dragon Ball** ran from 1984 to 1995 in Shueisha's **Weekly Shonen Jump** magazine. He is also known for his design work on video games such as **Dragon Warrior**, **Chrono Trigger** and **Tobal No. 1**. His recent manga works include **Cowa!**, **Kajika**, **Sand Land**, **Neko Majin**, and a children's book, **Toccio the Angel**. He lives with his family in Japan.

DRAGON BALL Z VOL.24
The SHONEN JUMP Manga Edition

STORY AND ART BY
AKIRA TORIYAMA

English Adaptation/Gerard Jones
Translation/Lillian Olsen
Touch-up Art & Lettering/Wayne Truman
Design/Sean Lee
Editor/Jason Thompson

Editor in Chief, Books/Alvin Lu
Editor in Chief, Magazines/Marc Weidenbaum
VP of Publishing Licensing/Rika Inouye
VP of Sales/Gonzalo Ferreyra
Sr. VP of Marketing/Liza Coppola
Publisher/Hyoe Narita

In the original Japanese edition, DRAGON BALL and DRAGON BALL Z
are known collectively as the 42-volume series DRAGON BALL. The
English DRAGON BALL Z was originally volumes 17-42 of the Japanese
DRAGON BALL.

Printed in the U.S.A.

Published by VIZ Media, LLC
P.O. Box 77010
San Francisco, CA 94107

SHONEN JUMP Manga Edition
10 9 8 7 6 5 4 3
First printing, January 2006
Third printing, October 2007

PARENTAL ADVISORY
DRAGON BALL Z is rated A for all Ages
and is recommended for any age group.
Contains violence.

ratings.viz.com

THE WORLD'S
MOST POPULAR MANGA

www.viz.com

www.shonenjump.com

SHONEN JUMP MANGA

DRAGON BALL Z

Vol. 24

DB: 40 of 42

STORY AND ART BY
AKIRA TORIYAMA

THE MAIN CHARACTERS

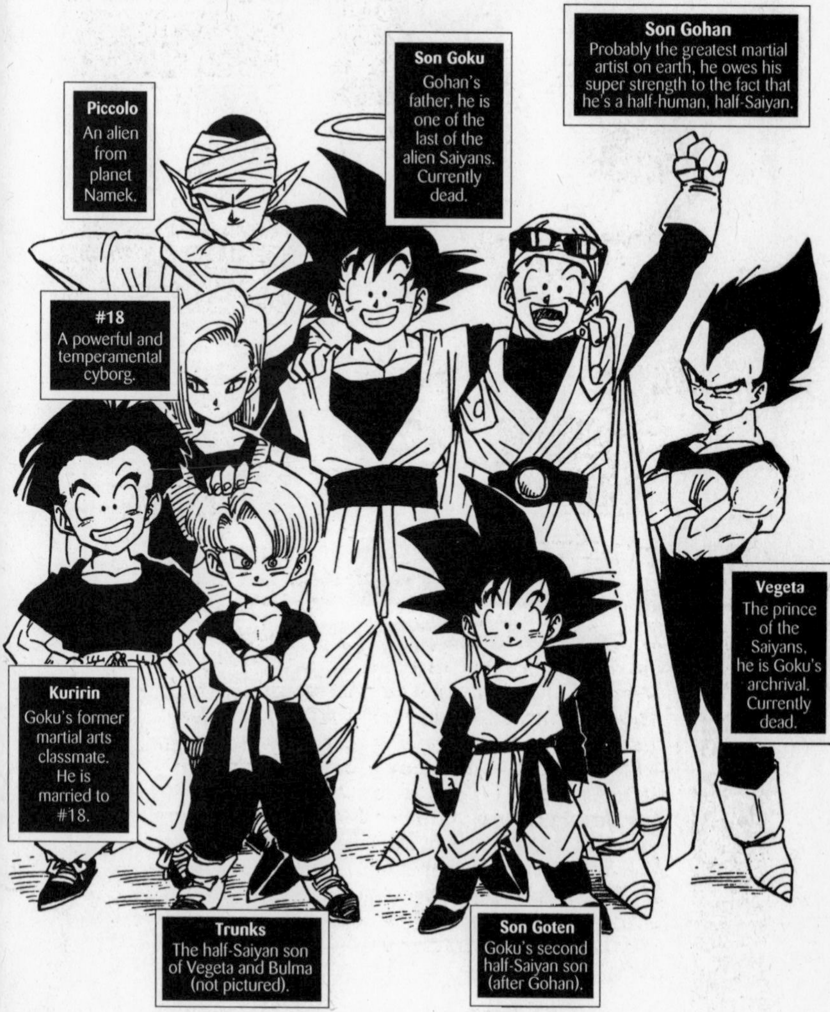
Son Gohan
Probably the greatest martial artist on earth, he owes his super strength to the fact that he's a half-human, half-Saiyan.
Son Goku
Gohan's father, he is one of the last of the alien Saiyans. Currently dead.
Piccolo
An alien from planet Namek.
#18
A powerful and temperamental cyborg.
Vegeta
The prince of the Saiyans, he is Goku's archrival. Currently dead.
Kuririn
Goku's former martial arts classmate. He is married to #18.
Son Goten
Goku's second half-Saiyan son (after Gohan).
Trunks
The half-Saiyan son of Vegeta and Bulma (not pictured).

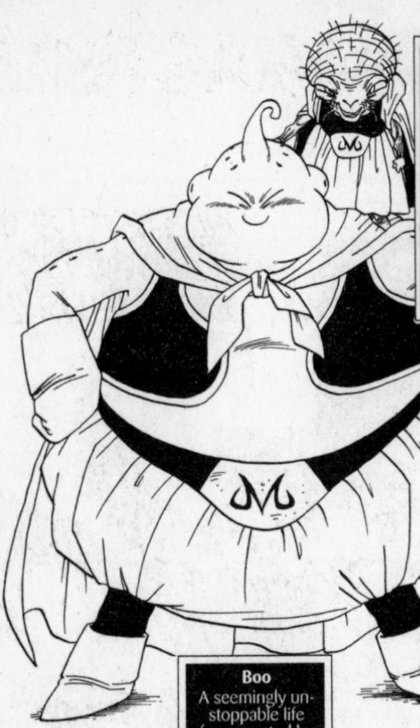

Bobbidi
The son of Bibbidi the Warlock, who fought Kaiô-shin thousands of years ago.

Boo
A seemingly unstoppable life form created by Bobbidi's father.

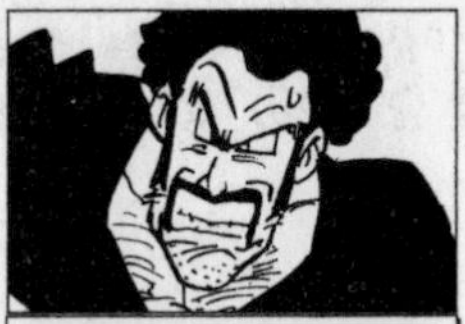

Hercule
An ordinary wrestler who became world-famous when he took credit for defeating Cell.

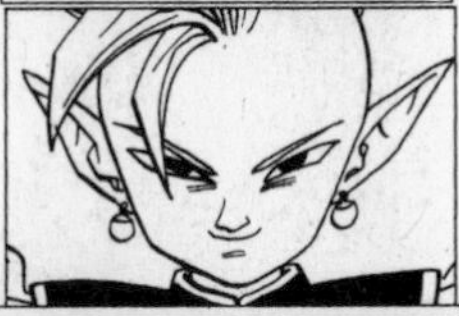

Kaiô-shin
The "Lord of Lords," he is the supreme deity of the Dragon Ball universe. He came to earth to stop Bobbidi.

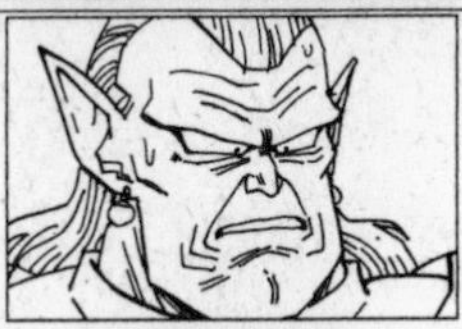

Kibito
Kaiô-shin's assistant.

Son Goku was earth's greatest hero, and the Dragon Balls, which can grant any wish, were earth's greatest treasure. After many adventures, Goku finally died saving the world from the monstrous Cell, but he left behind two sons, Gohan and Goten. Now the earth has been invaded by a new enemy: Bobbidi the Warlock and his terrible servant, Boo the Djinn. Gohan was the first to challenge Boo, but he was defeated and spirited away to an alien planet by Kaiô-shin. Vegeta was the second to challenge Boo, and died. Now, Bobbidi and Boo rampage across the planet, in search of Piccolo, Goten and Trunks, the last living heroes who might be able to oppose them. But even though he's not alive, Goku is back from heaven with a special day pass...
and he's ready to fight!

DRAGON BALL Z 24

CON TENTS PAGE

DRAGON BALL ドラゴンボール

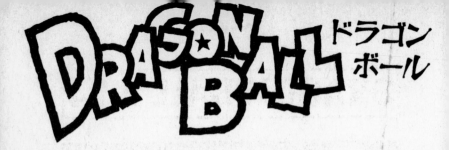

DBZ:279 · Goku Meets Boo!!

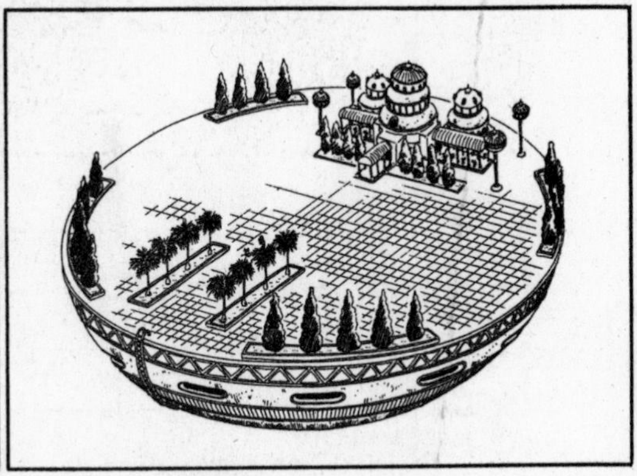

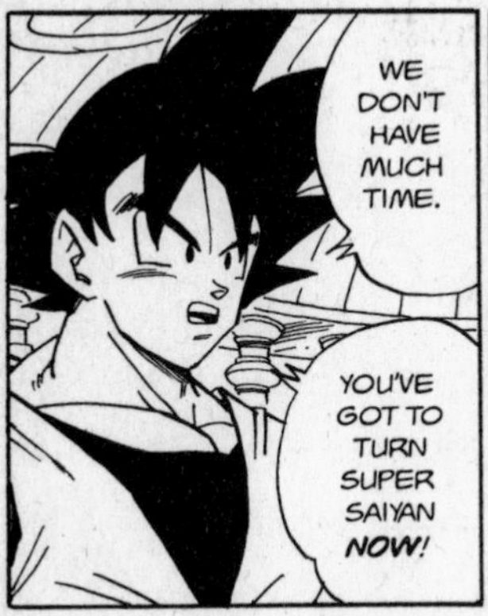
WE DON'T HAVE MUCH TIME.
YOU'VE GOT TO TURN SUPER SAIYAN *NOW*!

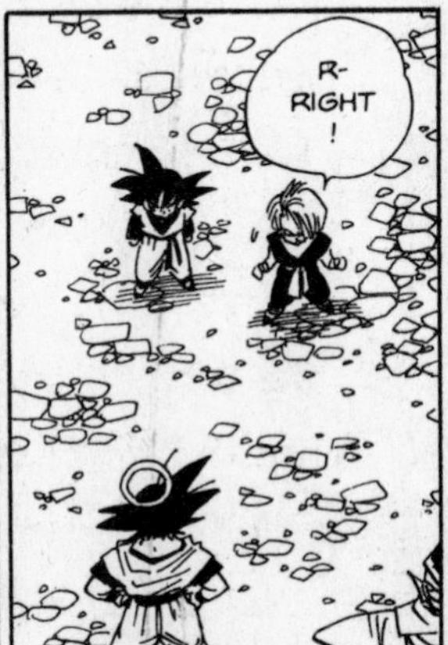
R-RIGHT!

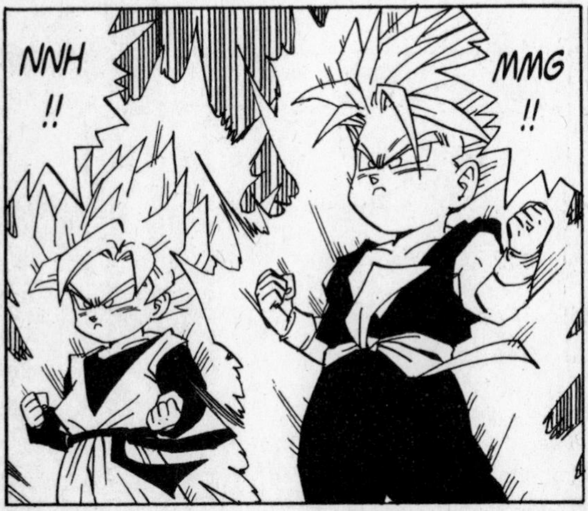
MMG!!
NNH!!

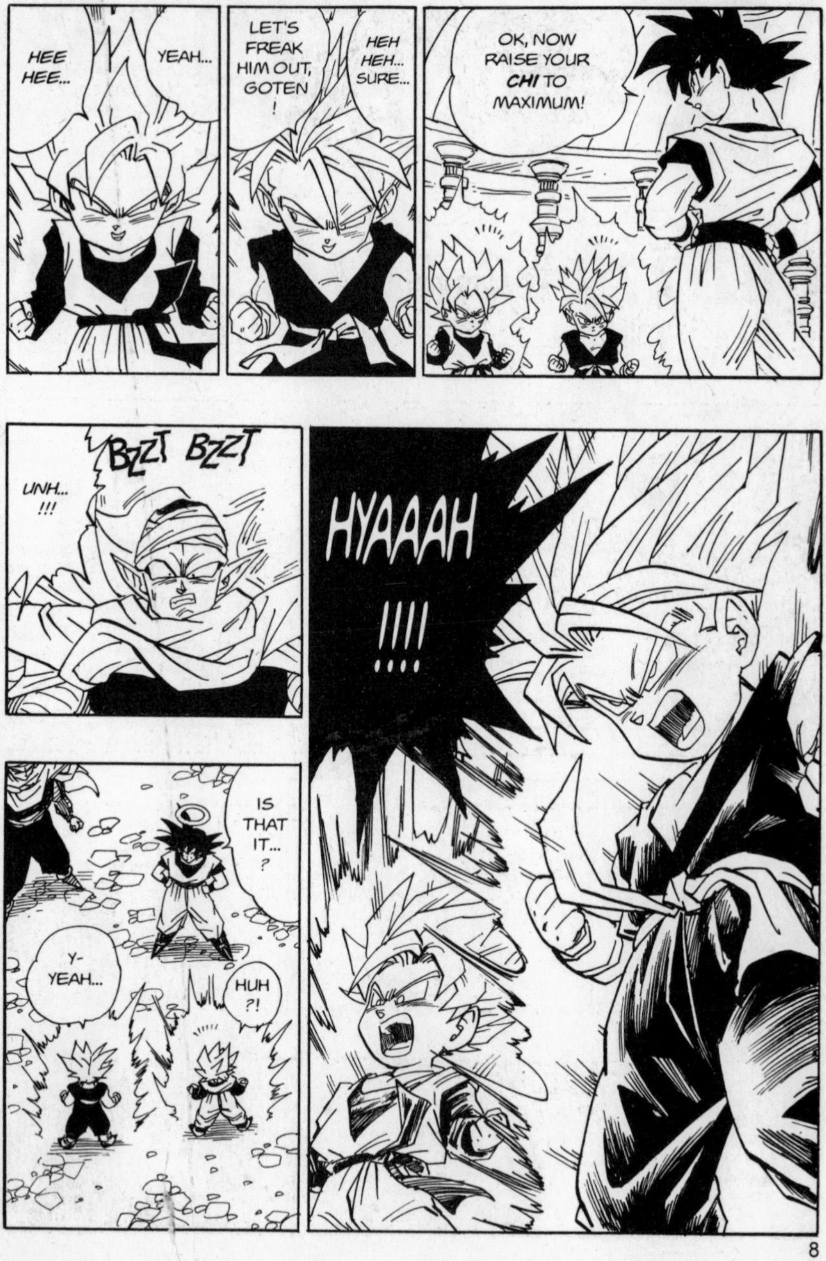
OK, NOW RAISE YOUR **CHI** TO MAXIMUM!
HEH HEH... SURE...
LET'S FREAK HIM OUT, GOTEN!
YEAH...
HEE HEE...
HYAAAH !!!!!!!!
BZZT BZZT
UNH... !!!
IS THAT IT...?
HUH ?!
Y-YEAH...

READ THIS WAY

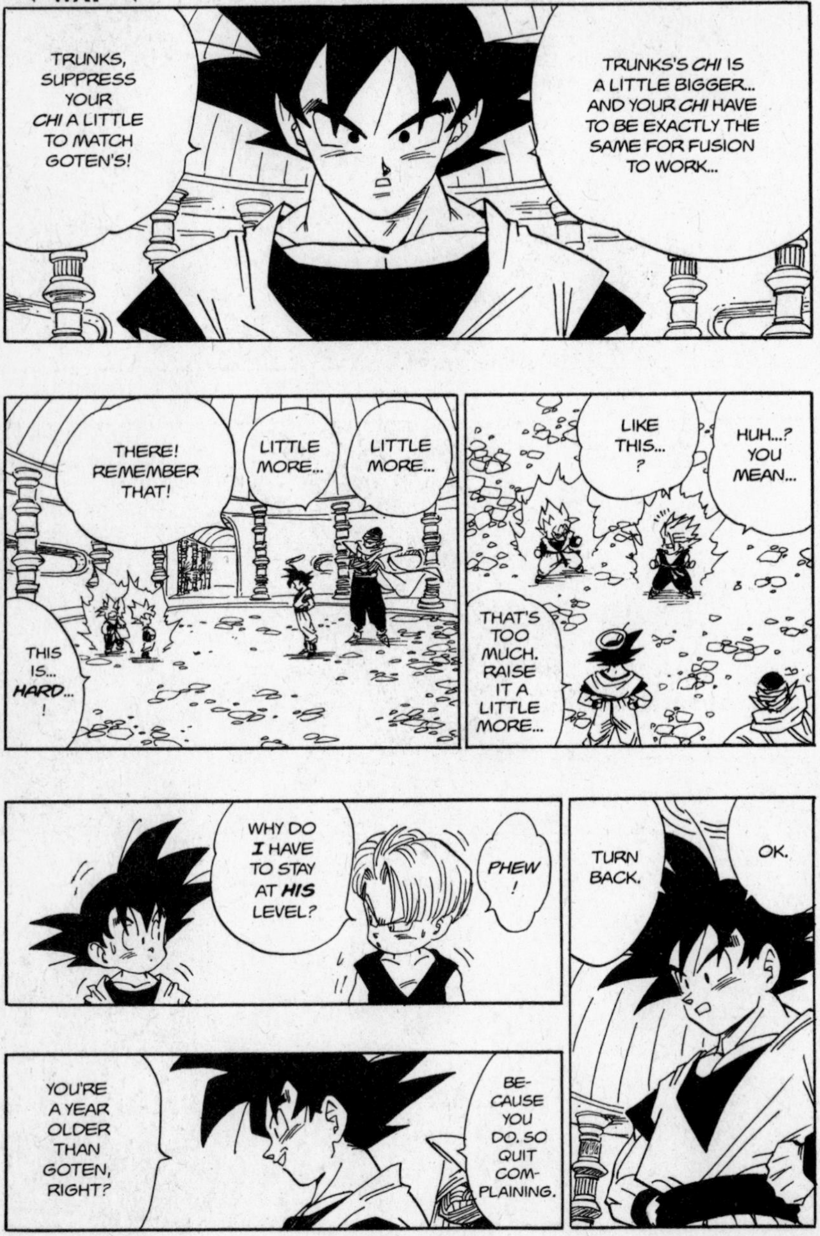

TRUNKS'S CHI IS A LITTLE BIGGER... AND YOUR CHI HAVE TO BE EXACTLY THE SAME FOR FUSION TO WORK...
TRUNKS, SUPPRESS YOUR CHI A LITTLE TO MATCH GOTEN'S!
HUH...? YOU MEAN...
LIKE THIS... ?
THAT'S TOO MUCH. RAISE IT A LITTLE MORE...
LITTLE MORE...
LITTLE MORE...
THERE! REMEMBER THAT!
THIS IS... HARD... !
OK.
TURN BACK.
PHEW !
WHY DO I HAVE TO STAY AT HIS LEVEL?
BE-CAUSE YOU DO. SO QUIT COM-PLAINING.
YOU'RE A YEAR OLDER THAN GOTEN, RIGHT?

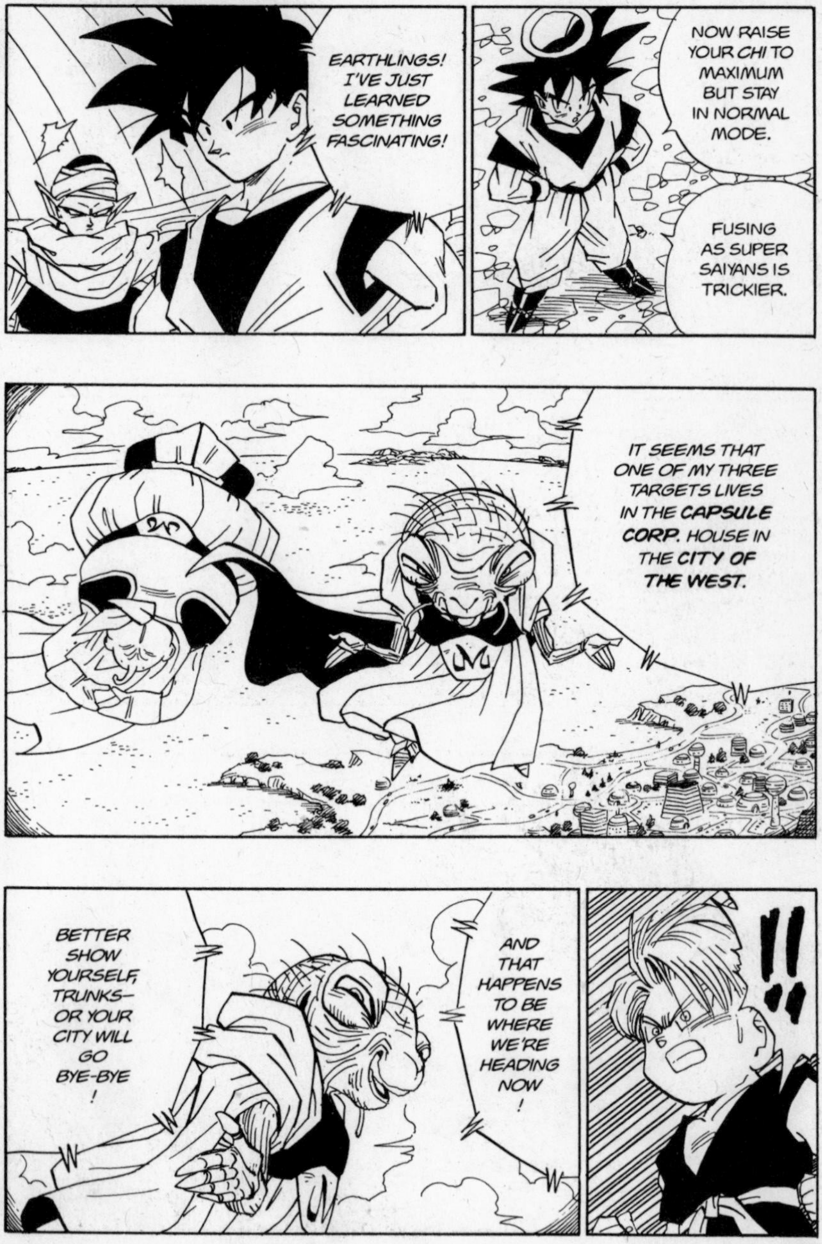
NOW RAISE YOUR CHI TO MAXIMUM BUT STAY IN NORMAL MODE.
FUSING AS SUPER SAIYANS IS TRICKIER.
EARTHLINGS! I'VE JUST LEARNED SOMETHING FASCINATING!
IT SEEMS THAT ONE OF MY THREE TARGETS LIVES IN THE CAPSULE CORP. HOUSE IN THE CITY OF THE WEST.
!!
AND THAT HAPPENS TO BE WHERE WE'RE HEADING NOW!
BETTER SHOW YOURSELF, TRUNKS— OR YOUR CITY WILL GO BYE-BYE!

READ THIS WAY

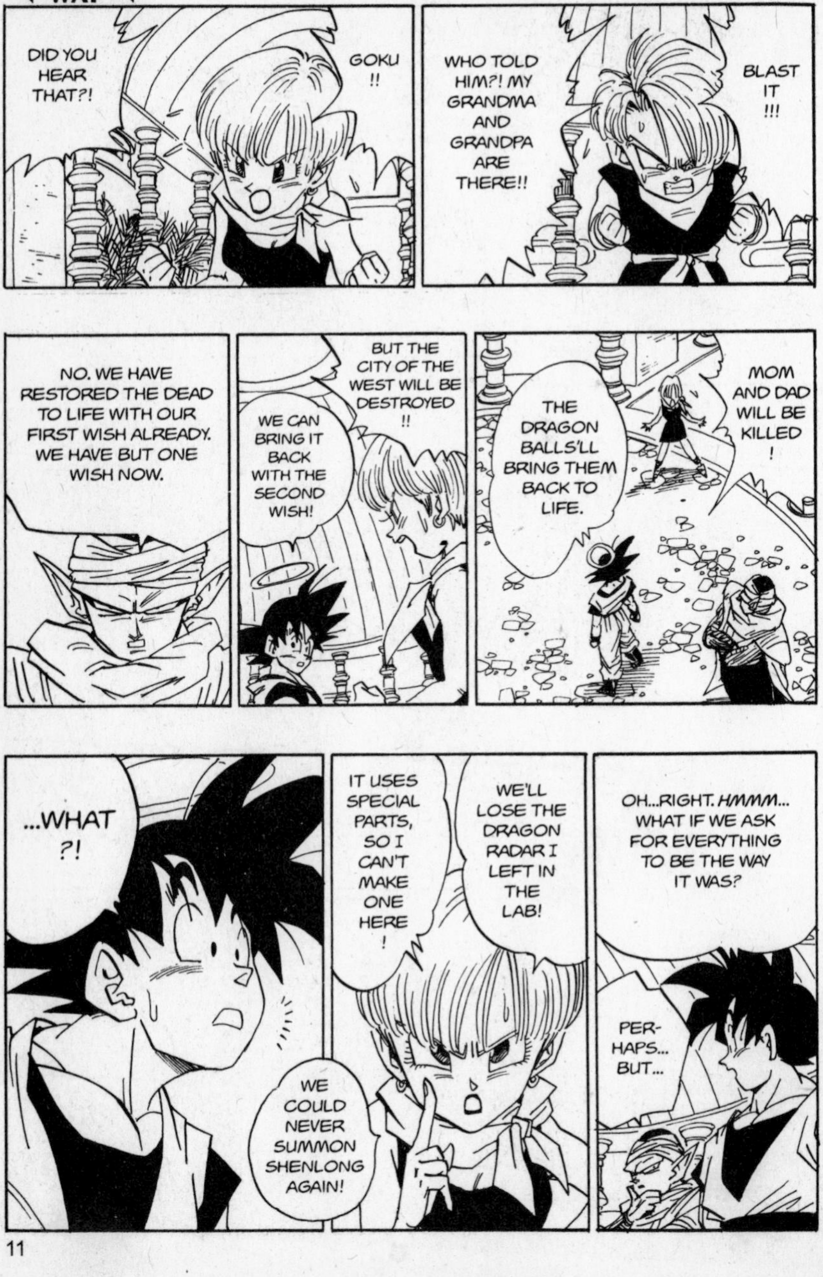
BLAST IT !!!
WHO TOLD HIM?! MY GRANDMA AND GRANDPA ARE THERE!!
GOKU !!
DID YOU HEAR THAT?!
MOM AND DAD WILL BE KILLED !
THE DRAGON BALLS'LL BRING THEM BACK TO LIFE.
BUT THE CITY OF THE WEST WILL BE DESTROYED !!
WE CAN BRING IT BACK WITH THE SECOND WISH!
NO. WE HAVE RESTORED THE DEAD TO LIFE WITH OUR FIRST WISH ALREADY. WE HAVE BUT ONE WISH NOW.
OH...RIGHT. *HMMM*... WHAT IF WE ASK FOR EVERYTHING TO BE THE WAY IT WAS?
PER-HAPS... BUT...
WE'LL LOSE THE DRAGON RADAR I LEFT IN THE LAB!
IT USES SPECIAL PARTS, SO I CAN'T MAKE ONE HERE !
WE COULD NEVER SUMMON SHENLONG AGAIN!
...WHAT ?!

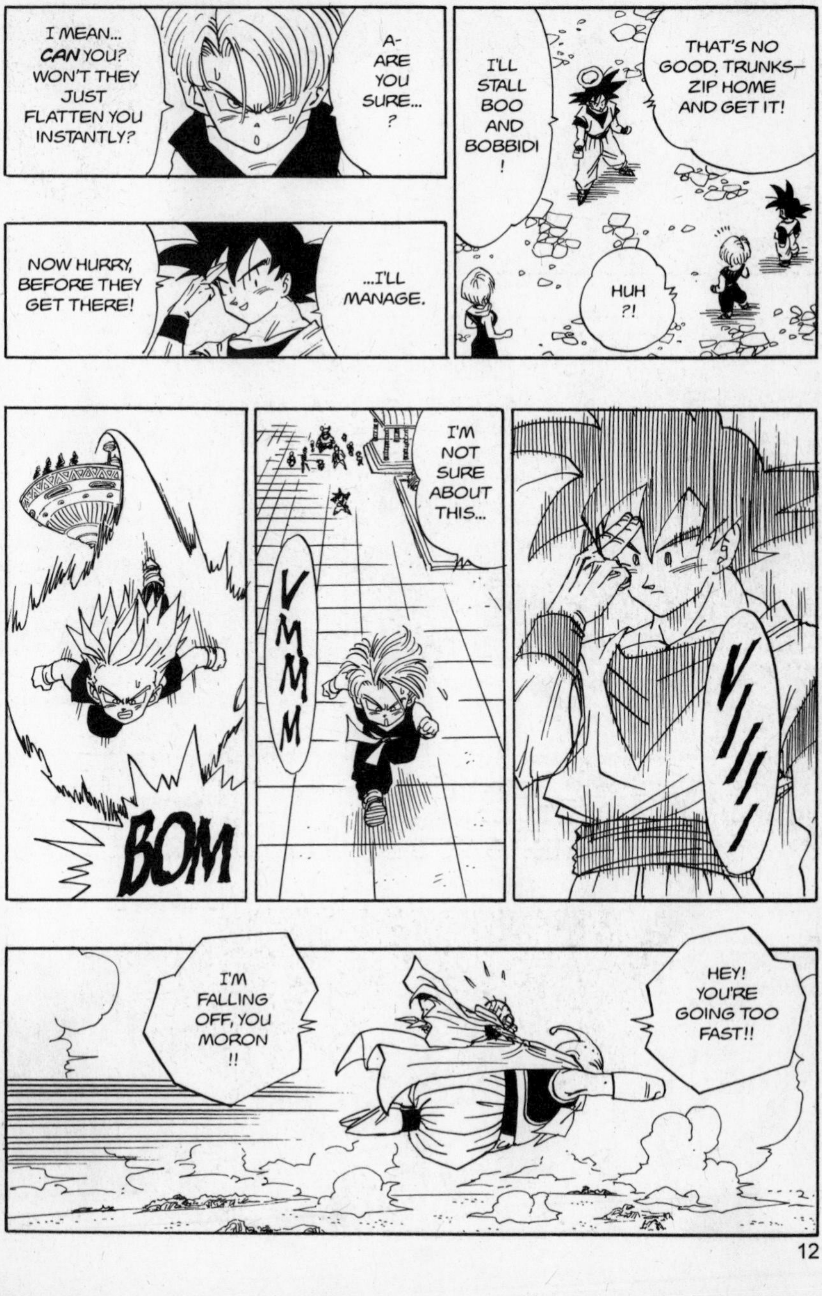
THAT'S NO GOOD. TRUNKS— ZIP HOME AND GET IT!
I'LL STALL BOO AND BOBBIDI!
HUH?!
A-ARE YOU SURE...?
I MEAN... **CAN** YOU? WON'T THEY JUST FLATTEN YOU INSTANTLY?
...I'LL MANAGE.
NOW HURRY, BEFORE THEY GET THERE!
I'M NOT SURE ABOUT THIS...
VMMM
BOM
HEY! YOU'RE GOING TOO FAST!!
I'M FALLING OFF, YOU MORON!!

READ THIS WAY

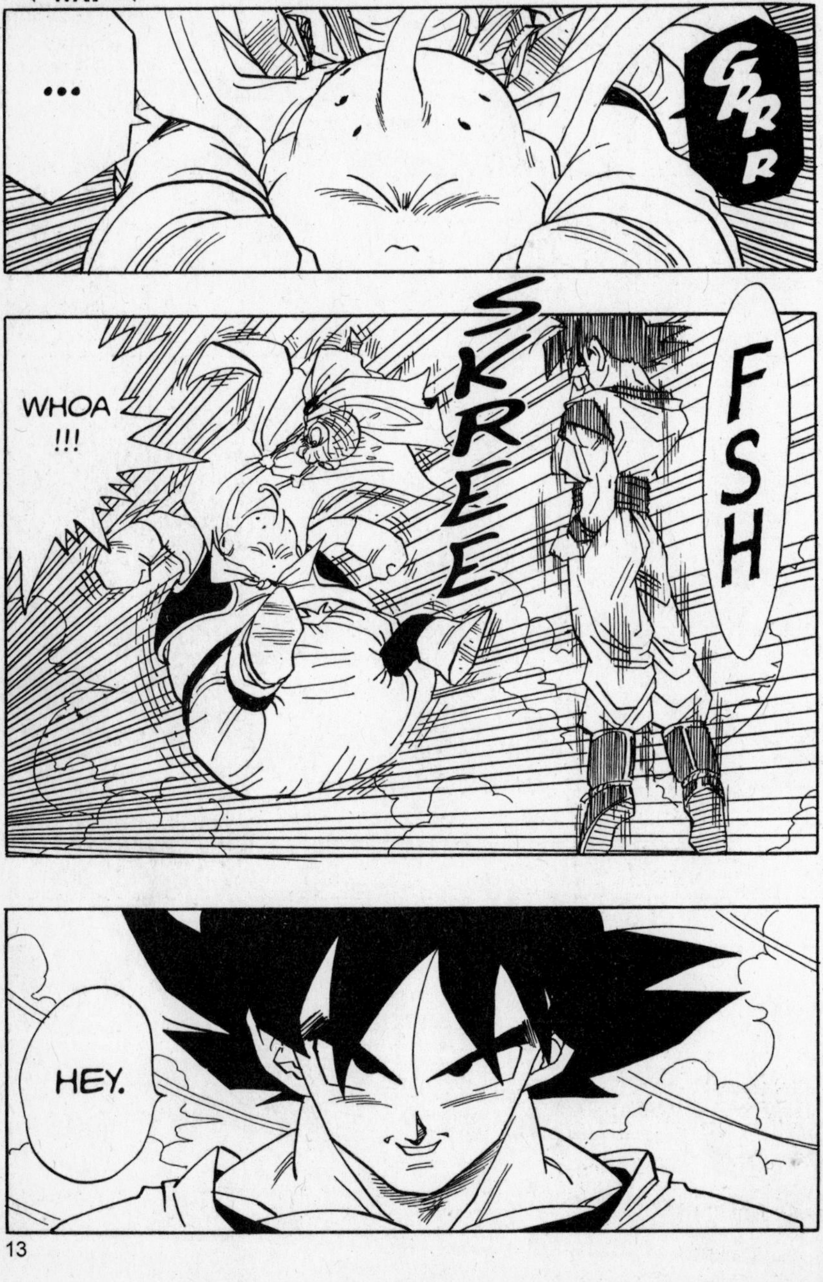

GRRR
...
FSH
SKREE
WHOA !!!
HEY.

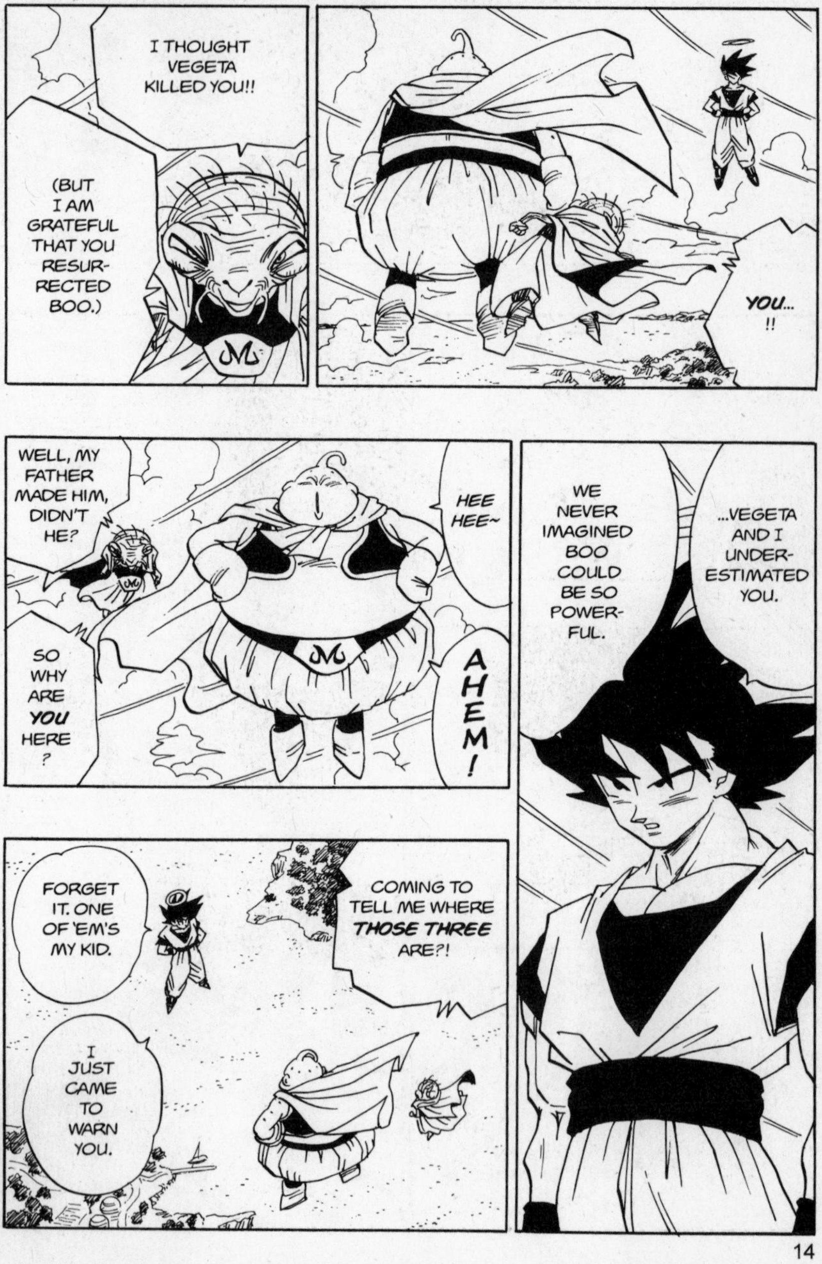
YOU... !!
I THOUGHT VEGETA KILLED YOU!!
(BUT I AM GRATEFUL THAT YOU RESURRECTED BOO.)
...VEGETA AND I UNDERESTIMATED YOU.
WE NEVER IMAGINED BOO COULD BE SO POWERFUL.
HEE HEE~
WELL, MY FATHER MADE HIM, DIDN'T HE?
AHEM!
SO WHY ARE *YOU* HERE?
COMING TO TELL ME WHERE *THOSE THREE* ARE?!
FORGET IT. ONE OF 'EM'S MY KID.
I JUST CAME TO WARN YOU.

READ THIS WAY

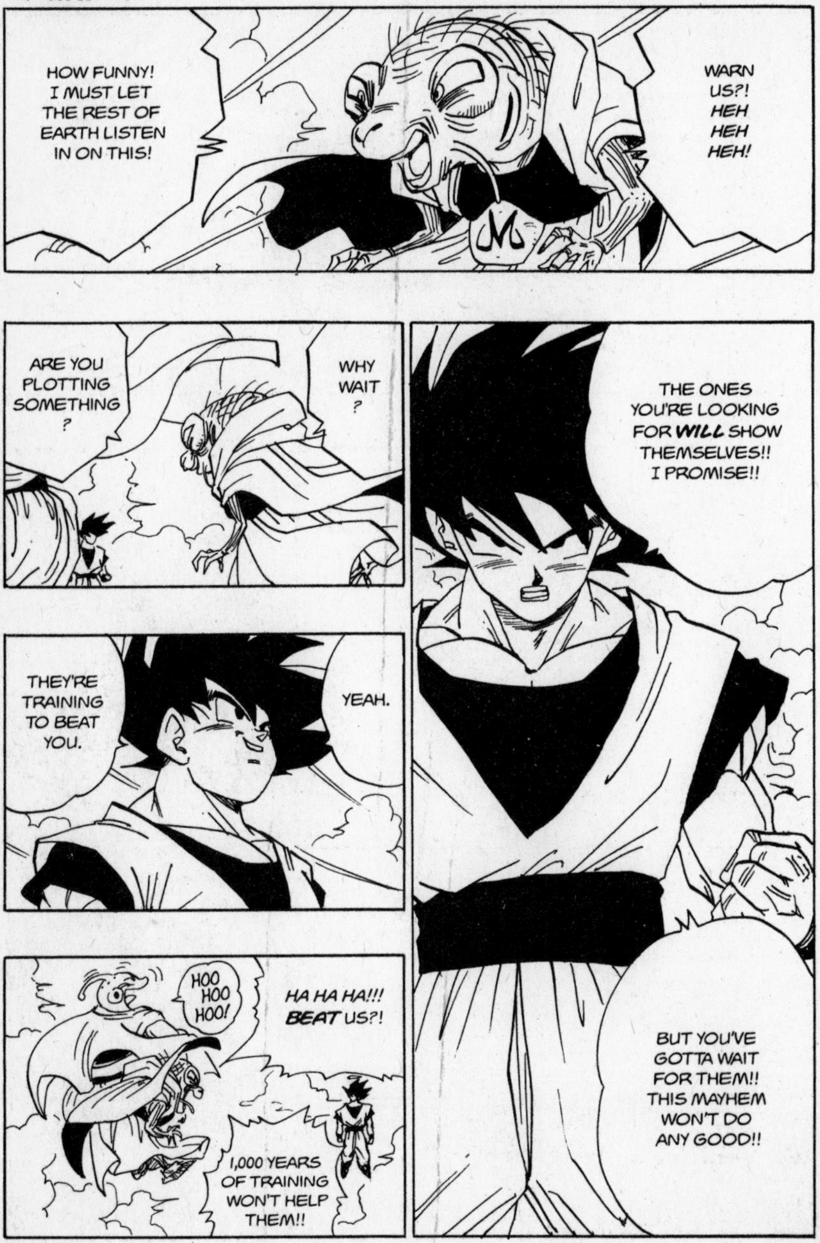
WARN US?! HEH HEH HEH!
HOW FUNNY! I MUST LET THE REST OF EARTH LISTEN IN ON THIS!
THE ONES YOU'RE LOOKING FOR WILL SHOW THEMSELVES!! I PROMISE!!
BUT YOU'VE GOTTA WAIT FOR THEM!! THIS MAYHEM WON'T DO ANY GOOD!!
WHY WAIT?
ARE YOU PLOTTING SOMETHING?
THEY'RE TRAINING TO BEAT YOU.
YEAH.
HA HA HA!!! BEAT US?!
HOO HOO HOO!
1,000 YEARS OF TRAINING WON'T HELP THEM!!

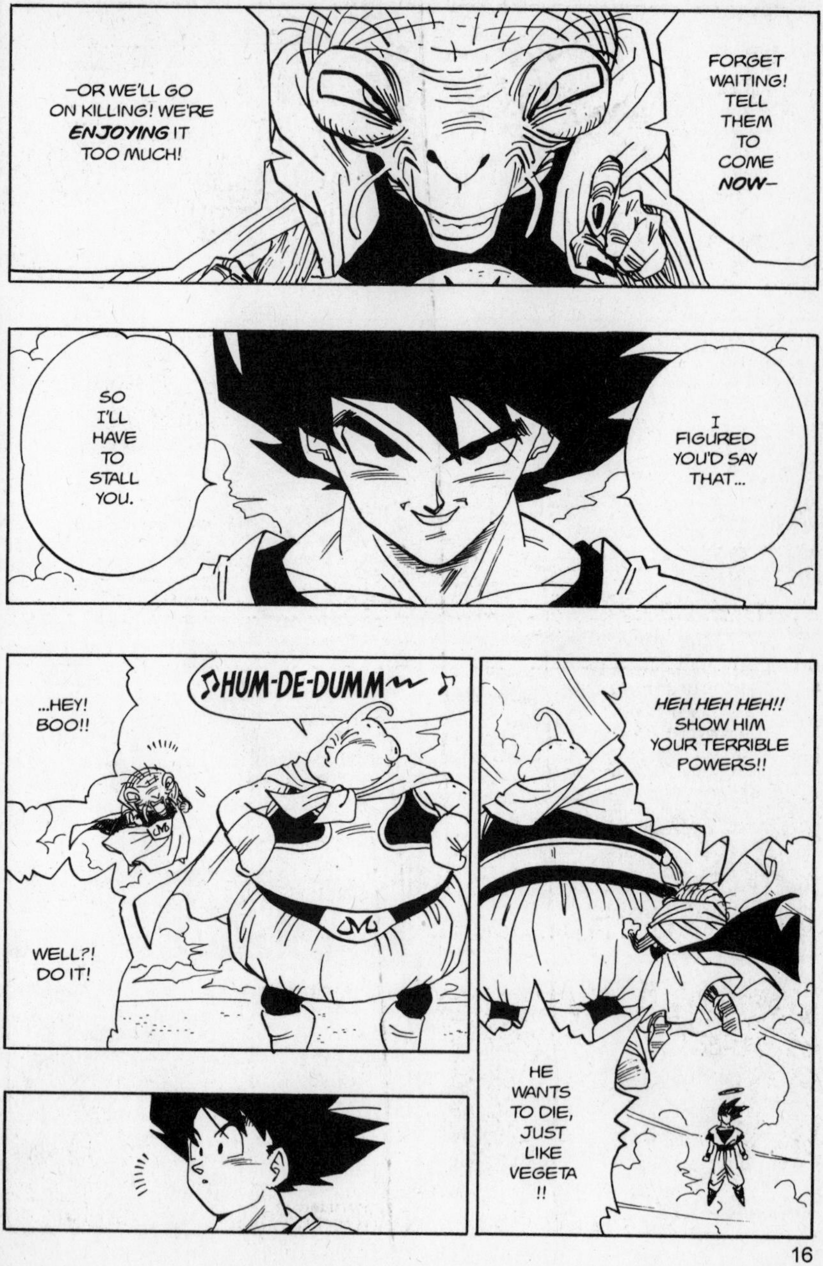
FORGET WAITING! TELL THEM TO COME *NOW*–
–OR WE'LL GO ON KILLING! WE'RE *ENJOYING* IT TOO MUCH!
I FIGURED YOU'D SAY THAT...
SO I'LL HAVE TO STALL YOU.
HEH HEH HEH!! SHOW HIM YOUR TERRIBLE POWERS!!
HE WANTS TO DIE, JUST LIKE VEGETA !!
♪HUM-DE-DUMM~ ♪
...HEY! BOO!!
WELL?! DO IT!

READ THIS WAY

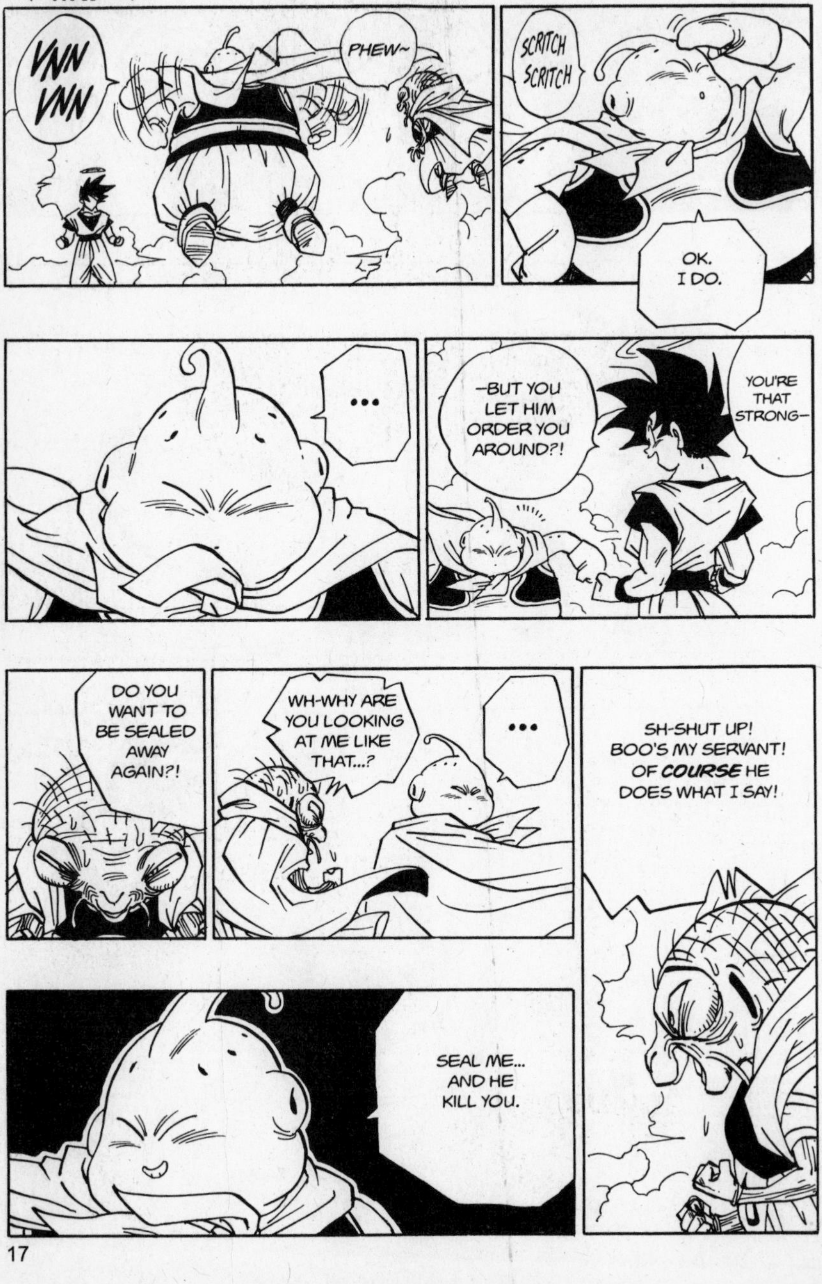
SCRITCH SCRITCH
OK. I DO.
PHEW~
VNN VNN
YOU'RE THAT STRONG—
—BUT YOU LET HIM ORDER YOU AROUND?!
...
SH-SHUT UP! BOO'S MY SERVANT! OF **COURSE** HE DOES WHAT I SAY!
...
WH-WHY ARE YOU LOOKING AT ME LIKE THAT...?
DO YOU WANT TO BE SEALED AWAY AGAIN?!
SEAL ME... AND HE KILL YOU.

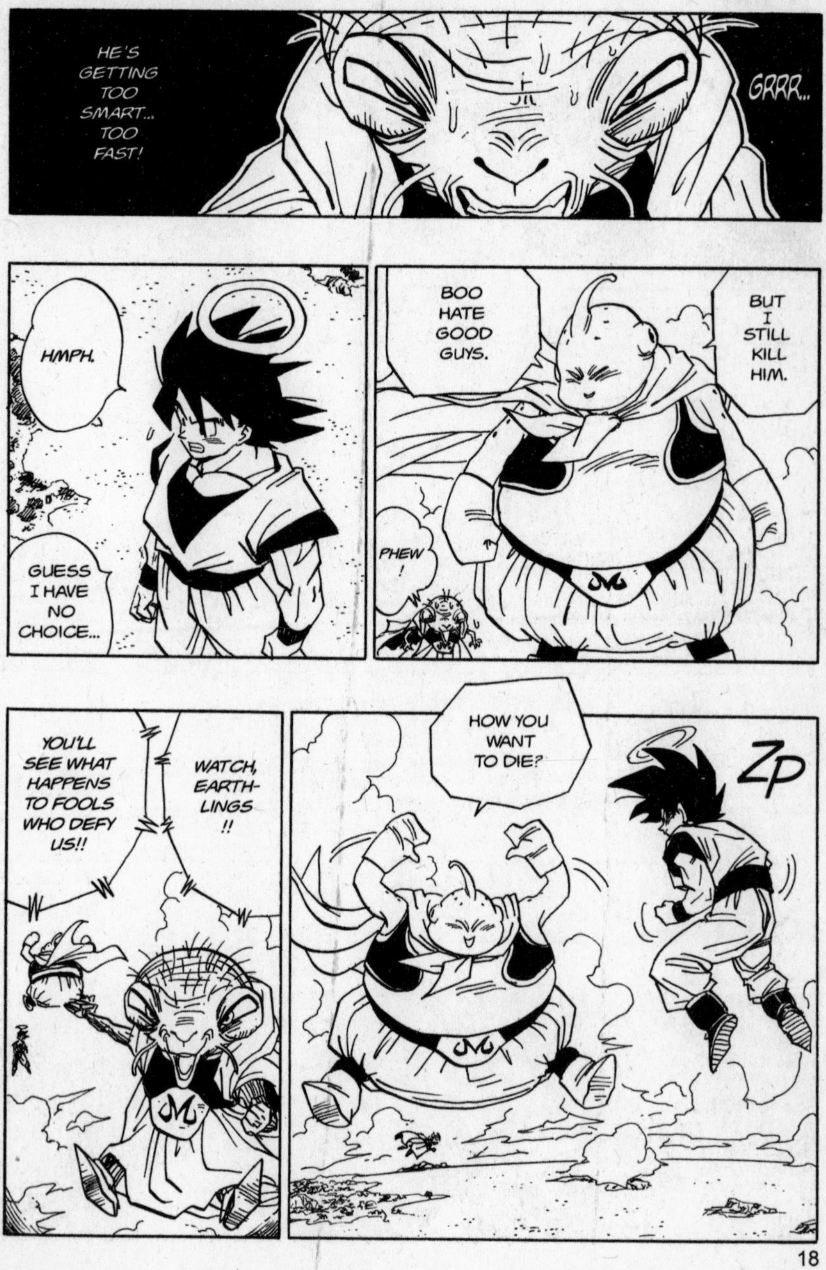
HE'S GETTING TOO SMART... TOO FAST!
GRRR...
HMPH.
GUESS I HAVE NO CHOICE...
BOO HATE GOOD GUYS.
BUT I STILL KILL HIM.
PHEW!
YOU'LL SEE WHAT HAPPENS TO FOOLS WHO DEFY US!!
WATCH, EARTH-LINGS!!
HOW YOU WANT TO DIE?
ZP

READ THIS WAY

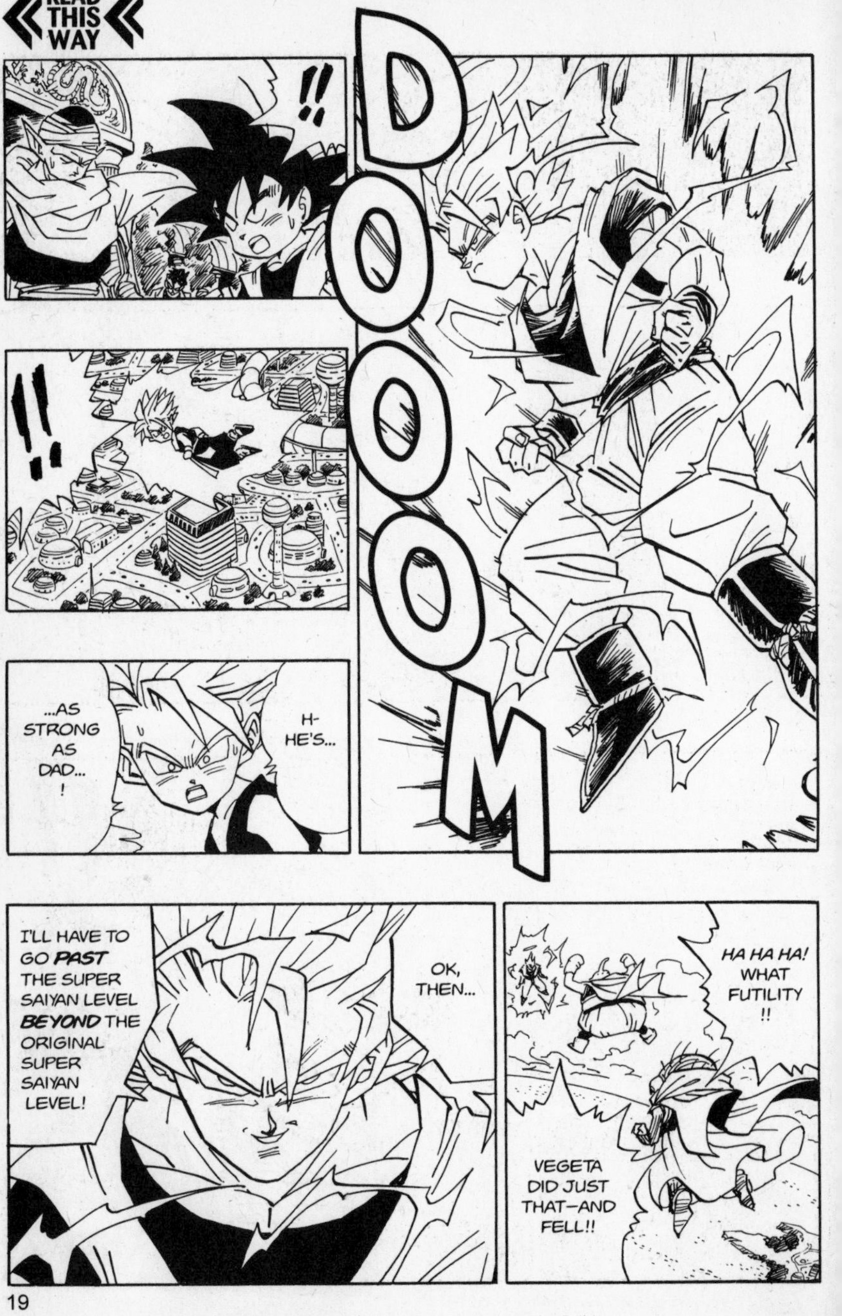

DOOOOM
!!
!!
H- HE'S...
...AS STRONG AS DAD... !
HA HA HA! WHAT FUTILITY !!
VEGETA DID JUST THAT—AND FELL!!
OK, THEN...
I'LL HAVE TO GO **PAST** THE SUPER SAIYAN LEVEL **BEYOND** THE ORIGINAL SUPER SAIYAN LEVEL!

DBZ:280 · Super Saiyan Level 3!!!

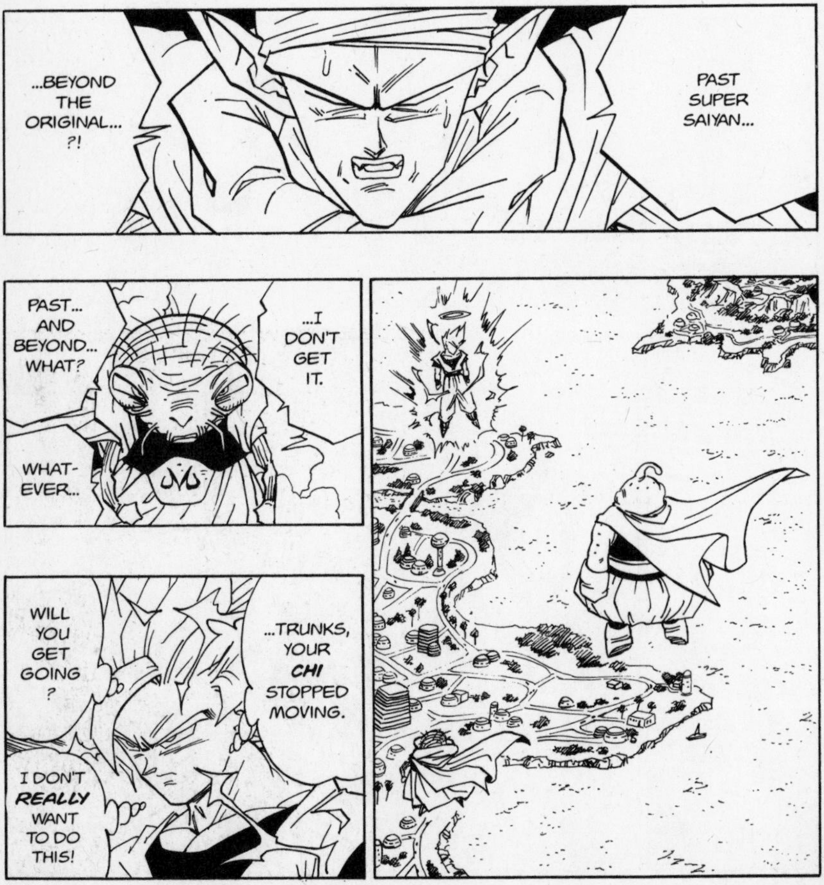
PAST SUPER SAIYAN...
...BEYOND THE ORIGINAL...?!
...I DON'T GET IT.
PAST... AND BEYOND... WHAT?
WHATEVER...
...TRUNKS, YOUR *CHI* STOPPED MOVING.
WILL YOU GET GOING?
I DON'T *REALLY* WANT TO DO THIS!

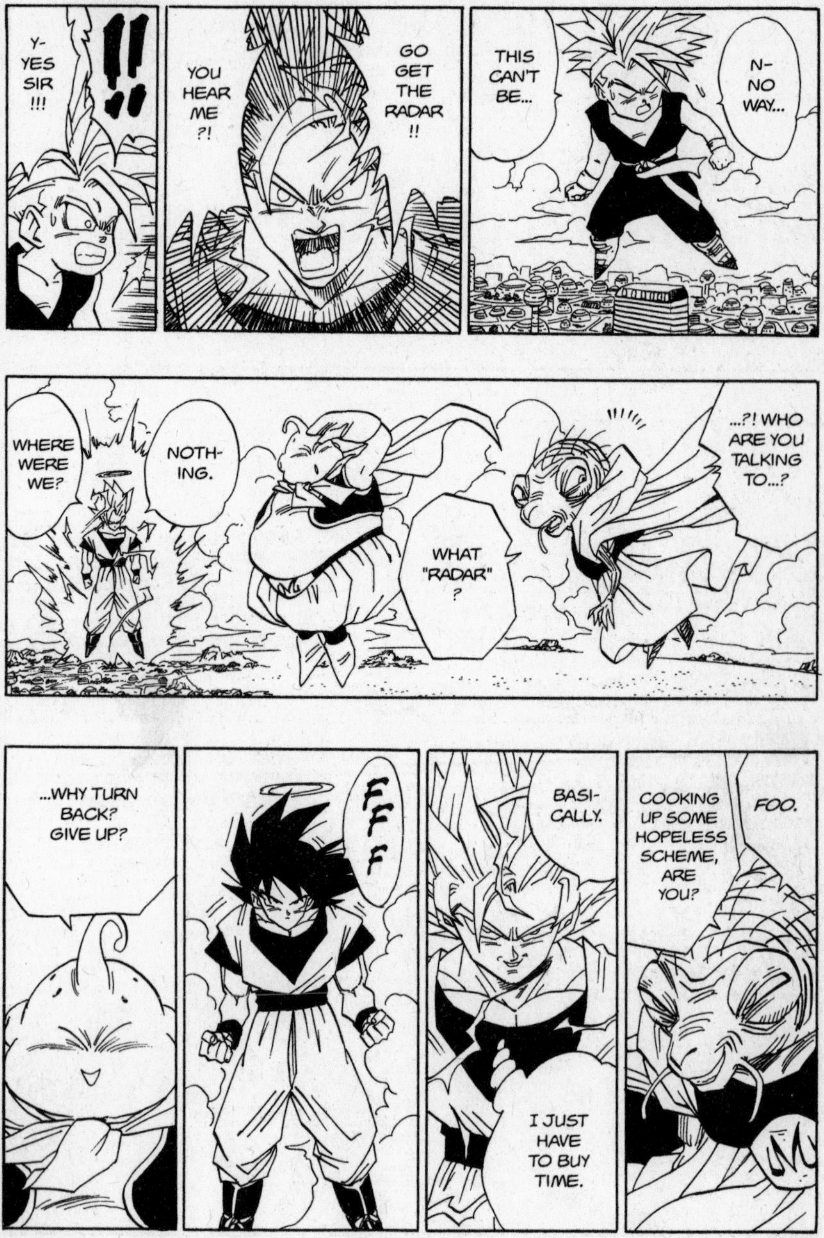
N- NO WAY...
THIS CAN'T BE...
GO GET THE RADAR !!
YOU HEAR ME ?!
!!
Y- YES SIR !!!
...?! WHO ARE YOU TALKING TO...?
WHAT "RADAR" ?
NOTH-ING.
WHERE WERE WE?
FOO.
COOKING UP SOME HOPELESS SCHEME, ARE YOU?
BASI-CALLY.
I JUST HAVE TO BUY TIME.
FFF
...WHY TURN BACK? GIVE UP?

READ THIS WAY

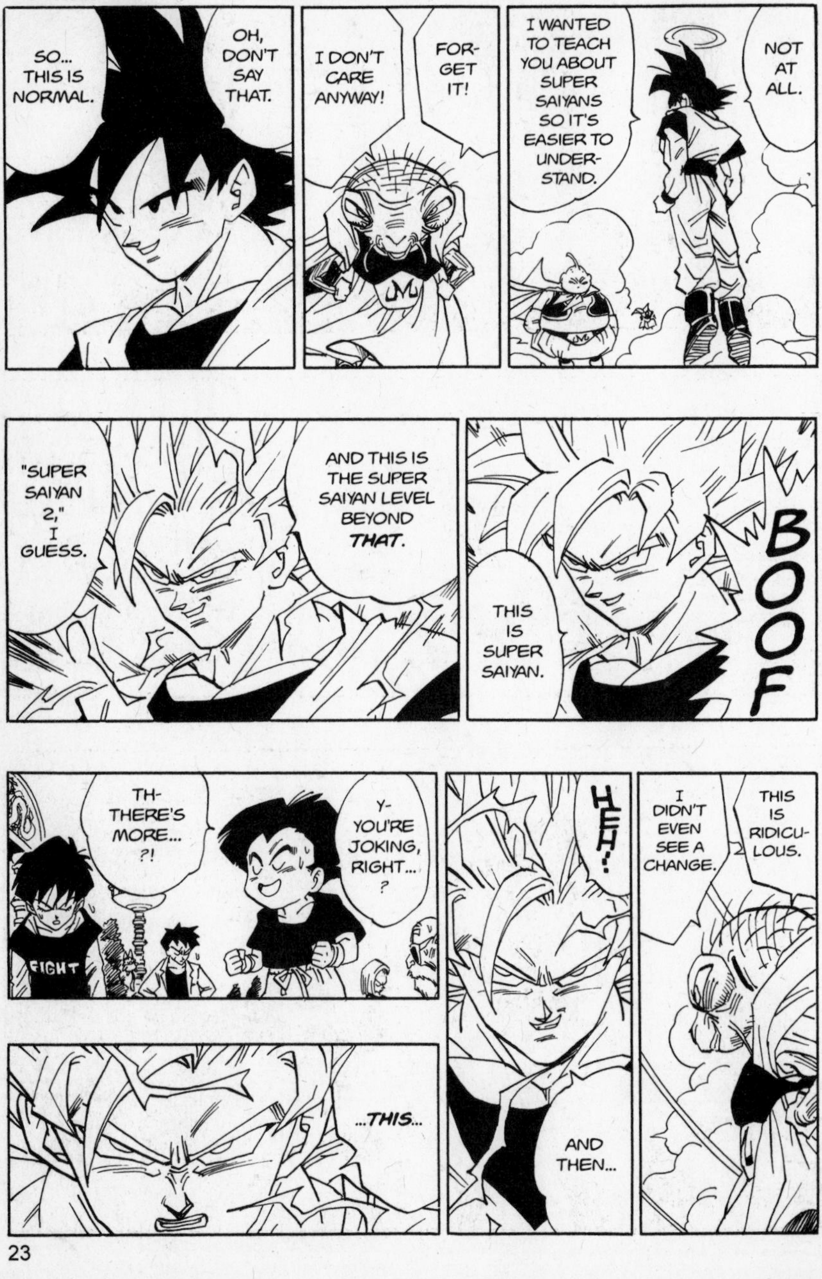
NOT AT ALL.
I WANTED TO TEACH YOU ABOUT SUPER SAIYANS SO IT'S EASIER TO UNDER-STAND.
FOR-GET IT!
I DON'T CARE ANYWAY!
OH, DON'T SAY THAT.
SO... THIS IS NORMAL.
BOOF
THIS IS SUPER SAIYAN.
AND THIS IS THE SUPER SAIYAN LEVEL BEYOND *THAT*.
"SUPER SAIYAN 2," I GUESS.
THIS IS RIDICU-LOUS.
I DIDN'T EVEN SEE A CHANGE.
HEH!
AND THEN...
Y-YOU'RE JOKING, RIGHT...?
TH-THERE'S MORE...?!
FIGHT
...*THIS*...

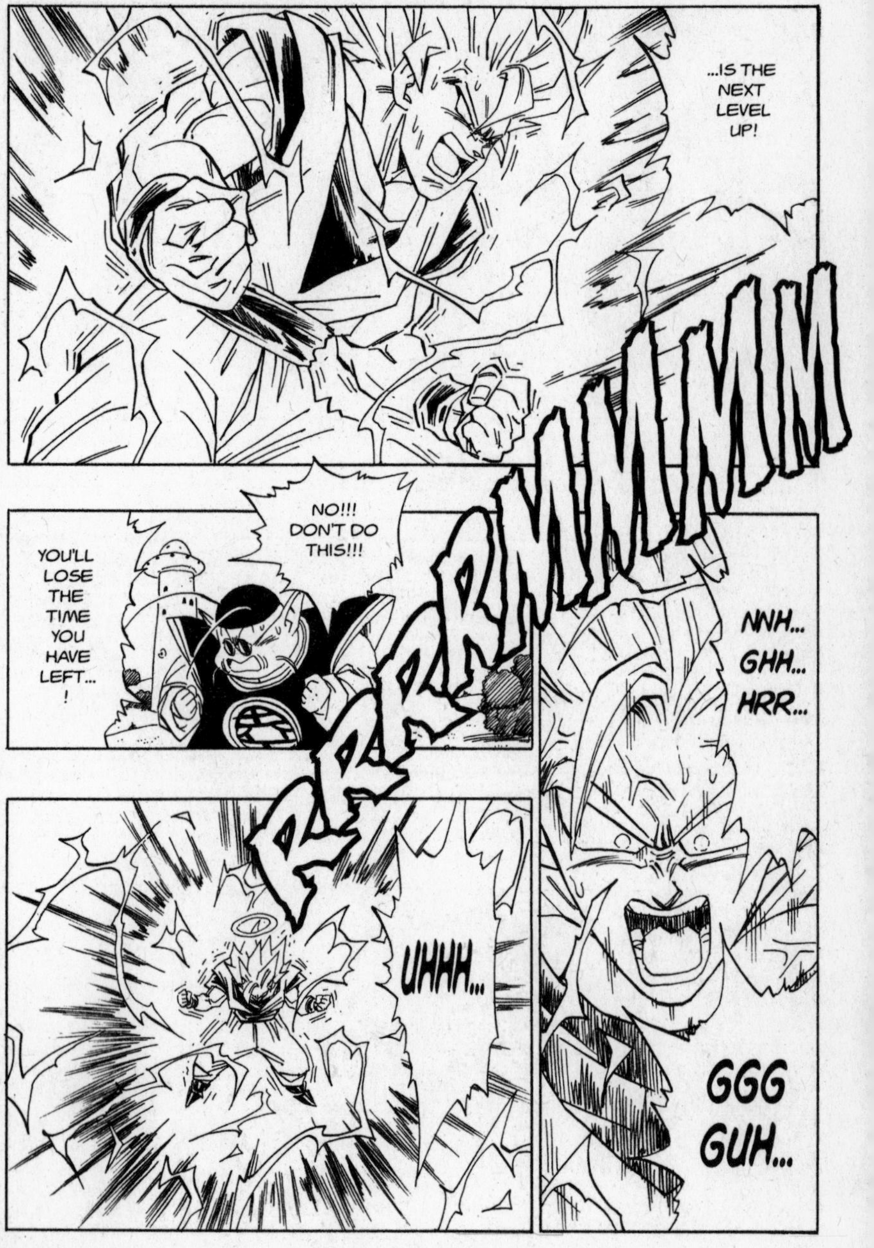
...IS THE NEXT LEVEL UP!
NNH... GHH... HRR...
RRRRMMMMMMM
GGG GUH...
NO!!! DON'T DO THIS!!!
YOU'LL LOSE THE TIME YOU HAVE LEFT...!
UHHH...

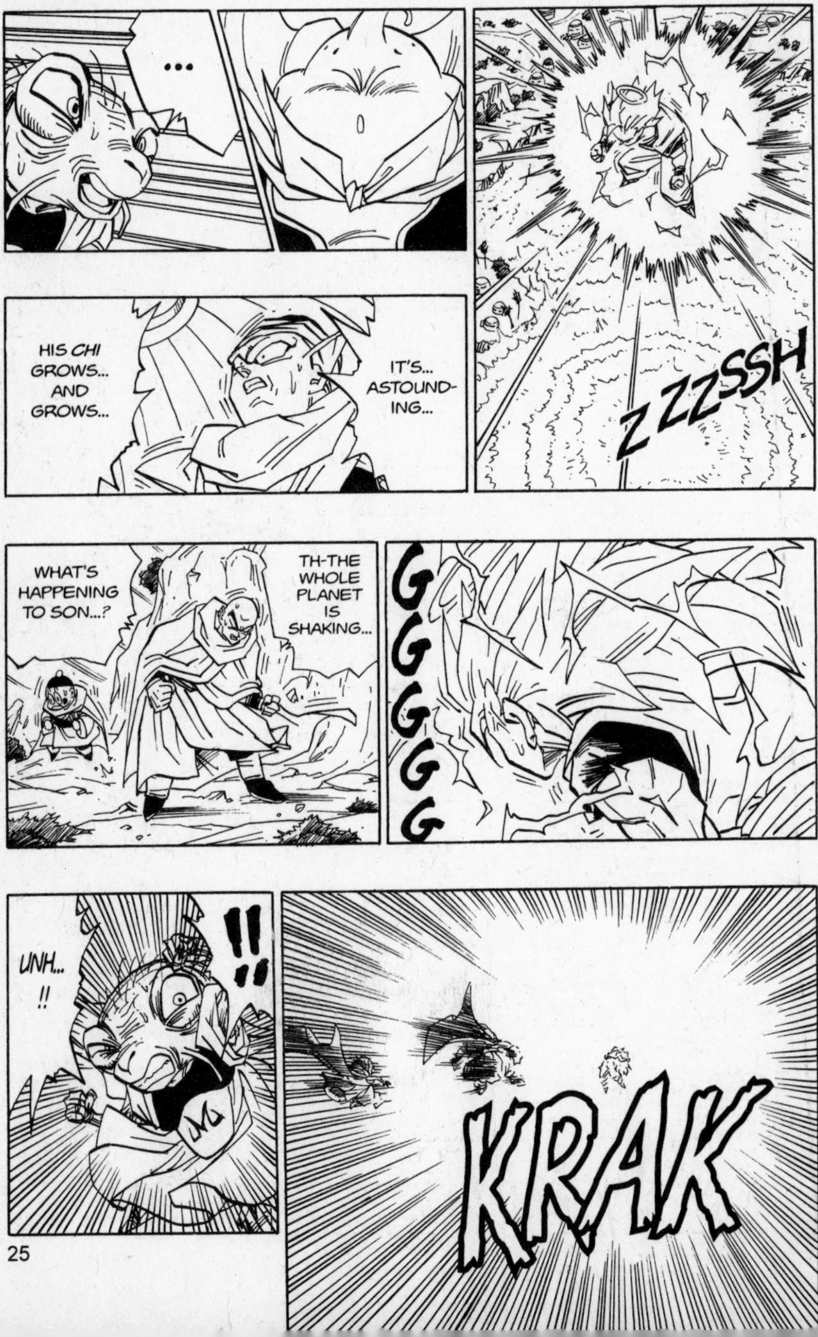
ZZZSSH
...
IT'S... ASTOUNDING...
HIS CHI GROWS... AND GROWS...
GGGGGG
TH-THE WHOLE PLANET IS SHAKING...
WHAT'S HAPPENING TO SON...?
KRAK
!!
UNH... !!

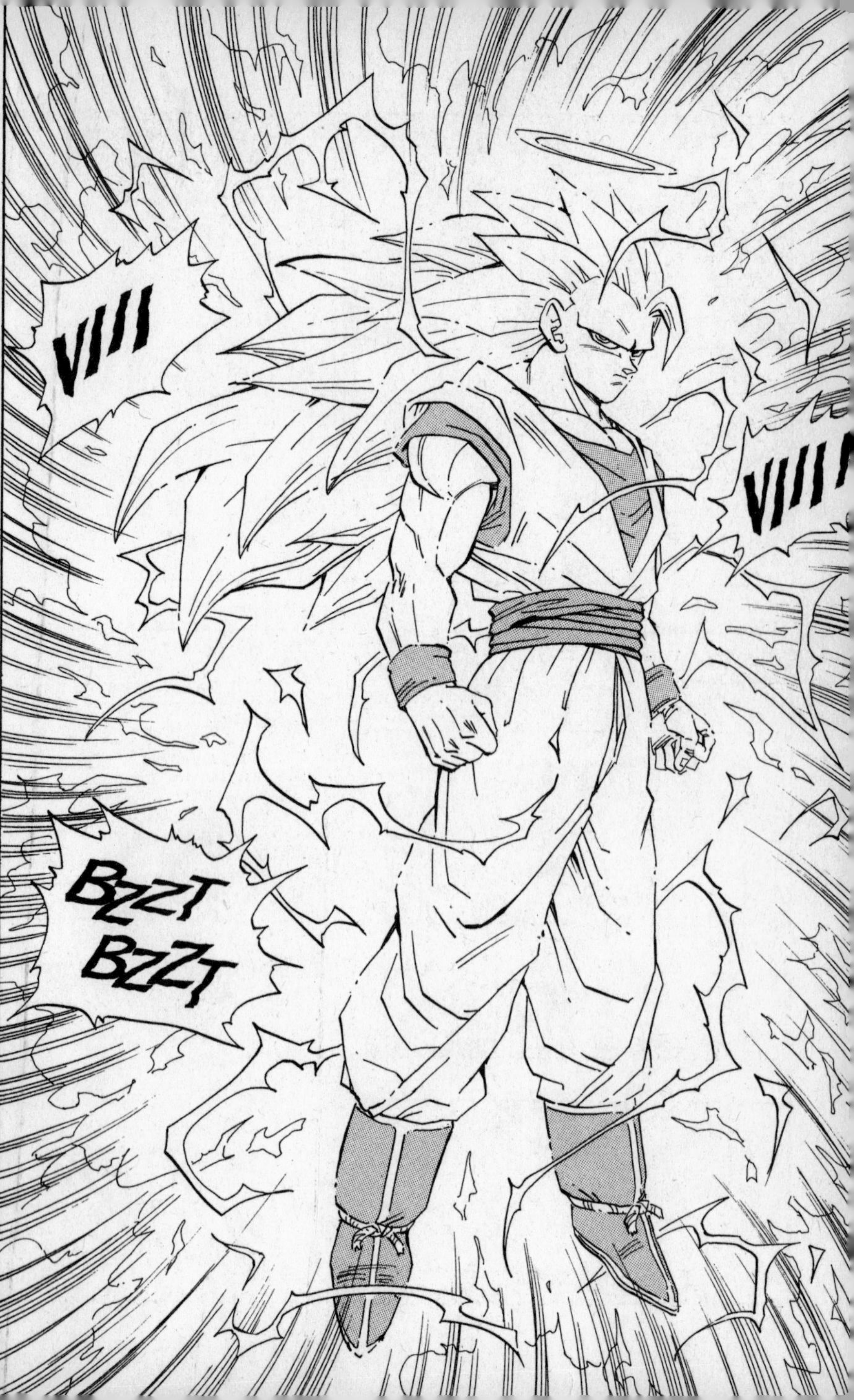
VIII
VIII
BZZT
BZZT

READ THIS WAY

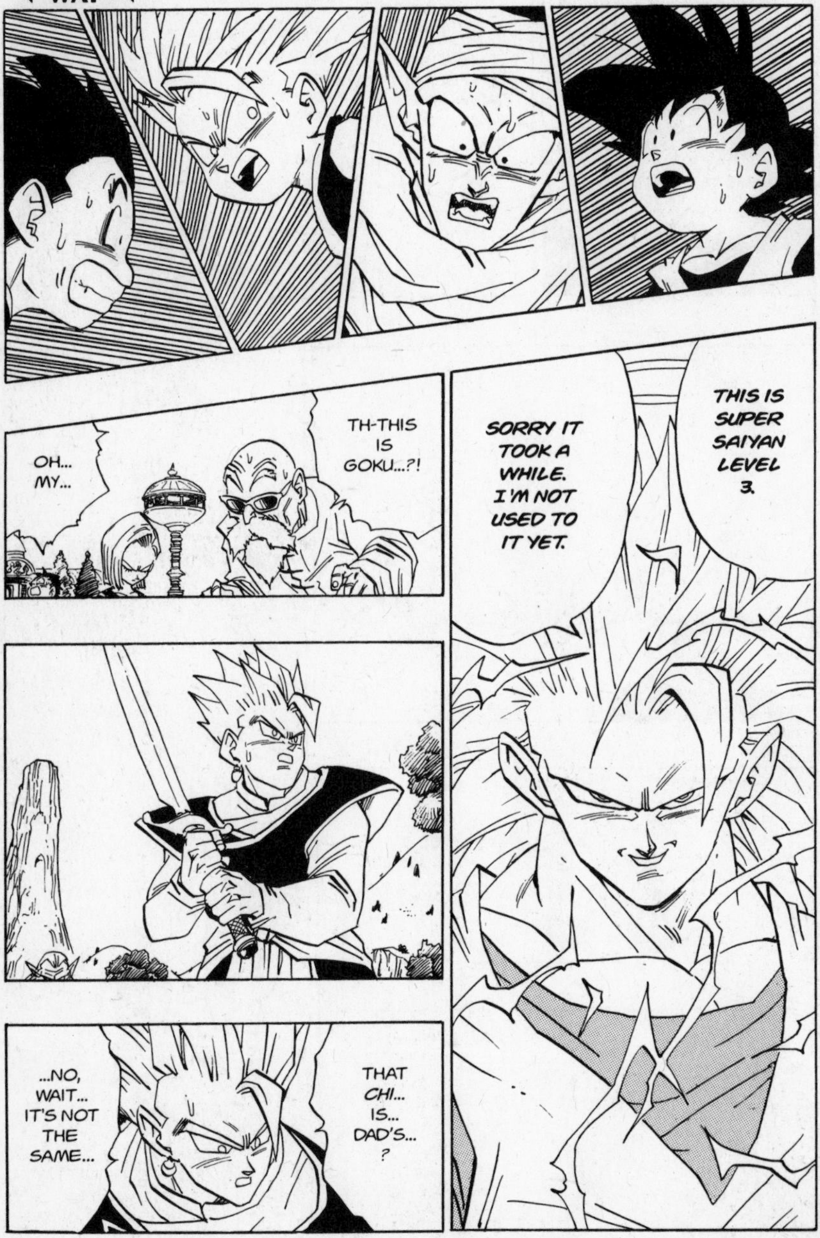
THIS IS SUPER SAIYAN LEVEL 3.
SORRY IT TOOK A WHILE. I'M NOT USED TO IT YET.
TH-THIS IS GOKU...?!
OH... MY...
THAT CHI... IS... DAD'S...?
...NO, WAIT... IT'S NOT THE SAME...

READ THIS WAY

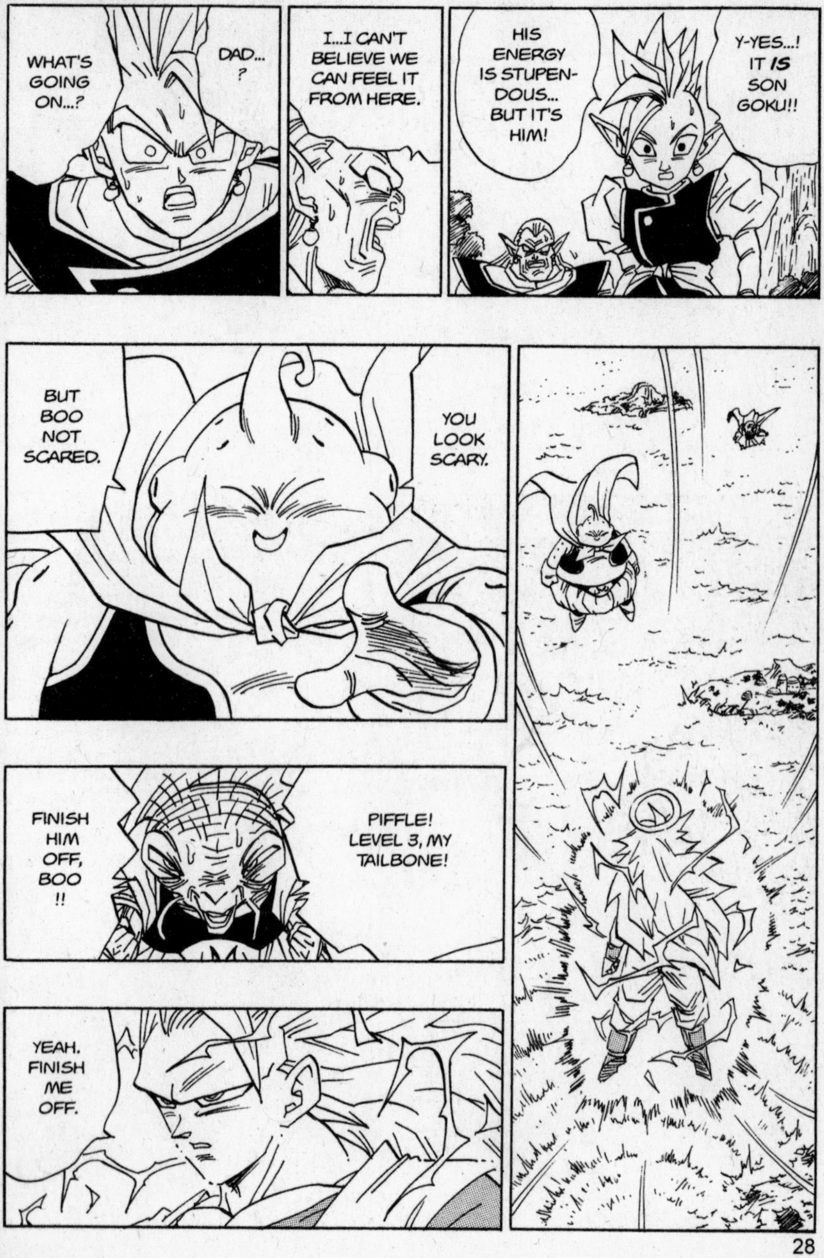
Y-YES...! IT **IS** SON GOKU!!
HIS ENERGY IS STUPENDOUS... BUT IT'S HIM!
I...I CAN'T BELIEVE WE CAN FEEL IT FROM HERE.
DAD...?
WHAT'S GOING ON...?
YOU LOOK SCARY.
BUT BOO NOT SCARED.
PIFFLE! LEVEL 3, MY TAILBONE!
FINISH HIM OFF, BOO!!
YEAH. FINISH ME OFF.

READ THIS WAY

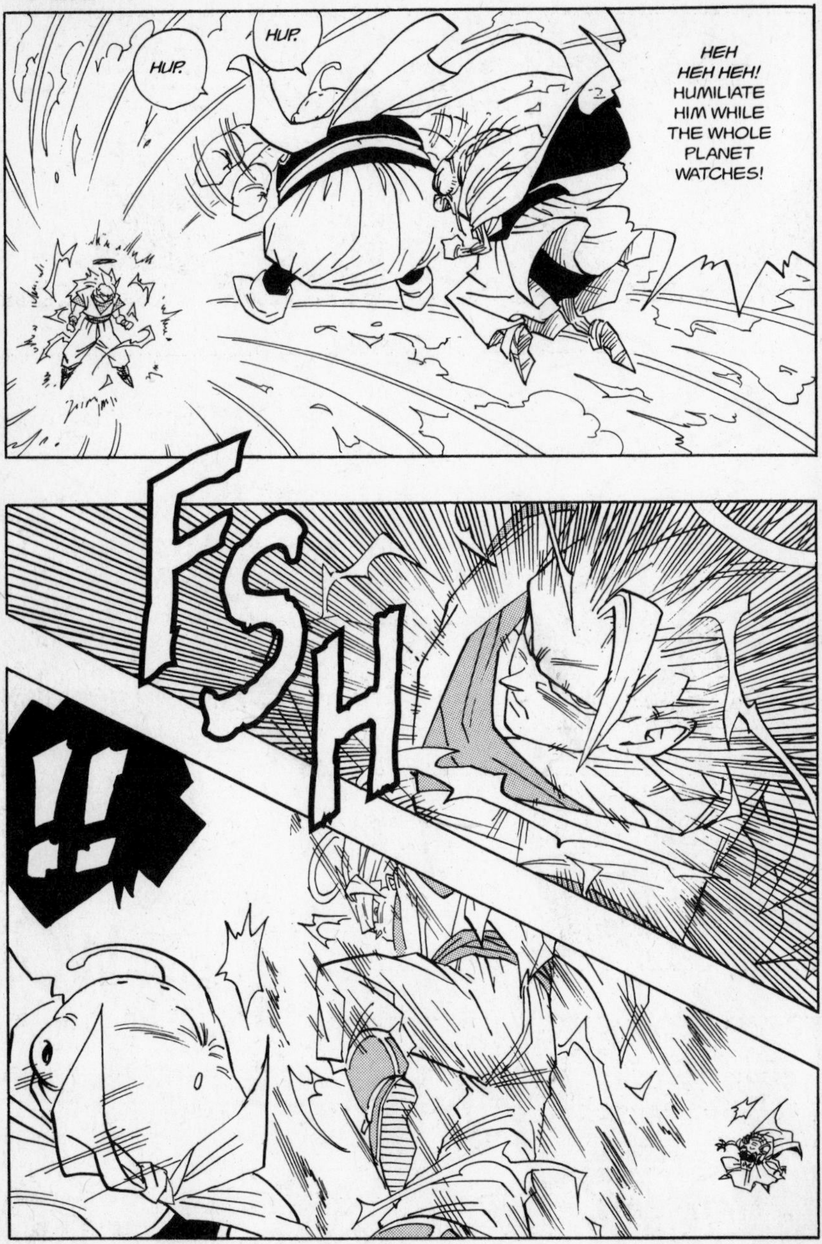
HEH HEH HEH! HUMILIATE HIM WHILE THE WHOLE PLANET WATCHES!
HUP.
HUP.
FSH
!!

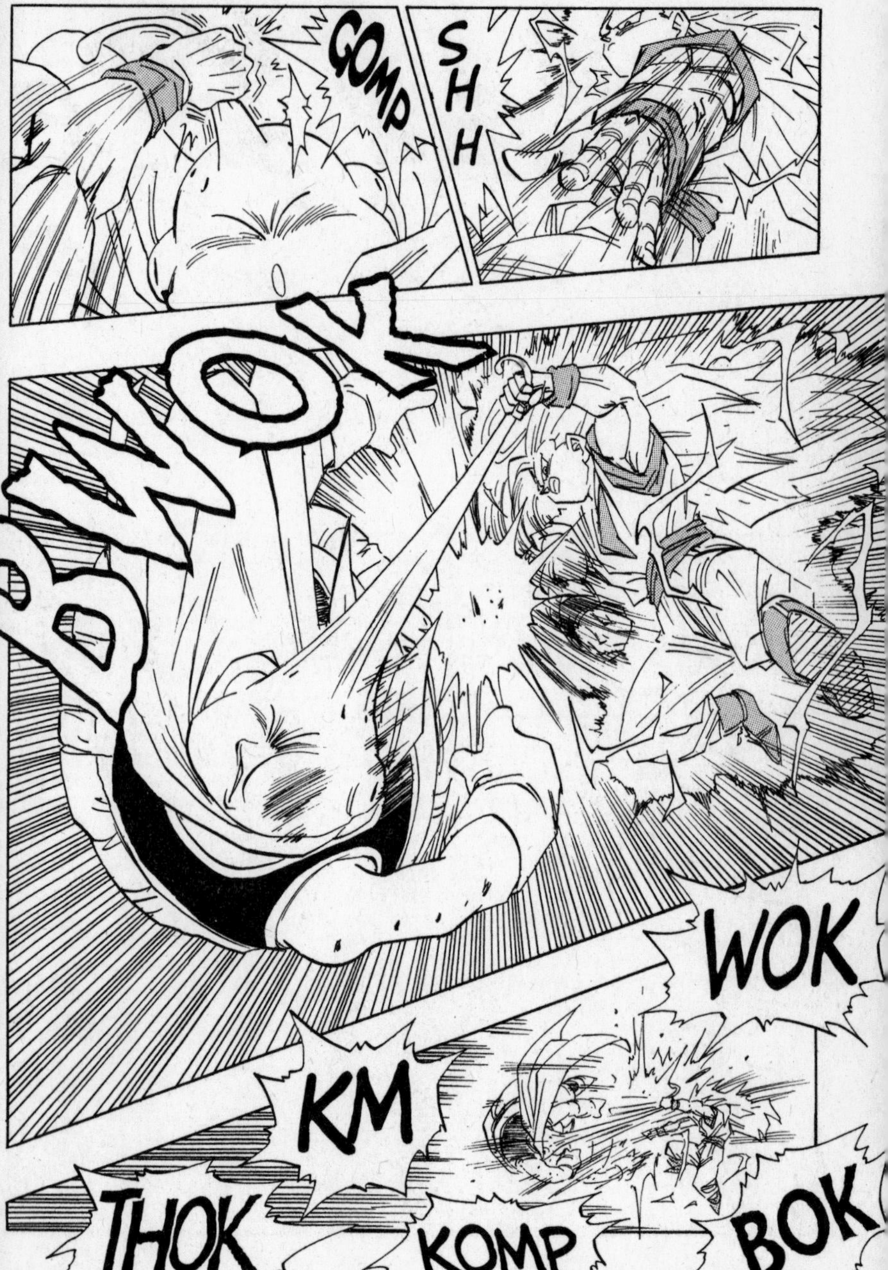
SHH
GOMP
BWOK
WOK
KM
BOK
KOMP
THOK

READ THIS WAY

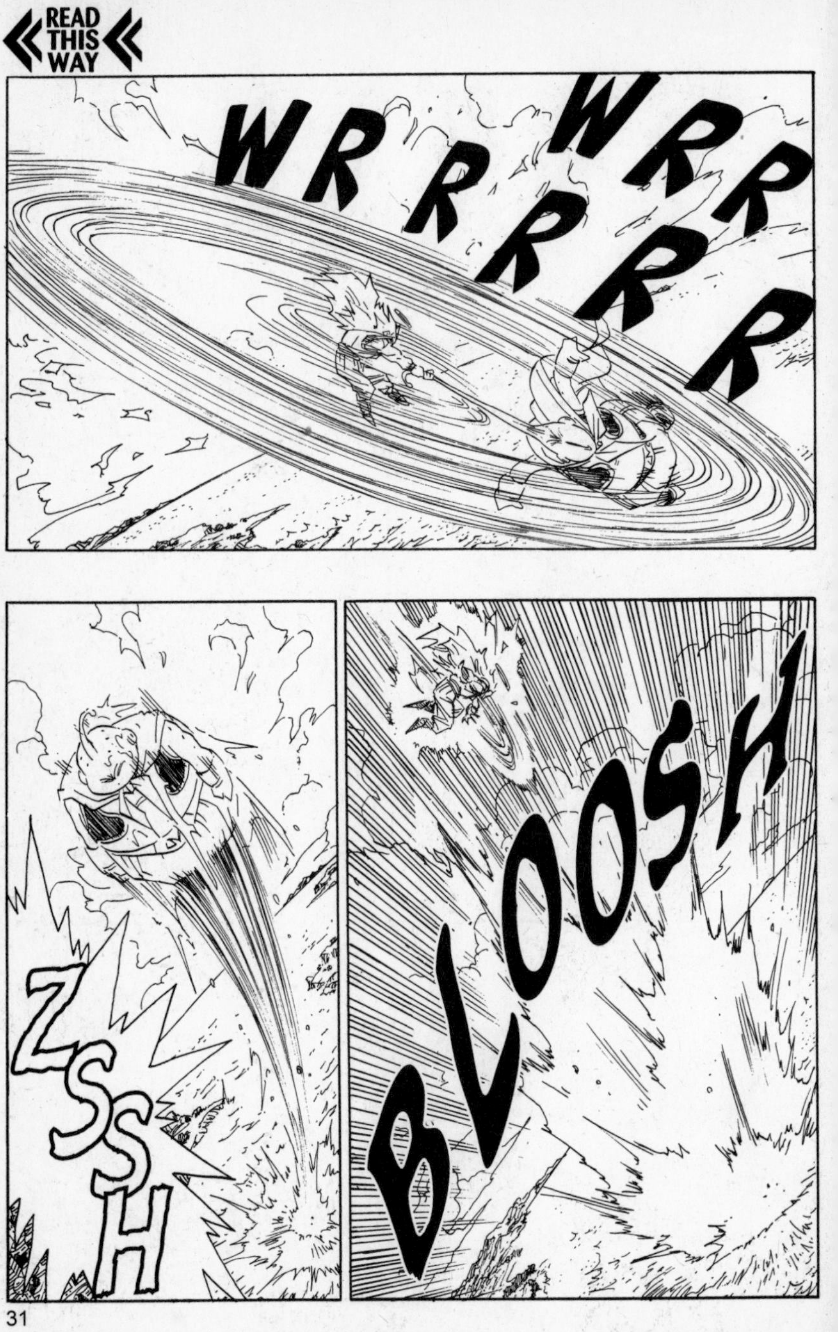
WRRRRRR
BLOOSH
ZSSH

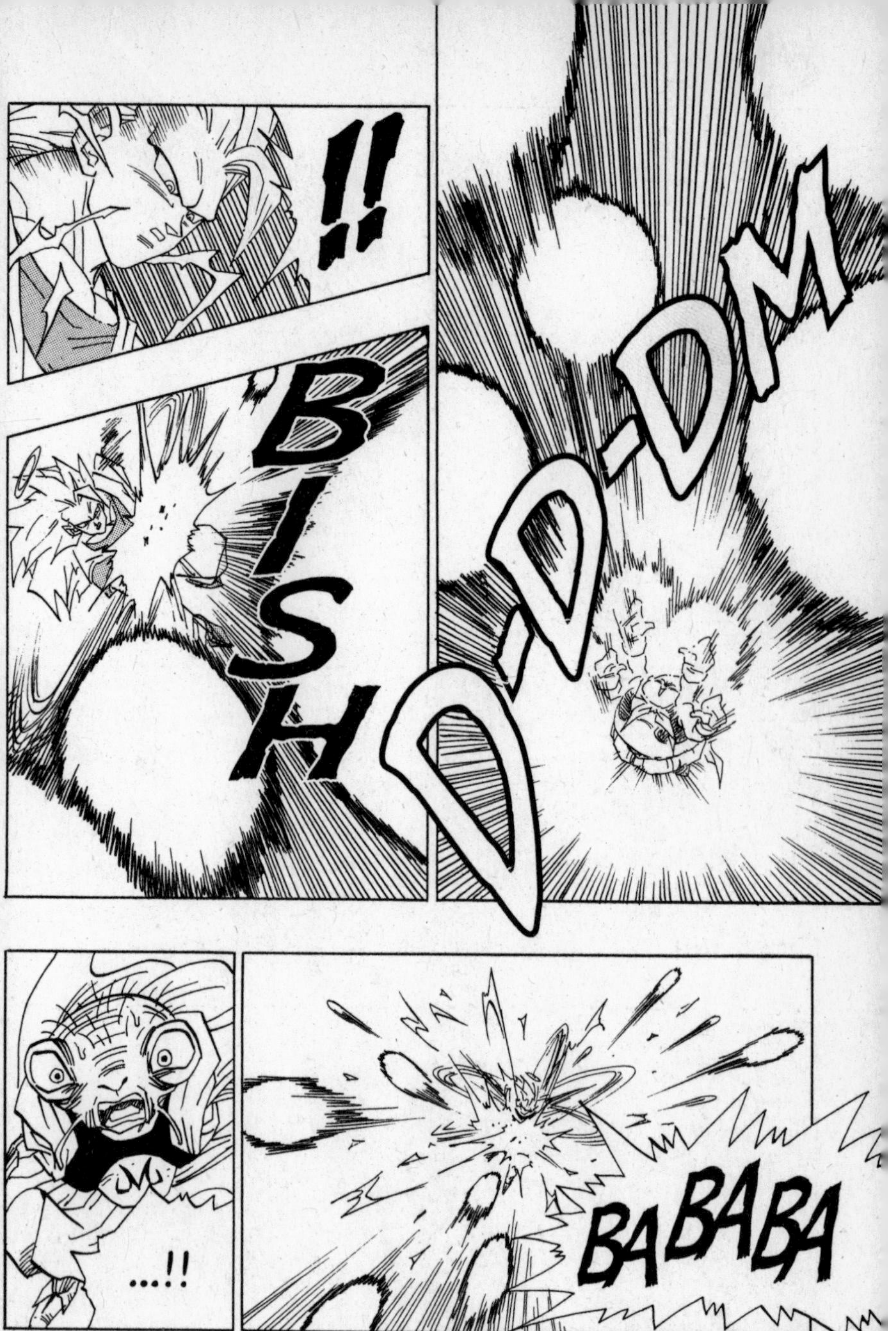
D-D-D-DM
!!
BISH
BABABA
...!!

READ THIS WAY

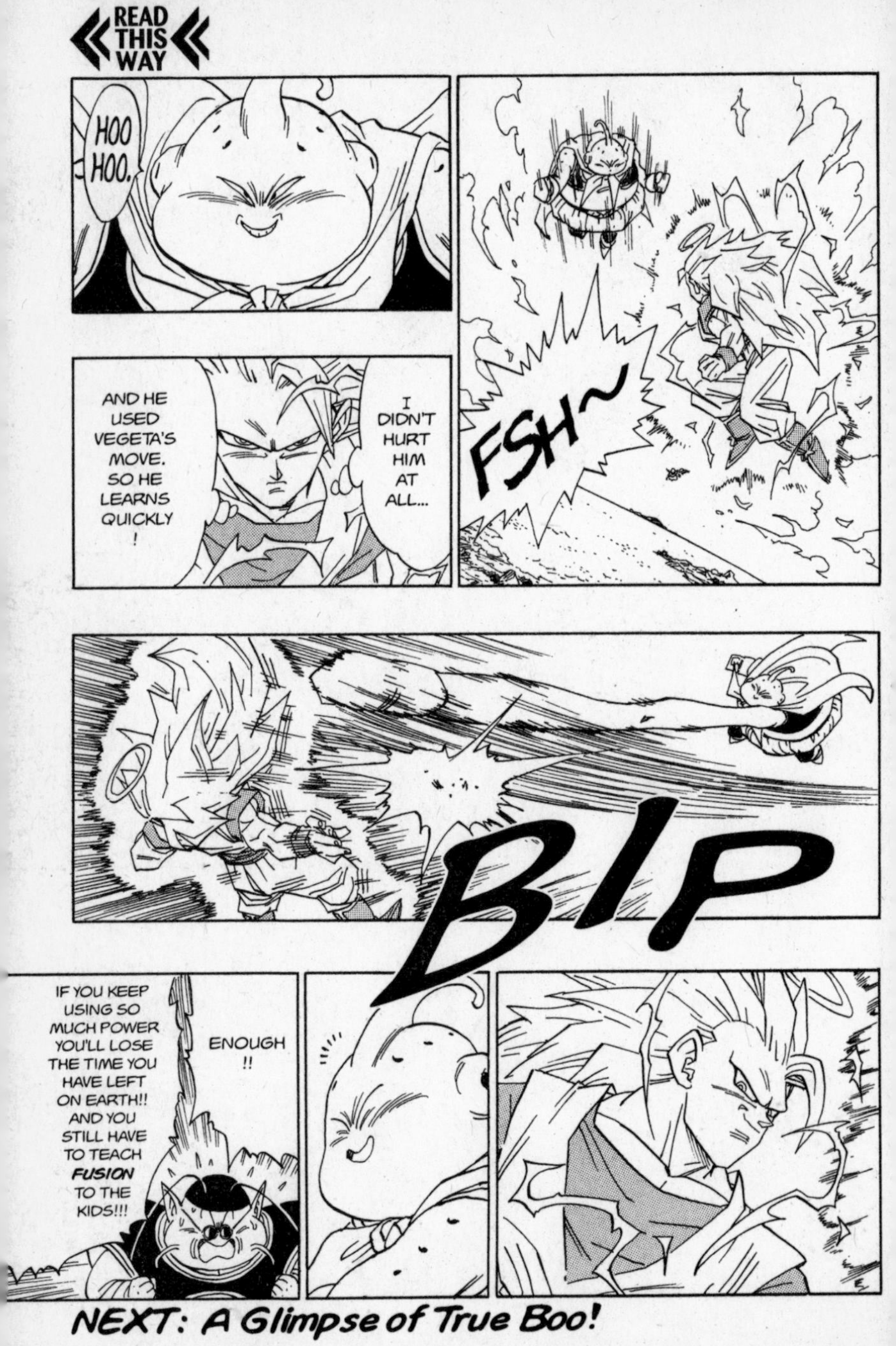
FSH~
HOO HOO.
I DIDN'T HURT HIM AT ALL...
AND HE USED VEGETA'S MOVE. SO HE LEARNS QUICKLY!
BIP
ENOUGH!!
IF YOU KEEP USING SO MUCH POWER YOU'LL LOSE THE TIME YOU HAVE LEFT ON EARTH!! AND YOU STILL HAVE TO TEACH **FUSION** TO THE KIDS!!!

NEXT: A Glimpse of True Boo!

DBZ:281 · Boo Unbound

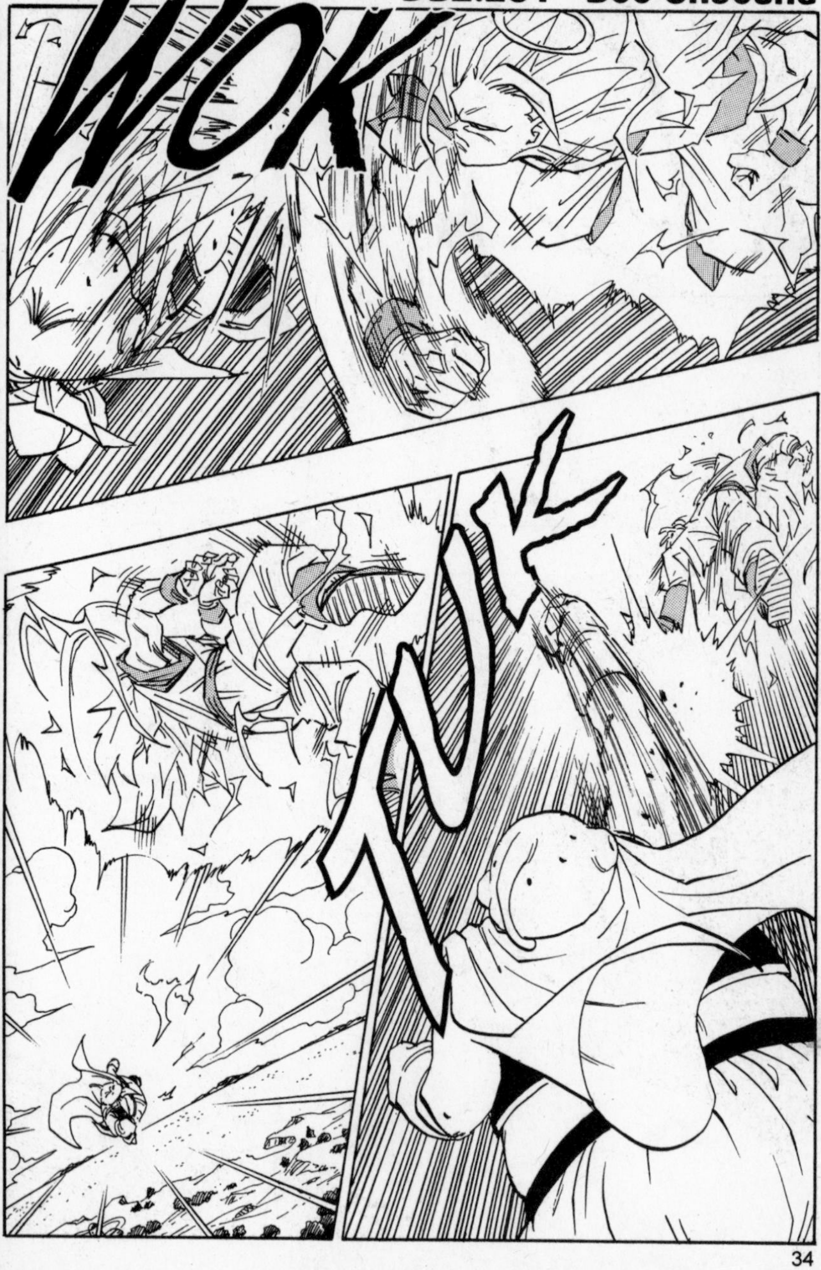
WOK
ZUK

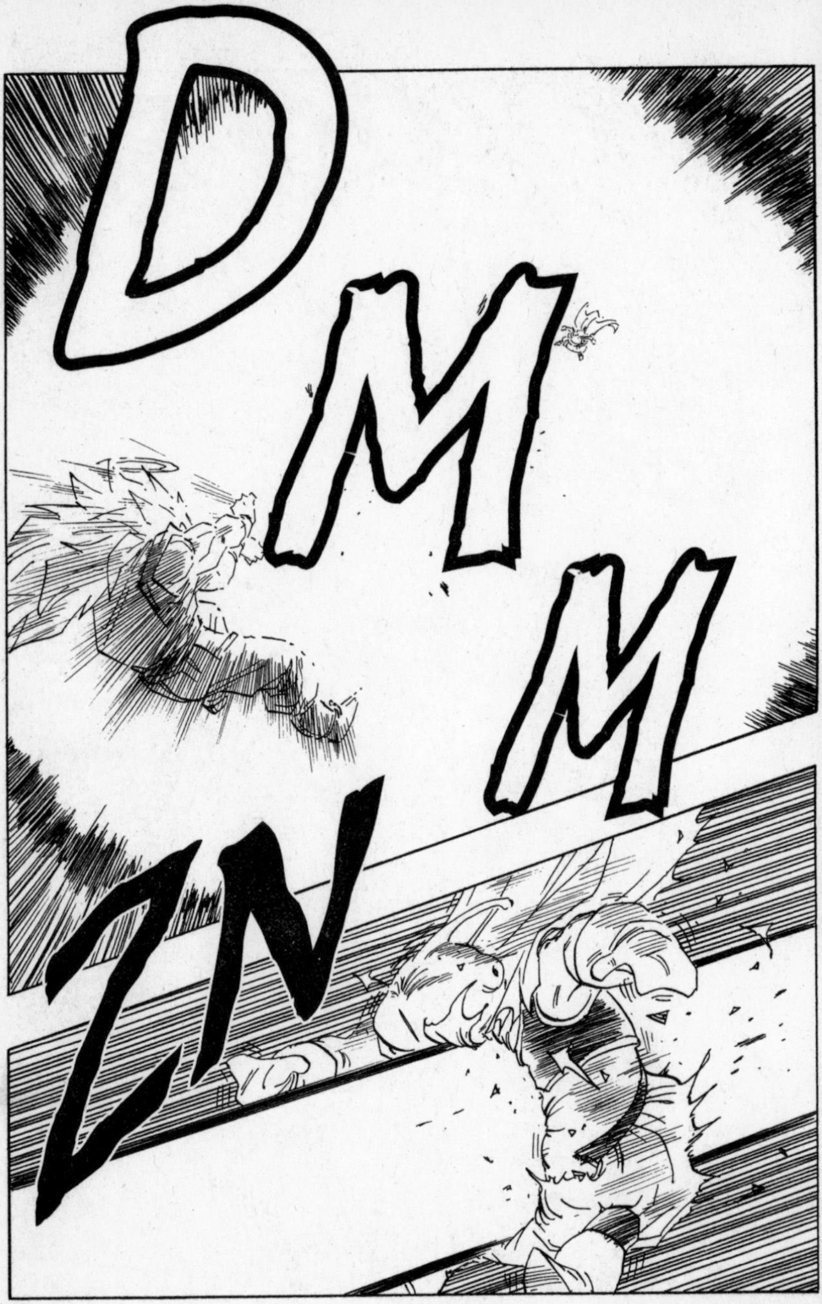
DMMM
ZN

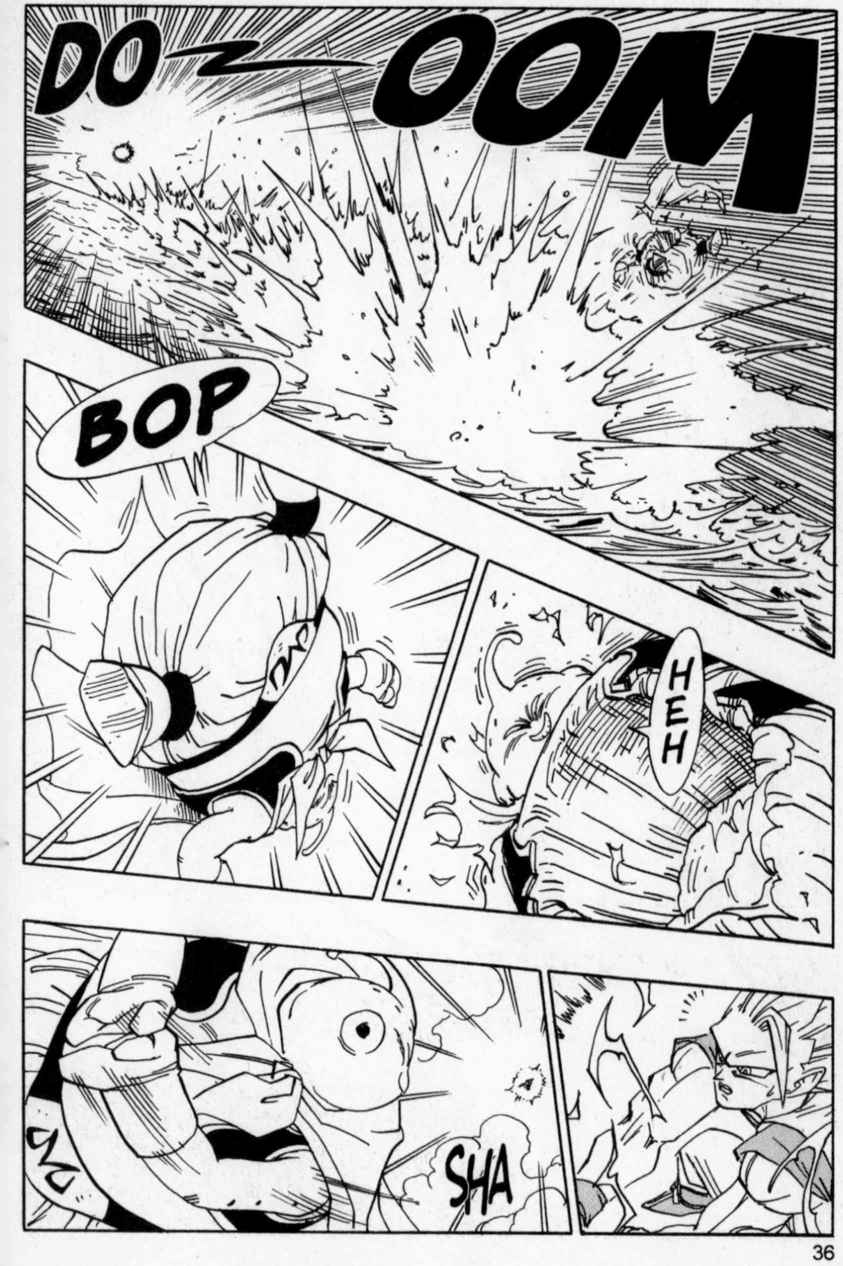
DO-OOM
HEH
BOP
SHA

READ THIS WAY

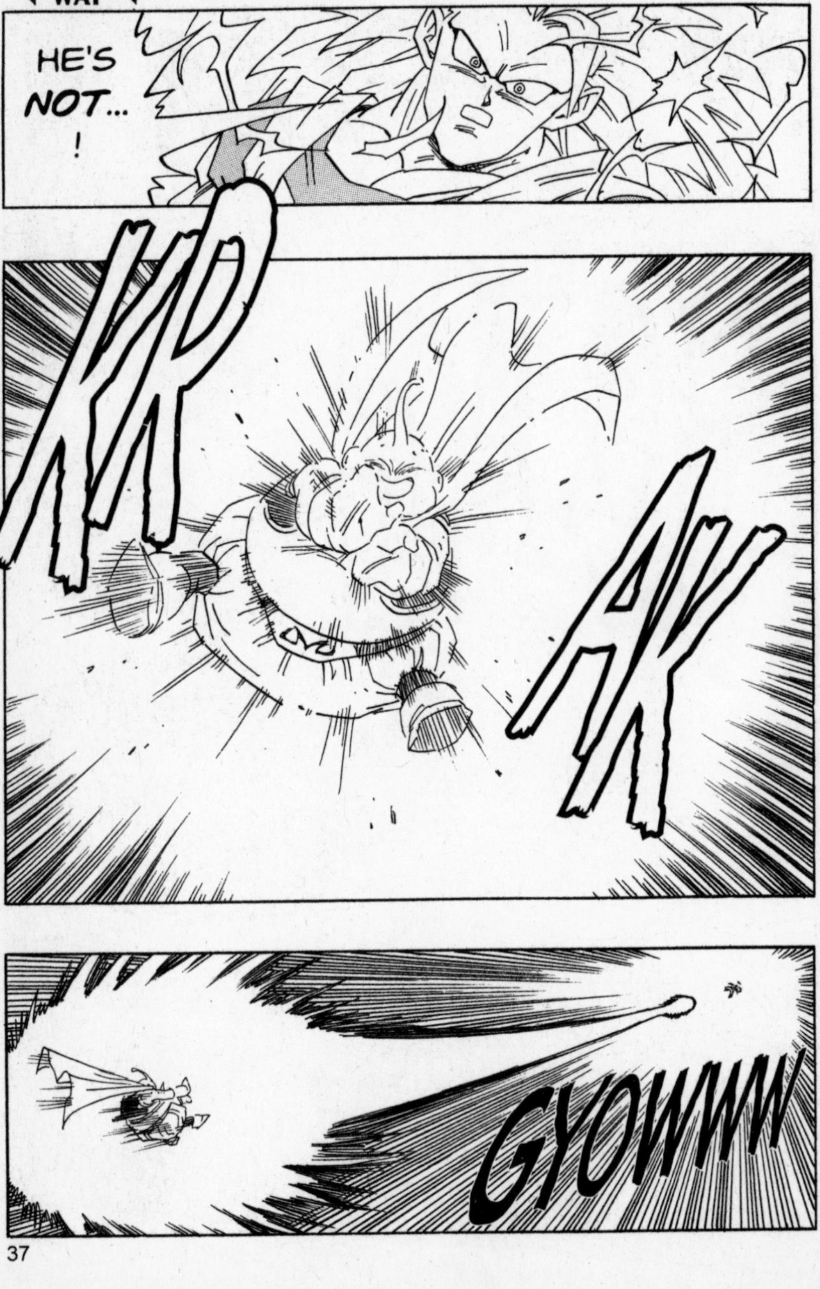

HE'S NOT... !
KRAK
GYOWWW

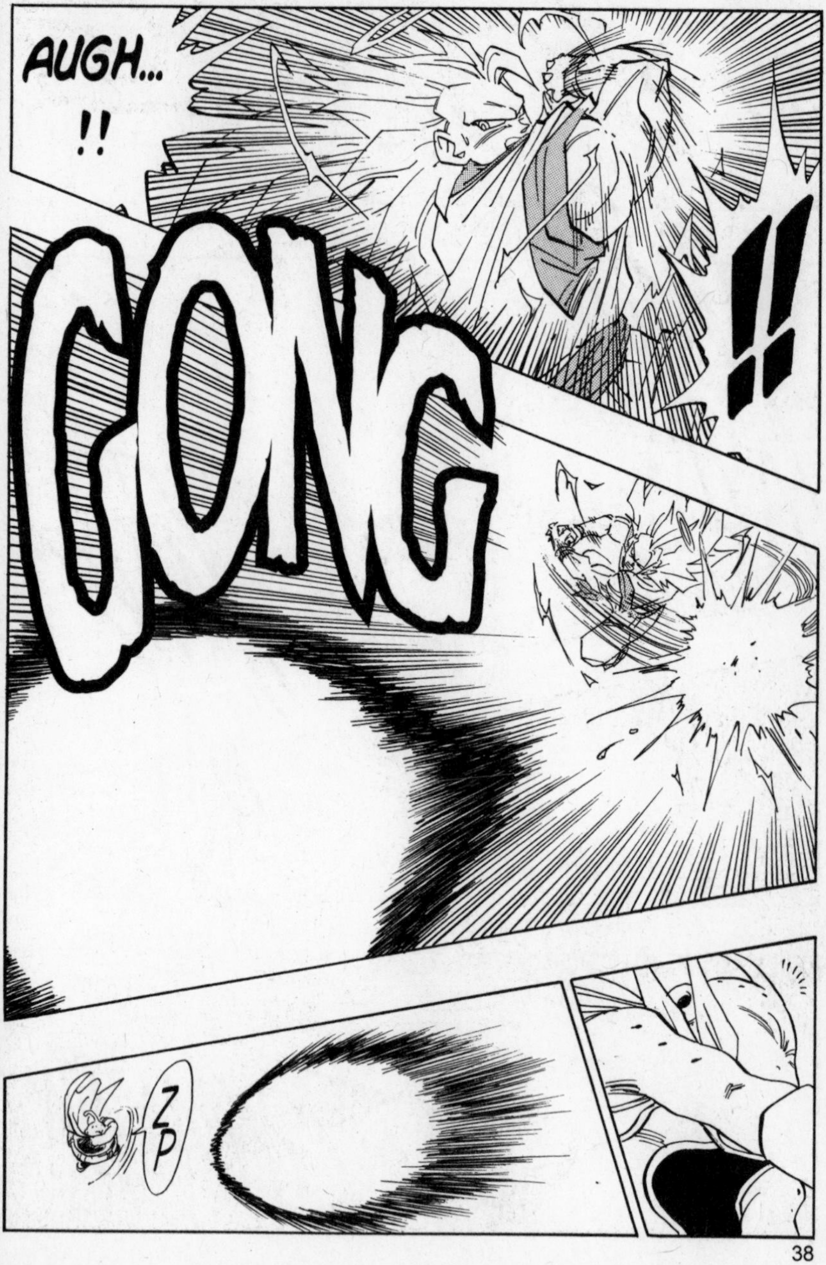
AUGH...
!!
GONG
!!
ZP

READ THIS WAY

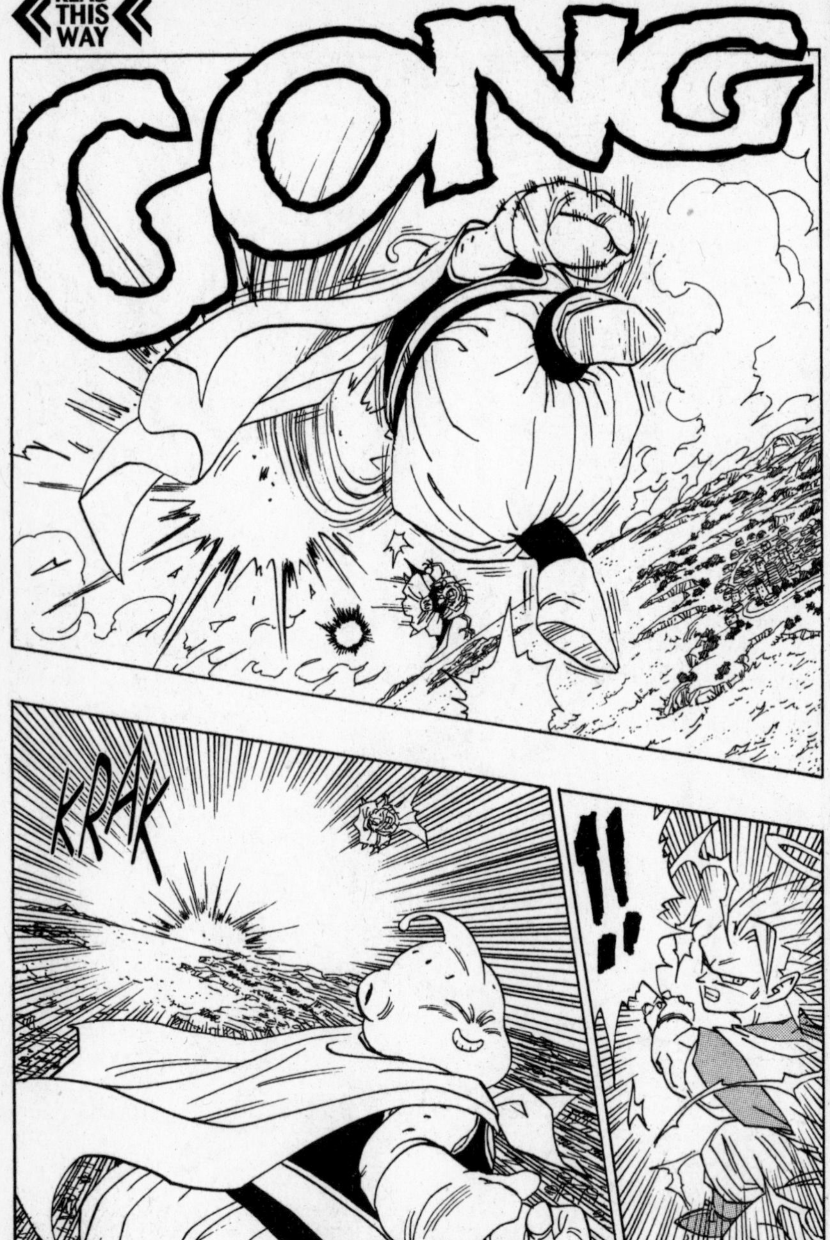
GONG
!!
KRAK

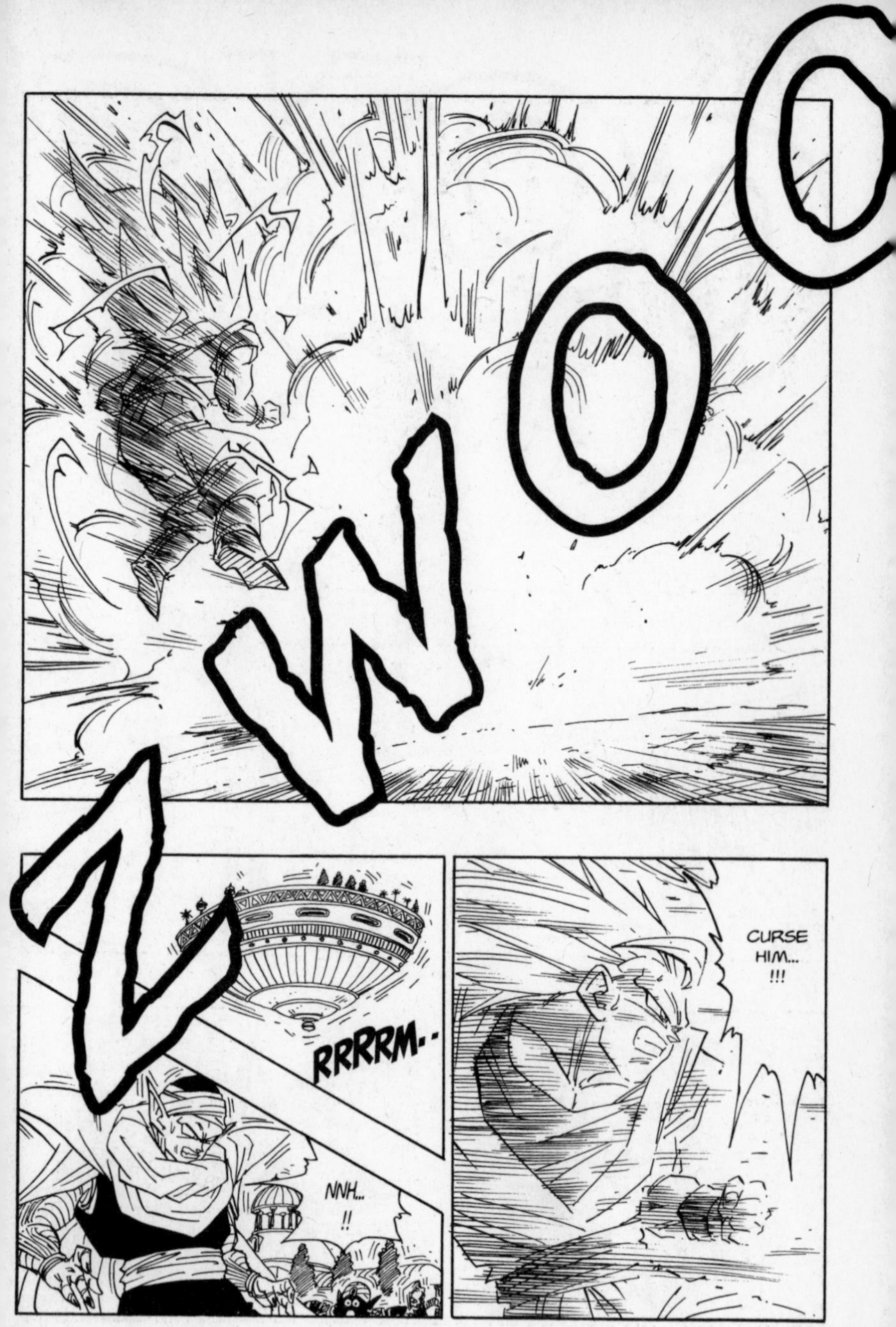
ZWOOO
CURSE HIM... !!!
RRRRM..
NNH... !!

READ THIS WAY

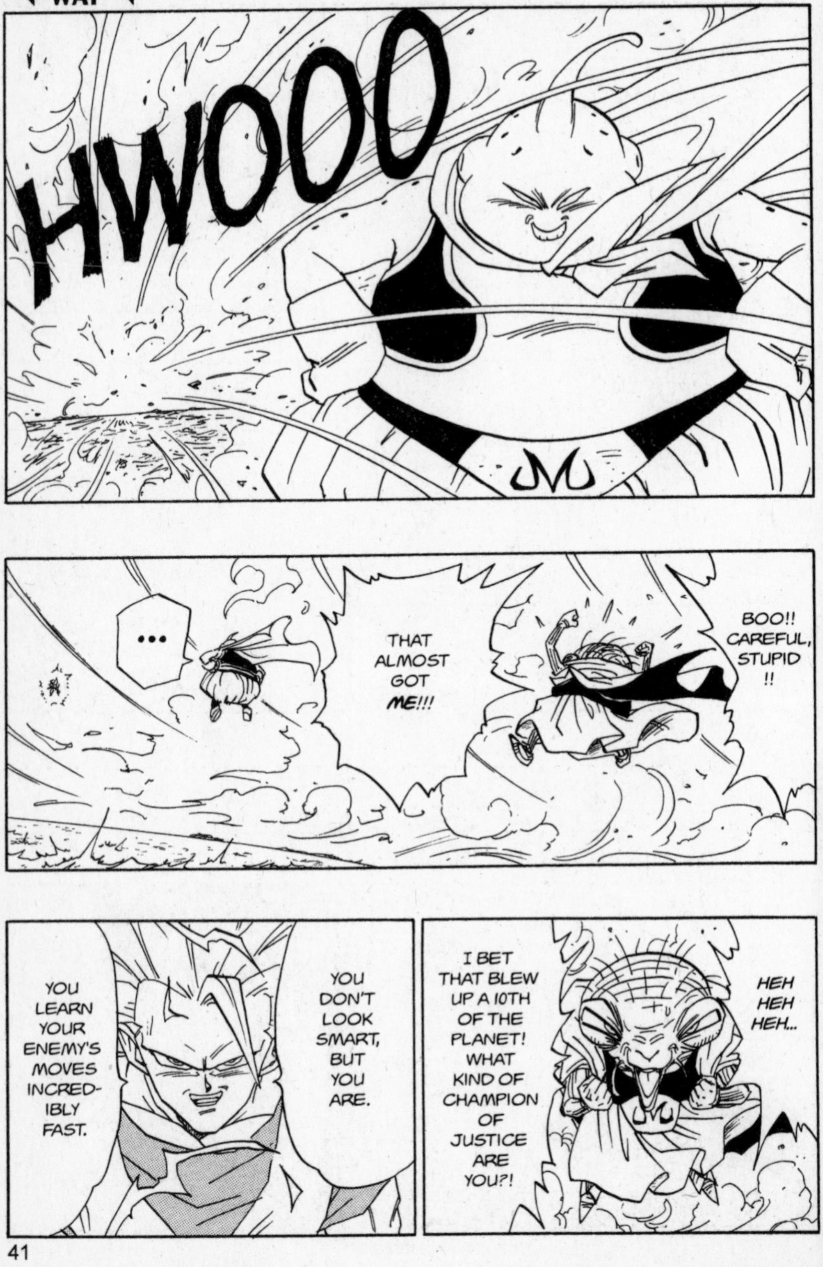
HWOOO
BOO!! CAREFUL, STUPID !!
THAT ALMOST GOT *ME*!!!
...
HEH HEH HEH...
I BET THAT BLEW UP A 10TH OF THE PLANET! WHAT KIND OF CHAMPION OF JUSTICE ARE YOU?!
YOU DON'T LOOK SMART, BUT YOU ARE.
YOU LEARN YOUR ENEMY'S MOVES INCRED-IBLY FAST.

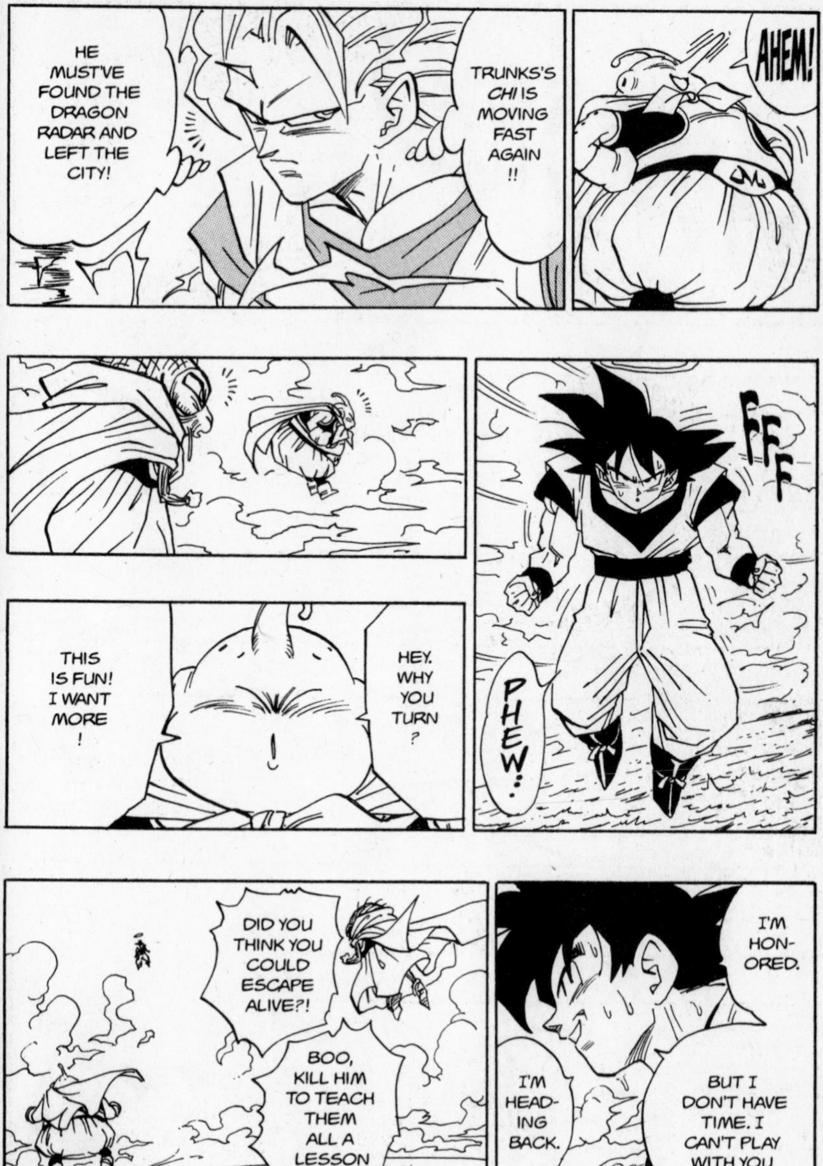
AHEM!
TRUNKS'S CHI IS MOVING FAST AGAIN !!
HE MUST'VE FOUND THE DRAGON RADAR AND LEFT THE CITY!
FFF
PHEW!!
HEY. WHY YOU TURN?
THIS IS FUN! I WANT MORE!
I'M HONORED.
BUT I DON'T HAVE TIME. I CAN'T PLAY WITH YOU FOREVER.
I'M HEADING BACK.
DID YOU THINK YOU COULD ESCAPE ALIVE?!
BOO, KILL HIM TO TEACH THEM ALL A LESSON !!

READ THIS WAY

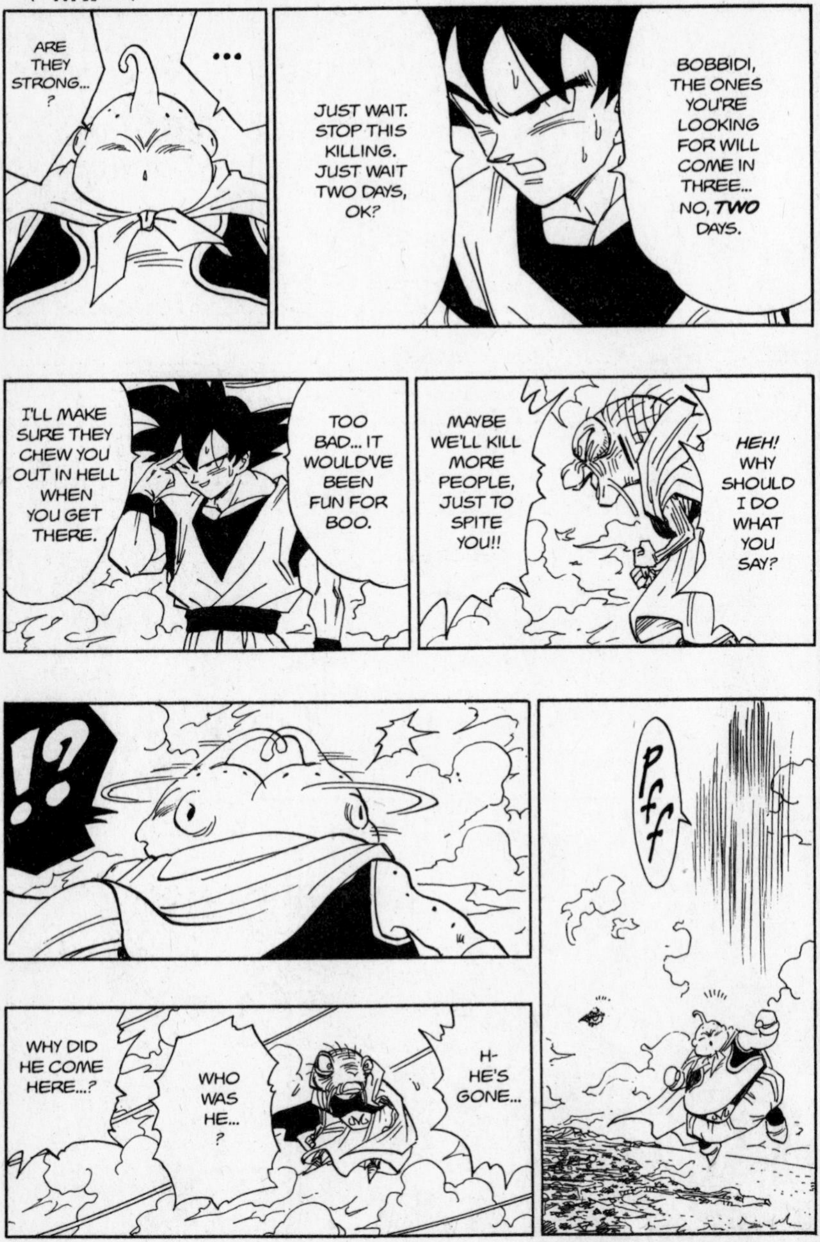
BOBBIDI, THE ONES YOU'RE LOOKING FOR WILL COME IN THREE... NO, **TWO** DAYS.
JUST WAIT. STOP THIS KILLING. JUST WAIT TWO DAYS, OK?
...
ARE THEY STRONG...?
HEH! WHY SHOULD I DO WHAT YOU SAY?
MAYBE WE'LL KILL MORE PEOPLE, JUST TO SPITE YOU!!
TOO BAD... IT WOULD'VE BEEN FUN FOR BOO.
I'LL MAKE SURE THEY CHEW YOU OUT IN HELL WHEN YOU GET THERE.
Pff
!?
H-HE'S GONE...
WHO WAS HE...?
WHY DID HE COME HERE...?

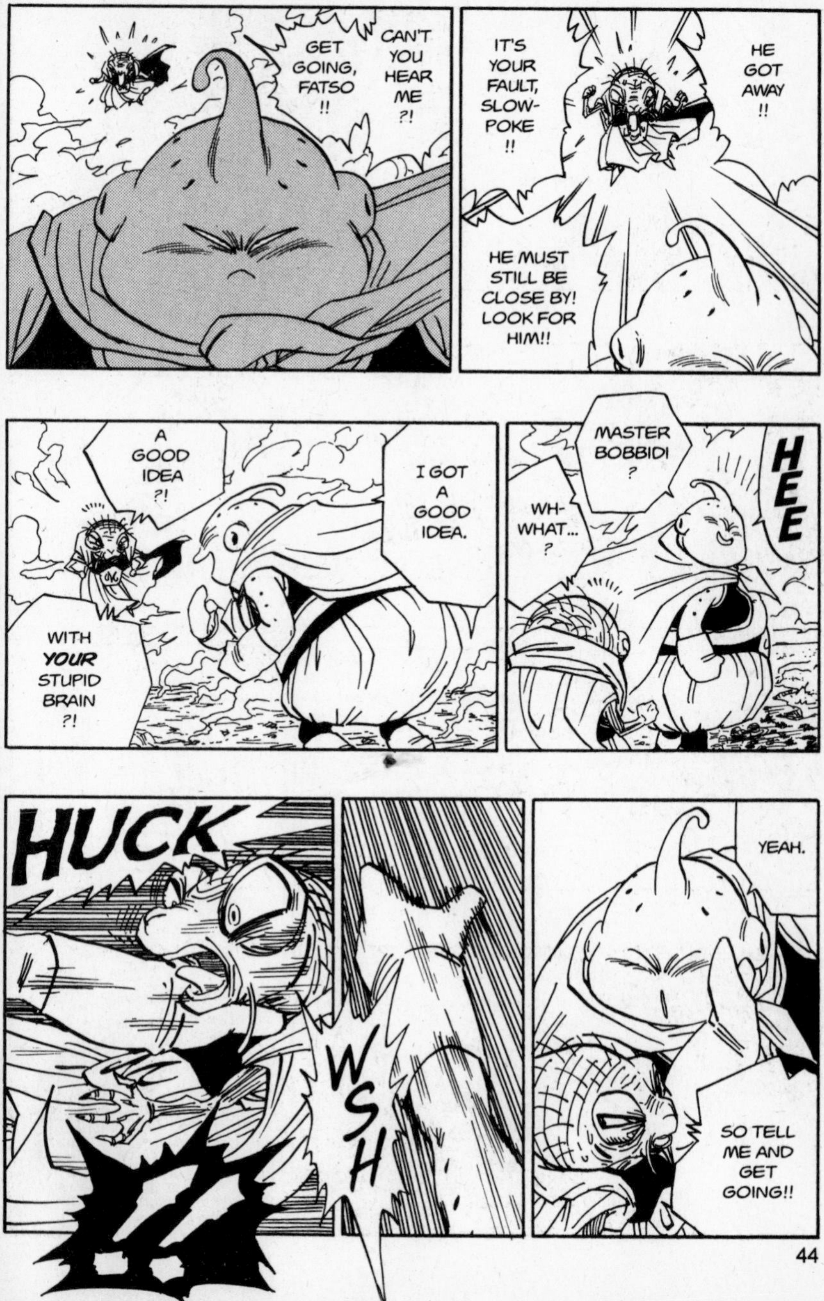
HE GOT AWAY!!
IT'S YOUR FAULT, SLOW-POKE!!
HE MUST STILL BE CLOSE BY! LOOK FOR HIM!!
CAN'T YOU HEAR ME?!
GET GOING, FATSO!!
HEE
MASTER BOBBIDI?
WH-WHAT...?
I GOT A GOOD IDEA.
A GOOD IDEA?!
WITH ***YOUR*** STUPID BRAIN?!
YEAH.
SO TELL ME AND GET GOING!!
WSH
HUCK
!?

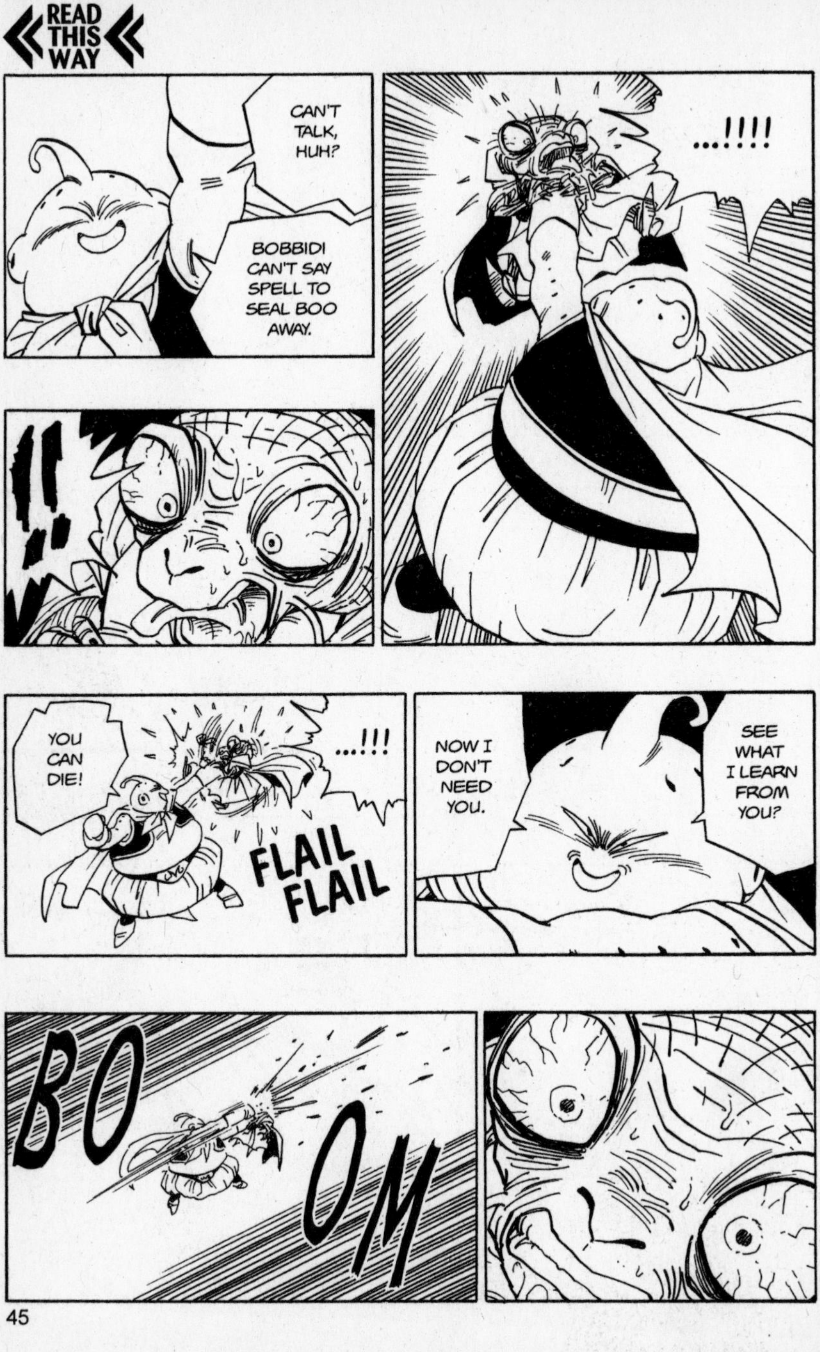
READ THIS WAY
...!!!!
CAN'T TALK, HUH?
BOBBIDI CAN'T SAY SPELL TO SEAL BOO AWAY.
!!
SEE WHAT I LEARN FROM YOU?
NOW I DON'T NEED YOU.
...!!!
YOU CAN DIE!
FLAIL FLAIL
BOOM

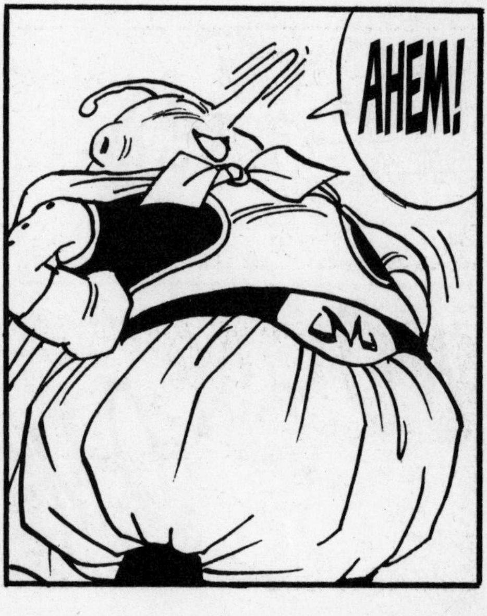
AHEM!

DBZ:282 · Goku's Time

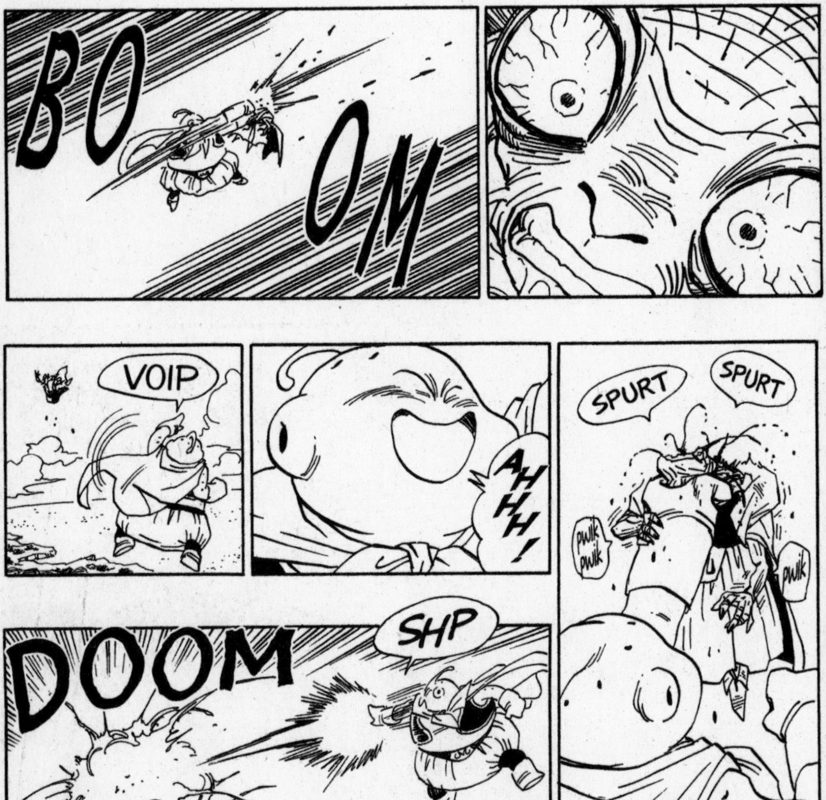
BOOM
SPURT
SPURT
pwik pwik
pwik
AHHH!
VOIP
SHP
DOOM

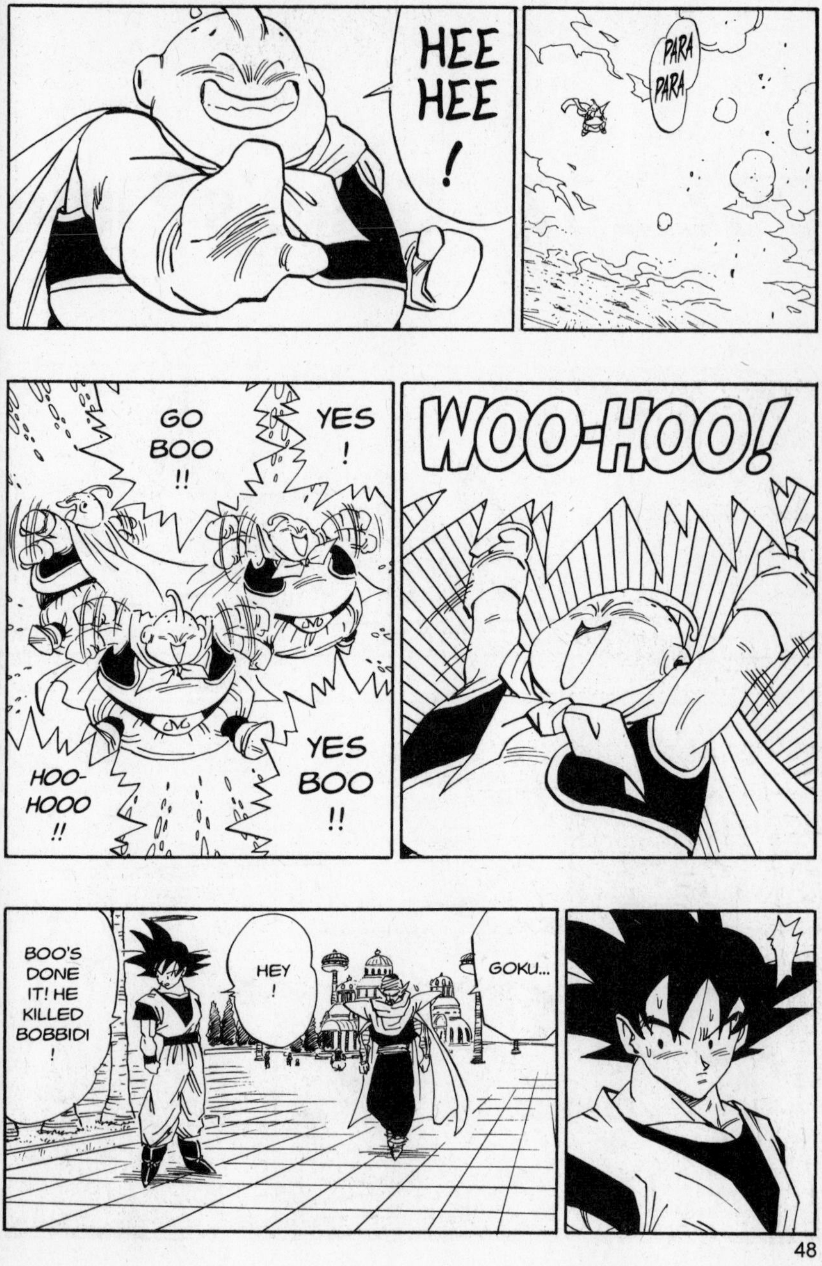
PARA PARA
HEE HEE !
WOO-HOO!
YES !
GO BOO !!
YES BOO !!
HOO-HOOO !!
GOKU...
HEY !
BOO'S DONE IT! HE KILLED BOBBIDI !

READ THIS WAY

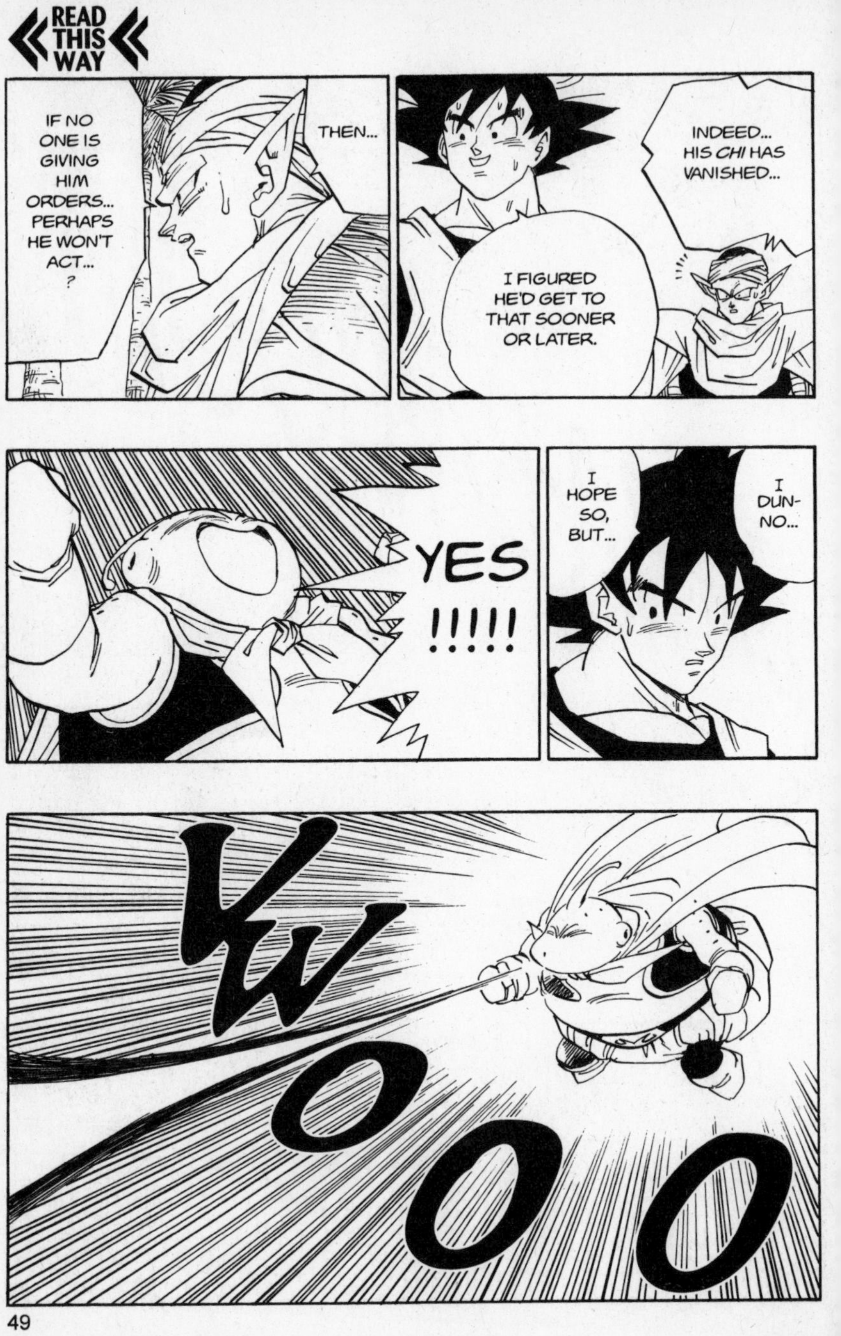
INDEED... HIS *CHI* HAS VANISHED...
I FIGURED HE'D GET TO THAT SOONER OR LATER.
THEN...
IF NO ONE IS GIVING HIM ORDERS... PERHAPS HE WON'T ACT...?
I DUN-NO...
I HOPE SO, BUT...
YES!!!!!
WOOO

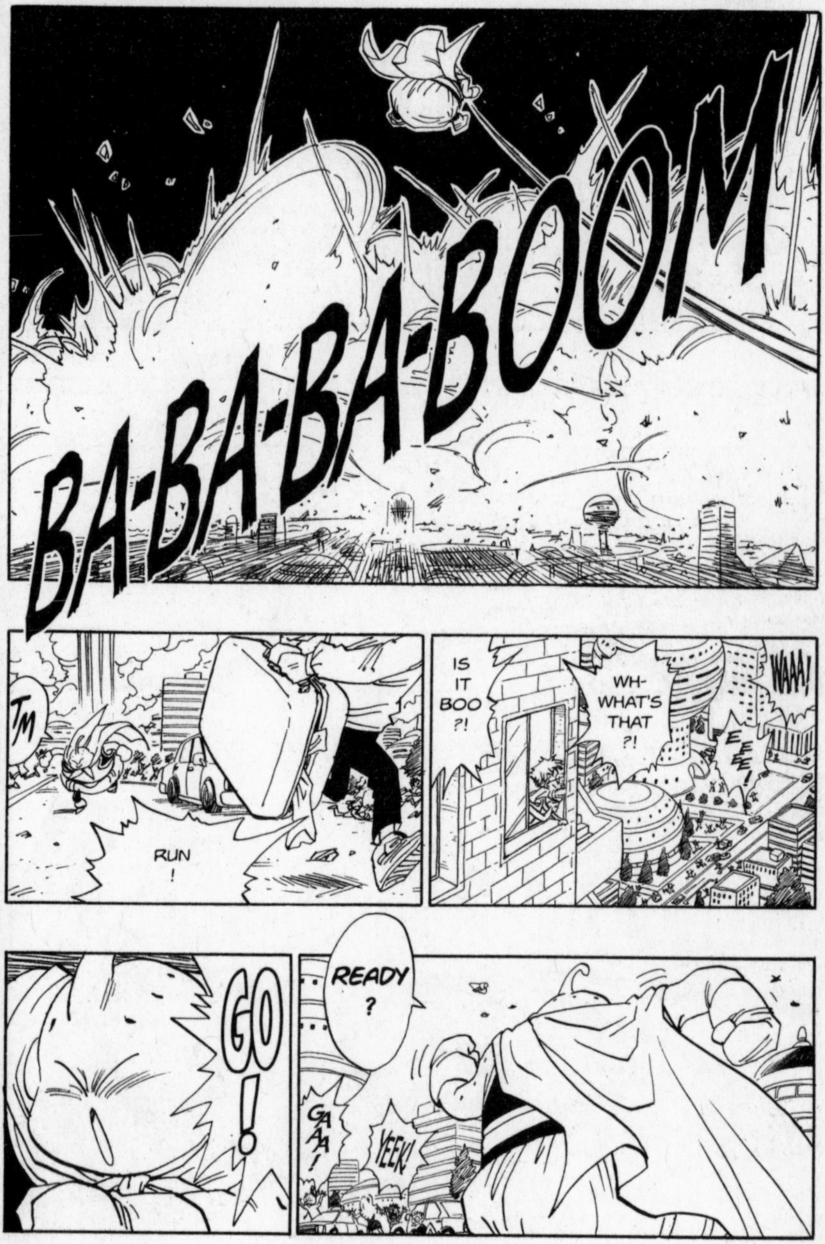
BA-BA-BA-BOOM
WAAA!
WH-WHAT'S THAT?!
IS IT BOO?!
EEEE!
TM
RUN!
READY?
YEEK!
GAAA!
GO!

READ THIS WAY

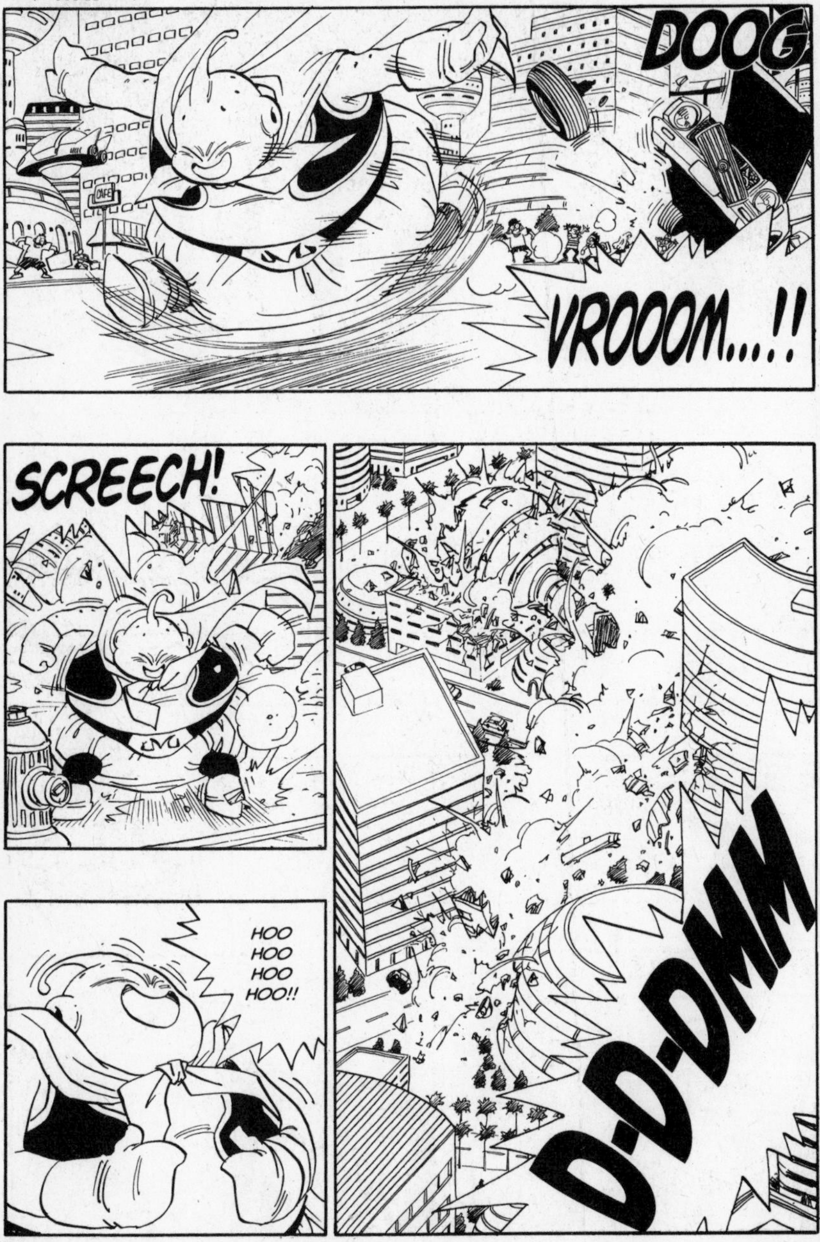
DOOG
VROOOM...!!
D-D-DMM
SCREECH!
HOO HOO HOO HOO!!

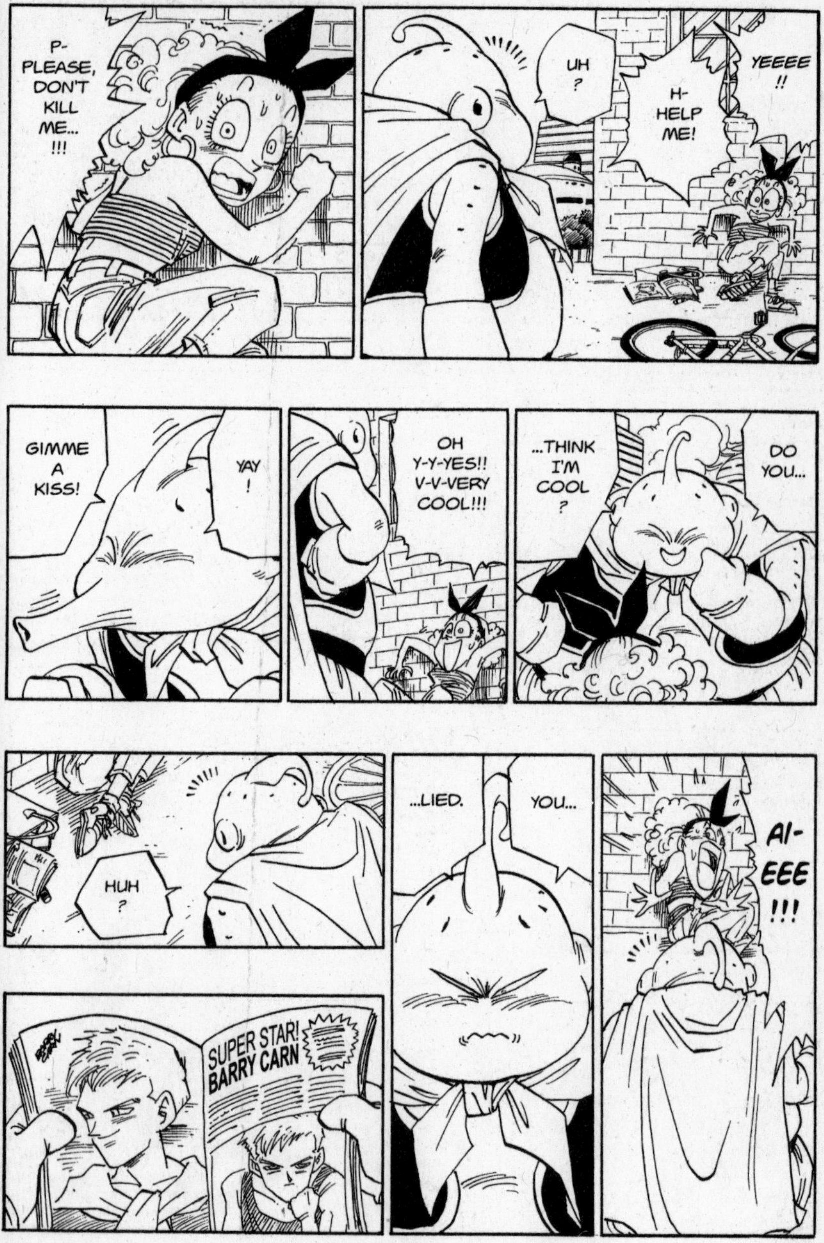
YEEEE !!
H- HELP ME!
UH ?
P- PLEASE, DON'T KILL ME... !!!
DO YOU...
...THINK I'M COOL ?
OH Y-Y-YES!! V-V-VERY COOL!!!
YAY !
GIMME A KISS!
AI- EEE !!!
YOU...
...LIED.
HUH ?
SUPER STAR! BARRY CARN

READ THIS WAY

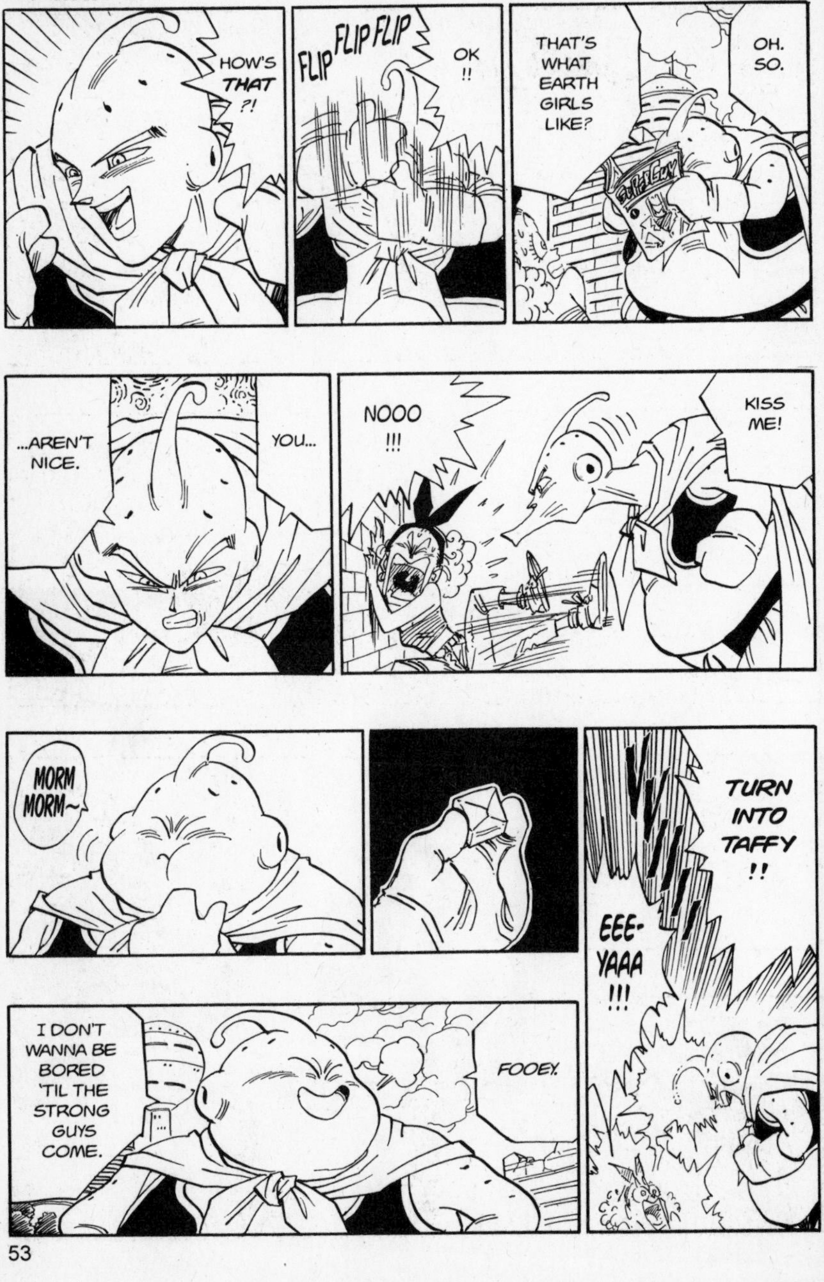

OH. SO.
THAT'S WHAT EARTH GIRLS LIKE?
FLIP FLIP FLIP
OK !!
HOW'S THAT ?!
KISS ME!
NOOO !!!
YOU...
...AREN'T NICE.
TURN INTO TAFFY !!
EEE-YAAA !!!
MORM MORM~
FOOEY.
I DON'T WANNA BE BORED 'TIL THE STRONG GUYS COME.

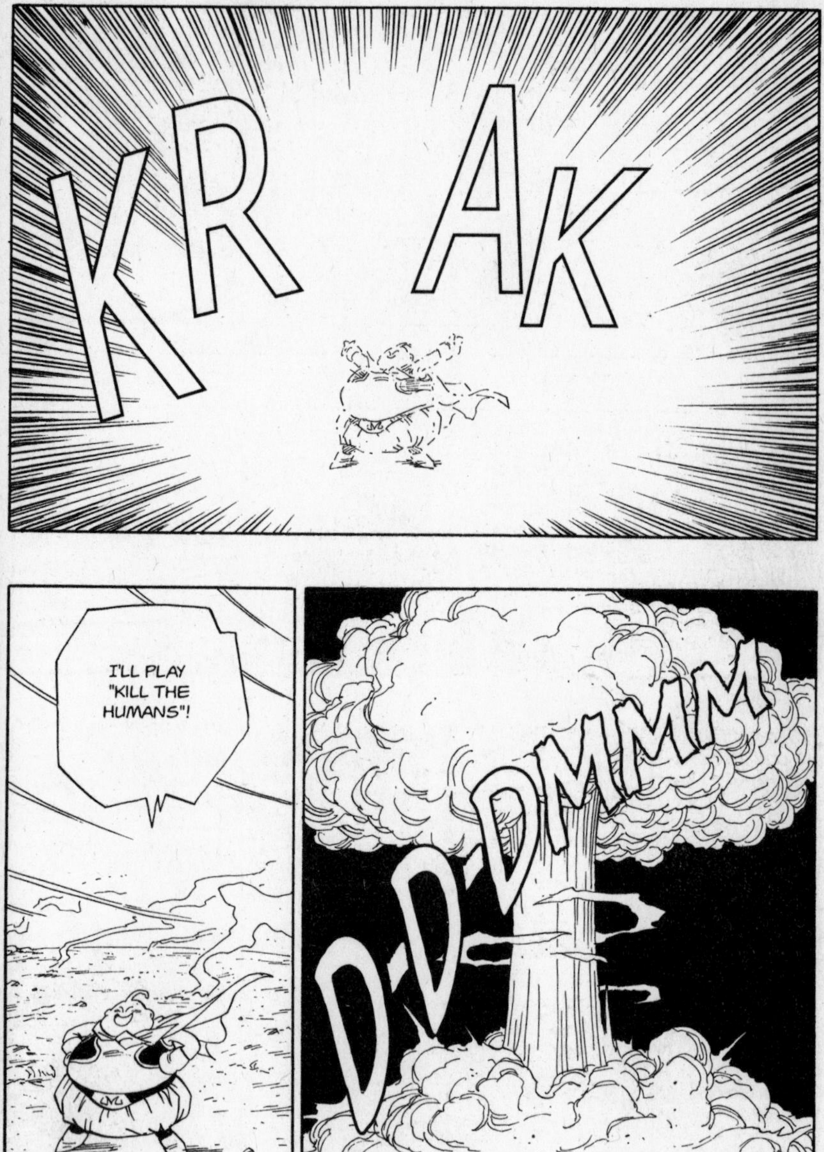
KRAK
D-D-DMMMM
I'LL PLAY "KILL THE HUMANS"!

READ THIS WAY

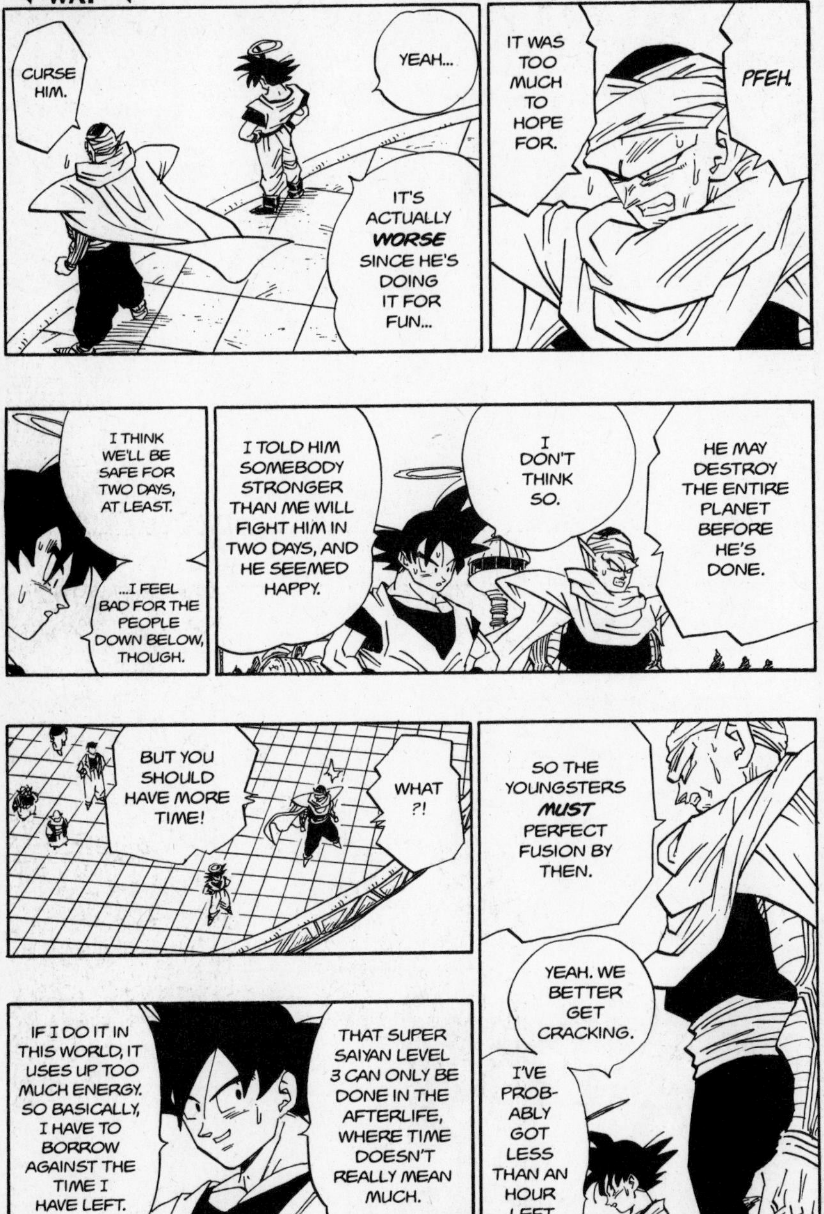
PFEH.
IT WAS TOO MUCH TO HOPE FOR.
YEAH...
IT'S ACTUALLY WORSE SINCE HE'S DOING IT FOR FUN...
CURSE HIM.
HE MAY DESTROY THE ENTIRE PLANET BEFORE HE'S DONE.
I DON'T THINK SO.
I TOLD HIM SOMEBODY STRONGER THAN ME WILL FIGHT HIM IN TWO DAYS, AND HE SEEMED HAPPY.
I THINK WE'LL BE SAFE FOR TWO DAYS, AT LEAST.
...I FEEL BAD FOR THE PEOPLE DOWN BELOW, THOUGH.
SO THE YOUNGSTERS MUST PERFECT FUSION BY THEN.
YEAH. WE BETTER GET CRACKING.
I'VE PROB-ABLY GOT LESS THAN AN HOUR LEFT.
WHAT ?!
BUT YOU SHOULD HAVE MORE TIME!
THAT SUPER SAIYAN LEVEL 3 CAN ONLY BE DONE IN THE AFTERLIFE, WHERE TIME DOESN'T REALLY MEAN MUCH.
IF I DO IT IN THIS WORLD, IT USES UP TOO MUCH ENERGY. SO BASICALLY, I HAVE TO BORROW AGAINST THE TIME I HAVE LEFT.

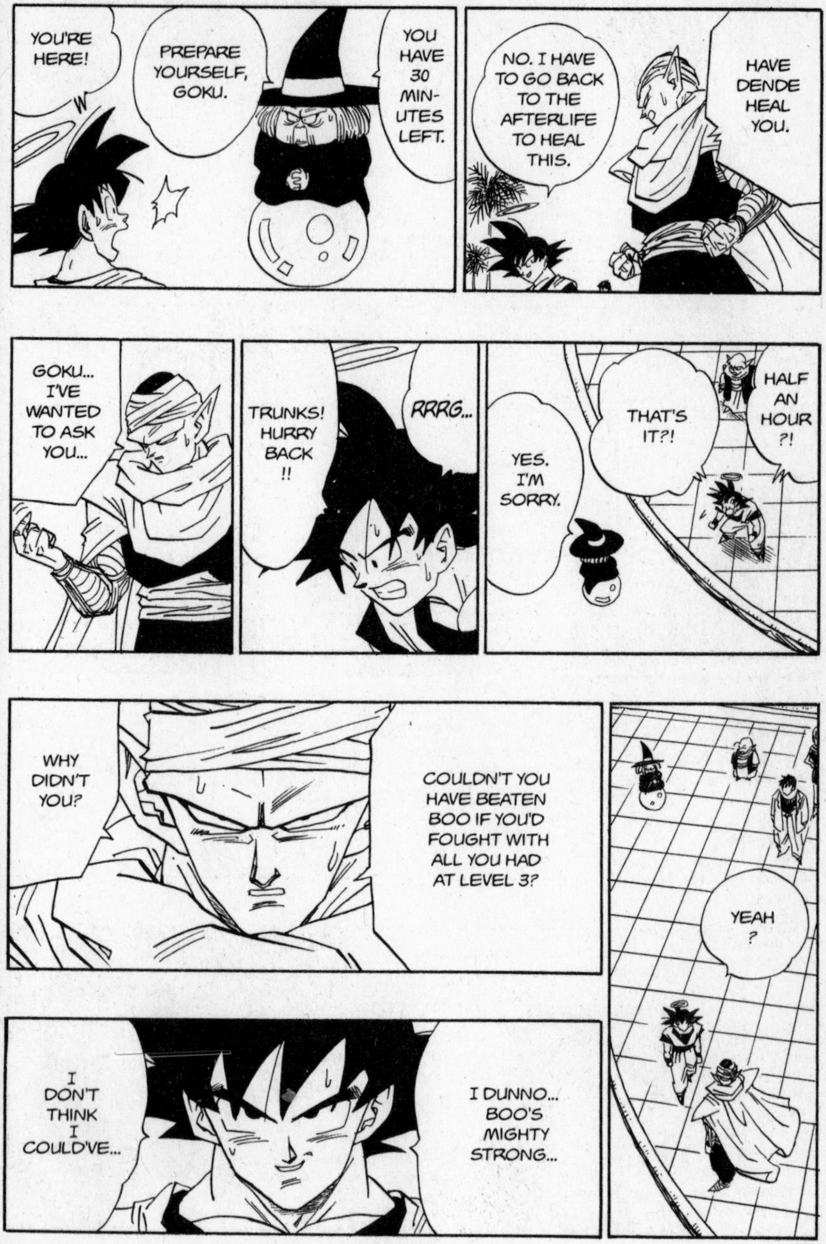
HAVE DENDE HEAL YOU.
NO. I HAVE TO GO BACK TO THE AFTERLIFE TO HEAL THIS.
YOU HAVE 30 MIN-UTES LEFT.
PREPARE YOURSELF, GOKU.
YOU'RE HERE!
HALF AN HOUR?!
THAT'S IT?!
YES. I'M SORRY.
RRRG...
TRUNKS! HURRY BACK!!
GOKU... I'VE WANTED TO ASK YOU...
YEAH?
COULDN'T YOU HAVE BEATEN BOO IF YOU'D FOUGHT WITH ALL YOU HAD AT LEVEL 3?
WHY DIDN'T YOU?
I DUNNO... BOO'S MIGHTY STRONG...
I DON'T THINK I COULD'VE...

READ THIS WAY

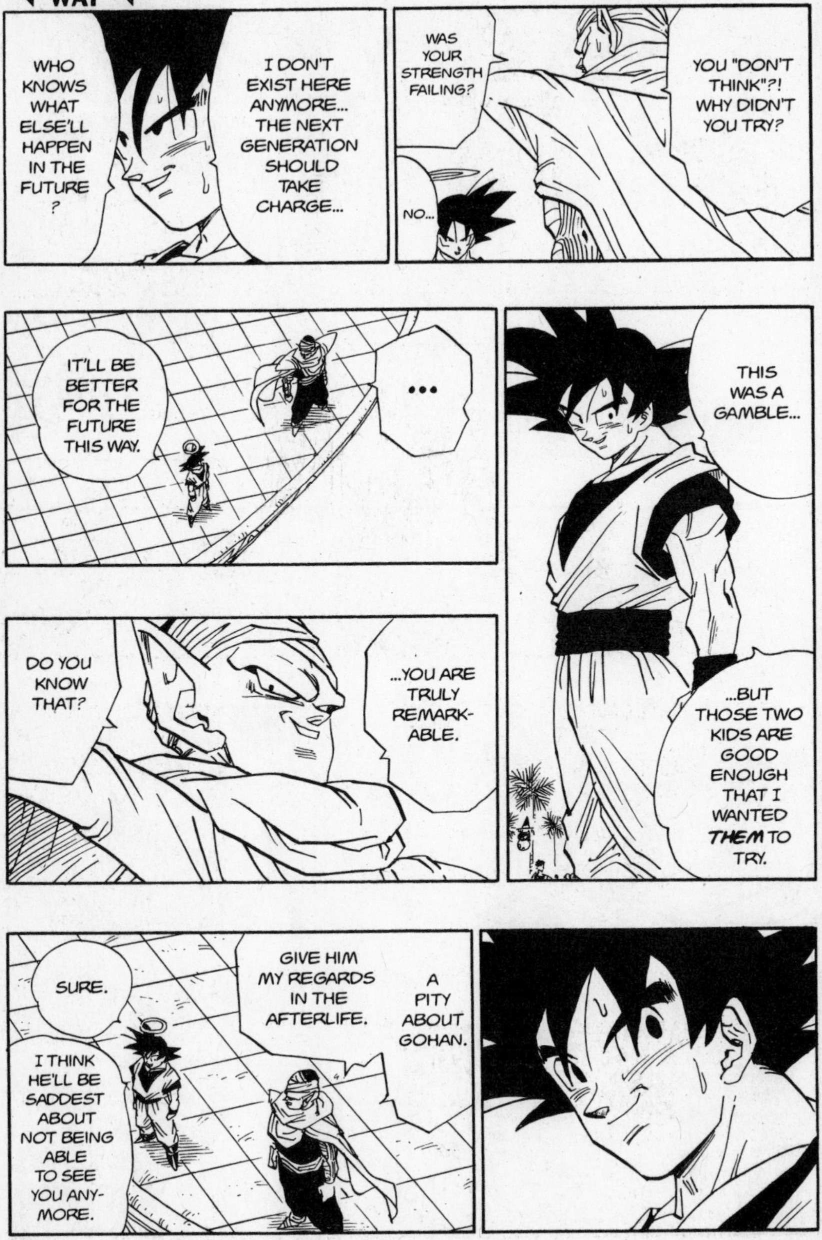
YOU "DON'T THINK"?! WHY DIDN'T YOU TRY?
WAS YOUR STRENGTH FAILING?
NO...
I DON'T EXIST HERE ANYMORE... THE NEXT GENERATION SHOULD TAKE CHARGE...
WHO KNOWS WHAT ELSE'LL HAPPEN IN THE FUTURE?
THIS WAS A GAMBLE...
...BUT THOSE TWO KIDS ARE GOOD ENOUGH THAT I WANTED *THEM* TO TRY.
...
IT'LL BE BETTER FOR THE FUTURE THIS WAY.
...YOU ARE TRULY REMARK-ABLE.
DO YOU KNOW THAT?
A PITY ABOUT GOHAN.
GIVE HIM MY REGARDS IN THE AFTERLIFE.
SURE.
I THINK HE'LL BE SADDEST ABOUT NOT BEING ABLE TO SEE YOU ANY-MORE.

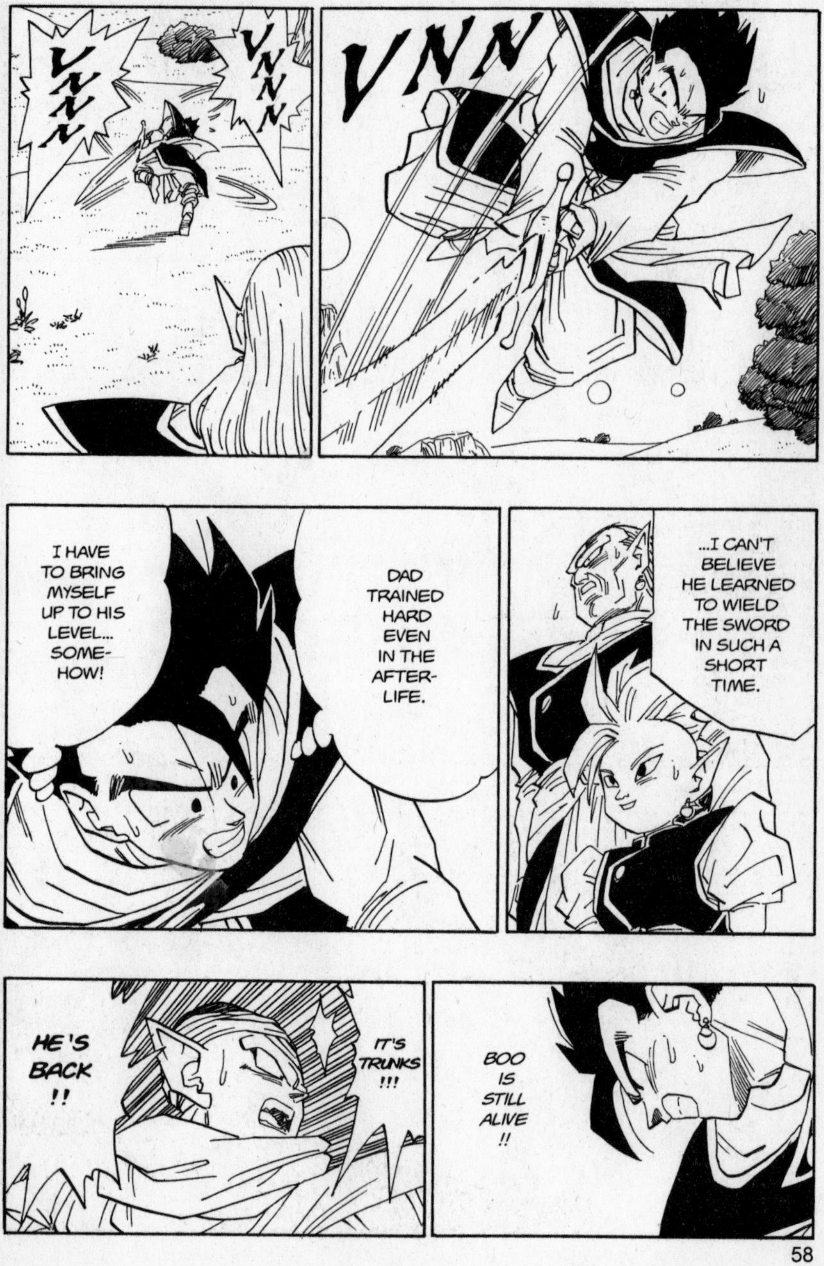
VNN
VNNN
VNNNN
...I CAN'T BELIEVE HE LEARNED TO WIELD THE SWORD IN SUCH A SHORT TIME.
DAD TRAINED HARD EVEN IN THE AFTER-LIFE.
I HAVE TO BRING MYSELF UP TO HIS LEVEL... SOME-HOW!
BOO IS STILL ALIVE !!
IT'S TRUNKS !!!
HE'S BACK !!

READ THIS WAY

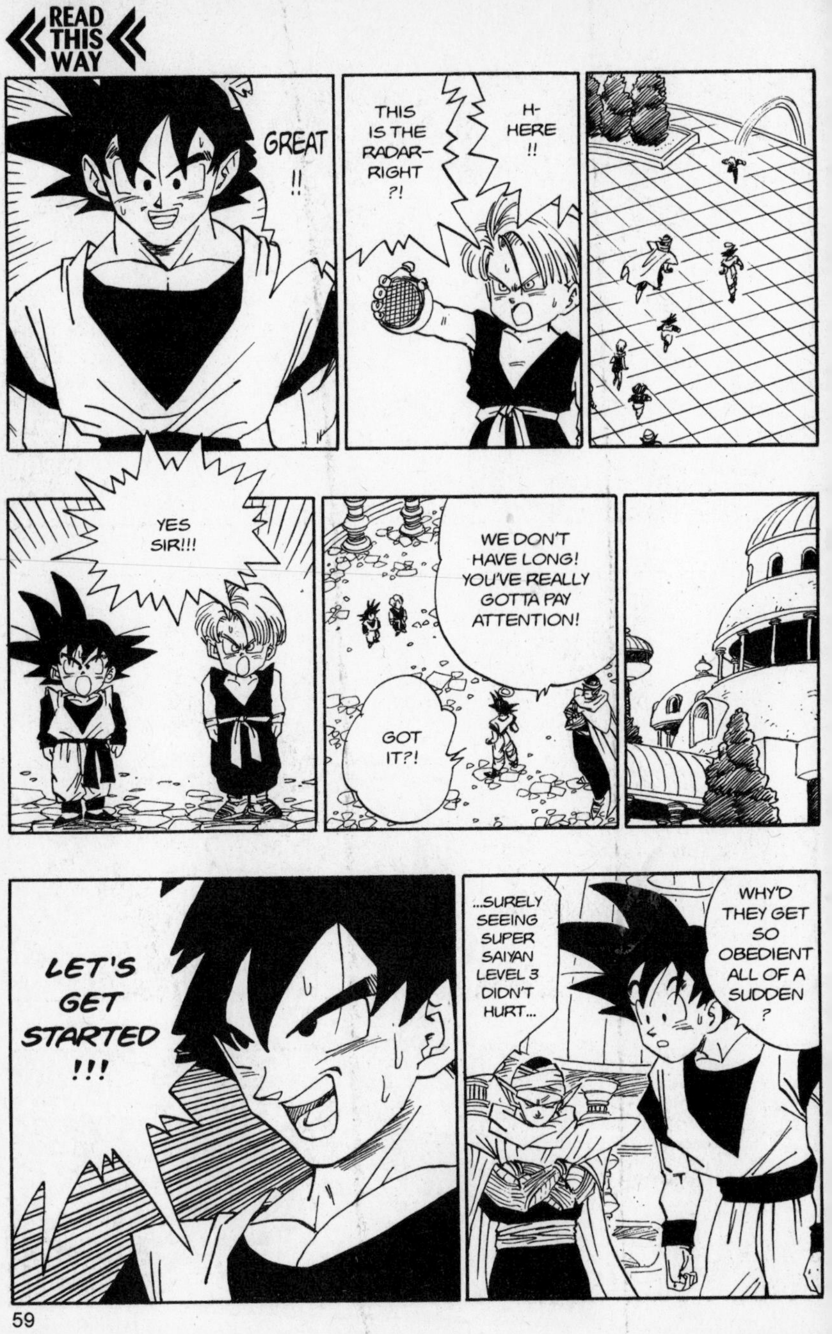
H- HERE !!
THIS IS THE RADAR- RIGHT ?!
GREAT !!
WE DON'T HAVE LONG! YOU'VE REALLY GOTTA PAY ATTENTION!
GOT IT?!
YES SIR!!!
WHY'D THEY GET SO OBEDIENT ALL OF A SUDDEN ?
...SURELY SEEING SUPER SAIYAN LEVEL 3 DIDN'T HURT...
LET'S GET STARTED !!!

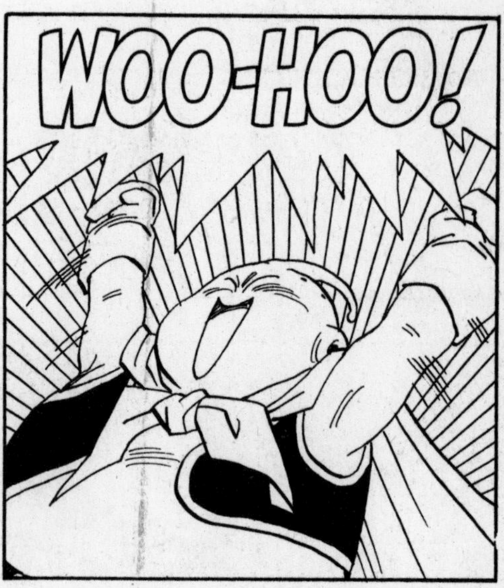
WOO-HOO!

DBZ:283 • Goku Goes Back

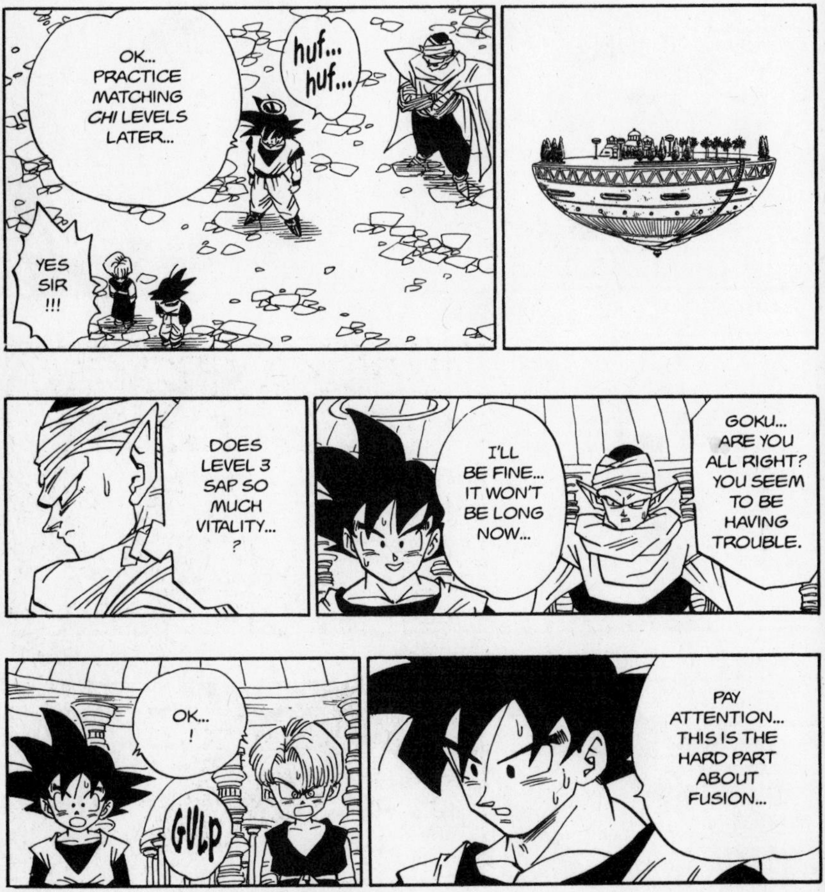
huf... huf...
OK... PRACTICE MATCHING CHI LEVELS LATER...
YES SIR !!!
GOKU... ARE YOU ALL RIGHT? YOU SEEM TO BE HAVING TROUBLE.
I'LL BE FINE... IT WON'T BE LONG NOW...
DOES LEVEL 3 SAP SO MUCH VITALITY...?
PAY ATTENTION... THIS IS THE HARD PART ABOUT FUSION...
OK...!
GULP

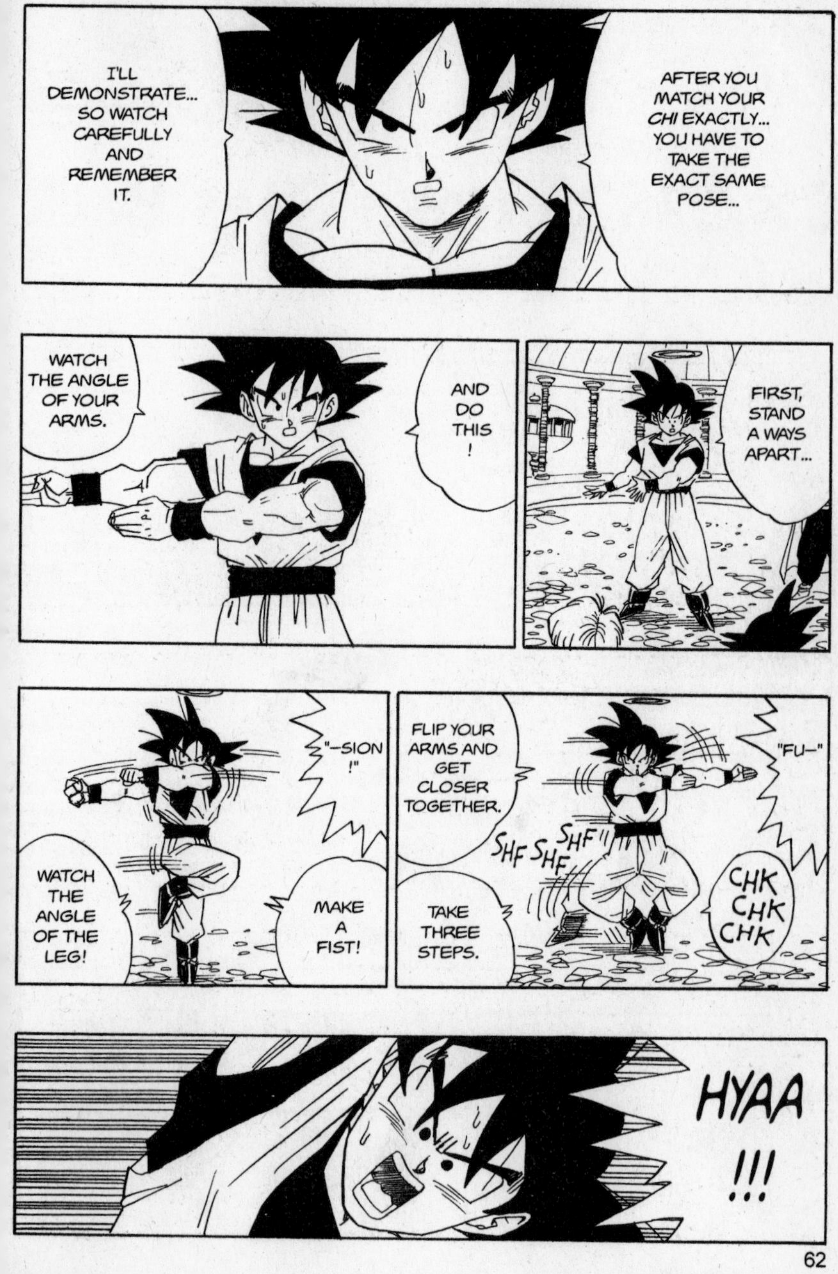

AFTER YOU MATCH YOUR *CHI* EXACTLY... YOU HAVE TO TAKE THE EXACT SAME POSE...
I'LL DEMONSTRATE... SO WATCH CAREFULLY AND REMEMBER IT.
FIRST, STAND A WAYS APART...
AND DO THIS!
WATCH THE ANGLE OF YOUR ARMS.
"FU–"
FLIP YOUR ARMS AND GET CLOSER TOGETHER.
SHF SHF SHF
CHK CHK CHK
TAKE THREE STEPS.
"–SION!"
MAKE A FIST!
WATCH THE ANGLE OF THE LEG!
HYAA!!!

READ THIS WAY

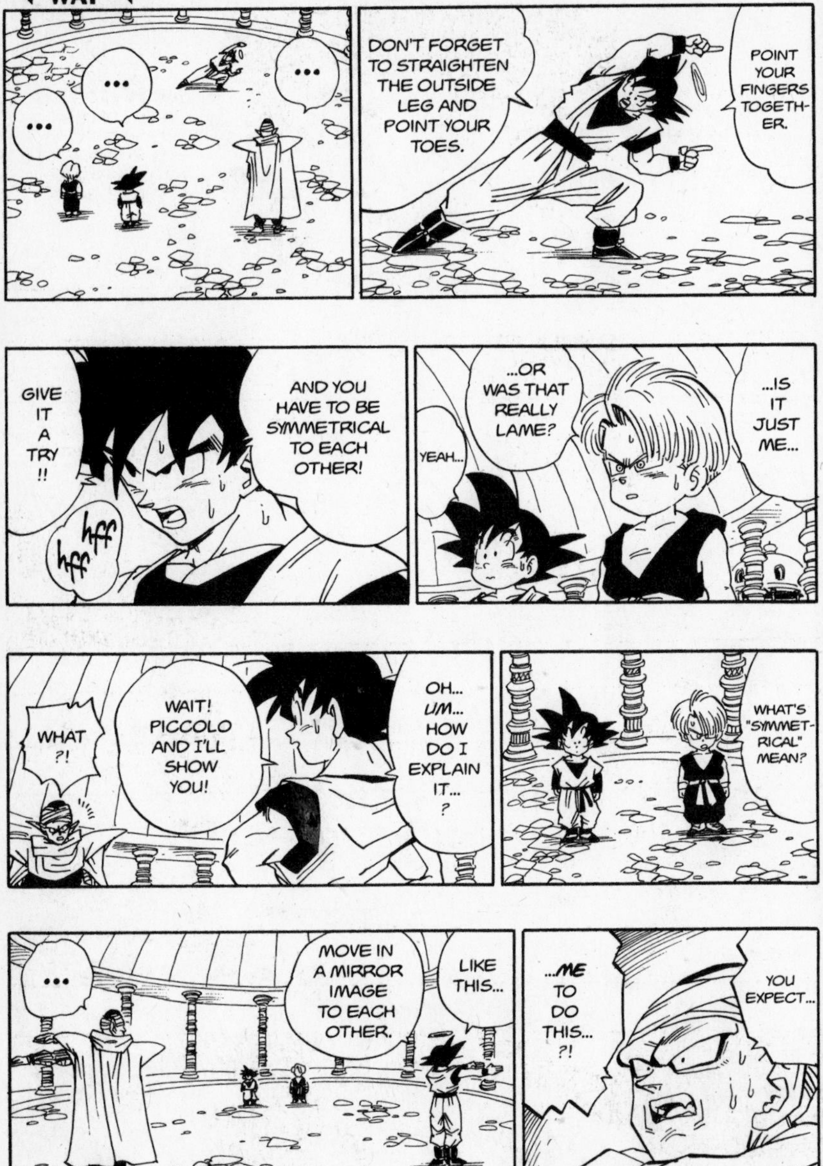
POINT YOUR FINGERS TOGETH-ER.
DON'T FORGET TO STRAIGHTEN THE OUTSIDE LEG AND POINT YOUR TOES.
...
...
...
...IS IT JUST ME...
...OR WAS THAT REALLY LAME?
YEAH...
AND YOU HAVE TO BE SYMMETRICAL TO EACH OTHER!
GIVE IT A TRY!!
hff hff
WHAT'S "SYMMET-RICAL" MEAN?
OH... UM... HOW DO I EXPLAIN IT...?
WAIT! PICCOLO AND I'LL SHOW YOU!
WHAT?!
YOU EXPECT...
...ME TO DO THIS...?!
LIKE THIS...
MOVE IN A MIRROR IMAGE TO EACH OTHER.
...

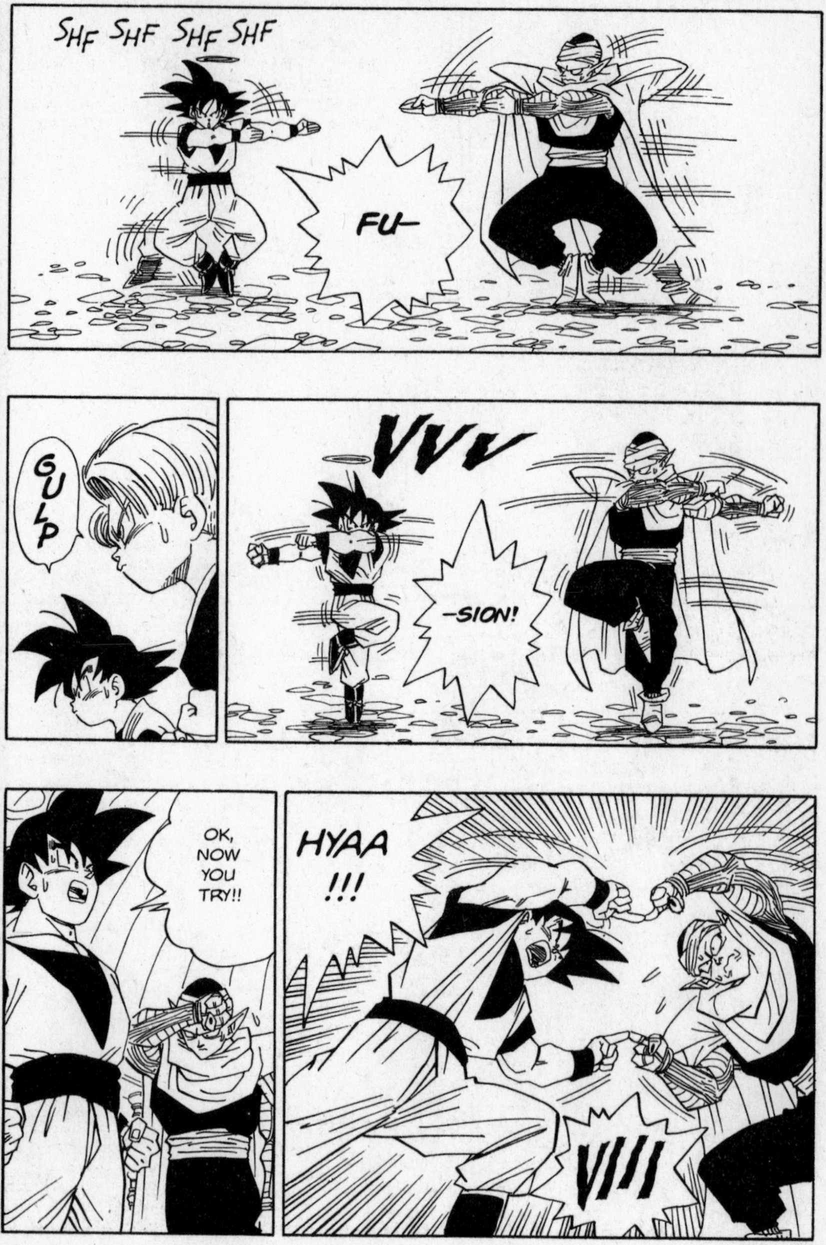

SHF SHF SHF SHF
FU—
VVV
—SION!
GULP
HYAA!!!
OK, NOW YOU TRY!!

READ THIS WAY

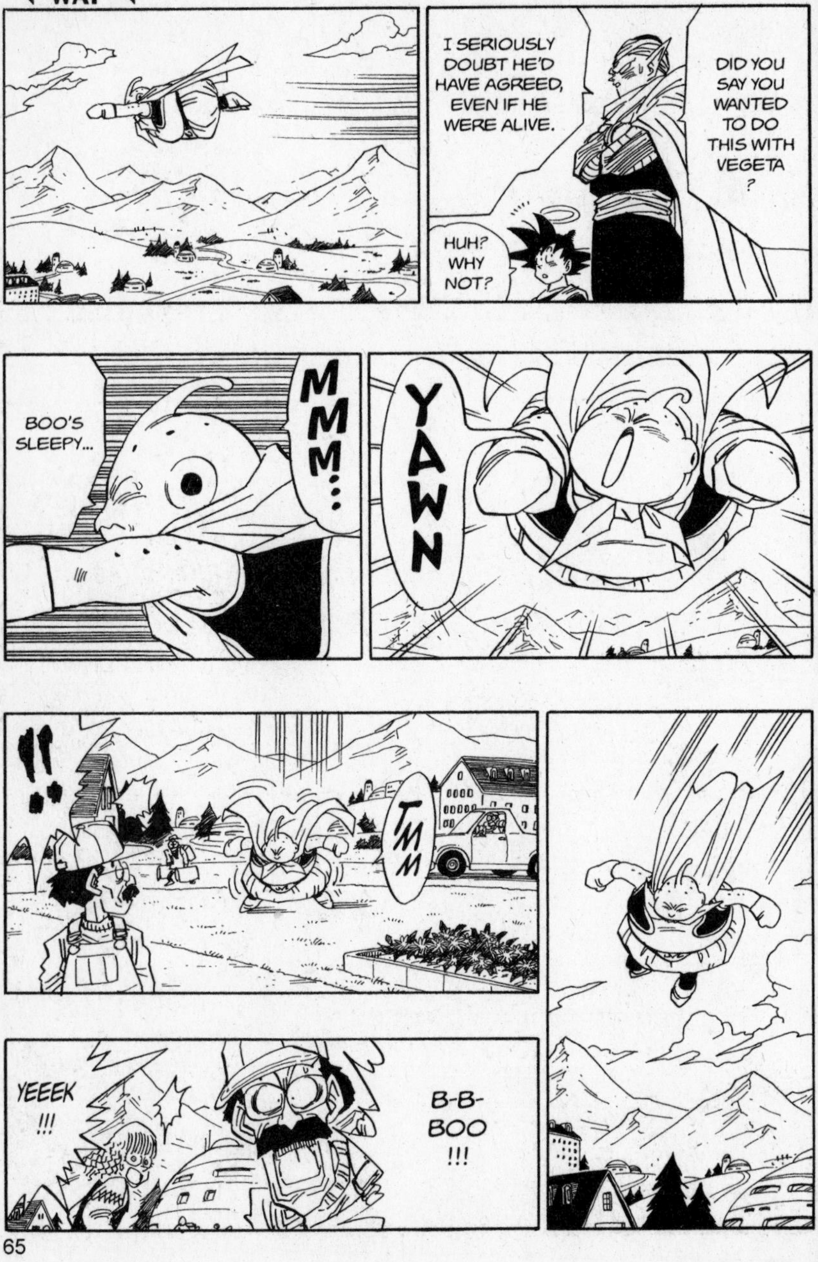

DID YOU SAY YOU WANTED TO DO THIS WITH VEGETA?
I SERIOUSLY DOUBT HE'D HAVE AGREED, EVEN IF HE WERE ALIVE.
HUH? WHY NOT?
YAWN
MMM...
BOO'S SLEEPY...
!!
TMM
B-B-BOO!!!
YEEEK!!!

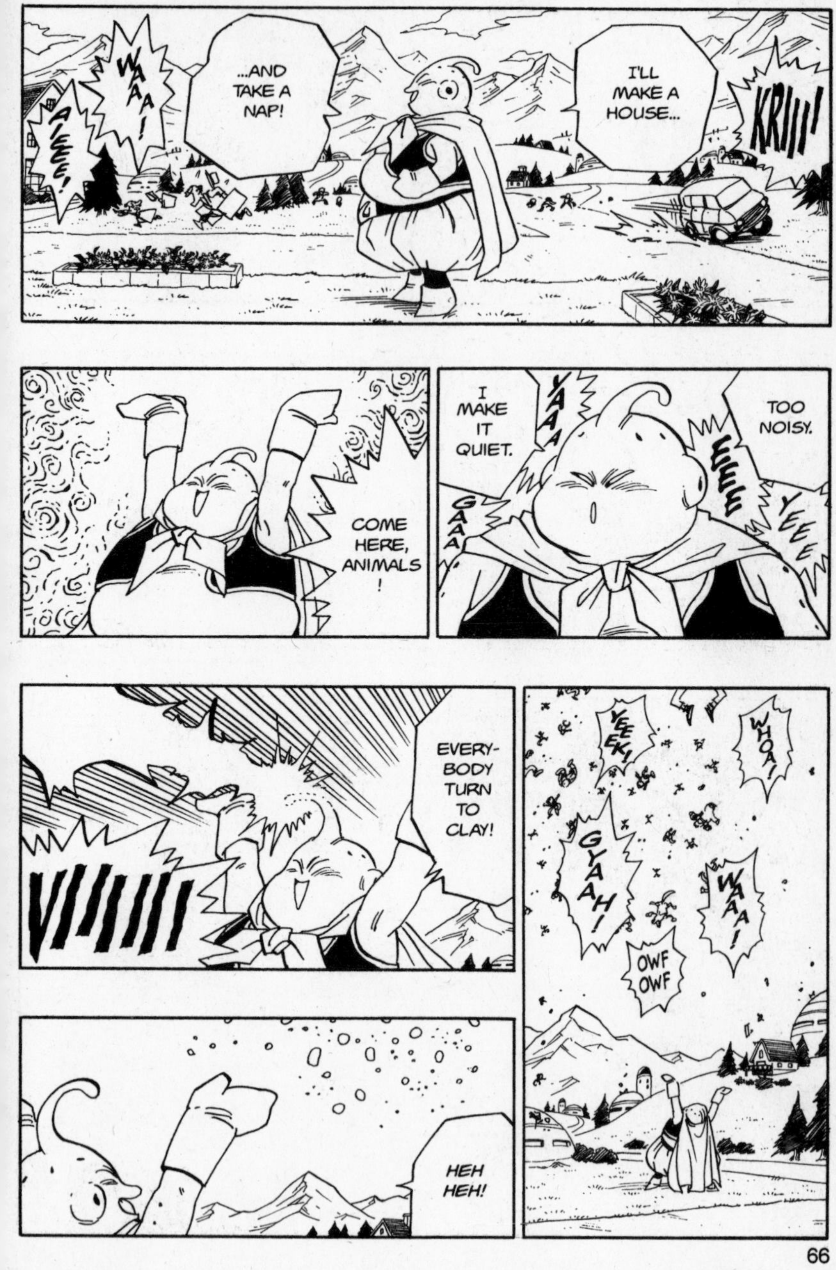
I'LL MAKE A HOUSE...
KRIIII
...AND TAKE A NAP!
WAAA!
AIEEE!
TOO NOISY.
YEEE
EEE
YAAA
I MAKE IT QUIET.
GAAAA
COME HERE, ANIMALS!
WHOA!
YEEEK!
GYAAH!
WAAA!
OWF OWF
EVERYBODY TURN TO CLAY!
VIIIII
HEH HEH!

READ THIS WAY

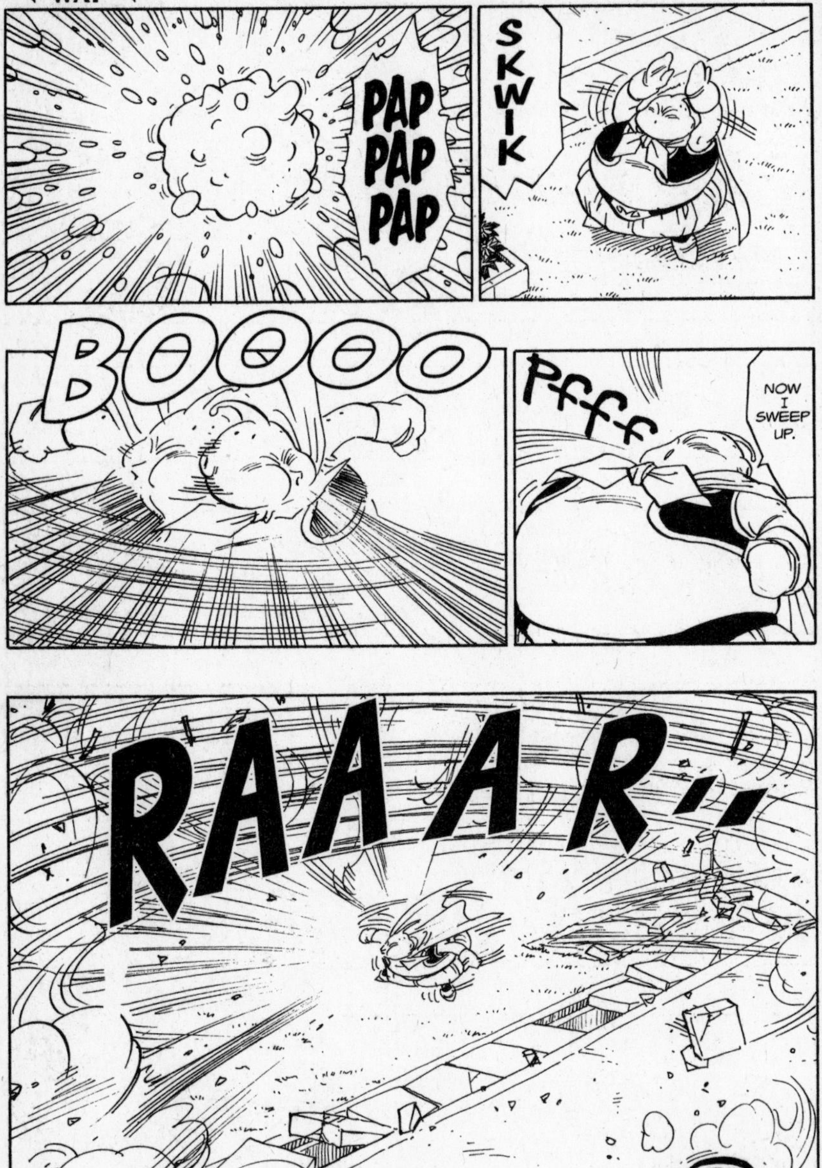
SKWIK
PAP PAP PAP
Pfff
NOW I SWEEP UP.
BOOOO
RAAAR!!

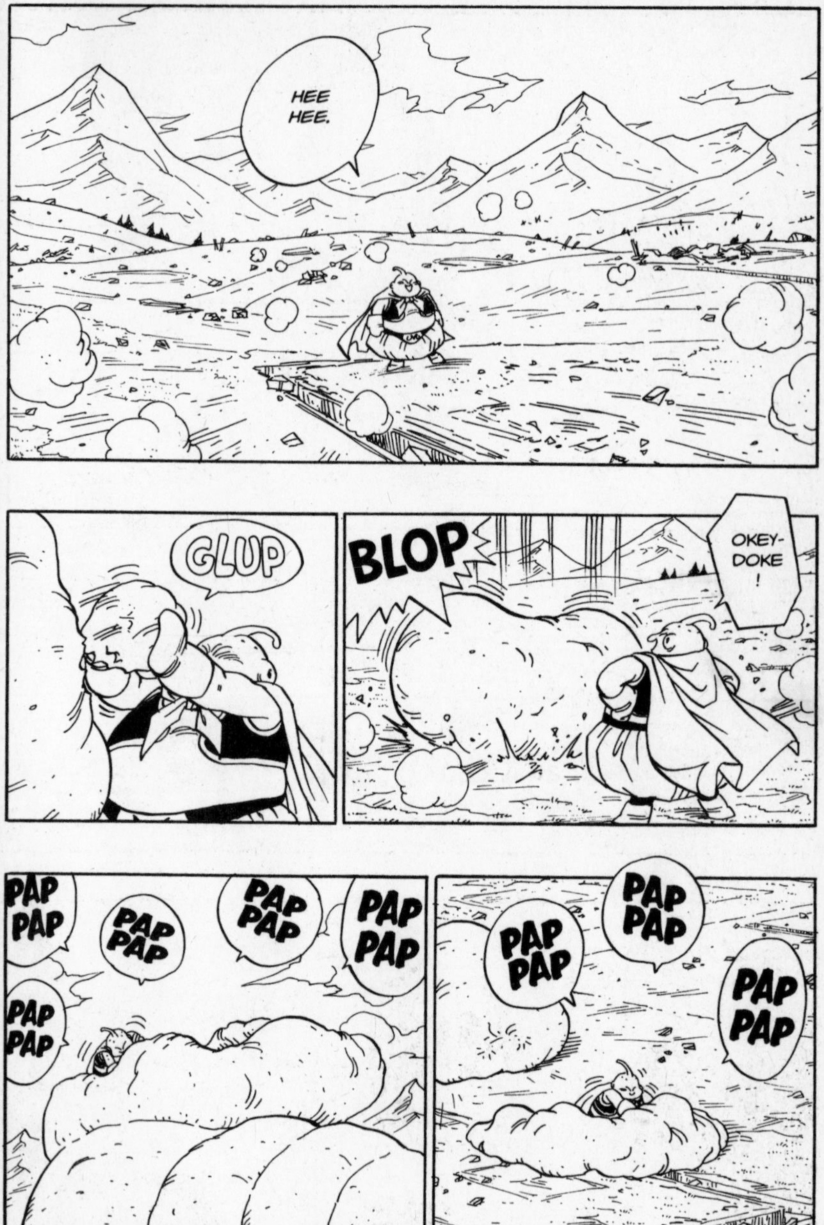
HEE HEE.
OKEY-DOKE!
BLOP
GLUP
PAP PAP
PAP PAP
PAP PAP
PAP PAP
PAP PAP
PAP PAP
PAP PAP
PAP PAP

READ THIS WAY

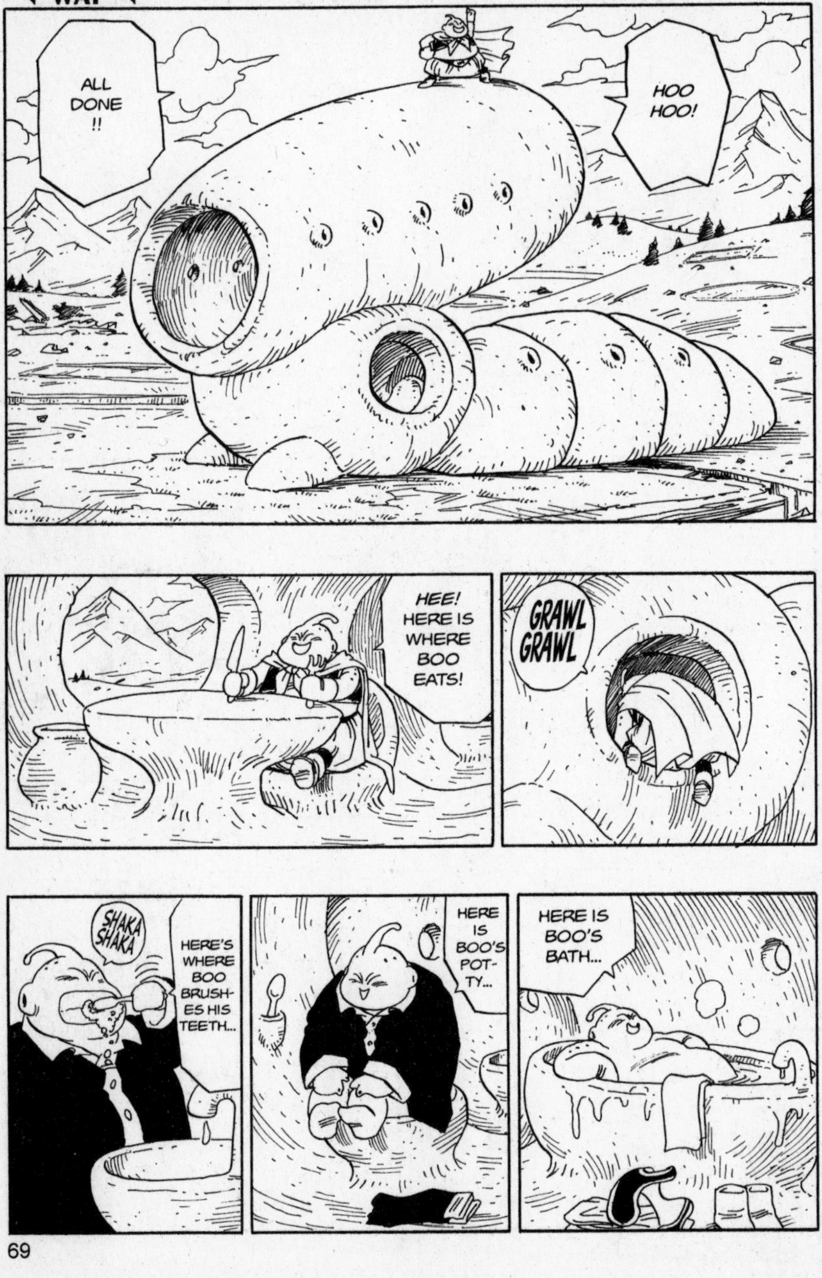

HOO HOO!
ALL DONE !!
GRAWL GRAWL
HEE! HERE IS WHERE BOO EATS!
HERE IS BOO'S BATH...
HERE IS BOO'S POT-TY...
HERE'S WHERE BOO BRUSH-ES HIS TEETH...
SHAKA SHAKA

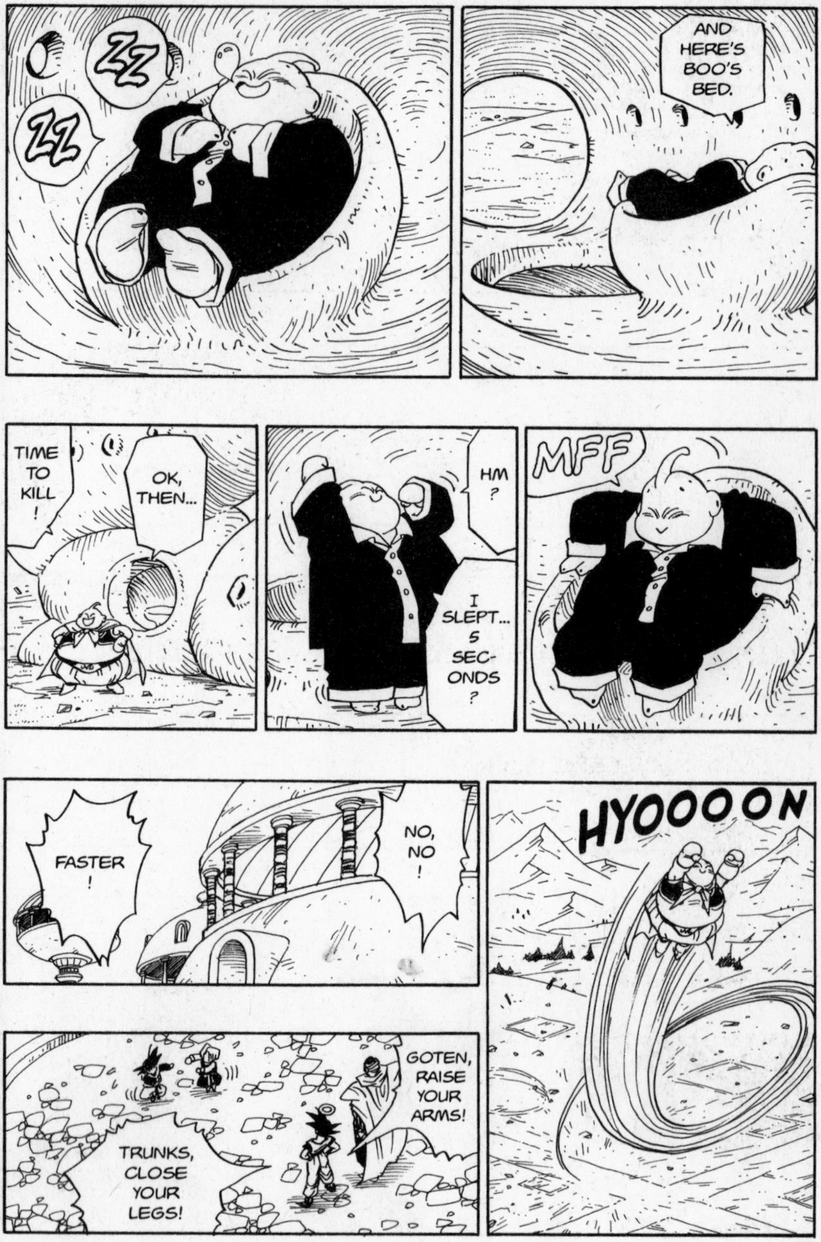
AND HERE'S BOO'S BED.
ZZ
ZZ
MFF
HM ?
I SLEPT... 5 SECONDS ?
OK, THEN...
TIME TO KILL !
HYOOOON
NO, NO !
FASTER !
GOTEN, RAISE YOUR ARMS!
TRUNKS, CLOSE YOUR LEGS!

READ THIS WAY

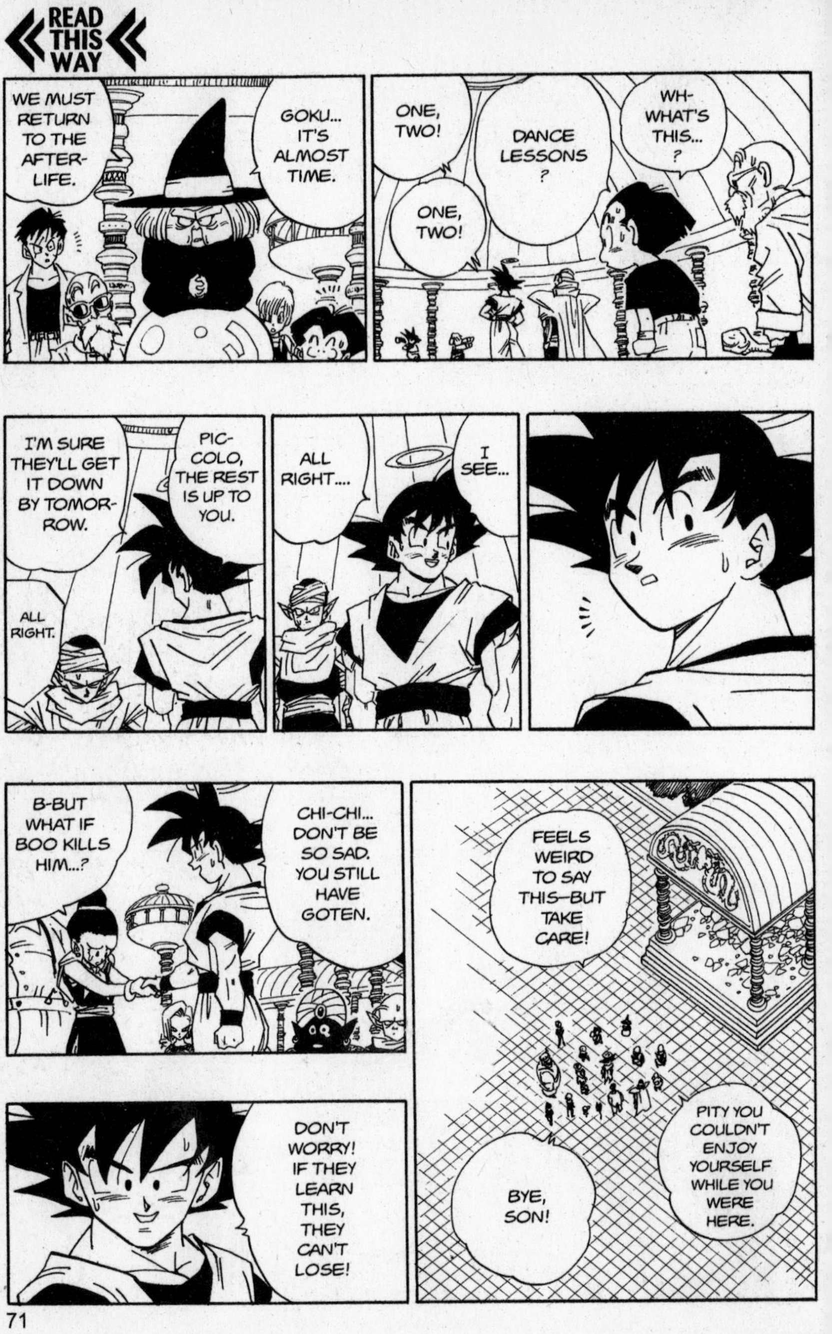
WH- WHAT'S THIS... ?
DANCE LESSONS ?
ONE, TWO!
ONE, TWO!
GOKU... IT'S ALMOST TIME.
WE MUST RETURN TO THE AFTER-LIFE.
I SEE...
ALL RIGHT....
PIC-COLO, THE REST IS UP TO YOU.
I'M SURE THEY'LL GET IT DOWN BY TOMOR-ROW.
ALL RIGHT.
FEELS WEIRD TO SAY THIS—BUT TAKE CARE!
PITY YOU COULDN'T ENJOY YOURSELF WHILE YOU WERE HERE.
BYE, SON!
CHI-CHI... DON'T BE SO SAD. YOU STILL HAVE GOTEN.
B-BUT WHAT IF BOO KILLS HIM...?
DON'T WORRY! IF THEY LEARN THIS, THEY CAN'T LOSE!

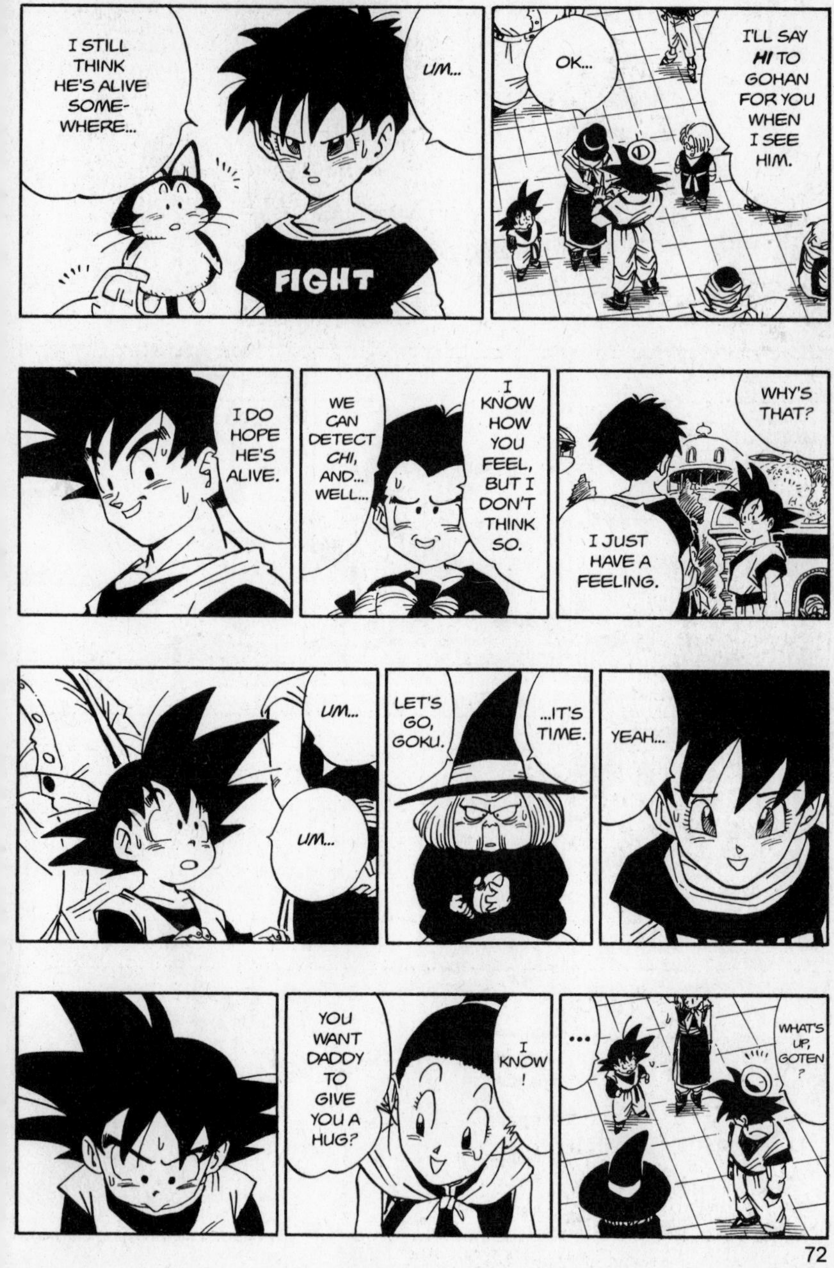
I'LL SAY HI TO GOHAN FOR YOU WHEN I SEE HIM.
OK...
UM...
I STILL THINK HE'S ALIVE SOME-WHERE...
WHY'S THAT?
I JUST HAVE A FEELING.
I KNOW HOW YOU FEEL, BUT I DON'T THINK SO.
WE CAN DETECT CHI, AND... WELL...
I DO HOPE HE'S ALIVE.
YEAH...
...IT'S TIME.
LET'S GO, GOKU.
UM...
UM...
WHAT'S UP, GOTEN?
...
I KNOW!
YOU WANT DADDY TO GIVE YOU A HUG?

READ THIS WAY

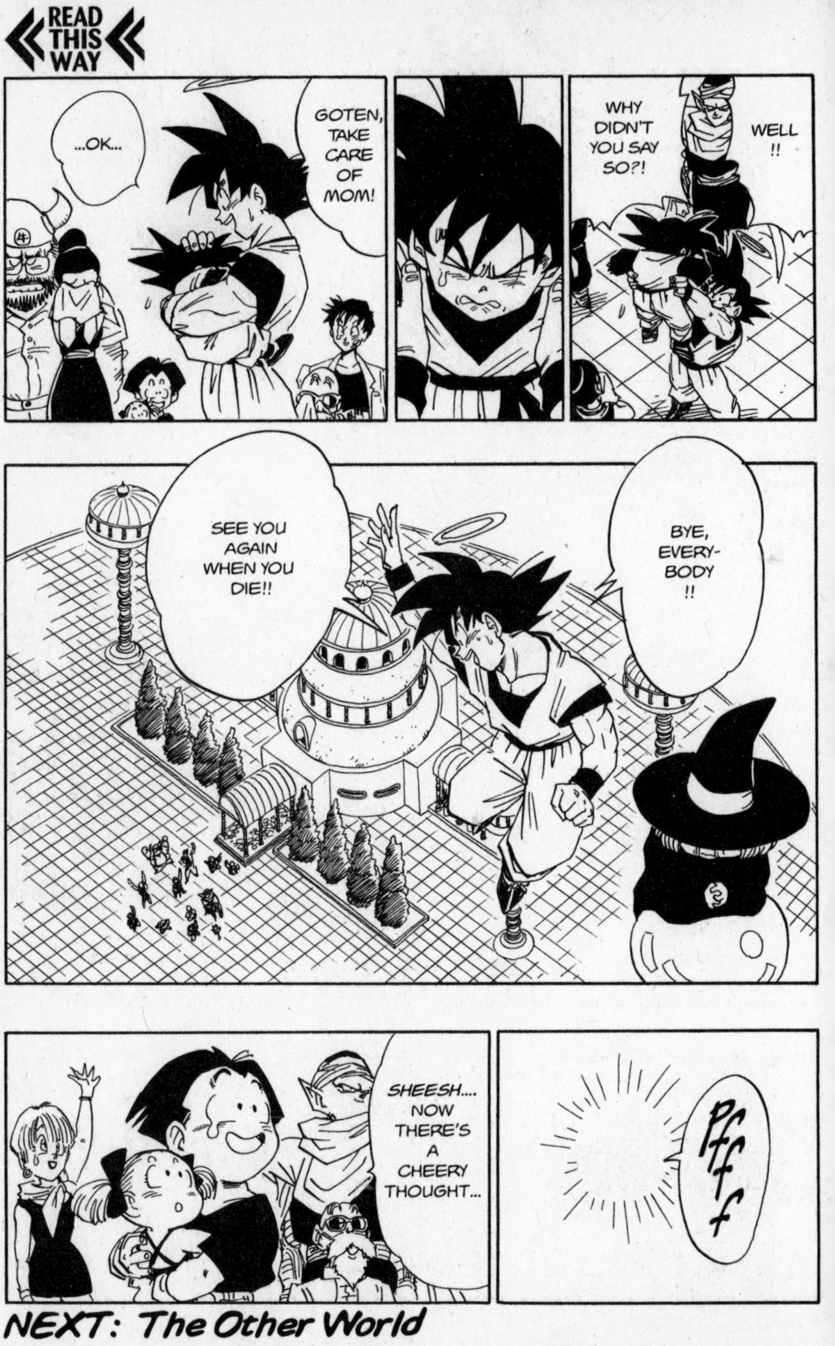
WELL !!
WHY DIDN'T YOU SAY SO?!
GOTEN, TAKE CARE OF MOM!
...OK...
BYE, EVERY-BODY !!
SEE YOU AGAIN WHEN YOU DIE!!
Pfff
SHEESH.... NOW THERE'S A CHEERY THOUGHT...

NEXT: The Other World

DBZ:284 · Where Is Gohan?

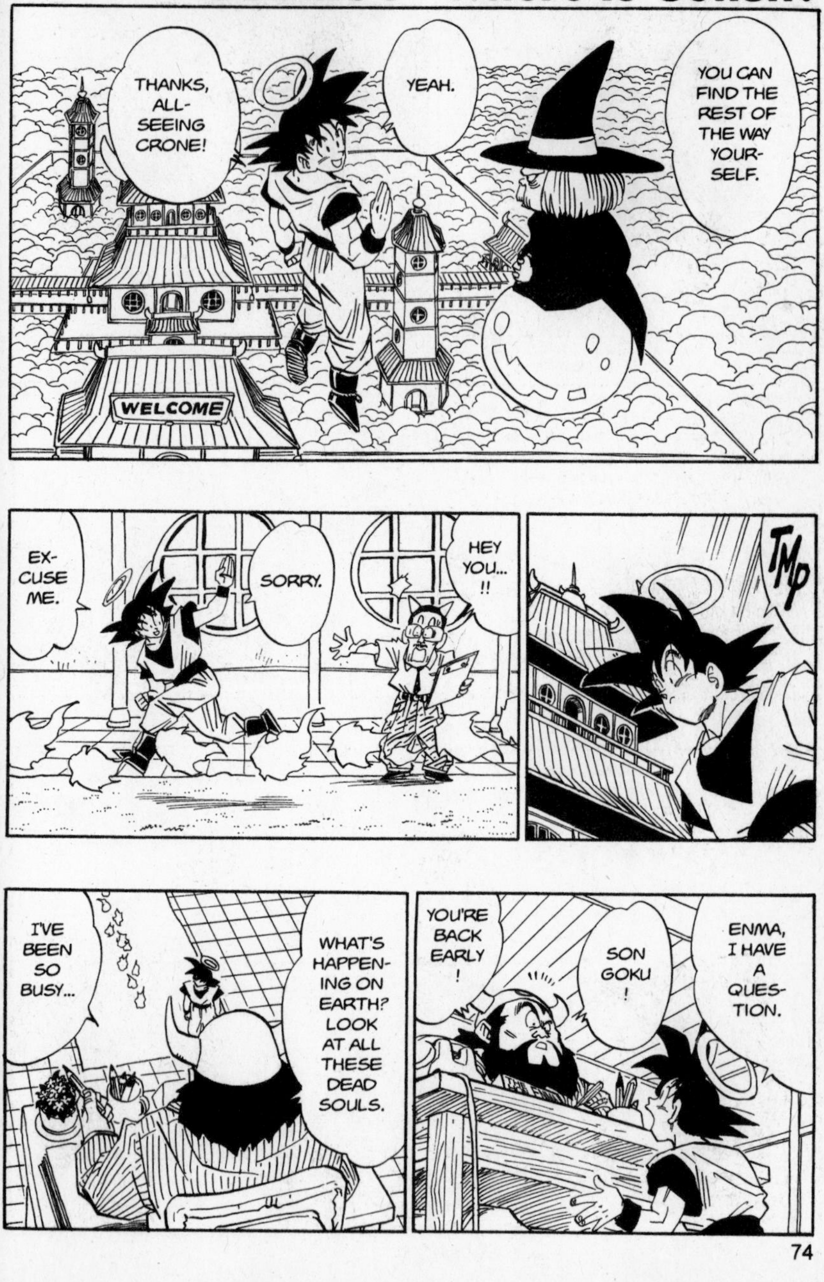
YOU CAN FIND THE REST OF THE WAY YOUR-SELF.
YEAH.
THANKS, ALL-SEEING CRONE!
WELCOME
TMP
HEY YOU... !!
SORRY.
EX-CUSE ME.
ENMA, I HAVE A QUES-TION.
SON GOKU !
YOU'RE BACK EARLY !
WHAT'S HAPPEN-ING ON EARTH? LOOK AT ALL THESE DEAD SOULS.
I'VE BEEN SO BUSY...

READ THIS WAY

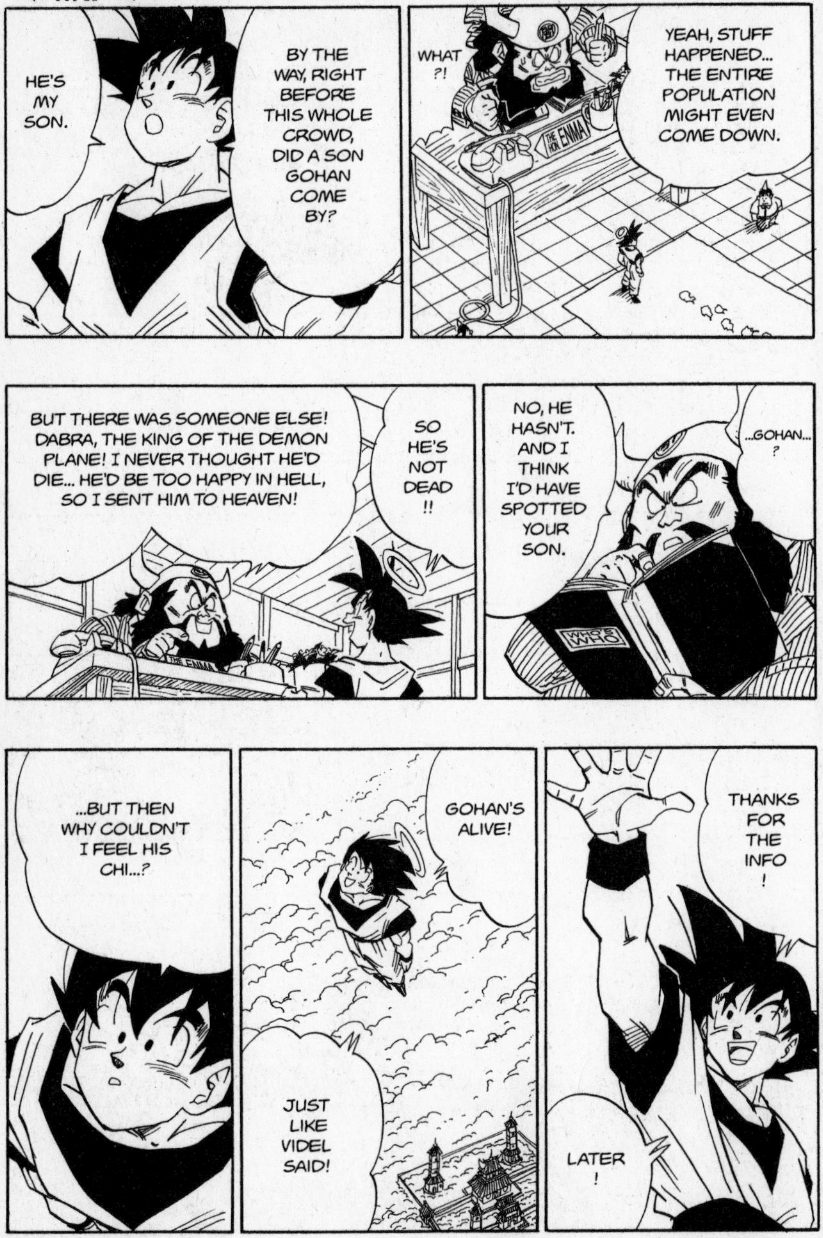
YEAH, STUFF HAPPENED... THE ENTIRE POPULATION MIGHT EVEN COME DOWN.
WHAT ?!
ENMA
BY THE WAY, RIGHT BEFORE THIS WHOLE CROWD, DID A SON GOHAN COME BY?
HE'S MY SON.
...GOHAN... ?
NO, HE HASN'T. AND I THINK I'D HAVE SPOTTED YOUR SON.
WHO'S WHO
SO HE'S NOT DEAD !!
BUT THERE WAS SOMEONE ELSE! DABRA, THE KING OF THE DEMON PLANE! I NEVER THOUGHT HE'D DIE... HE'D BE TOO HAPPY IN HELL, SO I SENT HIM TO HEAVEN!
THANKS FOR THE INFO !
LATER !
GOHAN'S ALIVE!
JUST LIKE VIDEL SAID!
...BUT THEN WHY COULDN'T I FEEL HIS CHI...?

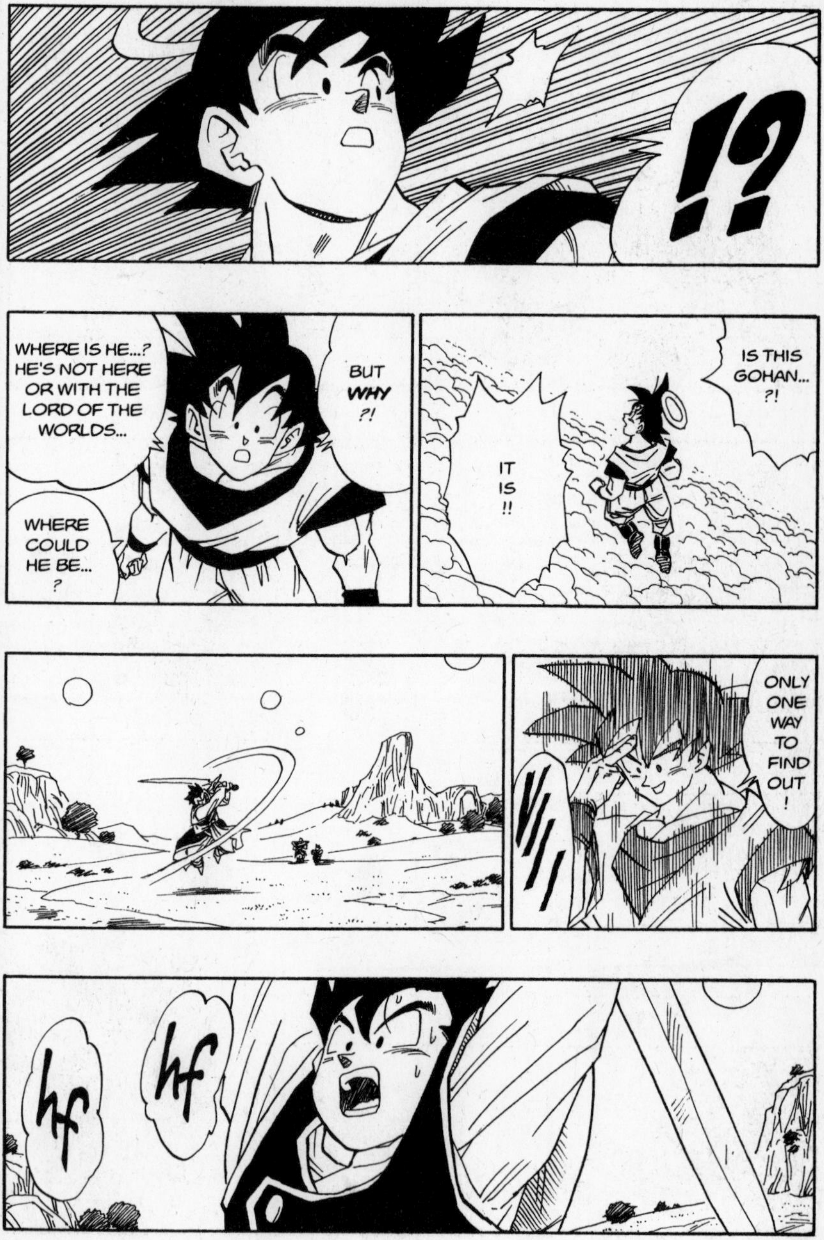
!?
IS THIS GOHAN...?!
IT IS!!
BUT WHY?!
WHERE IS HE...? HE'S NOT HERE OR WITH THE LORD OF THE WORLDS...
WHERE COULD HE BE...?
ONLY ONE WAY TO FIND OUT!
hf
hf

READ THIS WAY

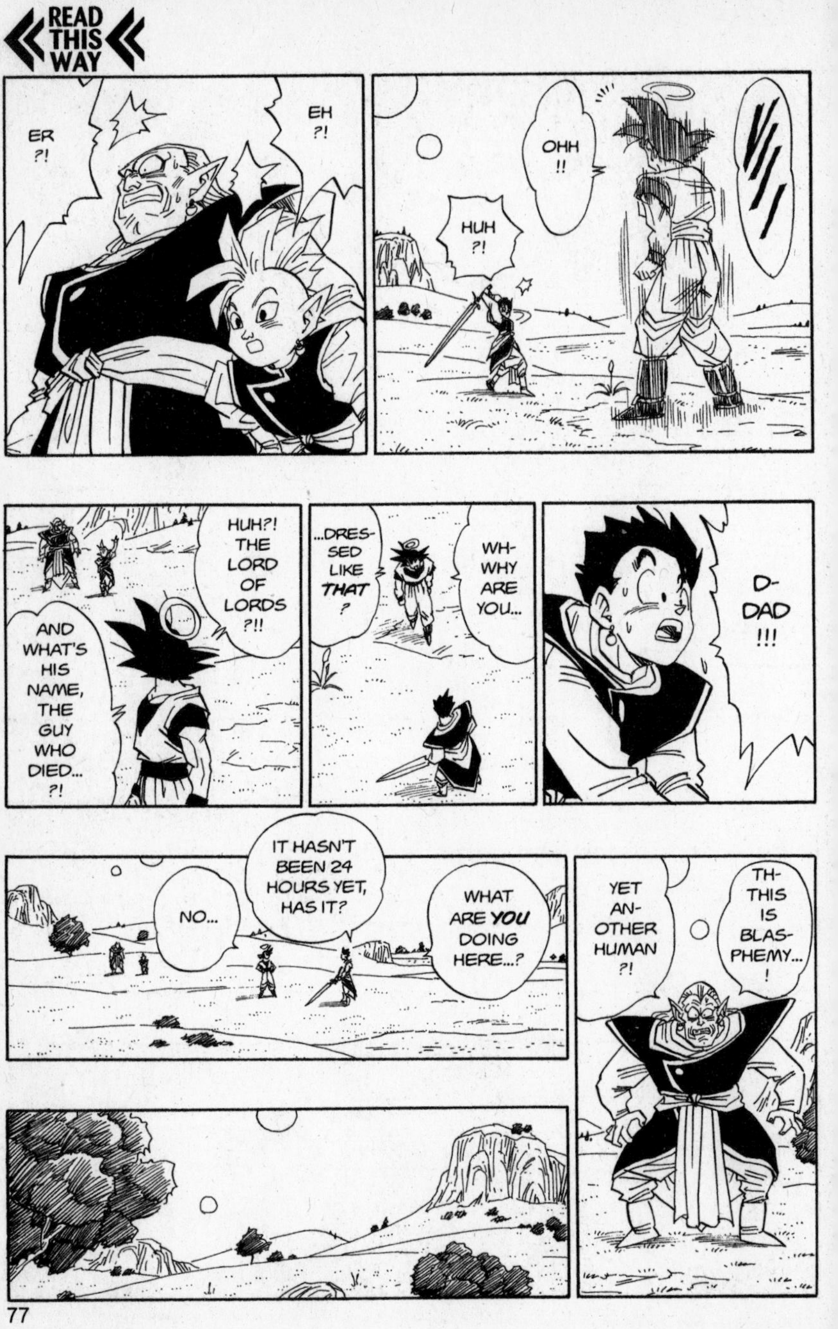

OHH !!
HUH ?!
EH ?!
ER ?!
D- DAD !!!
WH- WHY ARE YOU...
...DRES- SED LIKE *THAT* ?
HUH?! THE LORD OF LORDS ?!!
AND WHAT'S HIS NAME, THE GUY WHO DIED... ?!
TH- THIS IS BLAS- PHEMY... !
YET AN- OTHER HUMAN ?!
WHAT ARE *YOU* DOING HERE...?
IT HASN'T BEEN 24 HOURS YET, HAS IT?
NO...

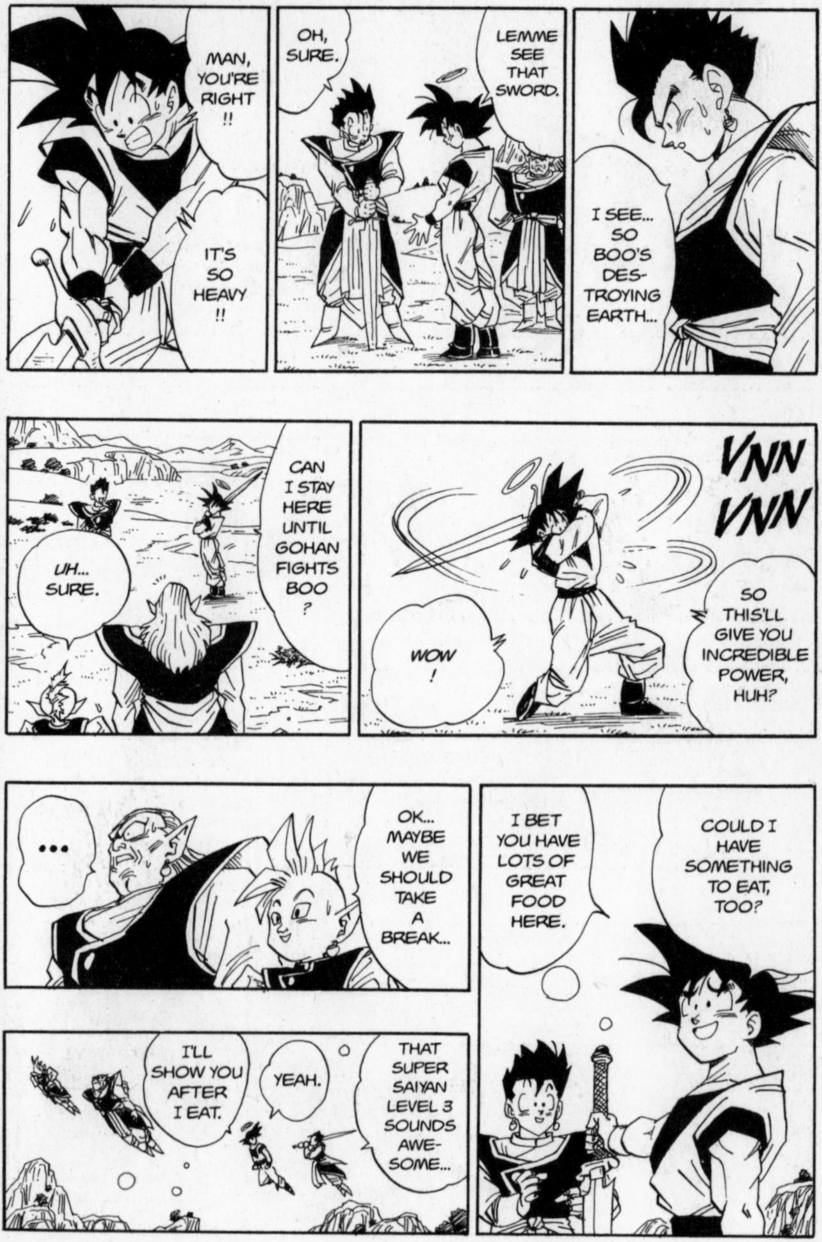
I SEE... SO BOO'S DES-TROYING EARTH...
LEMME SEE THAT SWORD.
OH, SURE.
MAN, YOU'RE RIGHT !!
IT'S SO HEAVY !!
VNN VNN
SO THIS'LL GIVE YOU INCREDIBLE POWER, HUH?
WOW !
CAN I STAY HERE UNTIL GOHAN FIGHTS BOO ?
UH... SURE.
COULD I HAVE SOMETHING TO EAT, TOO?
I BET YOU HAVE LOTS OF GREAT FOOD HERE.
OK... MAYBE WE SHOULD TAKE A BREAK...
...
THAT SUPER SAIYAN LEVEL 3 SOUNDS AWE-SOME...
YEAH.
I'LL SHOW YOU AFTER I EAT.

READ THIS WAY

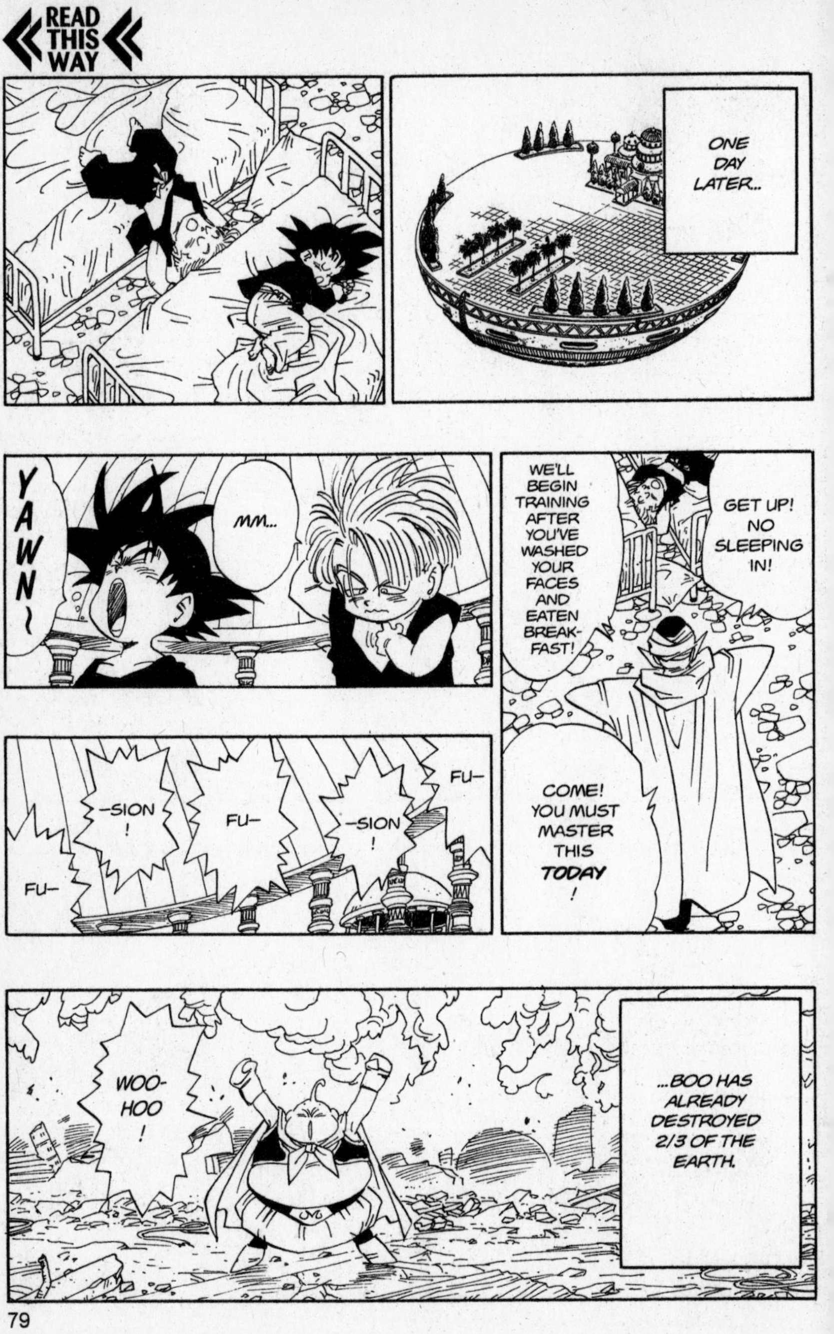
ONE DAY LATER...
GET UP! NO SLEEPING IN!
WE'LL BEGIN TRAINING AFTER YOU'VE WASHED YOUR FACES AND EATEN BREAKFAST!
COME! YOU MUST MASTER THIS TODAY!
MM...
YAWN~
FU–
–SION!
FU–
–SION!
FU–
...BOO HAS ALREADY DESTROYED 2/3 OF THE EARTH.
WOO-HOO!

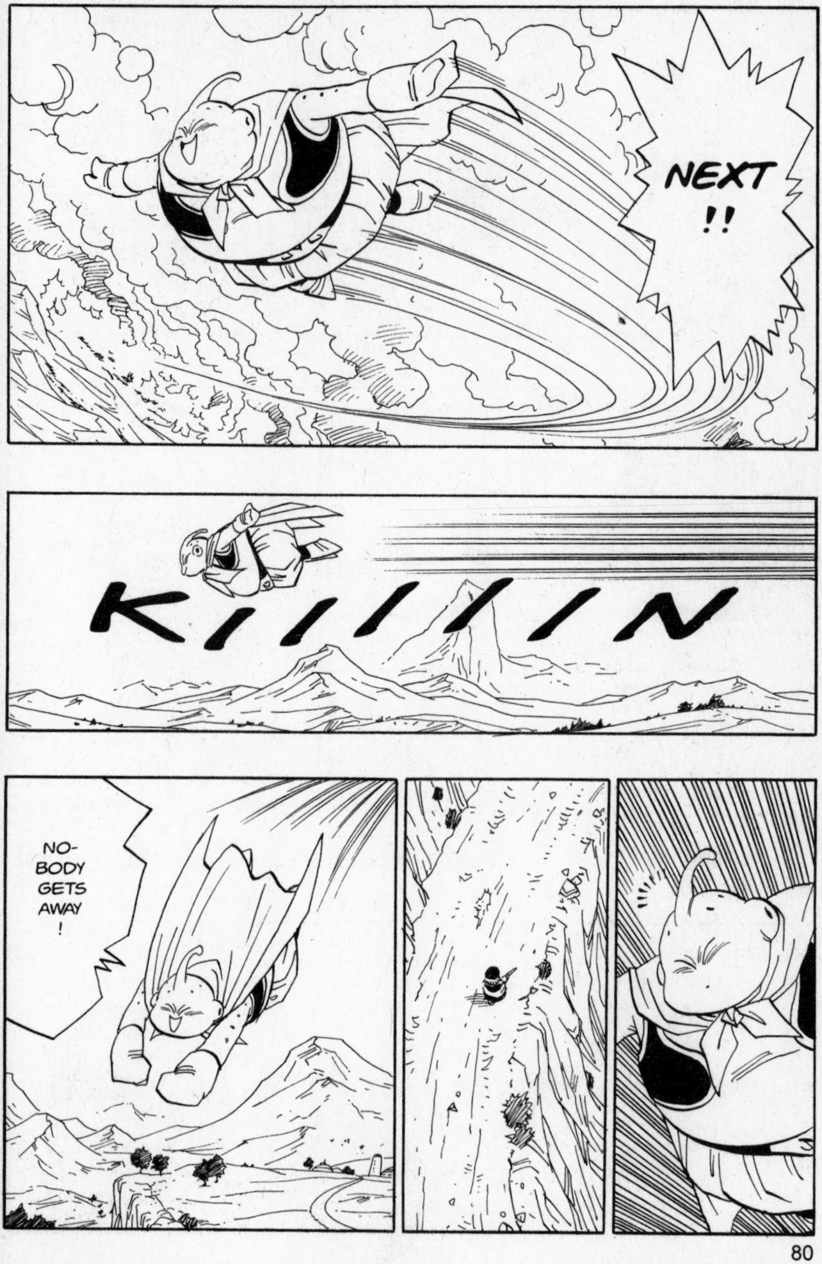
NEXT !!
KIIIIN
NO-BODY GETS AWAY !

READ THIS WAY

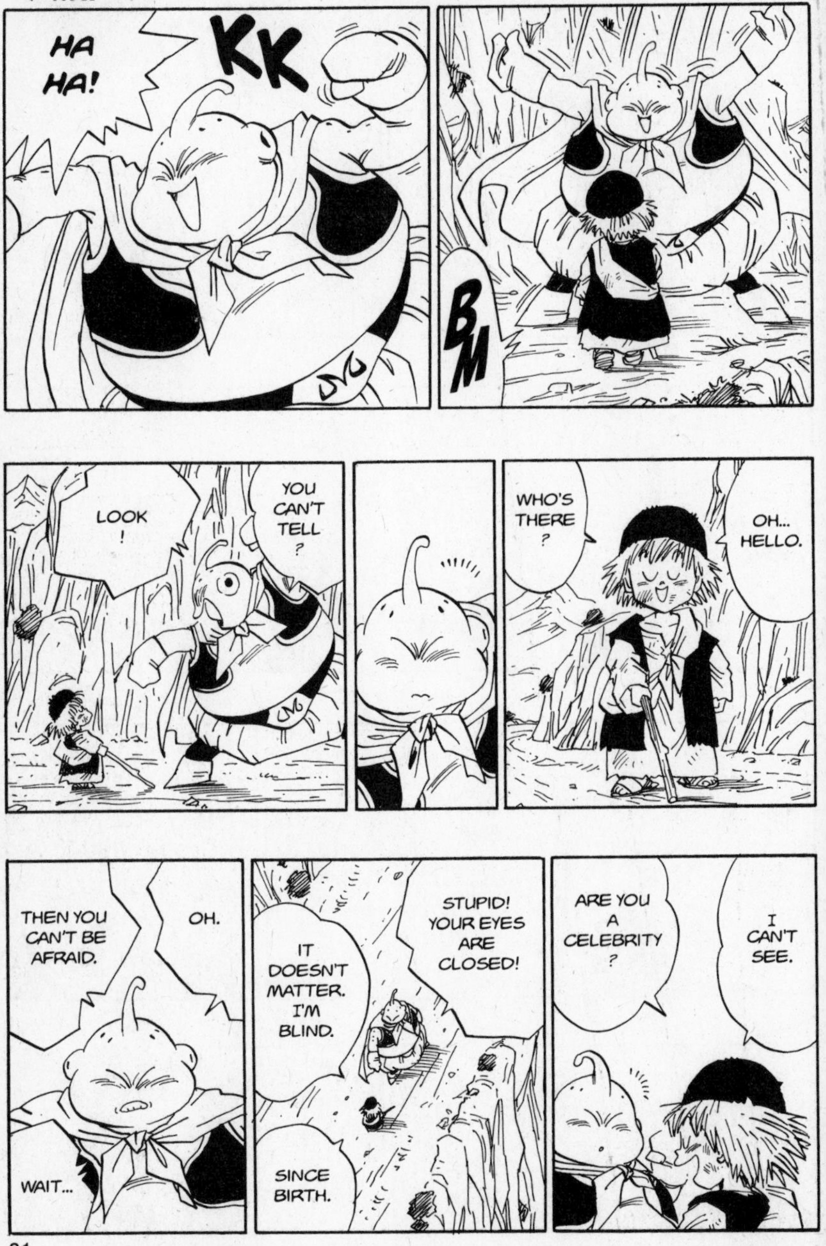

BM
HA HA!
KK
OH... HELLO.
WHO'S THERE?
YOU CAN'T TELL?
LOOK!
I CAN'T SEE.
ARE YOU A CELEBRITY?
STUPID! YOUR EYES ARE CLOSED!
IT DOESN'T MATTER. I'M BLIND.
SINCE BIRTH.
OH.
THEN YOU CAN'T BE AFRAID.
WAIT...

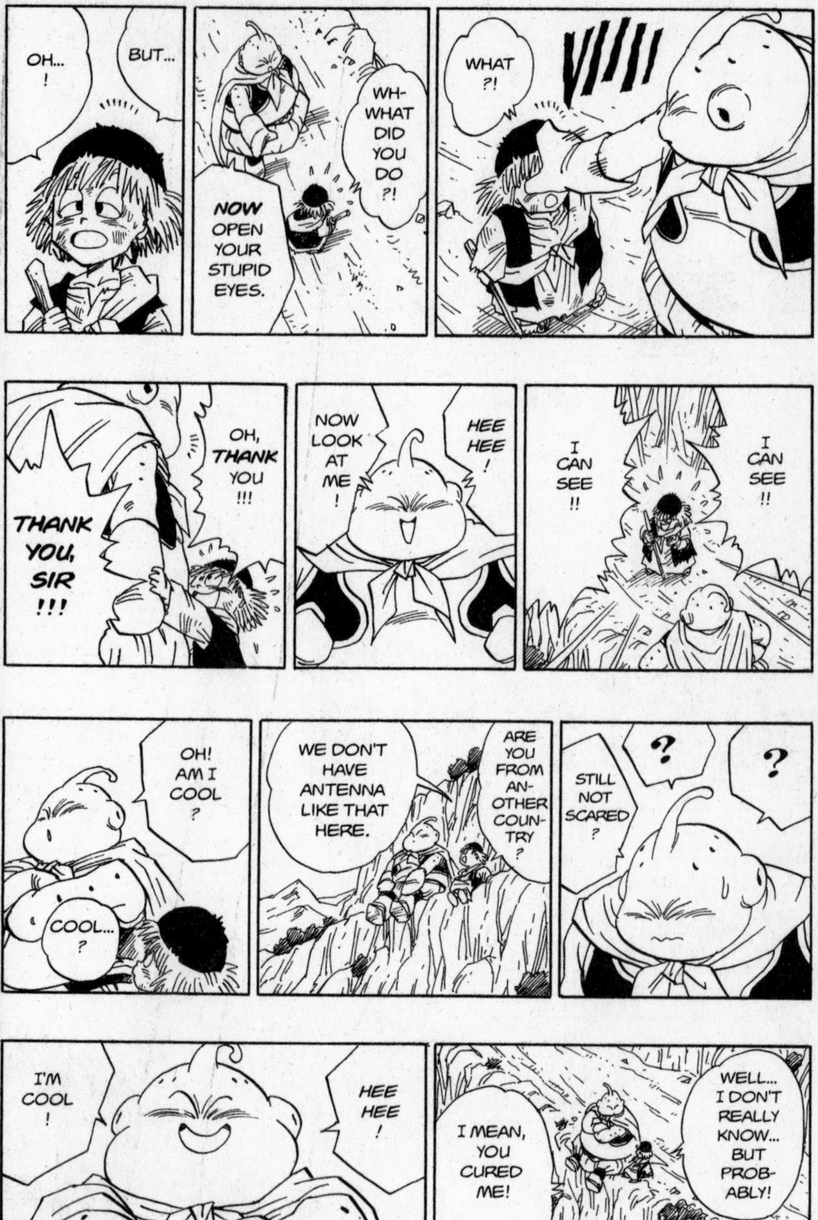
WHAT ?!
WH-WHAT DID YOU DO ?!
NOW OPEN YOUR STUPID EYES.
BUT...
OH... !
I CAN SEE !!
I CAN SEE !!
HEE HEE !
NOW LOOK AT ME !
OH, THANK YOU !!!
THANK YOU, SIR !!!
?
?
STILL NOT SCARED ?
ARE YOU FROM AN-OTHER COUN-TRY ?
WE DON'T HAVE ANTENNA LIKE THAT HERE.
OH! AM I COOL ?
COOL... ?
WELL... I DON'T REALLY KNOW... BUT PROB-ABLY!
I MEAN, YOU CURED ME!
HEE HEE !
I'M COOL !

READ THIS WAY

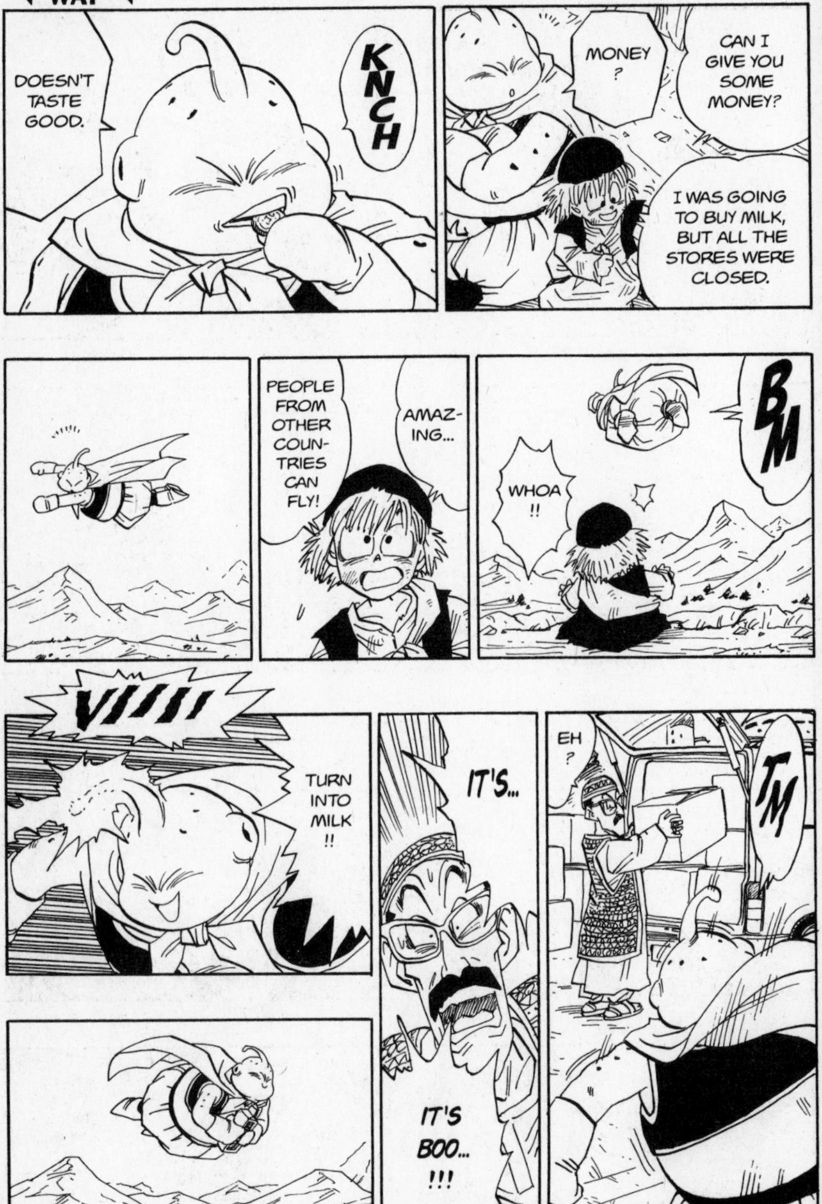

CAN I GIVE YOU SOME MONEY?
MONEY ?
I WAS GOING TO BUY MILK, BUT ALL THE STORES WERE CLOSED.
KNCH
DOESN'T TASTE GOOD.
BM
WHOA !!
AMAZ- ING...
PEOPLE FROM OTHER COUN- TRIES CAN FLY!
TM
EH ?
IT'S...
IT'S BOO... !!!
VIIII
TURN INTO MILK !!

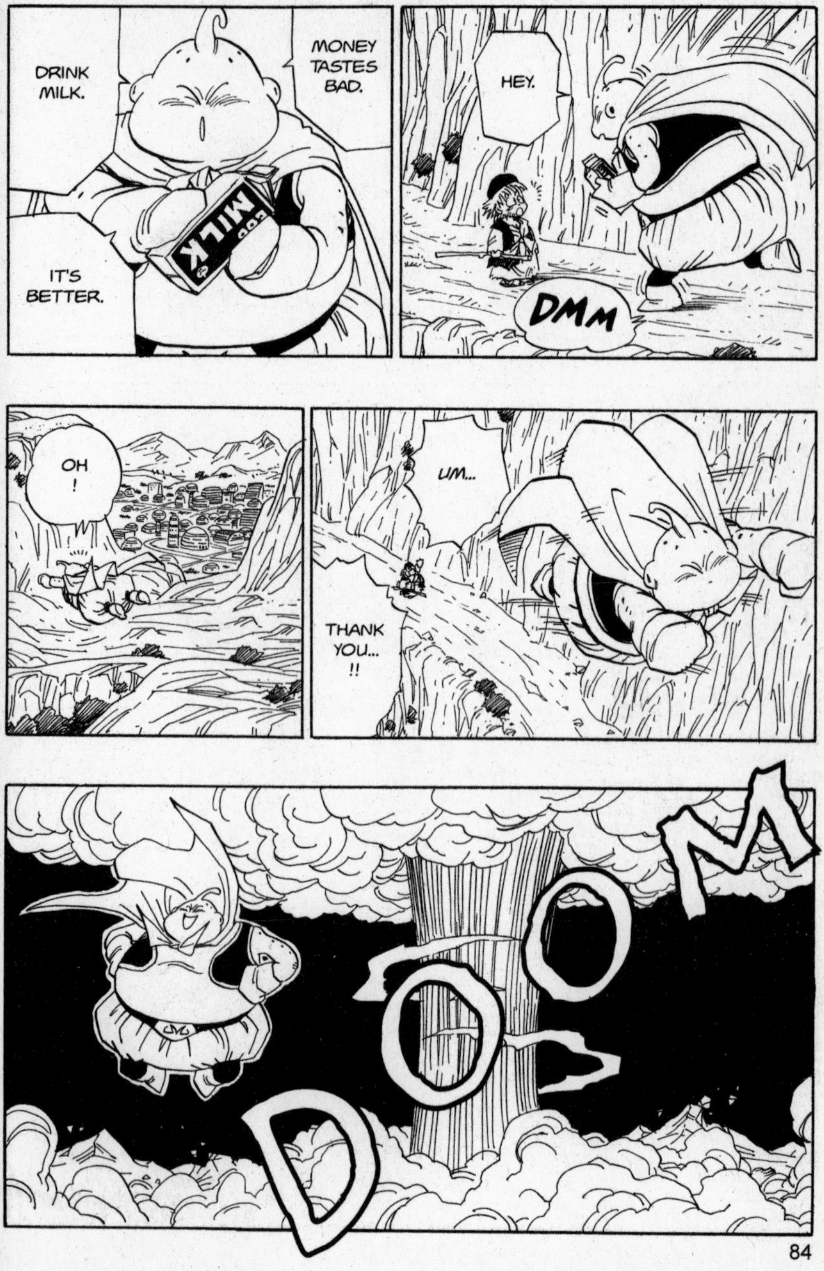
HEY.
DMM
MONEY TASTES BAD.
DRINK MILK.
MILK
IT'S BETTER.
UM...
THANK YOU...!!
OH!
DOOOM

READ THIS WAY

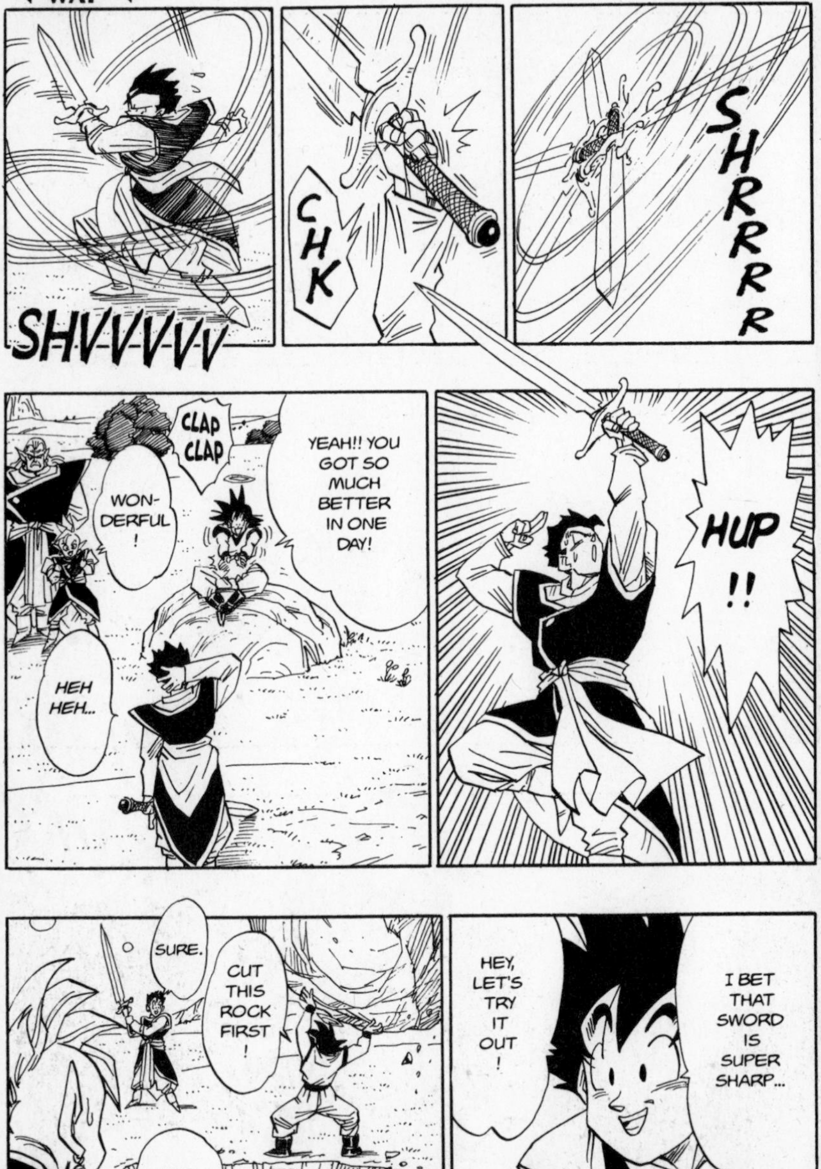
SHRRRR
CHK
SHVVVVV
HUP !!
YEAH!! YOU GOT SO MUCH BETTER IN ONE DAY!
CLAP CLAP
WON-DERFUL !
HEH HEH...
I BET THAT SWORD IS SUPER SHARP...
HEY, LET'S TRY IT OUT !
CUT THIS ROCK FIRST !
SURE.
...

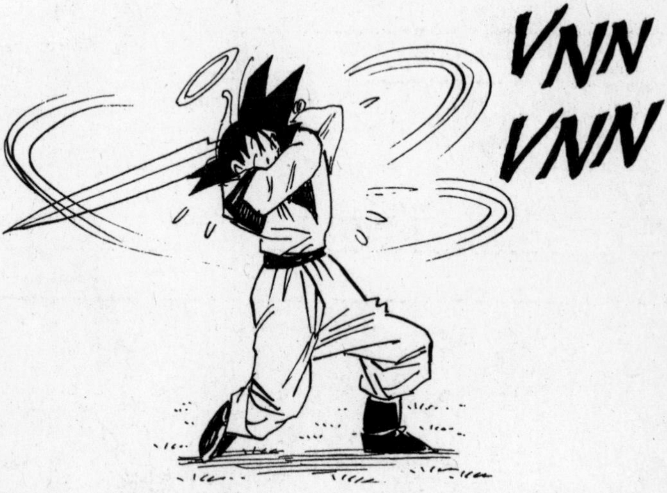
VNN
VNN

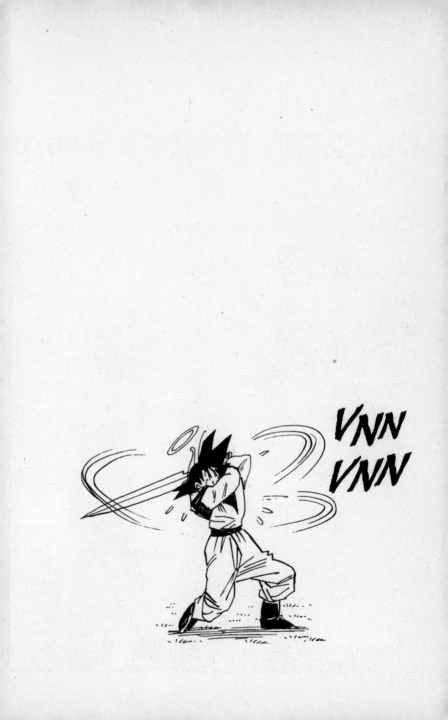

DBZ:285 • The Zeta Sword

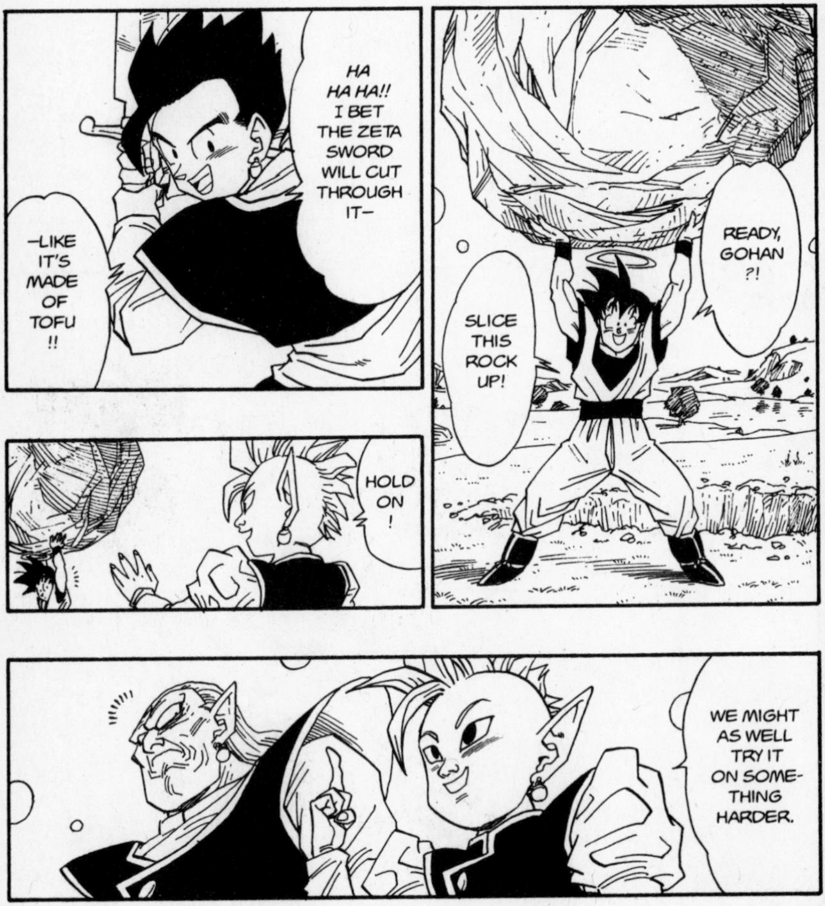
READY, GOHAN ?!
SLICE THIS ROCK UP!
HA HA HA!! I BET THE ZETA SWORD WILL CUT THROUGH IT—
—LIKE IT'S MADE OF TOFU !!
HOLD ON !
WE MIGHT AS WELL TRY IT ON SOME-THING HARDER.

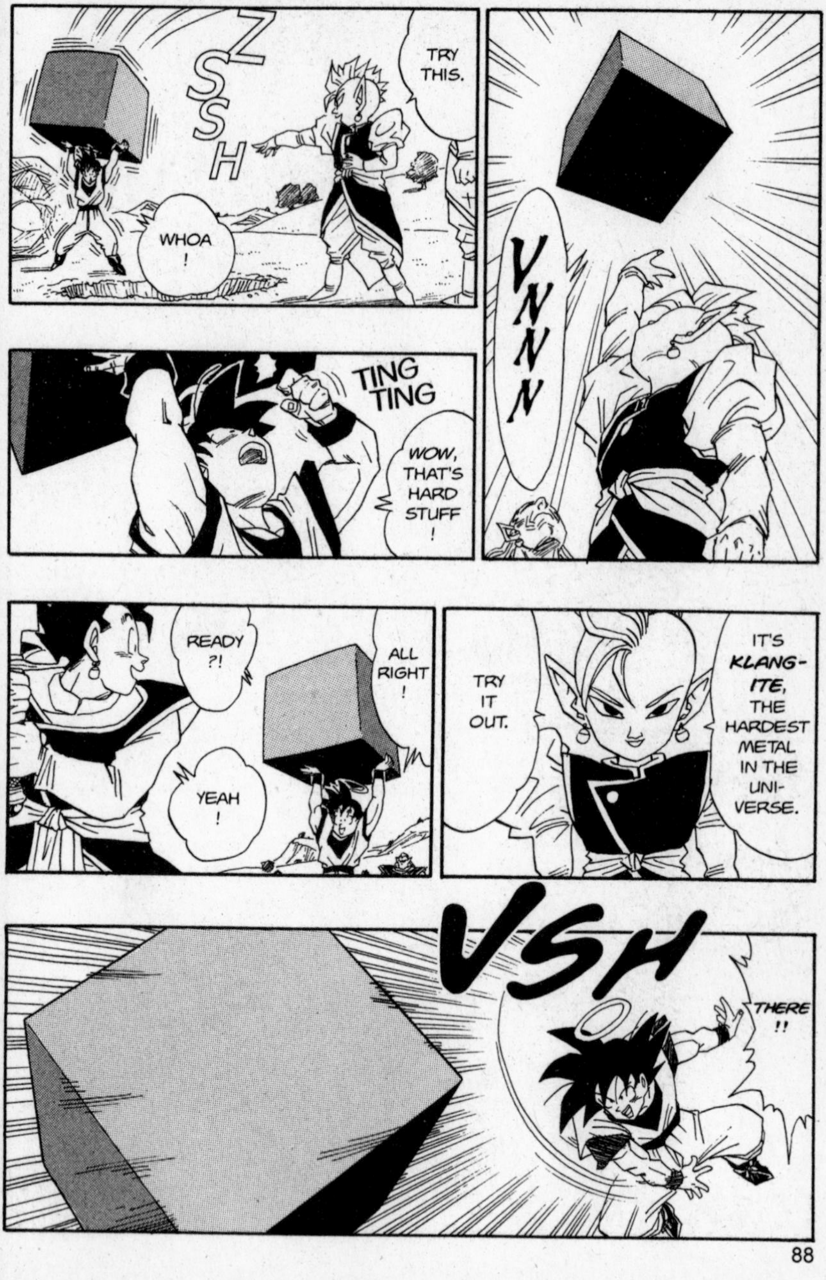
VNNN
TRY THIS.
ZSSH
WHOA!
TING TING
WOW, THAT'S HARD STUFF!
IT'S ***KLANGITE***, THE HARDEST METAL IN THE UNIVERSE.
TRY IT OUT.
ALL RIGHT!
READY?!
YEAH!
VSH
THERE!!

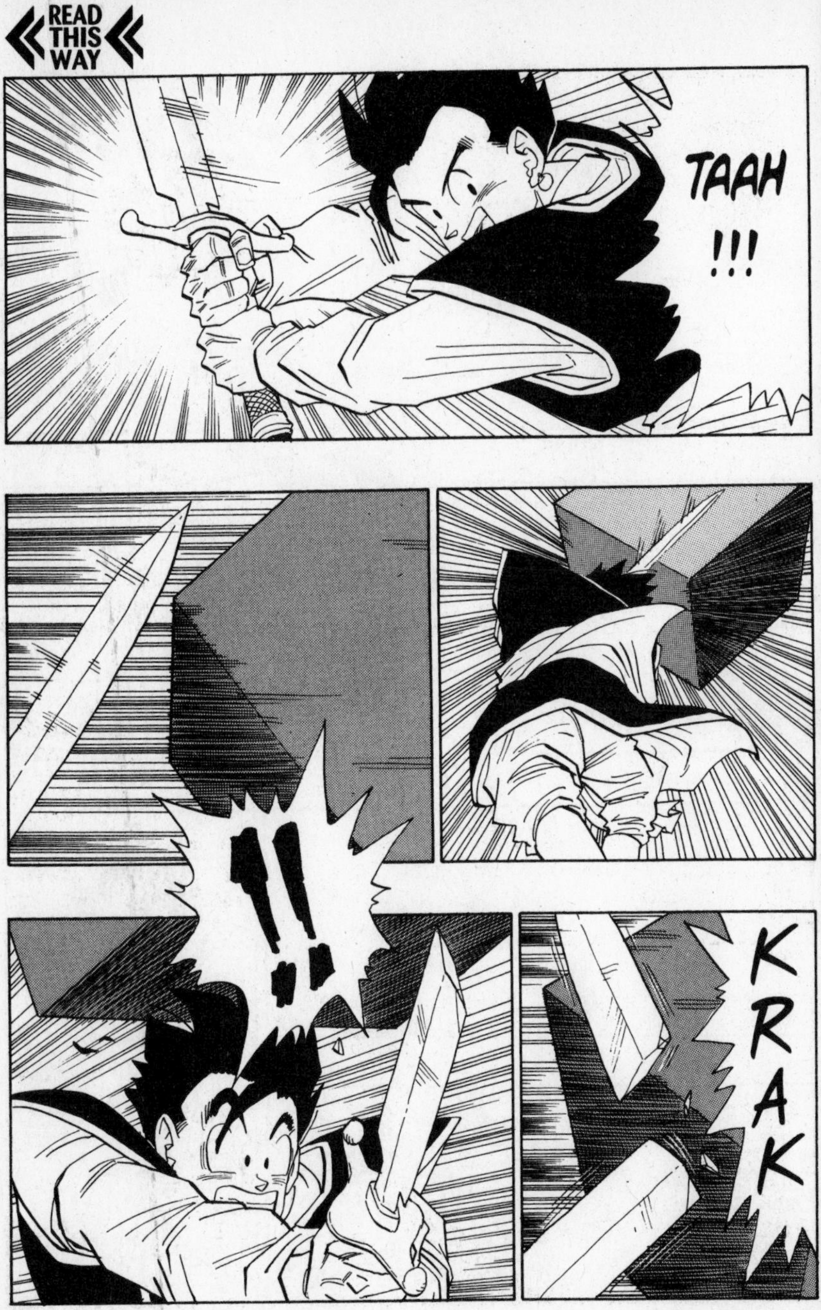
READ THIS WAY
TAAH !!!
!!
KRAK

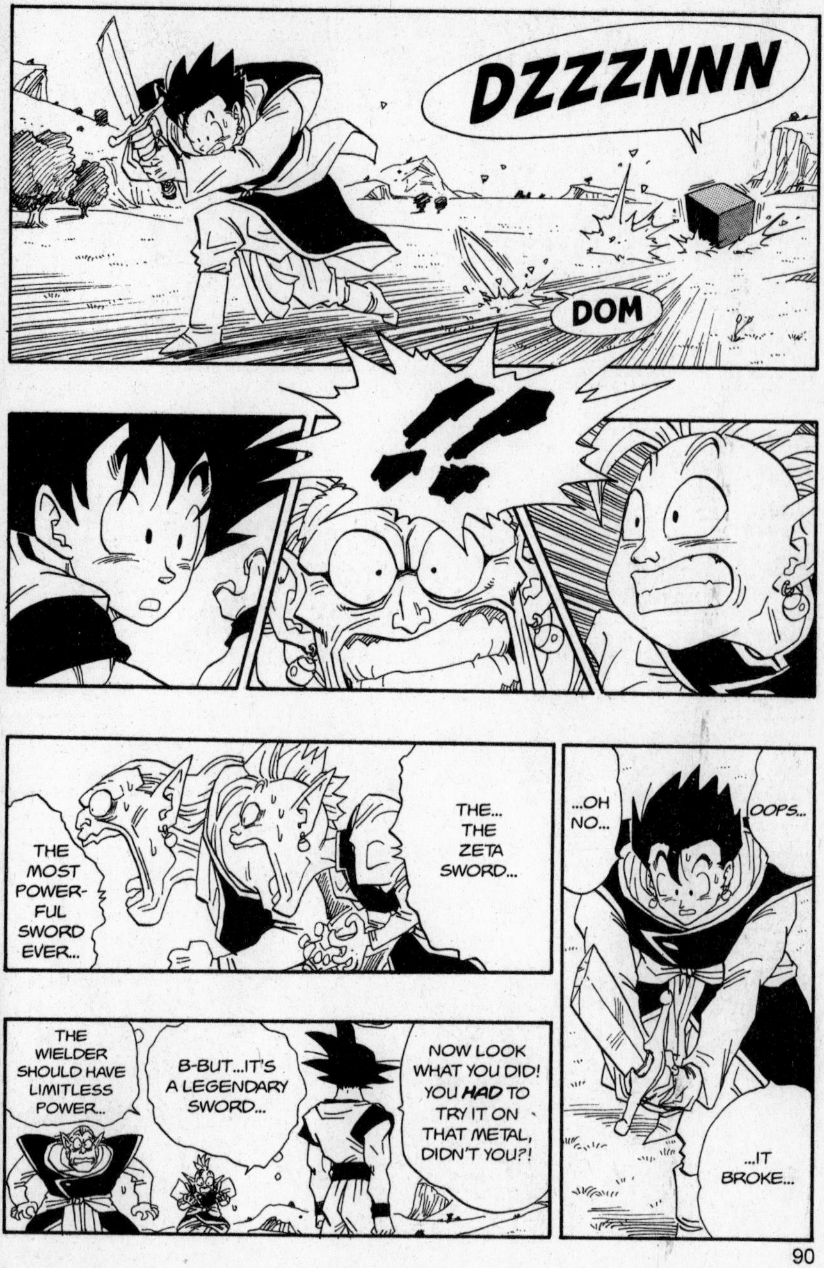
DZZZNNN
DOM
!!
OOPS...
...OH NO...
...IT BROKE...
THE... THE ZETA SWORD...
THE MOST POWER-FUL SWORD EVER...
NOW LOOK WHAT YOU DID! YOU ***HAD*** TO TRY IT ON THAT METAL, DIDN'T YOU?!
B-BUT...IT'S A LEGENDARY SWORD...
THE WIELDER SHOULD HAVE LIMITLESS POWER...

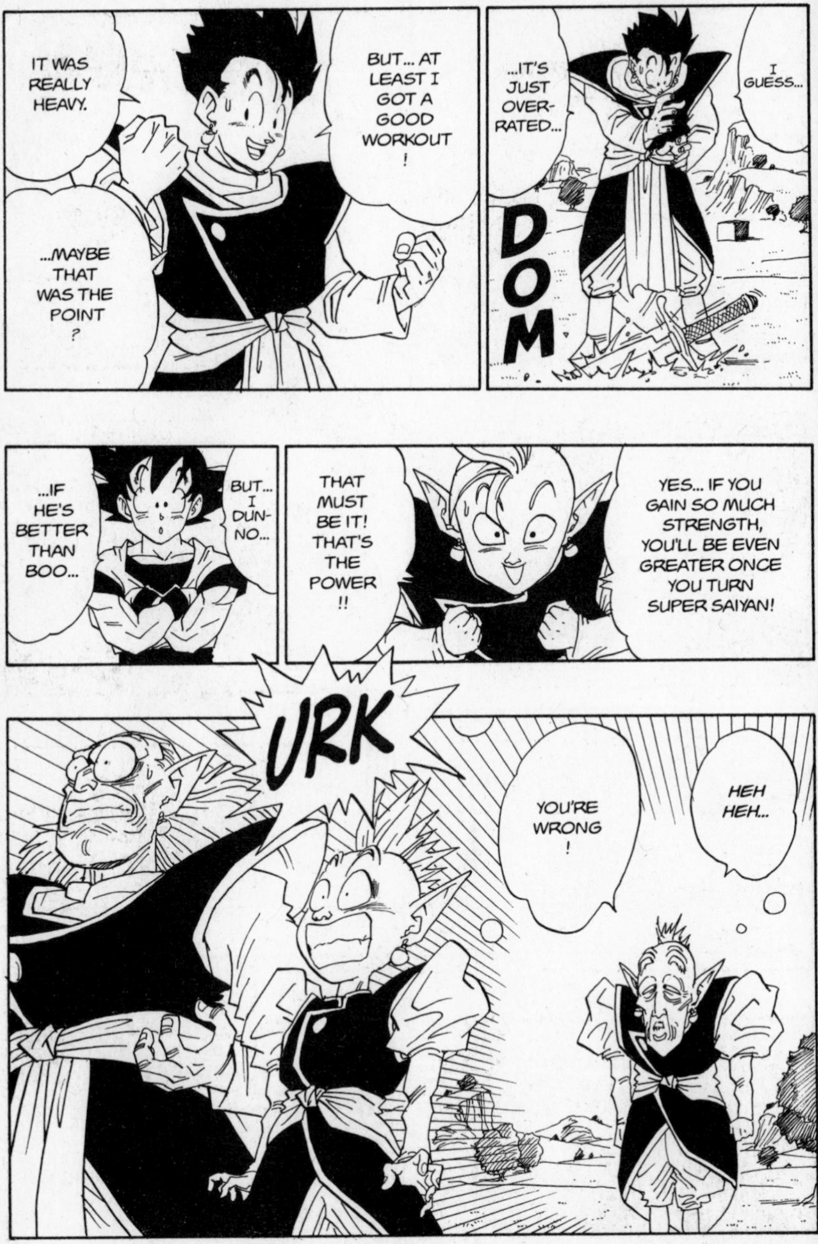
I GUESS...
...IT'S JUST OVER-RATED...
DOM
BUT... AT LEAST I GOT A GOOD WORKOUT!
IT WAS REALLY HEAVY.
...MAYBE THAT WAS THE POINT?
YES... IF YOU GAIN SO MUCH STRENGTH, YOU'LL BE EVEN GREATER ONCE YOU TURN SUPER SAIYAN!
THAT MUST BE IT! THAT'S THE POWER!!
BUT... I DUN-NO...
...IF HE'S BETTER THAN BOO...
HEH HEH...
YOU'RE WRONG!
URK

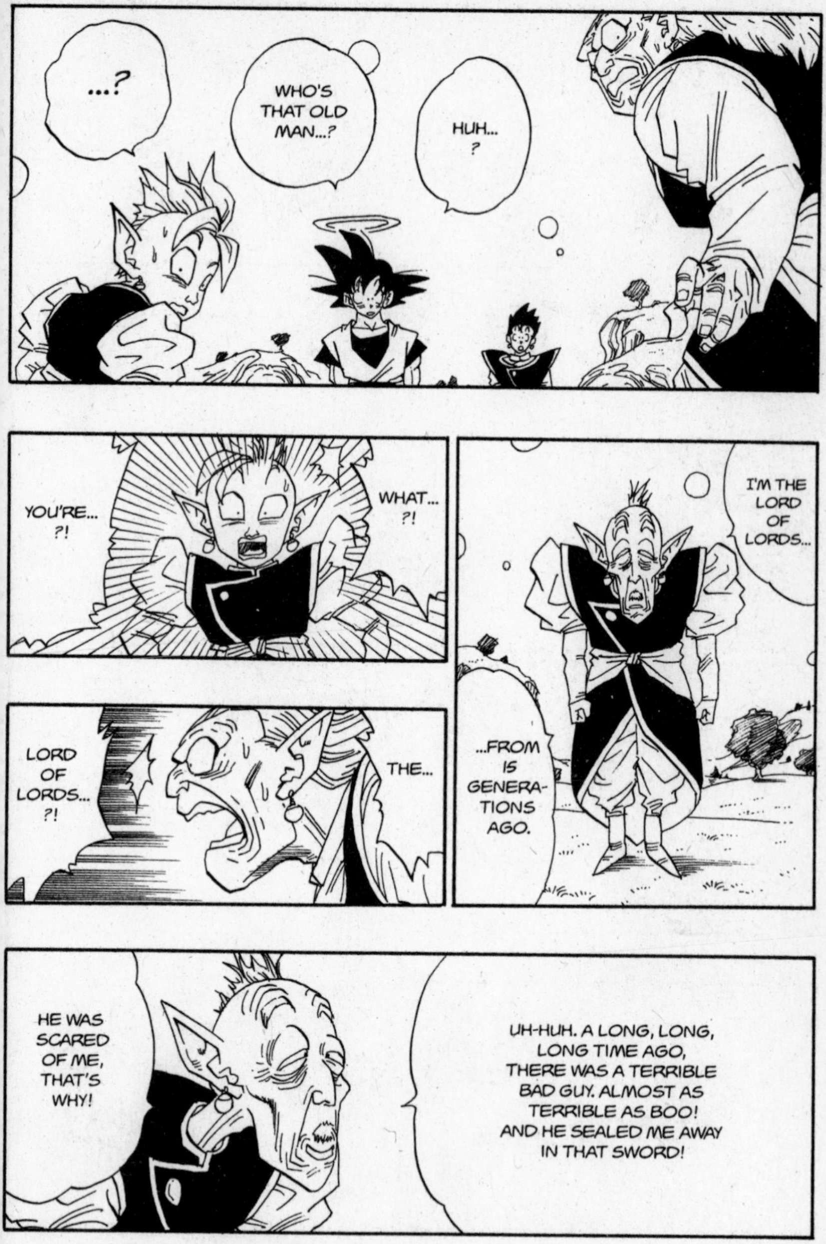
HUH... ?
WHO'S THAT OLD MAN...?
...?
I'M THE LORD OF LORDS...
...FROM 15 GENERATIONS AGO.
WHAT... ?!
YOU'RE... ?!
THE...
LORD OF LORDS... ?!
UH-HUH. A LONG, LONG, LONG TIME AGO, THERE WAS A TERRIBLE BAD GUY. ALMOST AS TERRIBLE AS BOO! AND HE SEALED ME AWAY IN THAT SWORD!
HE WAS SCARED OF ME, THAT'S WHY!

READ THIS WAY

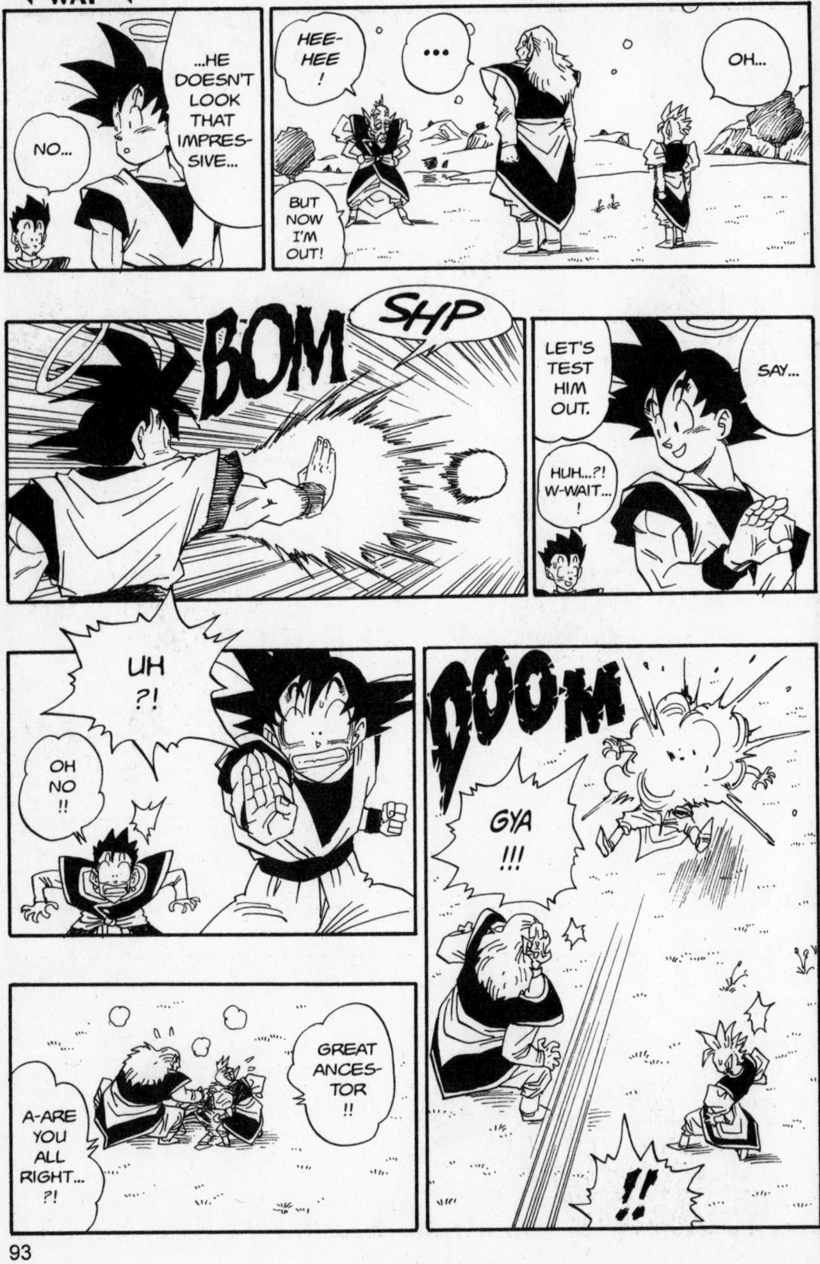

OH...
...
HEE-HEE!
BUT NOW I'M OUT!
...HE DOESN'T LOOK THAT IMPRES-SIVE...
NO...
SAY...
LET'S TEST HIM OUT.
HUH...?! W-WAIT...!
SHP
BOM
DOOM
GYA!!!
!!
UH?!
OH NO!!
GREAT ANCES-TOR!!
A-ARE YOU ALL RIGHT...?!

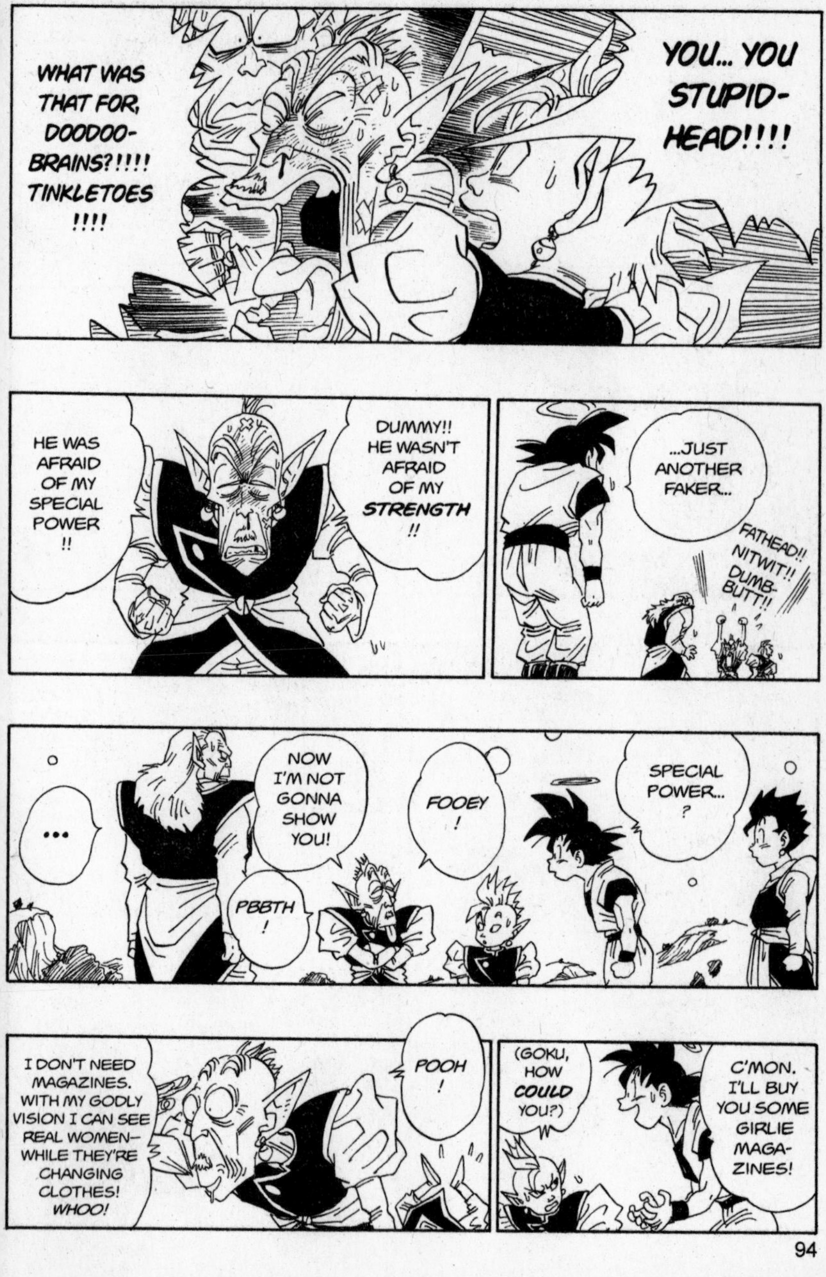
YOU... YOU STUPID-HEAD!!!!
WHAT WAS THAT FOR, DOODOO-BRAINS?!!!! TINKLETOES !!!!
...JUST ANOTHER FAKER...
FATHEAD!! NITWIT!! DUMB-BUTT!!
DUMMY!! HE WASN'T AFRAID OF MY STRENGTH !!
HE WAS AFRAID OF MY SPECIAL POWER !!
SPECIAL POWER... ?
FOOEY !
NOW I'M NOT GONNA SHOW YOU!
...
PBBTH !
C'MON. I'LL BUY YOU SOME GIRLIE MAGA-ZINES!
(GOKU, HOW COULD YOU?)
POOH !
I DON'T NEED MAGAZINES. WITH MY GODLY VISION I CAN SEE REAL WOMEN-WHILE THEY'RE CHANGING CLOTHES! WHOO!

READ THIS WAY

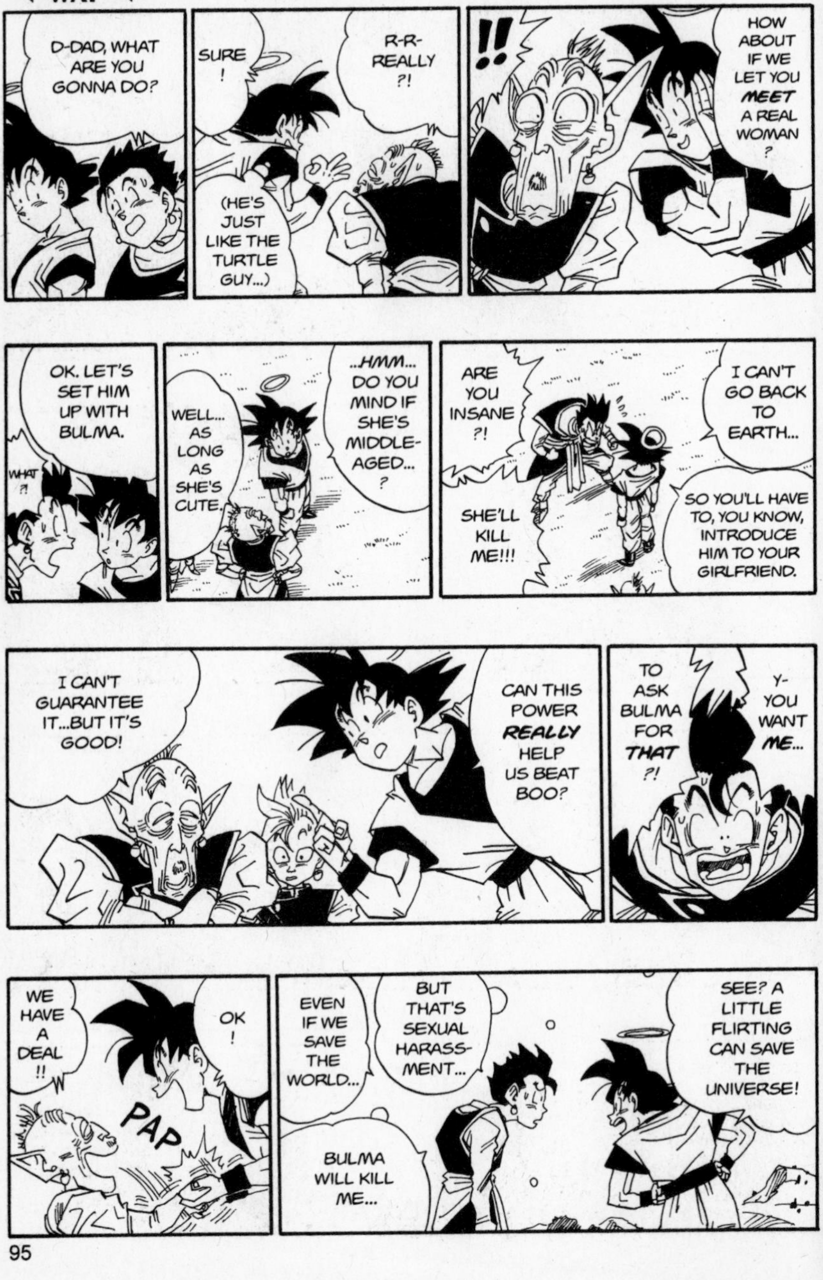
HOW ABOUT IF WE LET YOU MEET A REAL WOMAN ?
!!
R-R-REALLY ?!
SURE !
(HE'S JUST LIKE THE TURTLE GUY...)
D-DAD, WHAT ARE YOU GONNA DO?
I CAN'T GO BACK TO EARTH...
SO YOU'LL HAVE TO, YOU KNOW, INTRODUCE HIM TO YOUR GIRLFRIEND.
ARE YOU INSANE ?!
SHE'LL KILL ME!!!
...HMM... DO YOU MIND IF SHE'S MIDDLE-AGED... ?
WELL... AS LONG AS SHE'S CUTE.
OK. LET'S SET HIM UP WITH BULMA.
WHAT ?!
Y- YOU WANT ME...
TO ASK BULMA FOR THAT ?!
CAN THIS POWER REALLY HELP US BEAT BOO?
I CAN'T GUARANTEE IT...BUT IT'S GOOD!
SEE? A LITTLE FLIRTING CAN SAVE THE UNIVERSE!
BUT THAT'S SEXUAL HARASS-MENT...
EVEN IF WE SAVE THE WORLD...
BULMA WILL KILL ME...
OK !
WE HAVE A DEAL !!
PAP

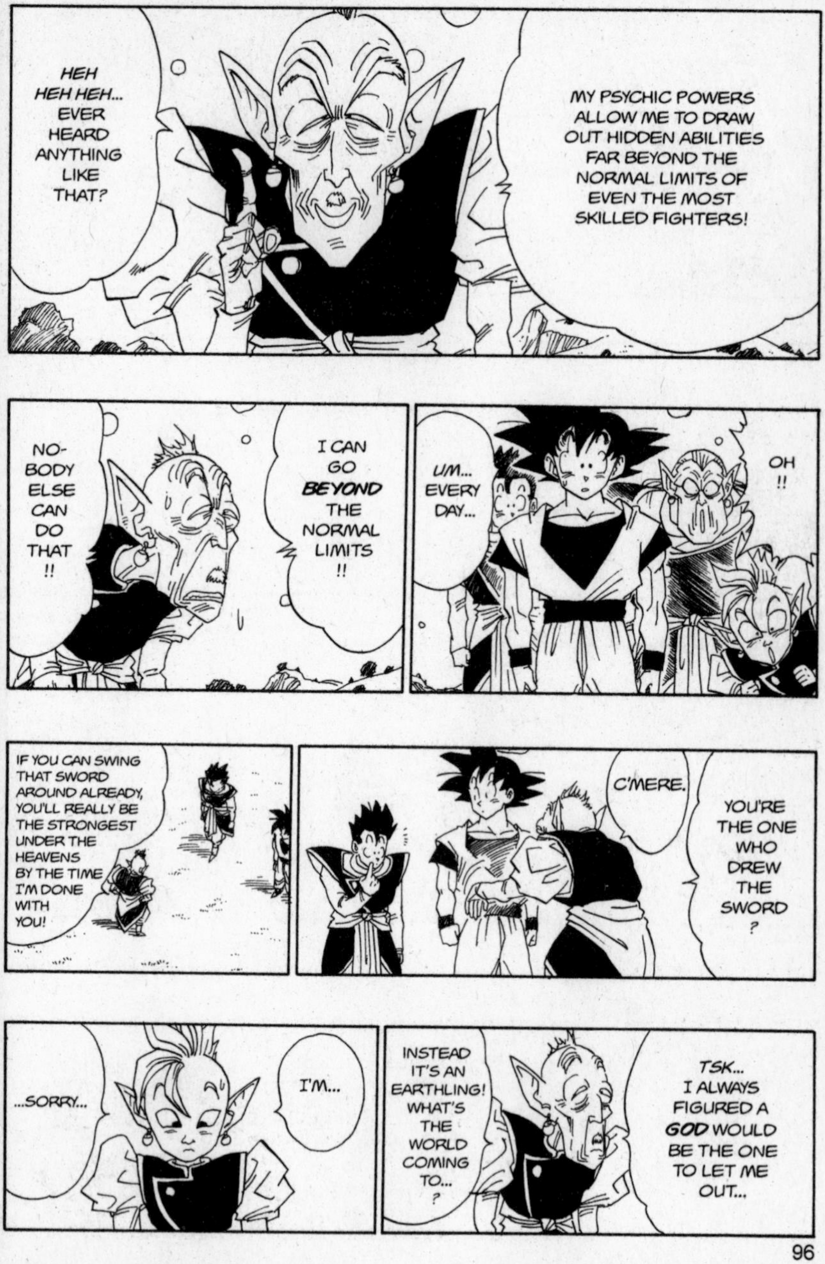
MY PSYCHIC POWERS ALLOW ME TO DRAW OUT HIDDEN ABILITIES FAR BEYOND THE NORMAL LIMITS OF EVEN THE MOST SKILLED FIGHTERS!
HEH HEH HEH... EVER HEARD ANYTHING LIKE THAT?
OH !!
UM... EVERY DAY...
I CAN GO **BEYOND** THE NORMAL LIMITS !!
NOBODY ELSE CAN DO THAT !!
YOU'RE THE ONE WHO DREW THE SWORD ?
C'MERE.
IF YOU CAN SWING THAT SWORD AROUND ALREADY, YOU'LL REALLY BE THE STRONGEST UNDER THE HEAVENS BY THE TIME I'M DONE WITH YOU!
TSK... I ALWAYS FIGURED A **GOD** WOULD BE THE ONE TO LET ME OUT...
INSTEAD IT'S AN EARTHLING! WHAT'S THE WORLD COMING TO... ?
I'M...
...SORRY...

READ THIS WAY

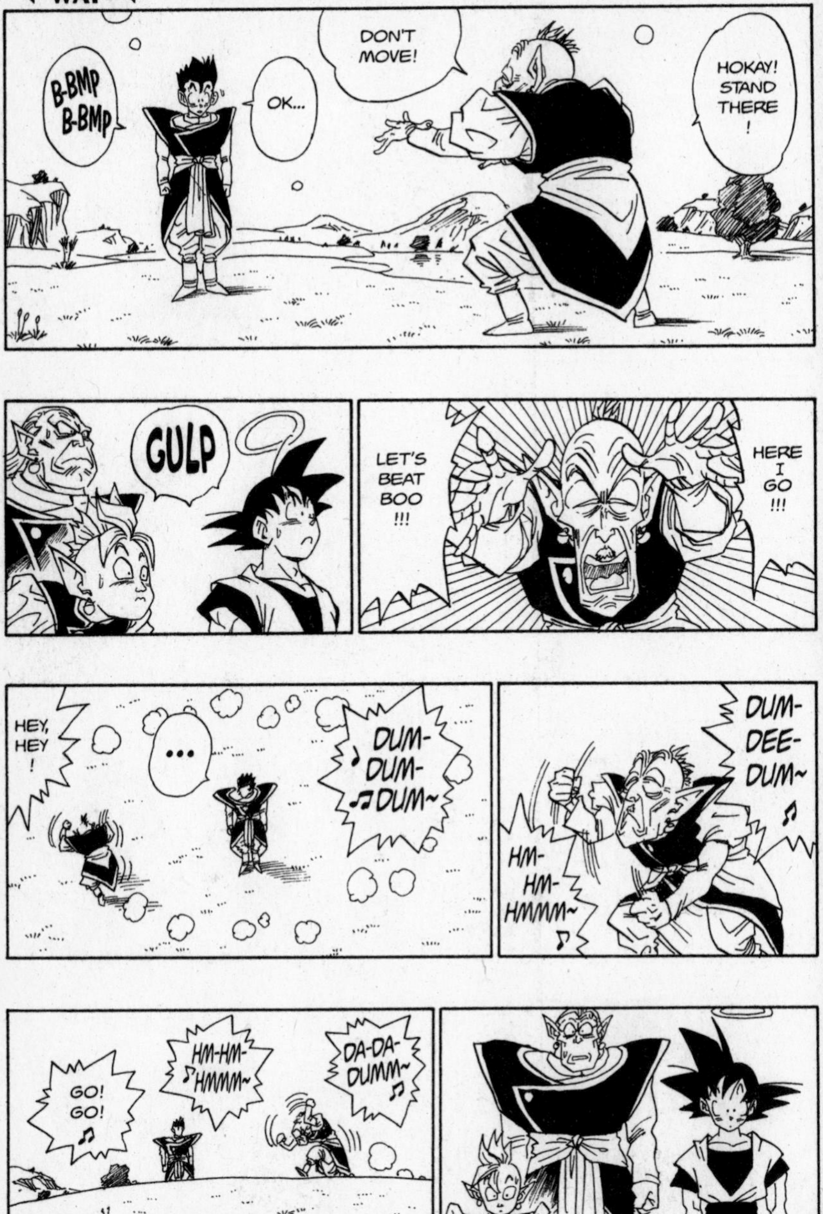
HOKAY! STAND THERE !
DON'T MOVE!
OK...
B-BMP B-BMP
HERE I GO !!!
LET'S BEAT BOO !!!
GULP
DUM-DEE-DUM~
HM-HM-HMMM~
DUM-DUM-DUM~
...
HEY, HEY !
DA-DA-DUMM~
HM-HM-HMMM~
GO! GO!

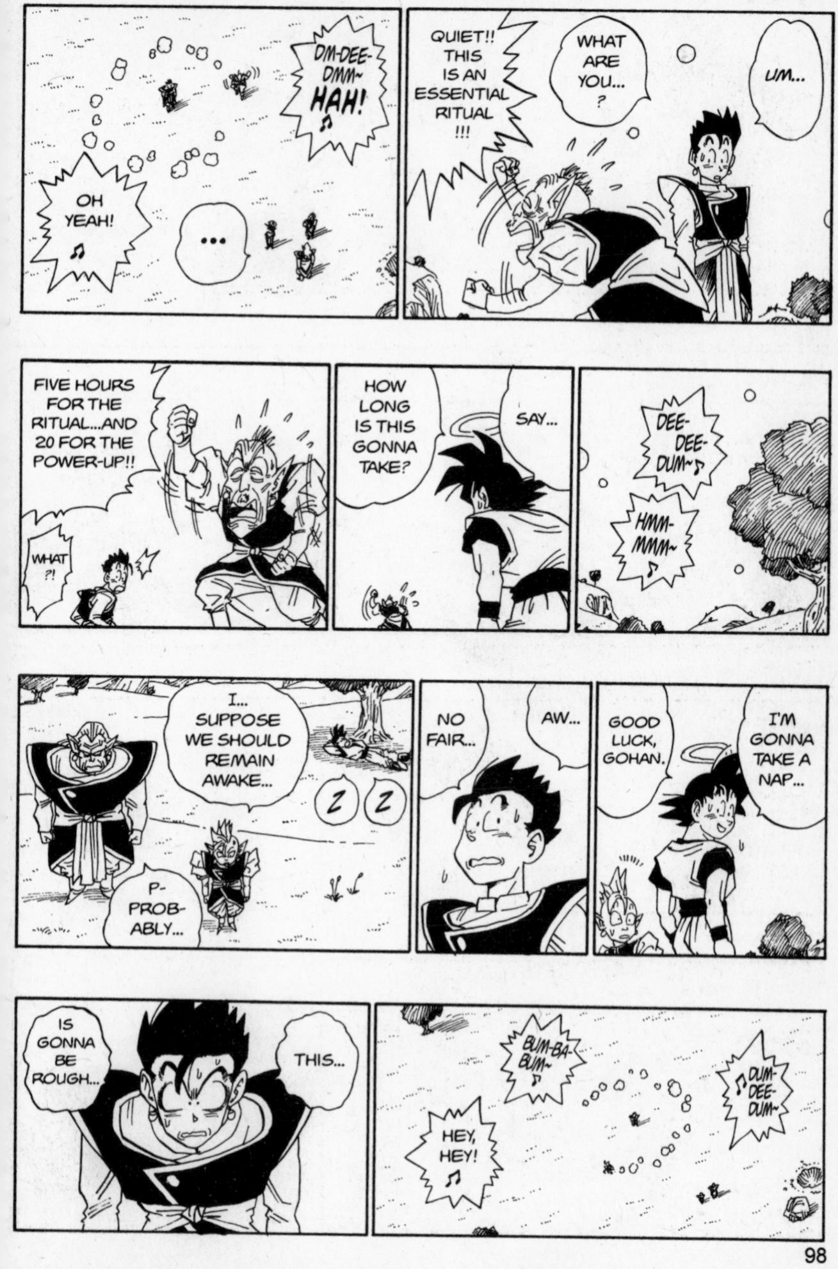
UM...
WHAT ARE YOU... ?
QUIET!! THIS IS AN ESSENTIAL RITUAL !!!
DM-DEE-DMM~ HAH! ♪
OH YEAH! ♪
...
DEE-DEE-DUM~♪
HMM-MMM~ ♪
SAY...
HOW LONG IS THIS GONNA TAKE?
FIVE HOURS FOR THE RITUAL...AND 20 FOR THE POWER-UP!!
WHAT ?!
I'M GONNA TAKE A NAP...
GOOD LUCK, GOHAN.
AW...
NO FAIR...
I... SUPPOSE WE SHOULD REMAIN AWAKE...
Z Z
P-PROBABLY...
DUM-DEE-DUM~ ♪
BUM-BA-BUM~ ♪
HEY, HEY! ♪
THIS...
IS GONNA BE ROUGH...

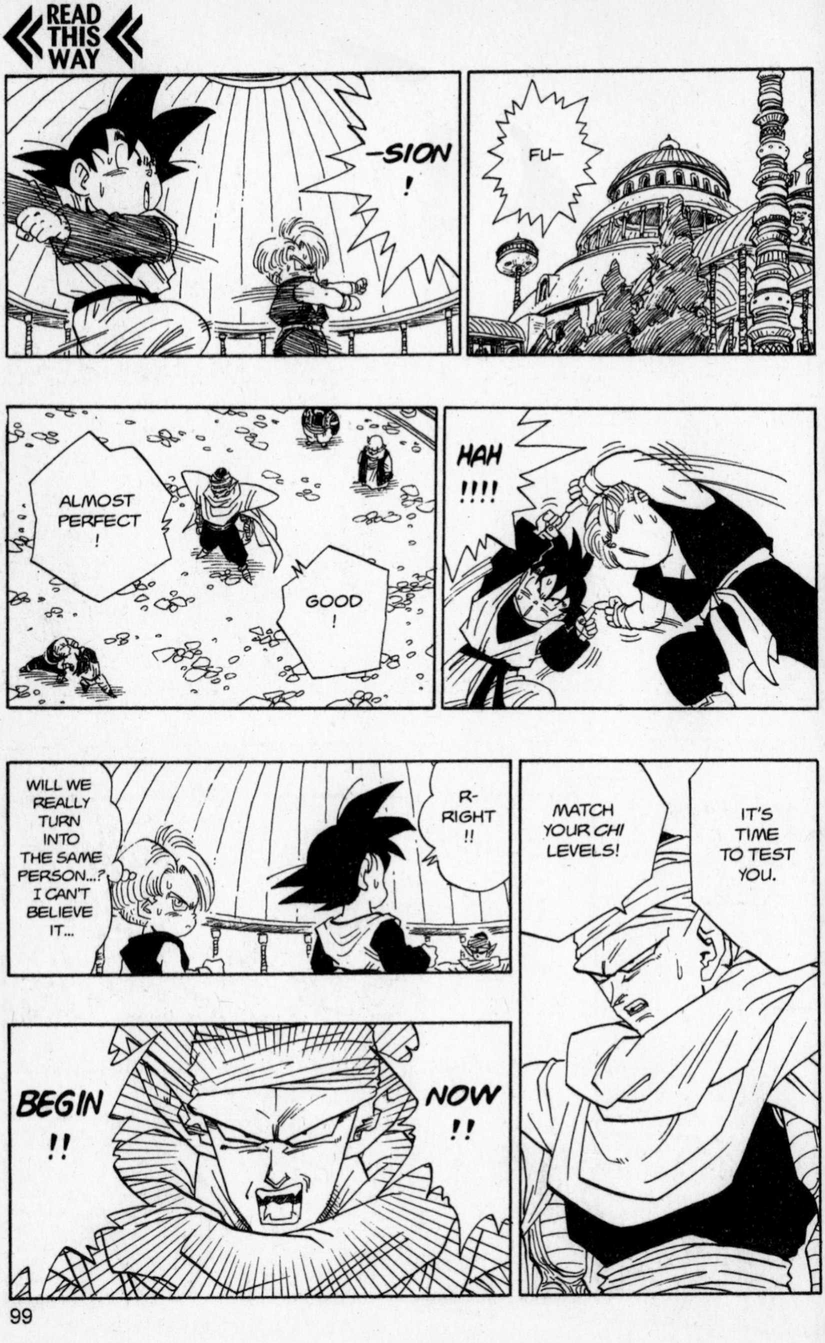
READ THIS WAY
FU–
–SION !
HAH !!!!
ALMOST PERFECT !
GOOD !
IT'S TIME TO TEST YOU.
MATCH YOUR *CHI* LEVELS!
R- RIGHT !!
WILL WE REALLY TURN INTO THE SAME PERSON...? I CAN'T BELIEVE IT...
BEGIN !!
NOW !!

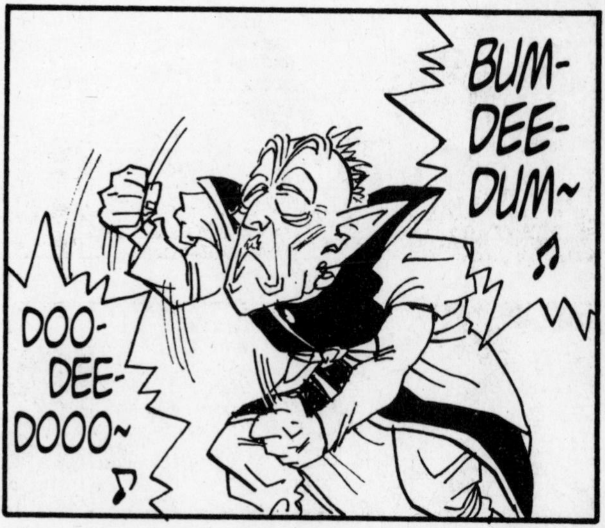
BUM- DEE- DUM~
DOO- DEE- DOOO~

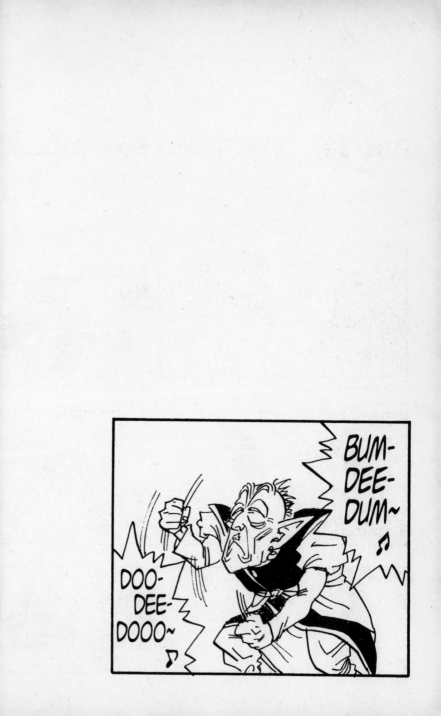

DBZ:286 • The Fusion Succeeds...?!

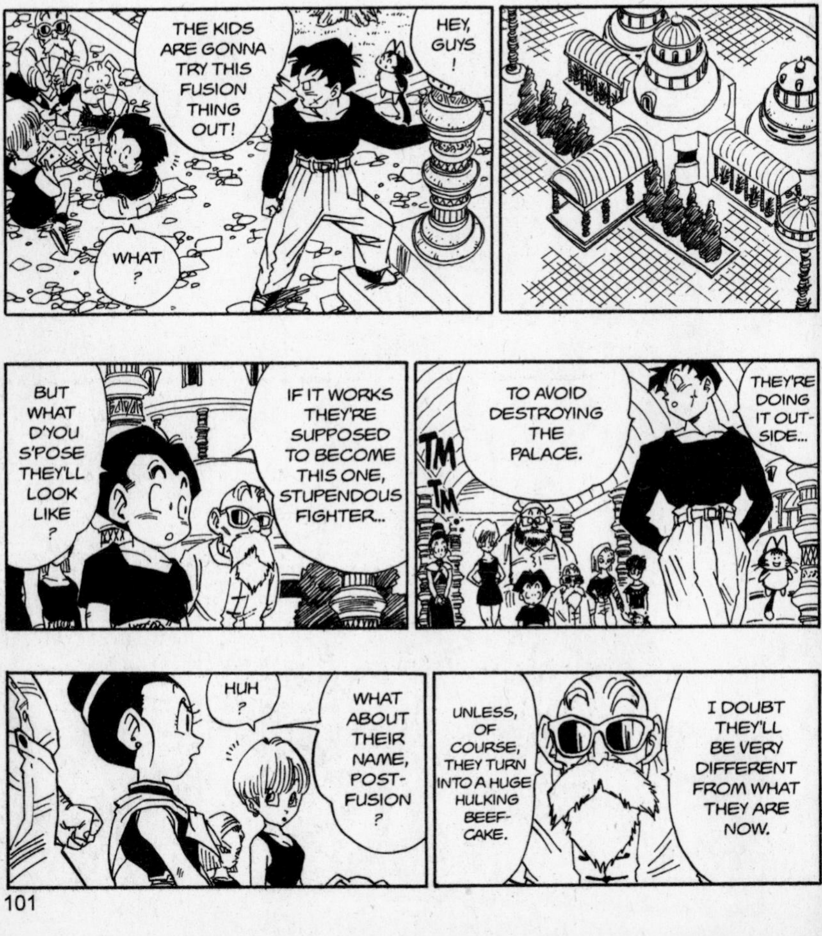
HEY, GUYS!
THE KIDS ARE GONNA TRY THIS FUSION THING OUT!
WHAT?
THEY'RE DOING IT OUT-SIDE...
TO AVOID DESTROYING THE PALACE.
TM TM
IF IT WORKS THEY'RE SUPPOSED TO BECOME THIS ONE, STUPENDOUS FIGHTER...
BUT WHAT D'YOU S'POSE THEY'LL LOOK LIKE?
I DOUBT THEY'LL BE VERY DIFFERENT FROM WHAT THEY ARE NOW.
UNLESS, OF COURSE, THEY TURN INTO A HUGE HULKING BEEF-CAKE.
WHAT ABOUT THEIR NAME, POST-FUSION?
HUH?

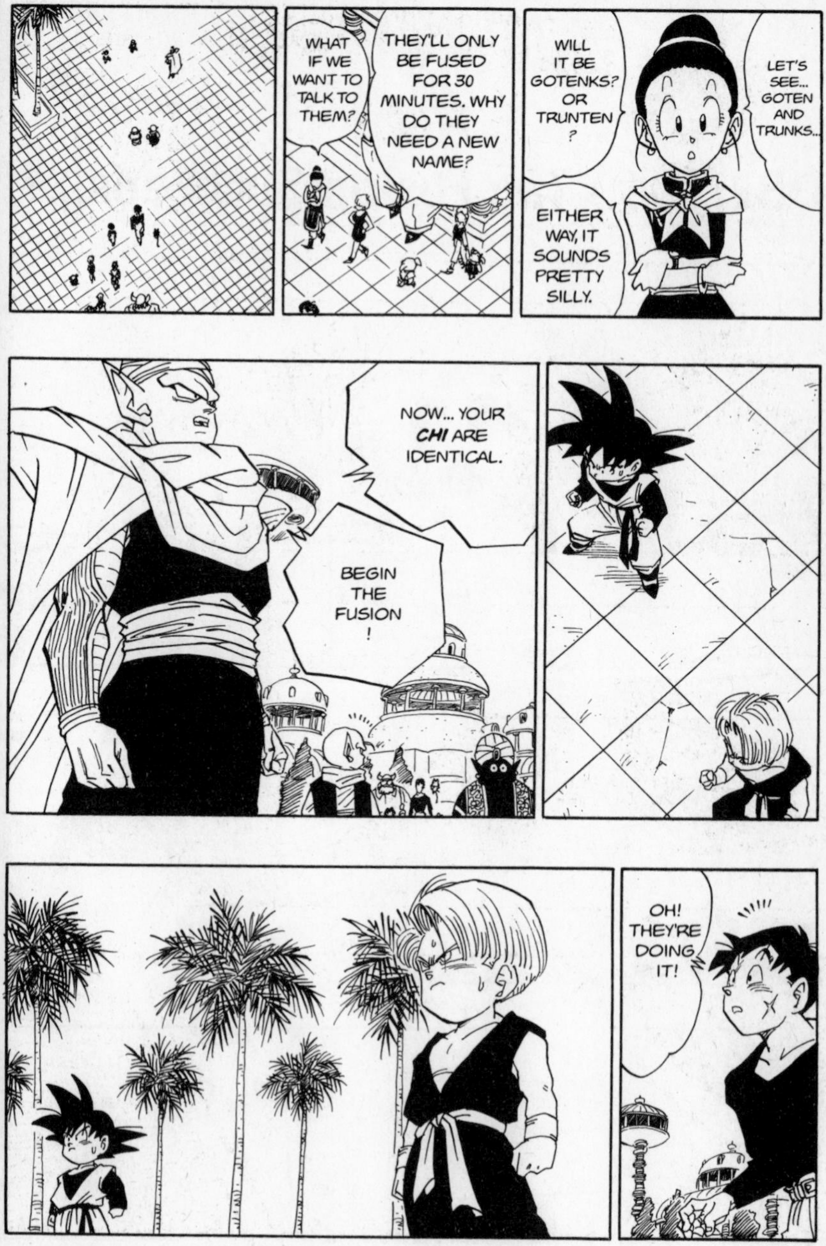
LET'S SEE... GOTEN AND TRUNKS...
WILL IT BE GOTENKS? OR TRUNTEN?
EITHER WAY, IT SOUNDS PRETTY SILLY.
THEY'LL ONLY BE FUSED FOR 30 MINUTES. WHY DO THEY NEED A NEW NAME?
WHAT IF WE WANT TO TALK TO THEM?
NOW... YOUR CHI ARE IDENTICAL.
BEGIN THE FUSION!
OH! THEY'RE DOING IT!

READ THIS WAY

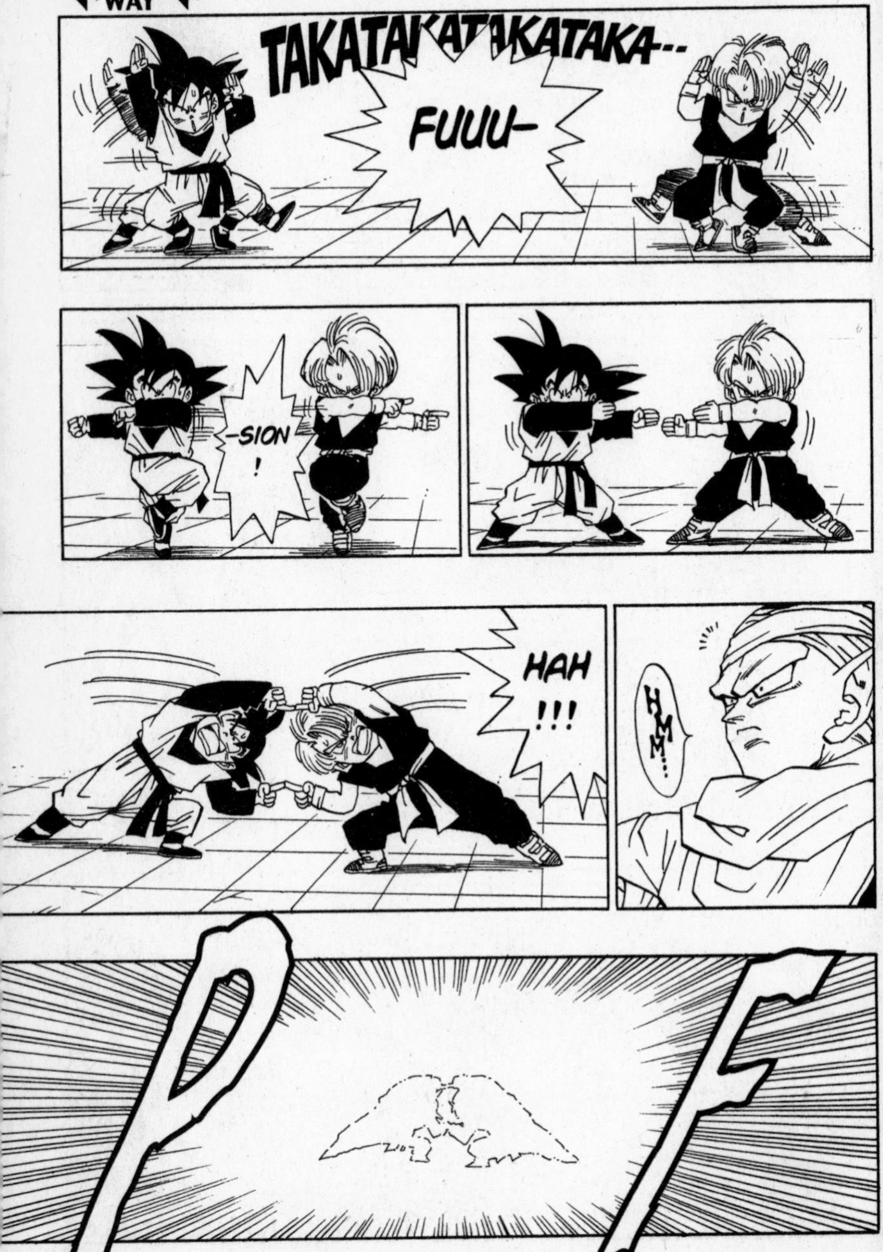
TAKATAKATAKATAKA...
FUUU-
-SION !
HMM...
HAH !!!
PF

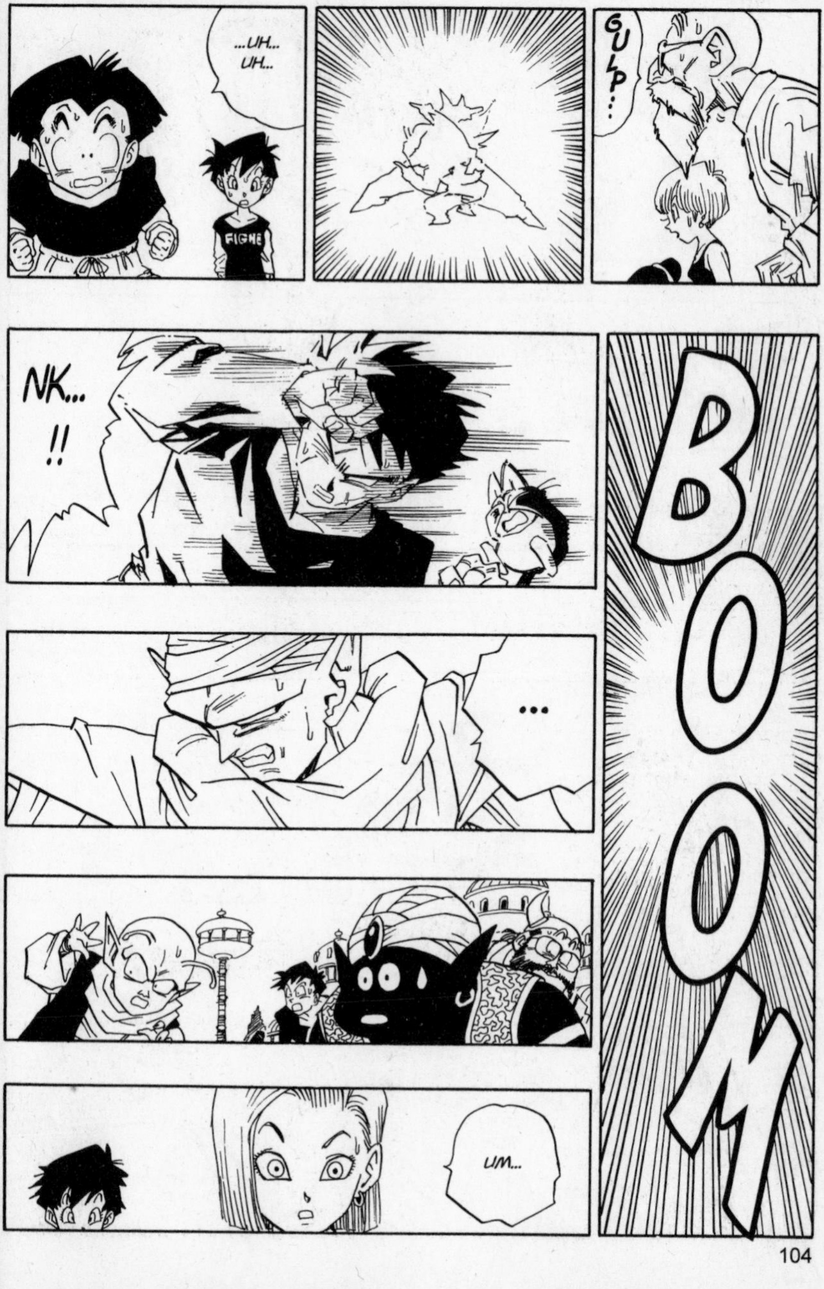
GULP...
...UH... UH...
BOOM
NK... !!
...
UM...

READ THIS WAY

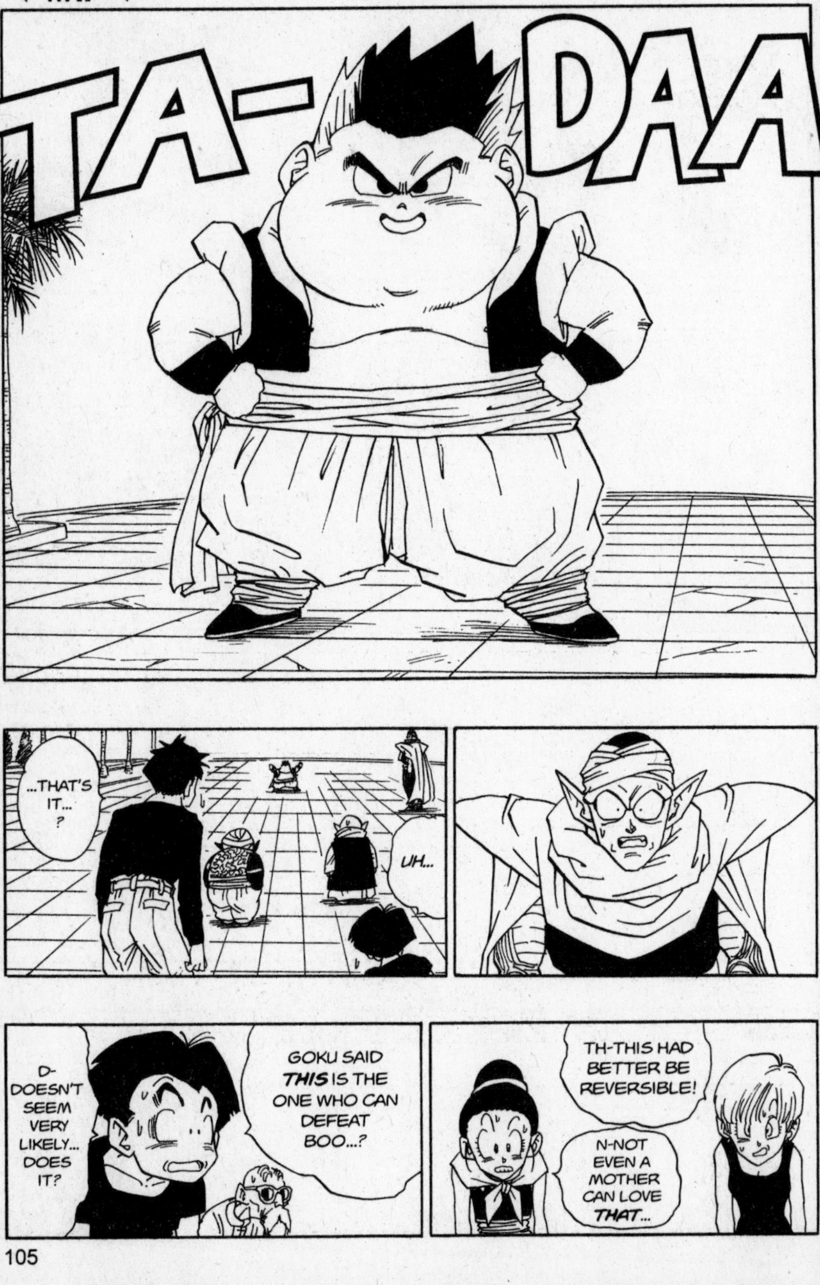
TA-DAA
...THAT'S IT... ?
UH...
TH-THIS HAD BETTER BE REVERSIBLE!
N-NOT EVEN A MOTHER CAN LOVE THAT...
GOKU SAID THIS IS THE ONE WHO CAN DEFEAT BOO...?
D-DOESN'T SEEM VERY LIKELY... DOES IT?

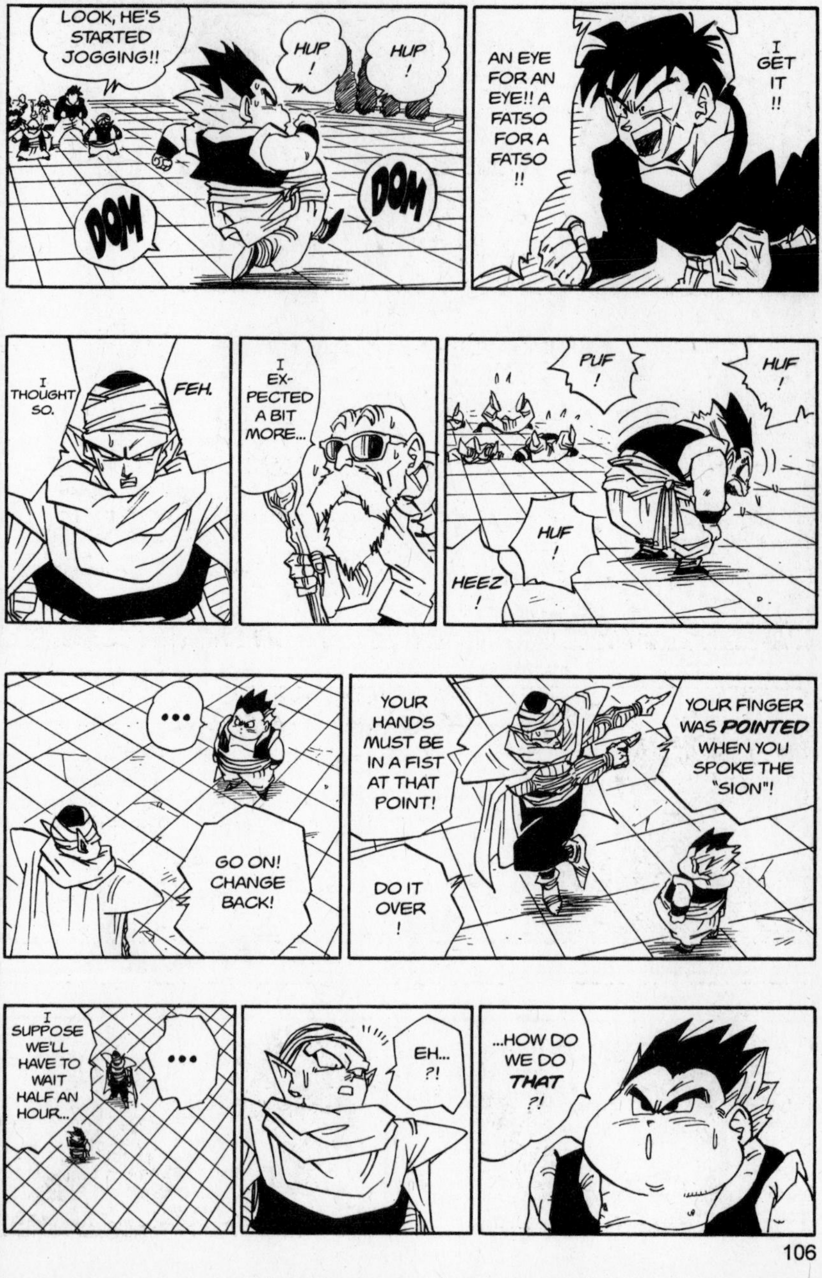
I GET IT!!
AN EYE FOR AN EYE!! A FATSO FOR A FATSO!!
HUP!
HUP!
LOOK, HE'S STARTED JOGGING!!
DOM
DOM
HUF!
PUF!
HUF!
HEEZ!
I EXPECTED A BIT MORE...
FEH.
I THOUGHT SO.
YOUR FINGER WAS POINTED WHEN YOU SPOKE THE "SION"!
YOUR HANDS MUST BE IN A FIST AT THAT POINT!
DO IT OVER!
...
GO ON! CHANGE BACK!
...HOW DO WE DO THAT?!
EH...?!
...
I SUPPOSE WE'LL HAVE TO WAIT HALF AN HOUR...

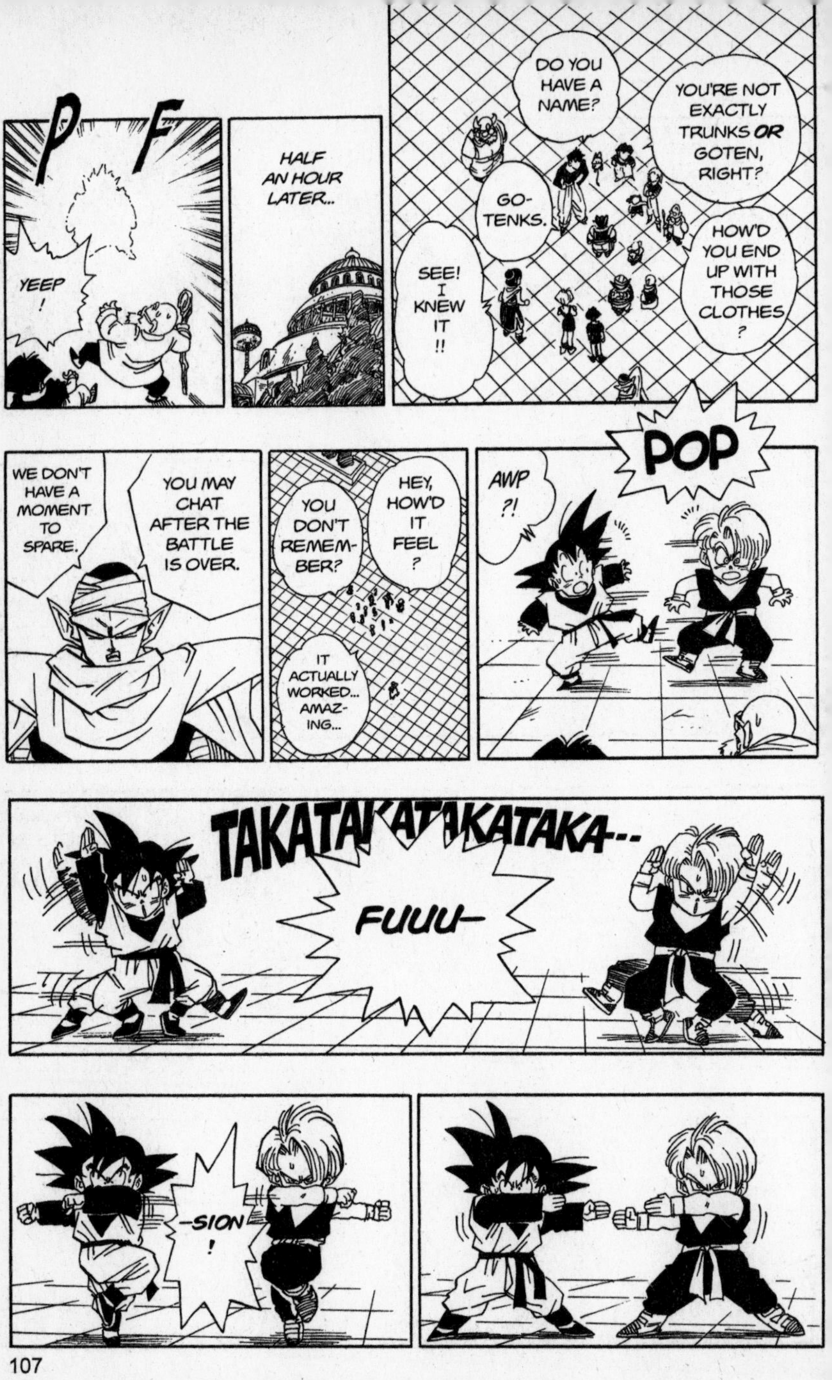
YOU'RE NOT EXACTLY TRUNKS OR GOTEN, RIGHT?
DO YOU HAVE A NAME?
HOW'D YOU END UP WITH THOSE CLOTHES?
GO-TENKS.
SEE! I KNEW IT!!
HALF AN HOUR LATER...
PF
YEEP!
POP
AWP?!
HEY, HOW'D IT FEEL?
YOU DON'T REMEMBER?
IT ACTUALLY WORKED... AMAZING...
YOU MAY CHAT AFTER THE BATTLE IS OVER.
WE DON'T HAVE A MOMENT TO SPARE.
TAKATAKATAKATAKA...
FUUU-
-SION!

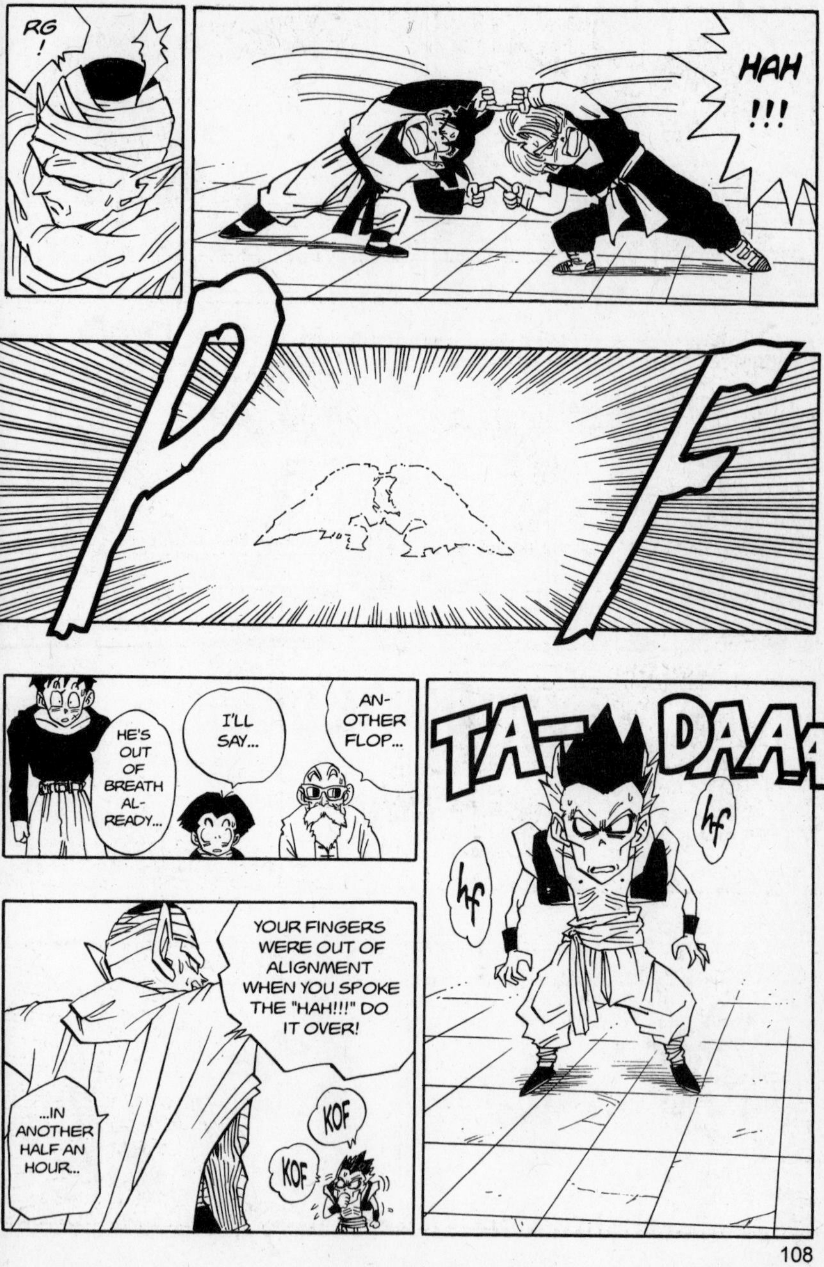
HAH!!!
RG!
PF
TA-DAAA
hf
hf
AN-OTHER FLOP...
I'LL SAY...
HE'S OUT OF BREATH AL-READY...
YOUR FINGERS WERE OUT OF ALIGNMENT WHEN YOU SPOKE THE "HAH!!!" DO IT OVER!
...IN ANOTHER HALF AN HOUR...
KOF
KOF

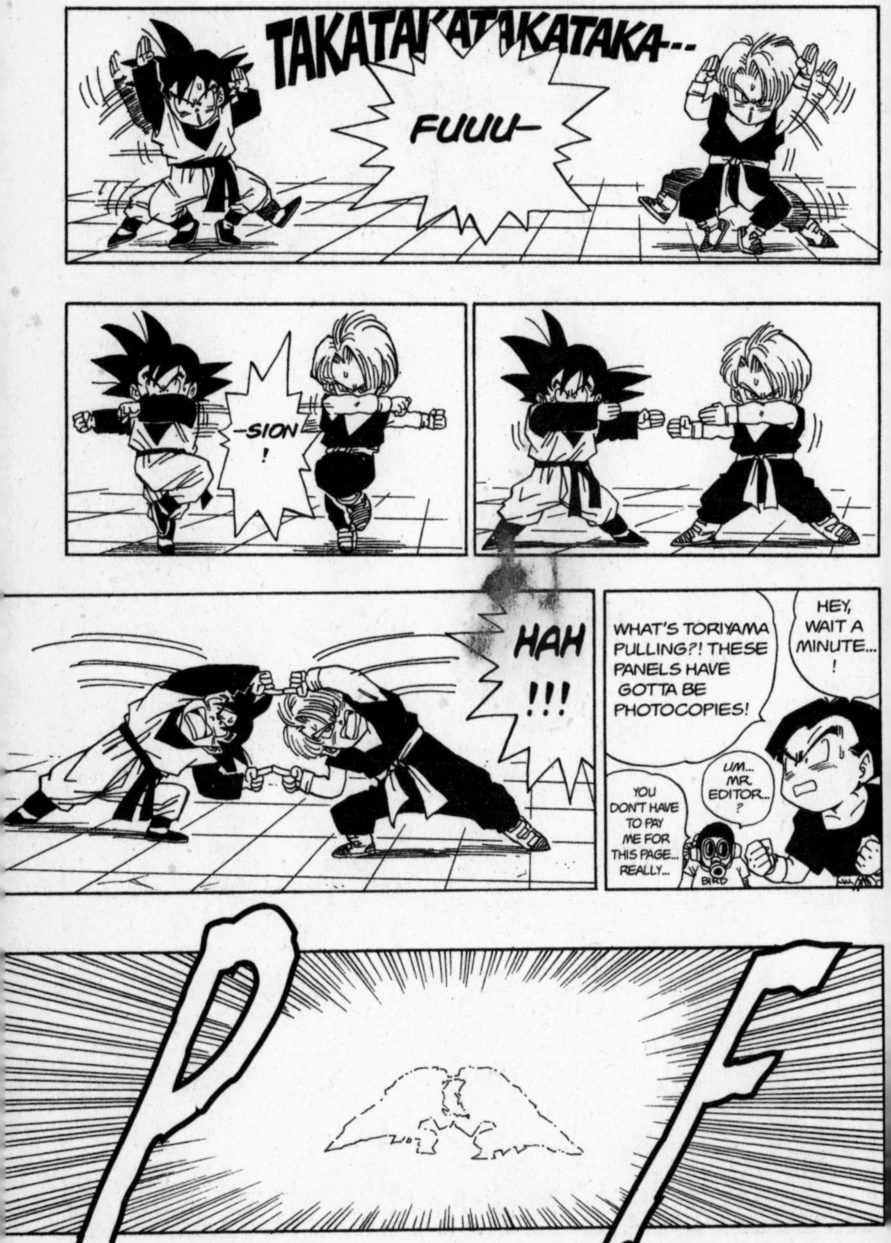
TAKATAKATAKATAKA...
FUUU-
-SION!
HEY, WAIT A MINUTE...!
WHAT'S TORIYAMA PULLING?! THESE PANELS HAVE GOTTA BE PHOTOCOPIES!
UM... MR. EDITOR...?
YOU DON'T HAVE TO PAY ME FOR THIS PAGE... REALLY...
BIRD
HAH!!!
PF

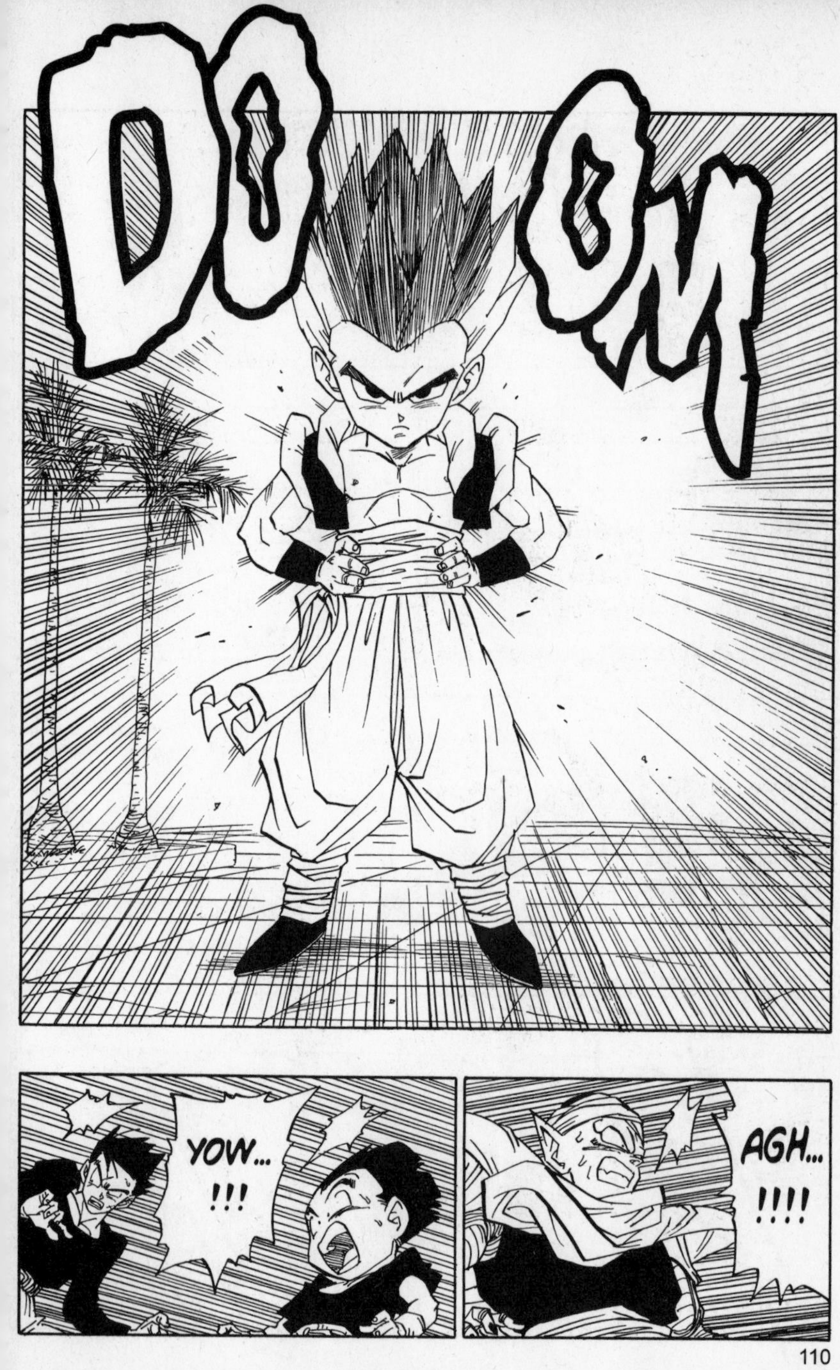
DOOM
AGH... !!!!
YOW... !!!

READ THIS WAY

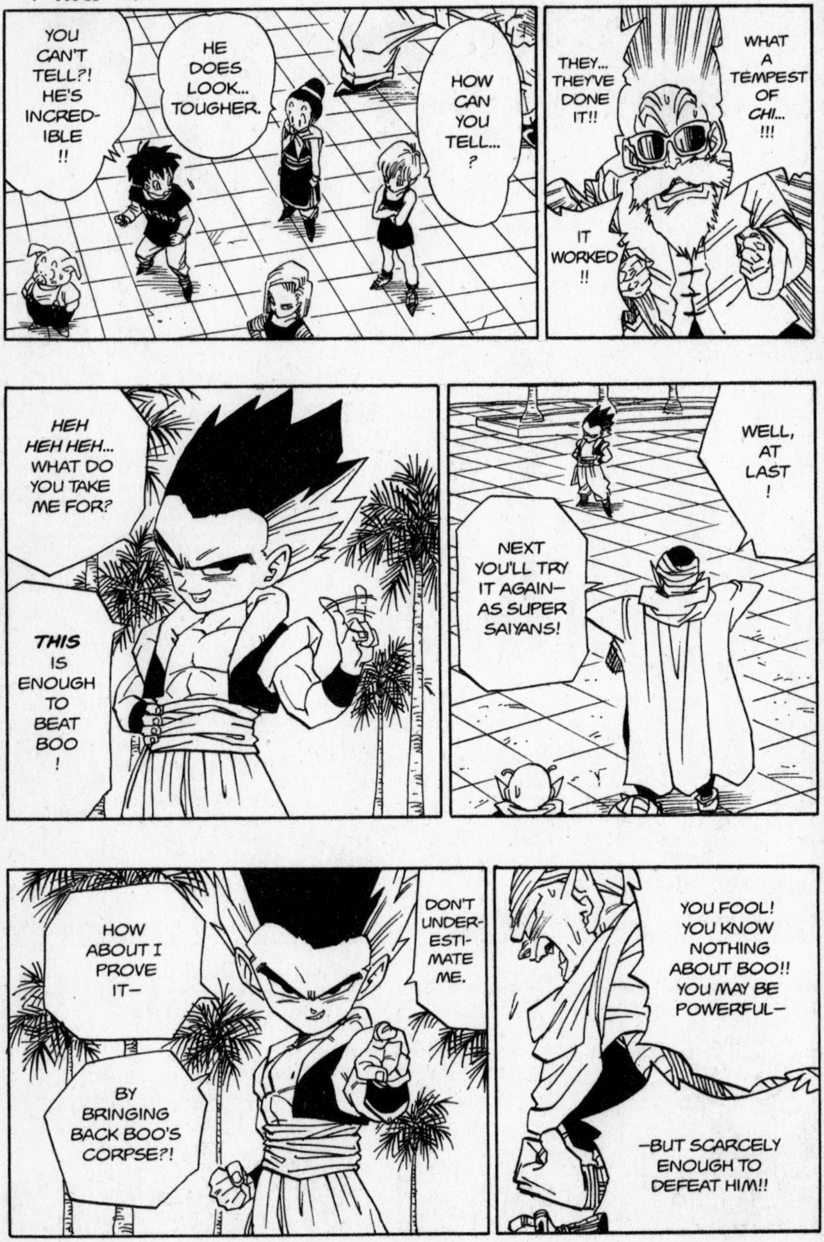
WHAT A TEMPEST OF CHI...!!!
THEY... THEY'VE DONE IT!!
IT WORKED!!
HOW CAN YOU TELL...?
HE DOES LOOK... TOUGHER.
YOU CAN'T TELL?! HE'S INCREDIBLE!!
WELL, AT LAST!
NEXT YOU'LL TRY IT AGAIN—AS SUPER SAIYANS!
HEH HEH HEH... WHAT DO YOU TAKE ME FOR?
THIS IS ENOUGH TO BEAT BOO!
YOU FOOL! YOU KNOW NOTHING ABOUT BOO!! YOU MAY BE POWERFUL—
—BUT SCARCELY ENOUGH TO DEFEAT HIM!!
DON'T UNDERESTIMATE ME.
HOW ABOUT I PROVE IT—
BY BRINGING BACK BOO'S CORPSE?!

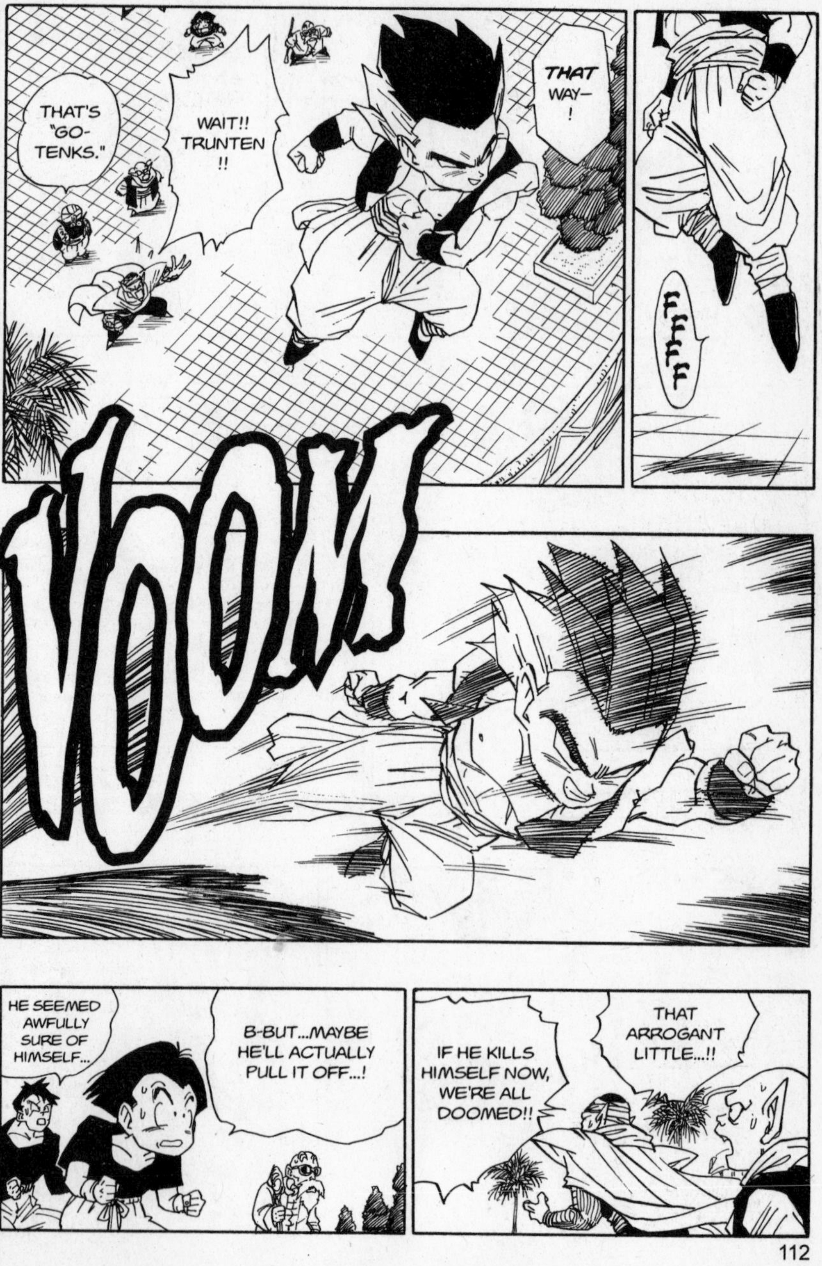
FFFF
THAT WAY—!
WAIT!! TRUNTEN!!
THAT'S "GO-TENKS."
VOOM
THAT ARROGANT LITTLE...!!
IF HE KILLS HIMSELF NOW, WE'RE ALL DOOMED!!
B-BUT...MAYBE HE'LL ACTUALLY PULL IT OFF...!
HE SEEMED AWFULLY SURE OF HIMSELF...

READ THIS WAY

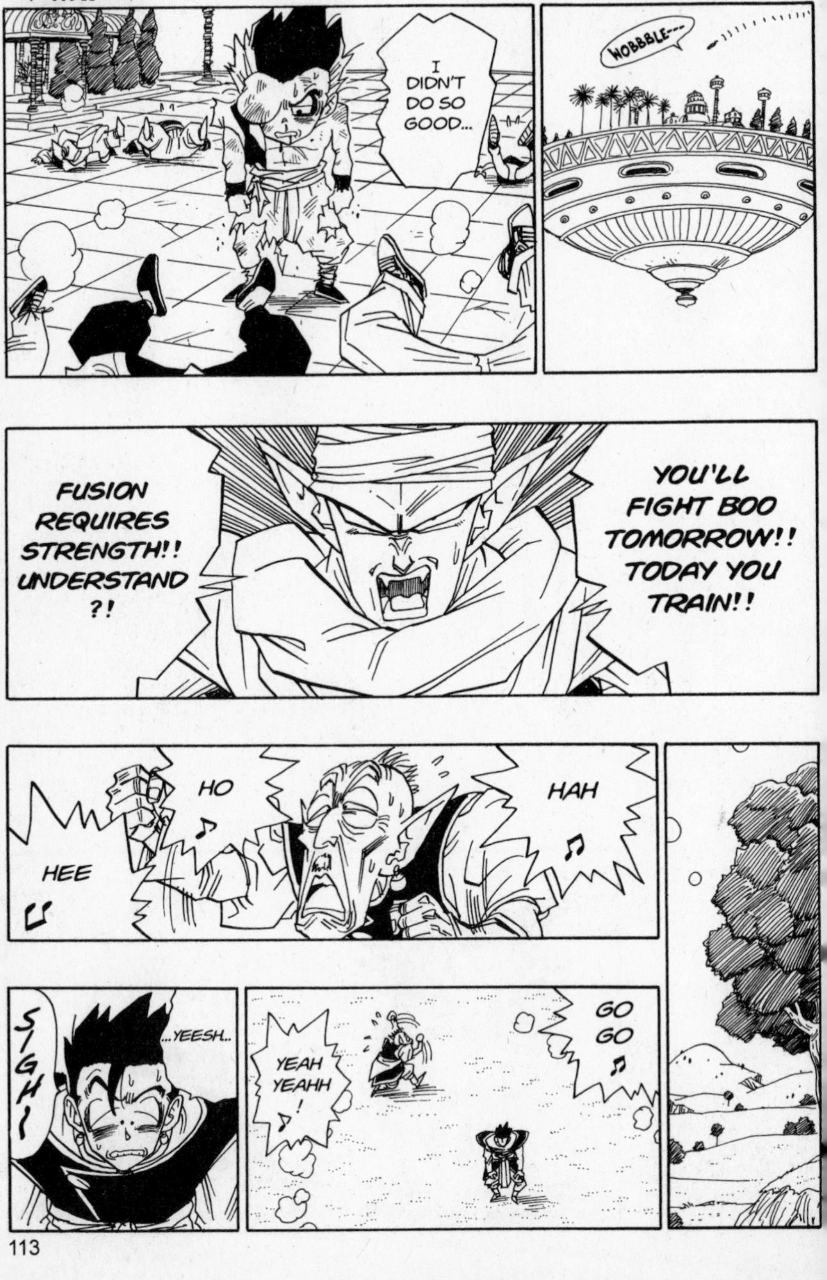
WOBBBLE---
I DIDN'T DO SO GOOD...
YOU'LL FIGHT BOO TOMORROW!! TODAY YOU TRAIN!!
FUSION REQUIRES STRENGTH!! UNDERSTAND?!
HAH ♪
HO ♪
HEE ♪
GO GO ♪
YEAH YEAHH ♪!
SIGH!
...YEESH...

DBZ:287 · The Earth's Secret Weapon!

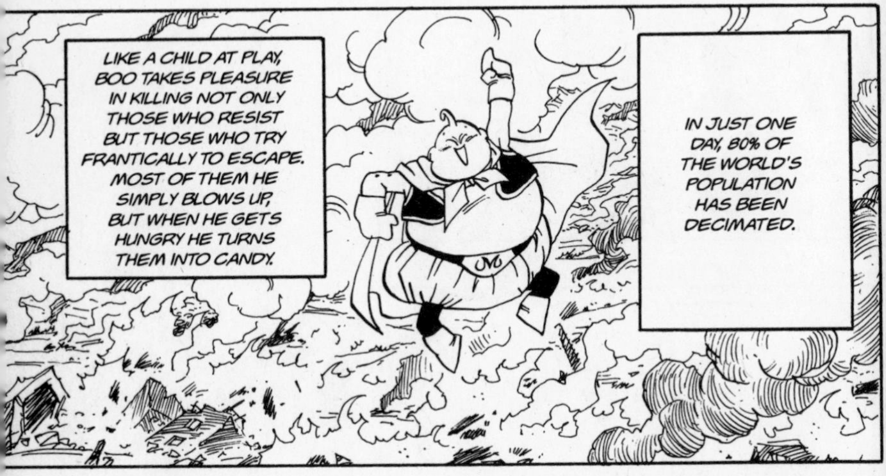
IN JUST ONE DAY, 80% OF THE WORLD'S POPULATION HAS BEEN DECIMATED.
LIKE A CHILD AT PLAY, BOO TAKES PLEASURE IN KILLING NOT ONLY THOSE WHO RESIST BUT THOSE WHO TRY FRANTICALLY TO ESCAPE. MOST OF THEM HE SIMPLY BLOWS UP, BUT WHEN HE GETS HUNGRY HE TURNS THEM INTO CANDY.

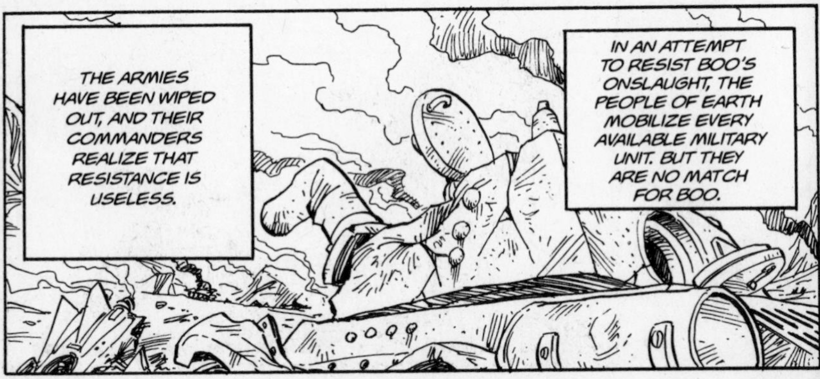
IN AN ATTEMPT TO RESIST BOO'S ONSLAUGHT, THE PEOPLE OF EARTH MOBILIZE EVERY AVAILABLE MILITARY UNIT. BUT THEY ARE NO MATCH FOR BOO.
THE ARMIES HAVE BEEN WIPED OUT, AND THEIR COMMANDERS REALIZE THAT RESISTANCE IS USELESS.

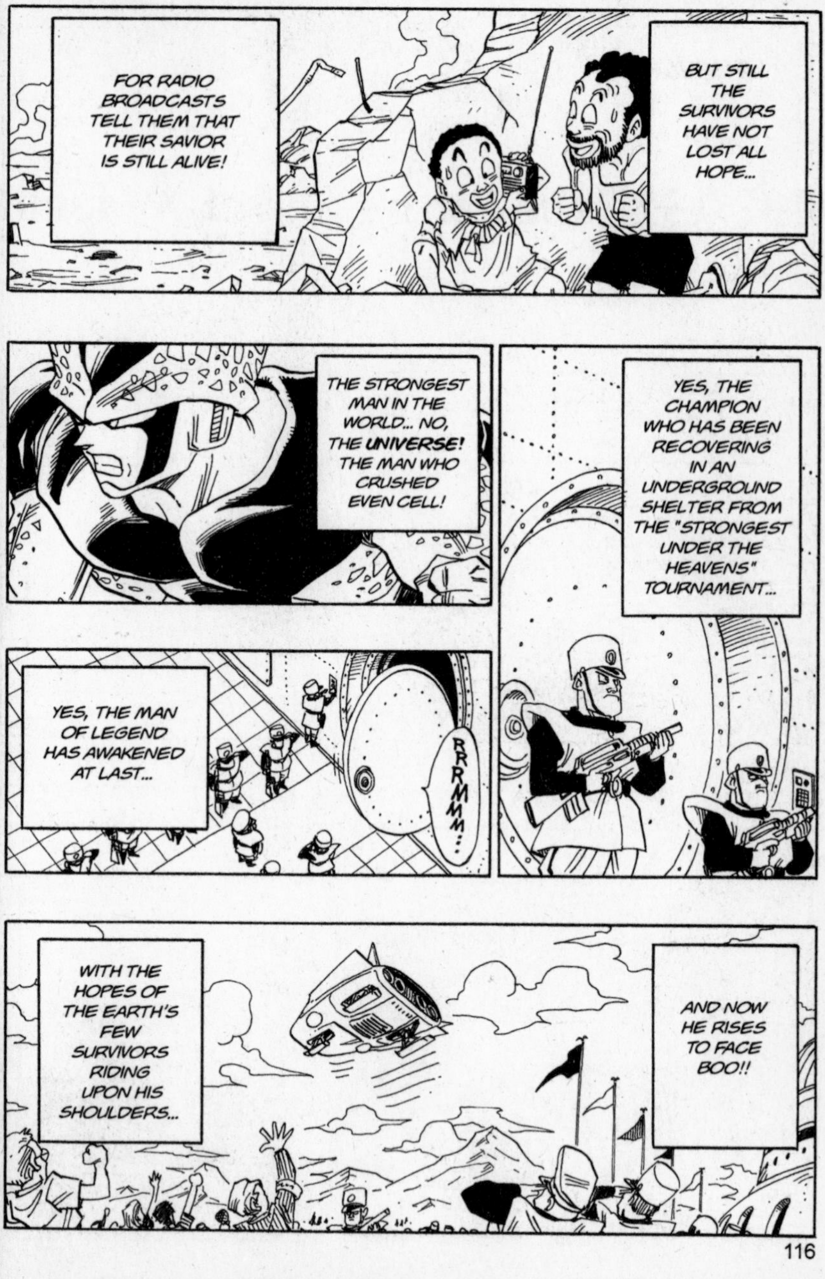
BUT STILL THE SURVIVORS HAVE NOT LOST ALL HOPE...
FOR RADIO BROADCASTS TELL THEM THAT THEIR SAVIOR IS STILL ALIVE!
YES, THE CHAMPION WHO HAS BEEN RECOVERING IN AN UNDERGROUND SHELTER FROM THE "STRONGEST UNDER THE HEAVENS" TOURNAMENT...
THE STRONGEST MAN IN THE WORLD... NO, THE **UNIVERSE!** THE MAN WHO CRUSHED EVEN CELL!
RRRMMM...
YES, THE MAN OF LEGEND HAS AWAKENED AT LAST...
AND NOW HE RISES TO FACE BOO!!
WITH THE HOPES OF THE EARTH'S FEW SURVIVORS RIDING UPON HIS SHOULDERS...

READ THIS WAY

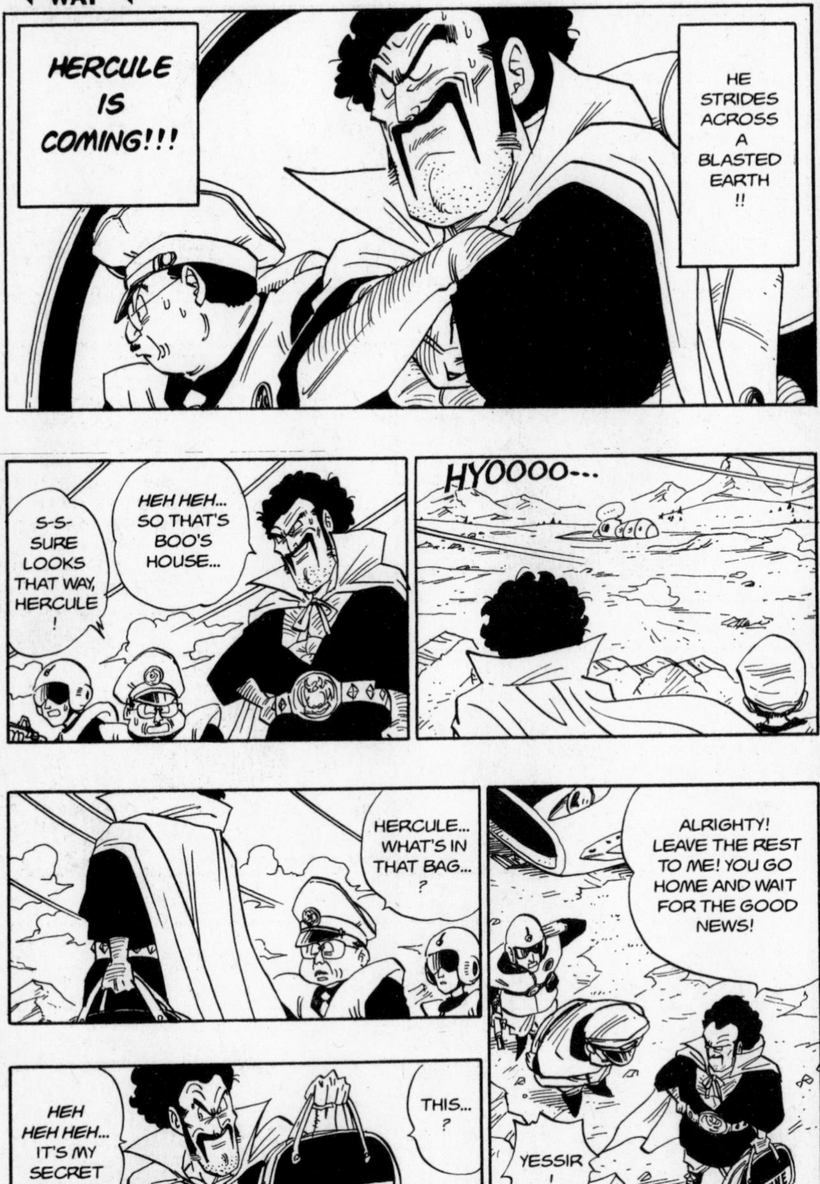
HE STRIDES ACROSS A BLASTED EARTH !!
HERCULE IS COMING!!!
HYOOOO---
HEH HEH... SO THAT'S BOO'S HOUSE...
S-S-SURE LOOKS THAT WAY, HERCULE!
ALRIGHTY! LEAVE THE REST TO ME! YOU GO HOME AND WAIT FOR THE GOOD NEWS!
YESSIR!
HERCULE
HERCULE... WHAT'S IN THAT BAG...?
THIS...?
HEH HEH HEH... IT'S MY SECRET WEAPON...
HERCULE

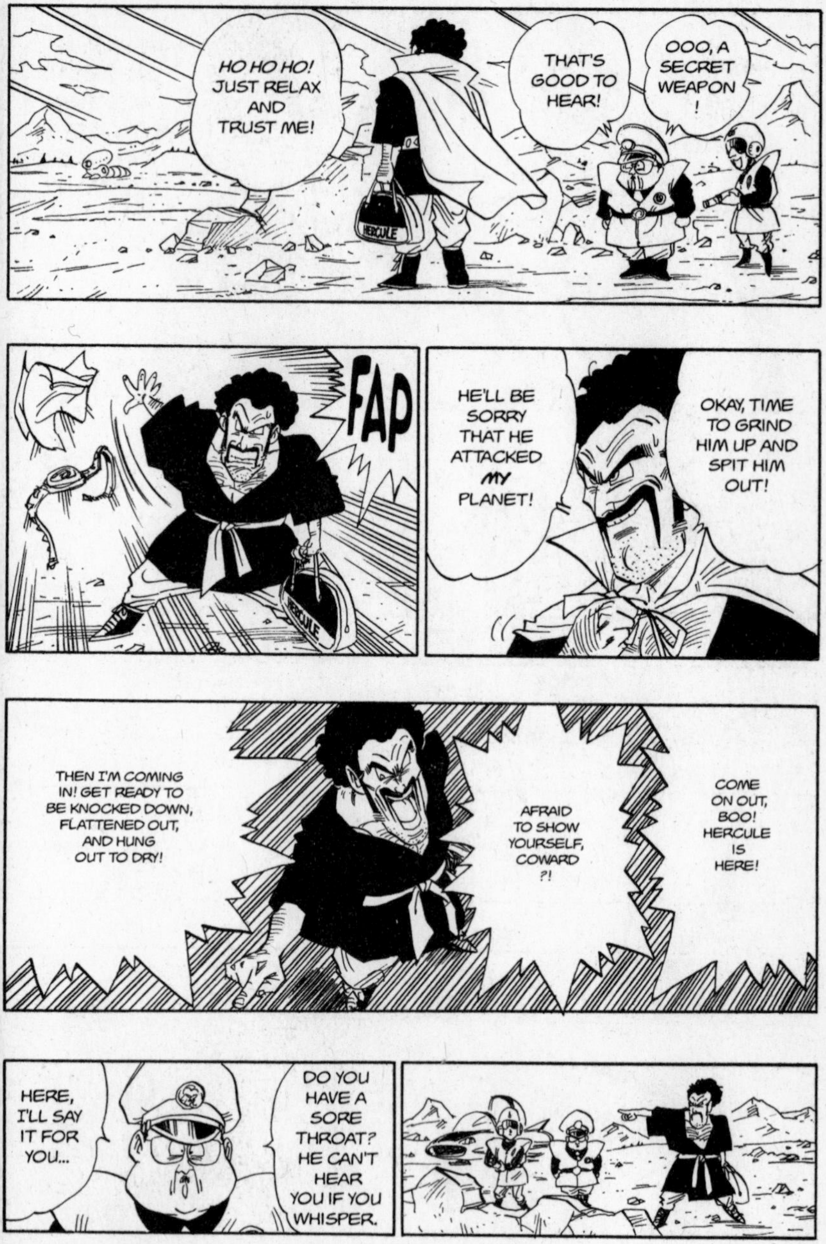
OOO, A SECRET WEAPON!
THAT'S GOOD TO HEAR!
HO HO HO! JUST RELAX AND TRUST ME!
HERCULE
OKAY, TIME TO GRIND HIM UP AND SPIT HIM OUT!
HE'LL BE SORRY THAT HE ATTACKED MY PLANET!
FAP
HERCULE
COME ON OUT, BOO! HERCULE IS HERE!
AFRAID TO SHOW YOURSELF, COWARD?!
THEN I'M COMING IN! GET READY TO BE KNOCKED DOWN, FLATTENED OUT, AND HUNG OUT TO DRY!
DO YOU HAVE A SORE THROAT? HE CAN'T HEAR YOU IF YOU WHISPER.
HERE, I'LL SAY IT FOR YOU...

READ THIS WAY

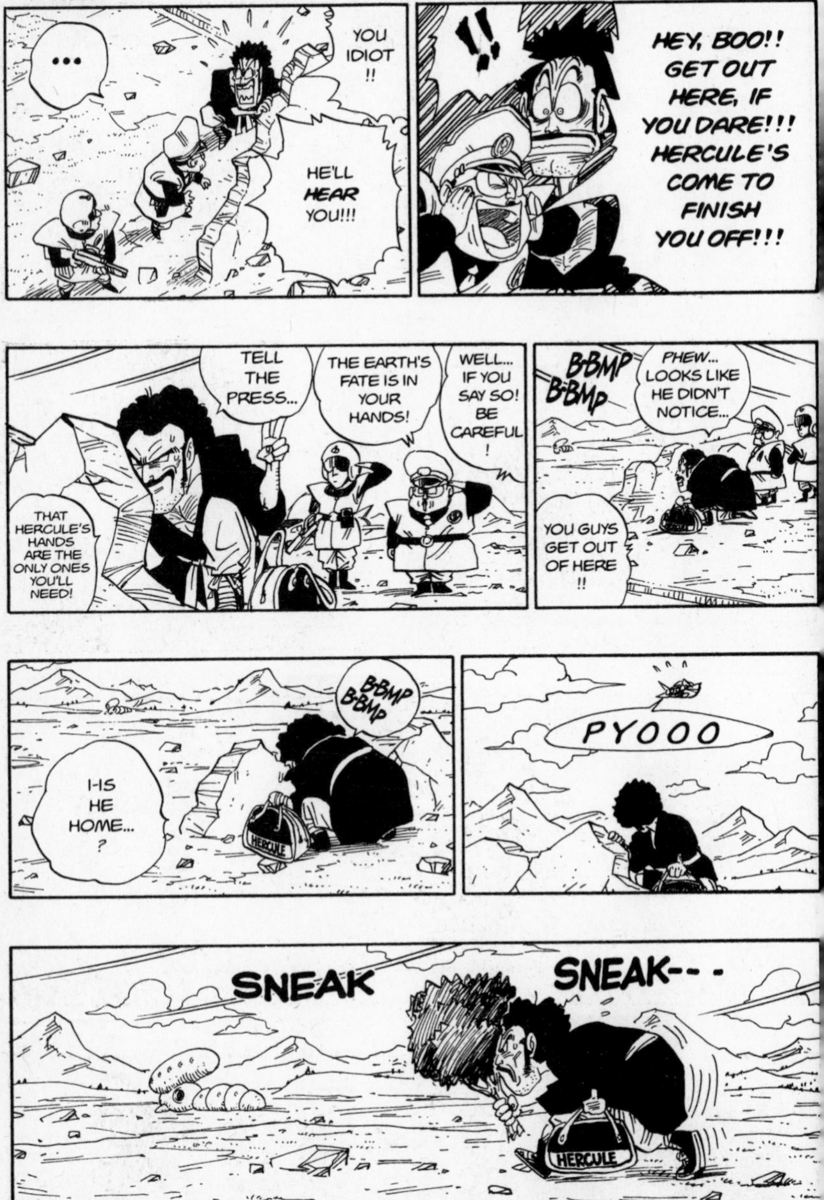
!!
HEY, BOO!! GET OUT HERE, IF YOU DARE!!! HERCULE'S COME TO FINISH YOU OFF!!!
YOU IDIOT !!
HE'LL HEAR YOU!!!
...
B-BMP B-BMP
PHEW... LOOKS LIKE HE DIDN'T NOTICE...
YOU GUYS GET OUT OF HERE !!
WELL... IF YOU SAY SO! BE CAREFUL !
THE EARTH'S FATE IS IN YOUR HANDS!
TELL THE PRESS...
THAT HERCULE'S HANDS ARE THE ONLY ONES YOU'LL NEED!
PYOOO
B-BMP B-BMP
I-IS HE HOME... ?
HERCULE
SNEAK---
SNEAK
HERCULE

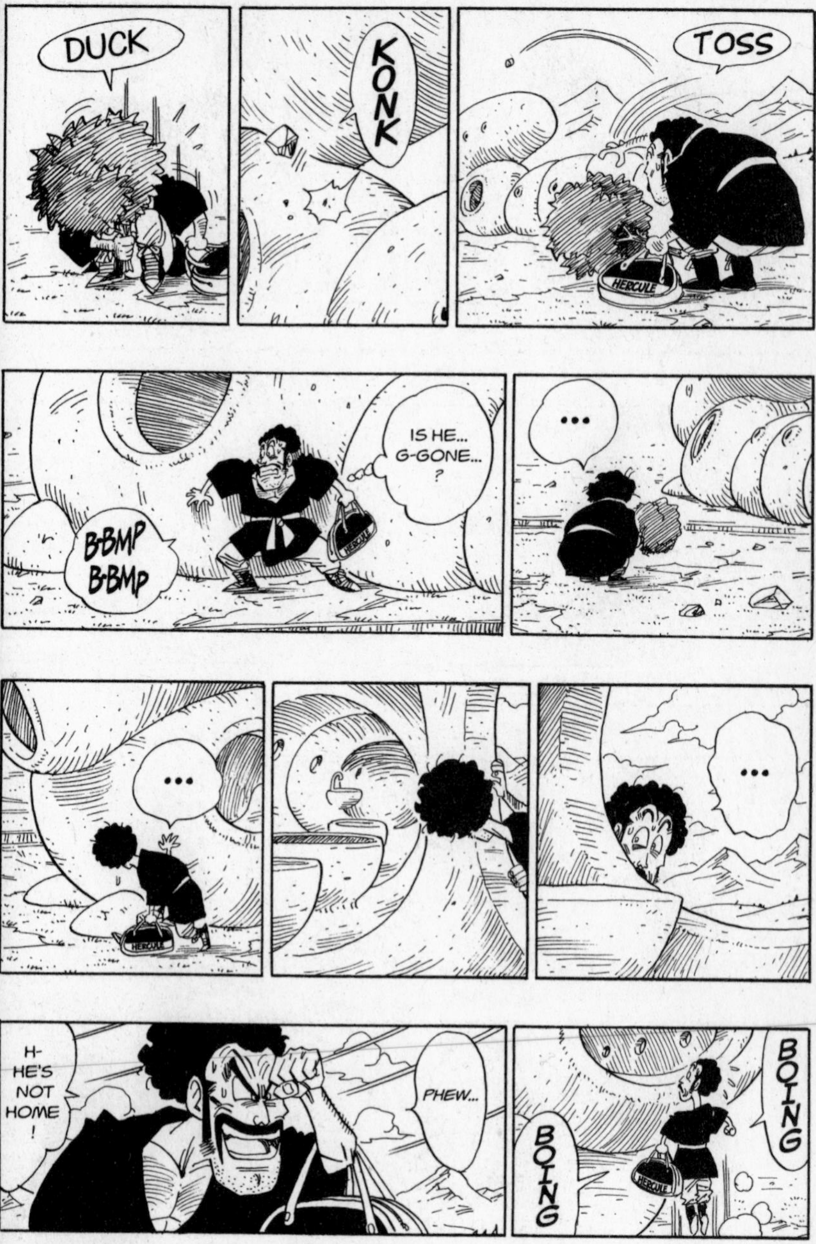
TOSS
KONK
DUCK
...
IS HE... G-GONE...?
B-BMP B-BMP
...
...
BOING
BOING
PHEW...
H-HE'S NOT HOME!

READ THIS WAY

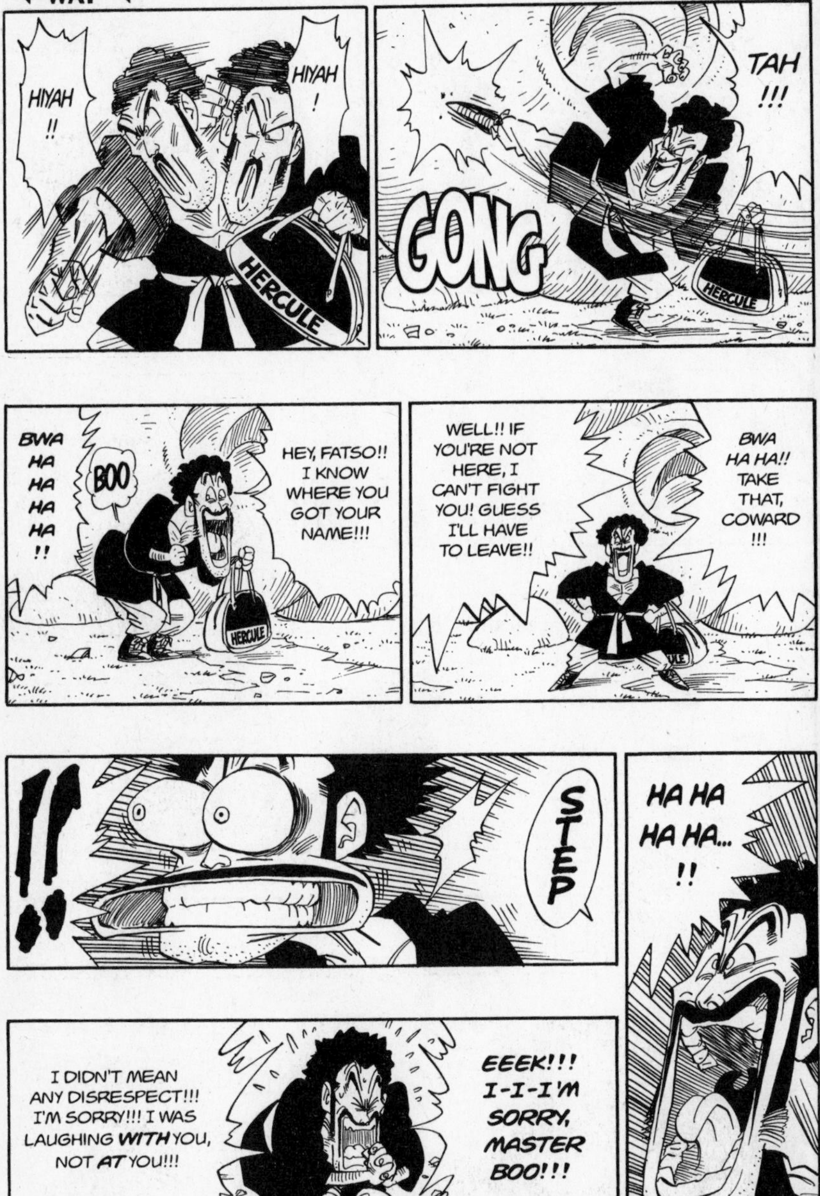
TAH!!!
GONG
HIYAH!
HIYAH!!
BWA HA HA!! TAKE THAT, COWARD!!!
WELL!! IF YOU'RE NOT HERE, I CAN'T FIGHT YOU! GUESS I'LL HAVE TO LEAVE!!
HEY, FATSO!! I KNOW WHERE YOU GOT YOUR NAME!!!
BOO
BWA HA HA HA HA!!
HA HA HA HA...!!
STEP
!!
EEEK!!! I-I-I'M SORRY, MASTER BOO!!!
I DIDN'T MEAN ANY DISRESPECT!!! I'M SORRY!!! I WAS LAUGHING **WITH** YOU, NOT **AT** YOU!!!

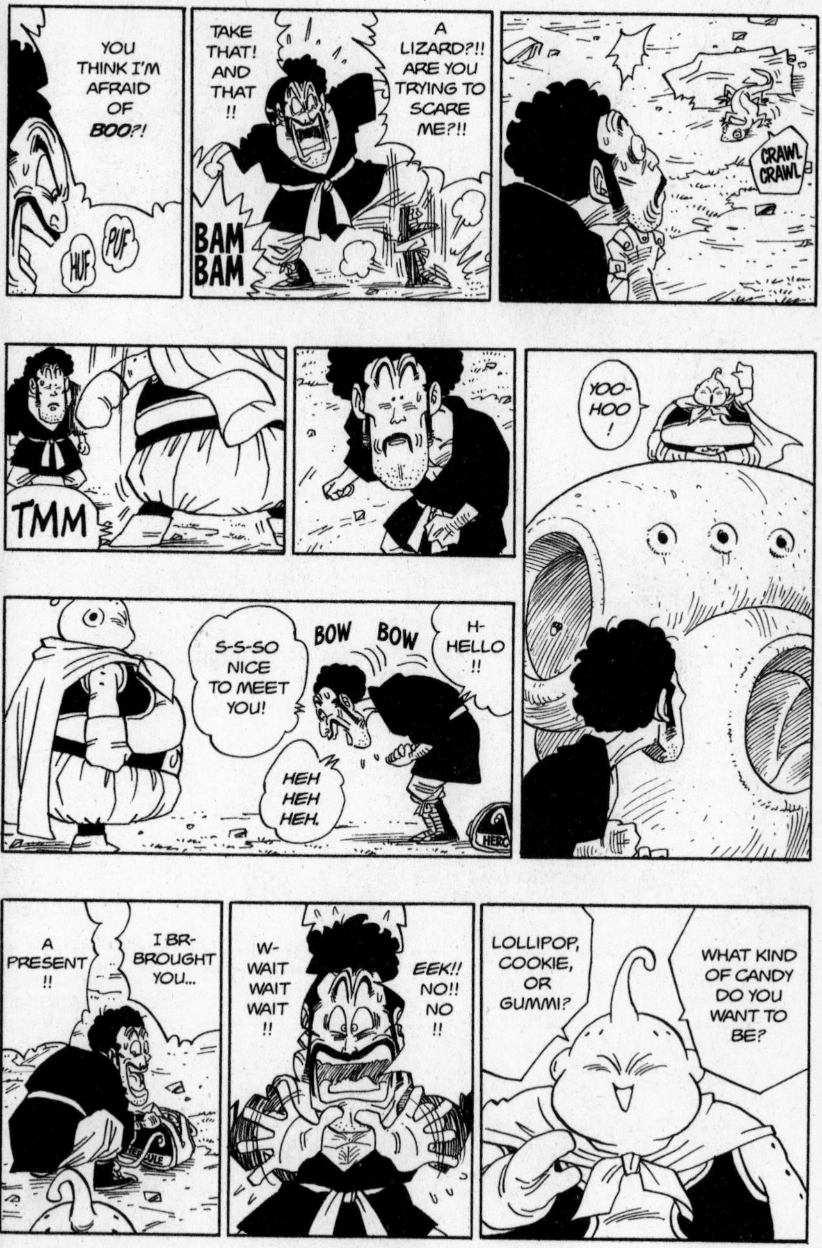
CRAWL CRAWL
A LIZARD?!! ARE YOU TRYING TO SCARE ME?!!
TAKE THAT! AND THAT !!
BAM BAM
YOU THINK I'M AFRAID OF BOO?!
PUF
HUF
YOO-HOO!
TMM
H-HELLO !!
BOW BOW
S-S-SO NICE TO MEET YOU!
HEH HEH HEH.
WHAT KIND OF CANDY DO YOU WANT TO BE?
LOLLIPOP, COOKIE, OR GUMMI?
EEK!! NO!! NO !!
W-WAIT WAIT WAIT !!
I BR-BROUGHT YOU...
A PRESENT !!
HERCULE

READ THIS WAY

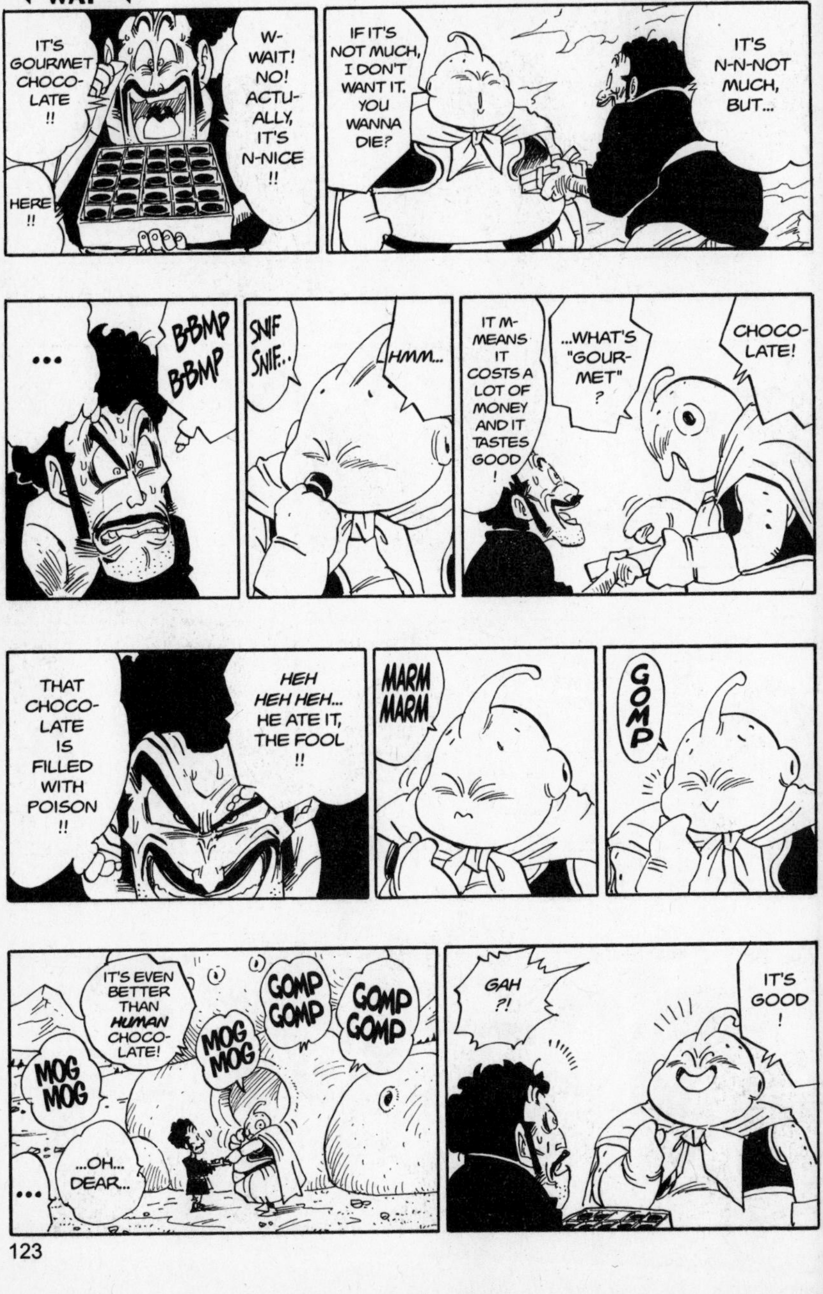
IT'S N-N-NOT MUCH, BUT...
IF IT'S NOT MUCH, I DON'T WANT IT. YOU WANNA DIE?
W-WAIT! NO! ACTUALLY, IT'S N-NICE !!
IT'S GOURMET CHOCOLATE !!
HERE !!
CHOCOLATE!
...WHAT'S "GOURMET"?
IT M-MEANS IT COSTS A LOT OF MONEY AND IT TASTES GOOD!
HMM...
SNIF SNIF...
B-BMP B-BMP
...
GOMP
MARM MARM
HEH HEH HEH... HE ATE IT, THE FOOL !!
THAT CHOCOLATE IS FILLED WITH POISON !!
IT'S GOOD!
GAH?!
GOMP GOMP
GOMP GOMP
IT'S EVEN BETTER THAN *HUMAN* CHOCOLATE!
MOG MOG
MOG MOG
...OH... DEAR...
...

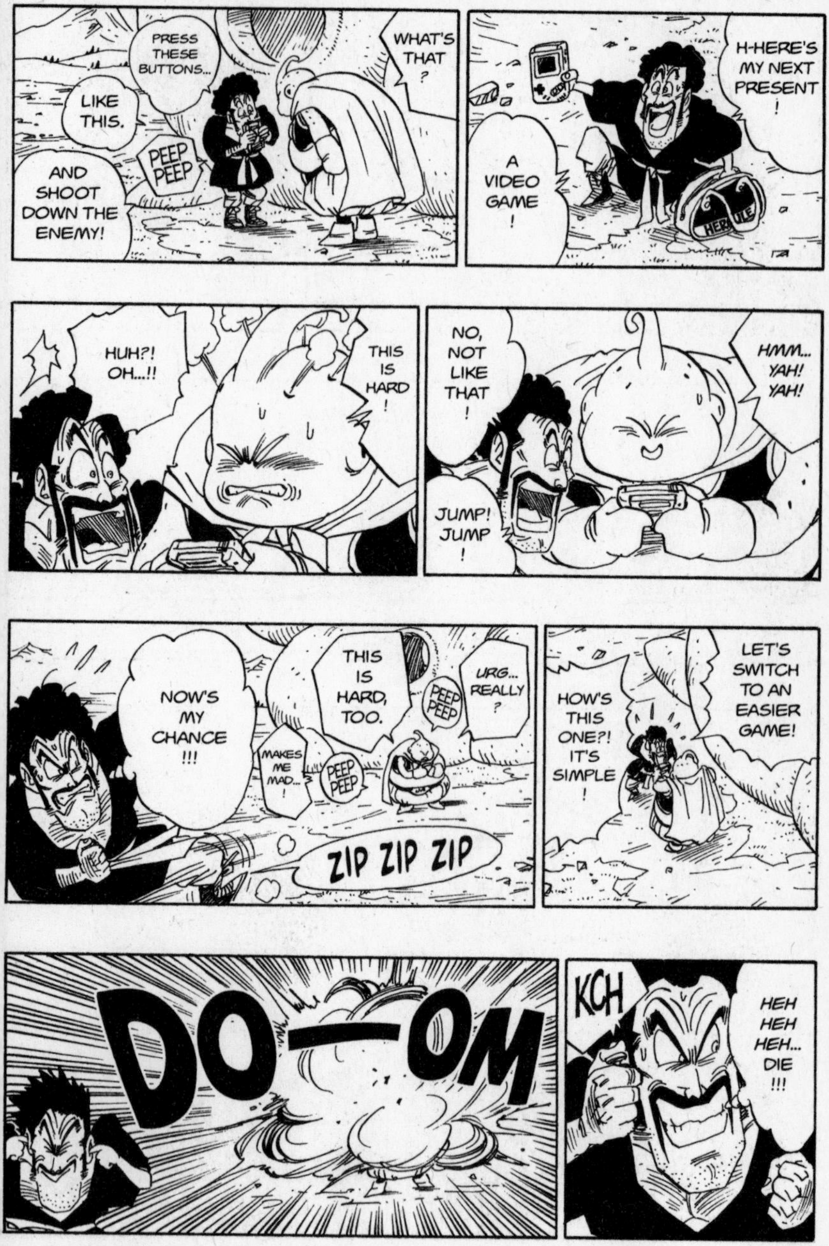
H-HERE'S MY NEXT PRESENT!
A VIDEO GAME!
WHAT'S THAT?
PRESS THESE BUTTONS...
LIKE THIS.
PEEP PEEP
AND SHOOT DOWN THE ENEMY!
HMM... YAH! YAH!
NO, NOT LIKE THAT!
JUMP! JUMP!
THIS IS HARD!
HUH?! OH...!!
LET'S SWITCH TO AN EASIER GAME!
HOW'S THIS ONE?! IT'S SIMPLE!
URG... REALLY?
PEEP PEEP
THIS IS HARD, TOO.
PEEP PEEP
MAKES ME MAD...!
NOW'S MY CHANCE!!!
ZIP ZIP ZIP
KCH
HEH HEH HEH... DIE!!!
DO—OM

READ THIS WAY

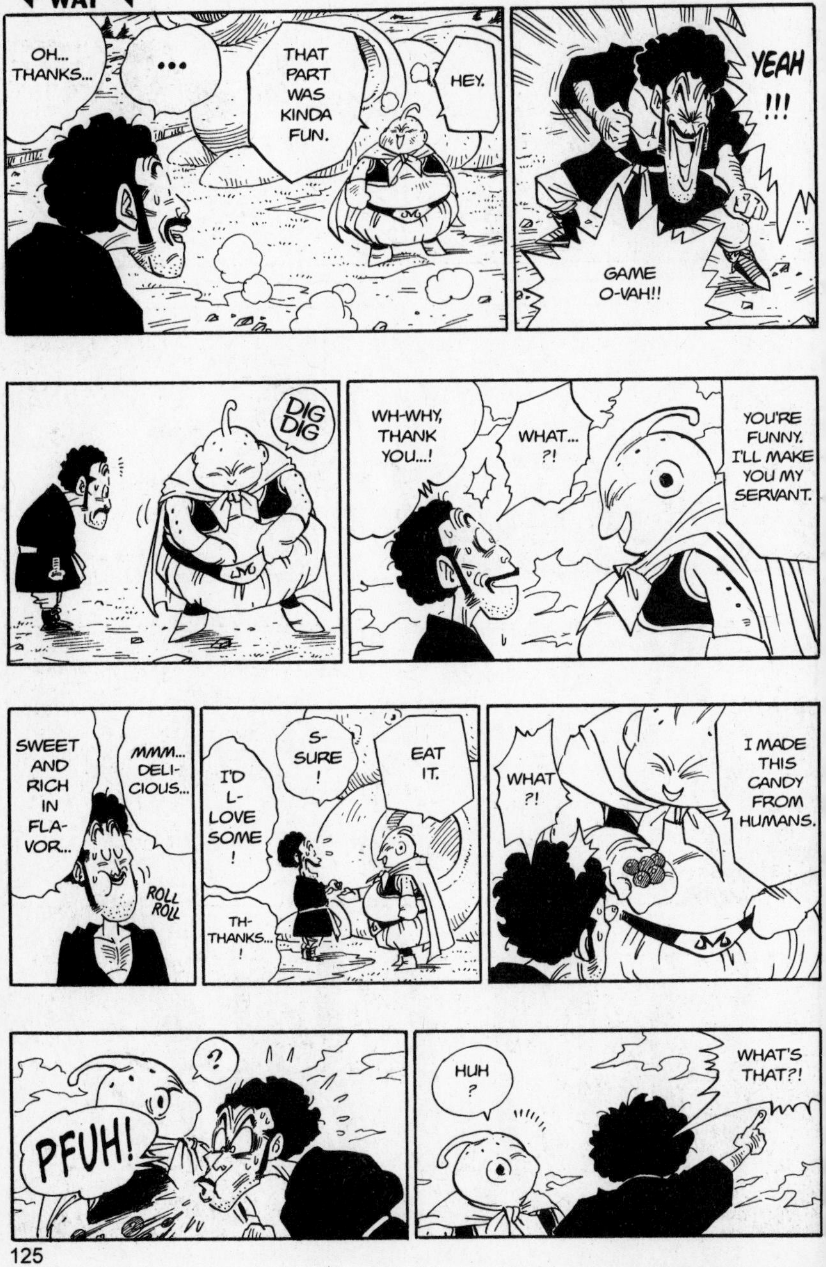
YEAH!!!
GAME O-VAH!!
HEY.
THAT PART WAS KINDA FUN.
...
OH... THANKS...
YOU'RE FUNNY. I'LL MAKE YOU MY SERVANT.
WHAT...?!
WH-WHY, THANK YOU...!
DIG DIG
I MADE THIS CANDY FROM HUMANS.
WHAT?!
EAT IT.
S-SURE!
I'D L-LOVE SOME!
TH-THANKS...!
MMM... DELICIOUS...
SWEET AND RICH IN FLAVOR...
ROLL ROLL
WHAT'S THAT?!
HUH?
?
PFUH!

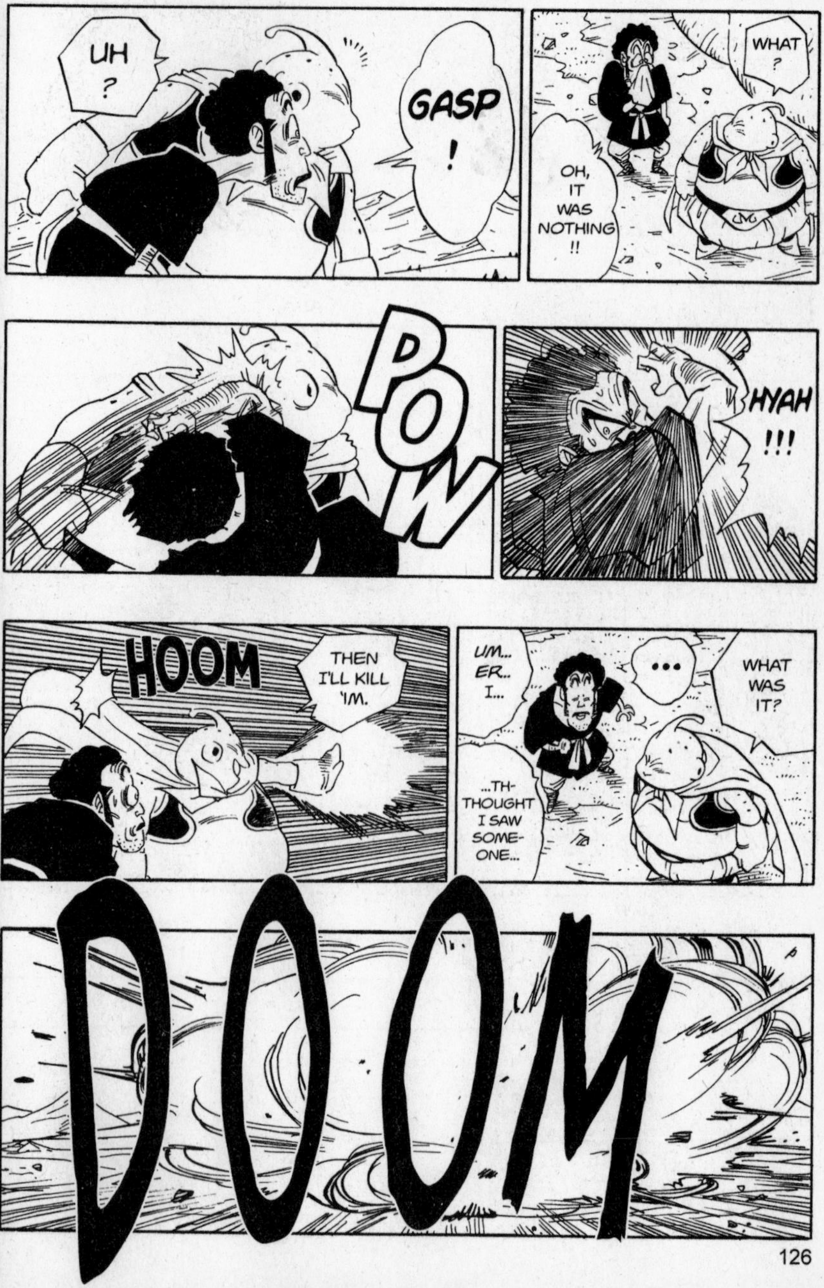
WHAT ?
OH, IT WAS NOTHING !!
GASP !
UH ?
HYAH !!!
POW
WHAT WAS IT?
...
UM... ER... I...
...TH-THOUGHT I SAW SOME-ONE...
THEN I'LL KILL 'IM.
HOOM
DOOM

READ THIS WAY

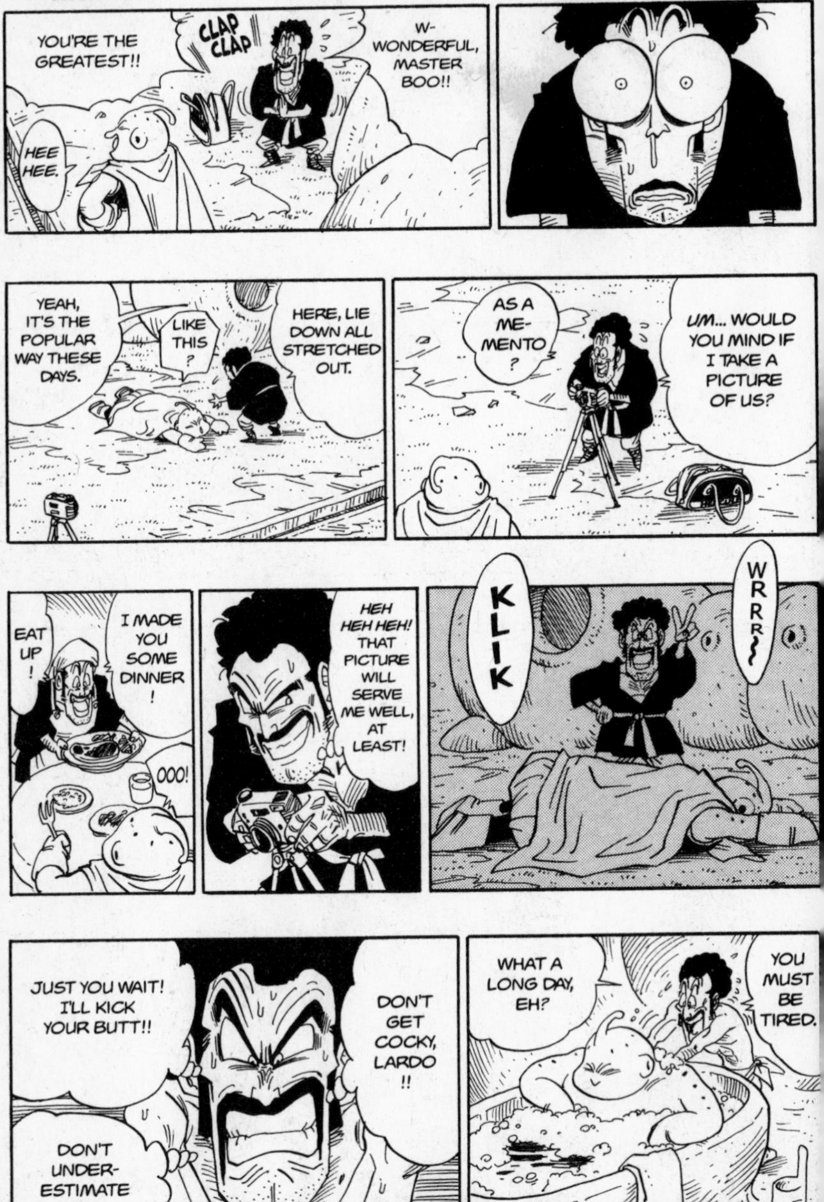
W-WONDERFUL, MASTER BOO!!
CLAP CLAP
YOU'RE THE GREATEST!!
HEE HEE.
UM... WOULD YOU MIND IF I TAKE A PICTURE OF US?
AS A MEMENTO ?
HERE, LIE DOWN ALL STRETCHED OUT.
LIKE THIS ?
YEAH, IT'S THE POPULAR WAY THESE DAYS.
WRRR~
KLIK
HEH HEH HEH! THAT PICTURE WILL SERVE ME WELL, AT LEAST!
I MADE YOU SOME DINNER !
EAT UP !
OOO!
YOU MUST BE TIRED.
WHAT A LONG DAY, EH?
DON'T GET COCKY, LARDO !!
JUST YOU WAIT! I'LL KICK YOUR BUTT!!
DON'T UNDER-ESTIMATE ME!!

DBZ:288
Super Fusion!!

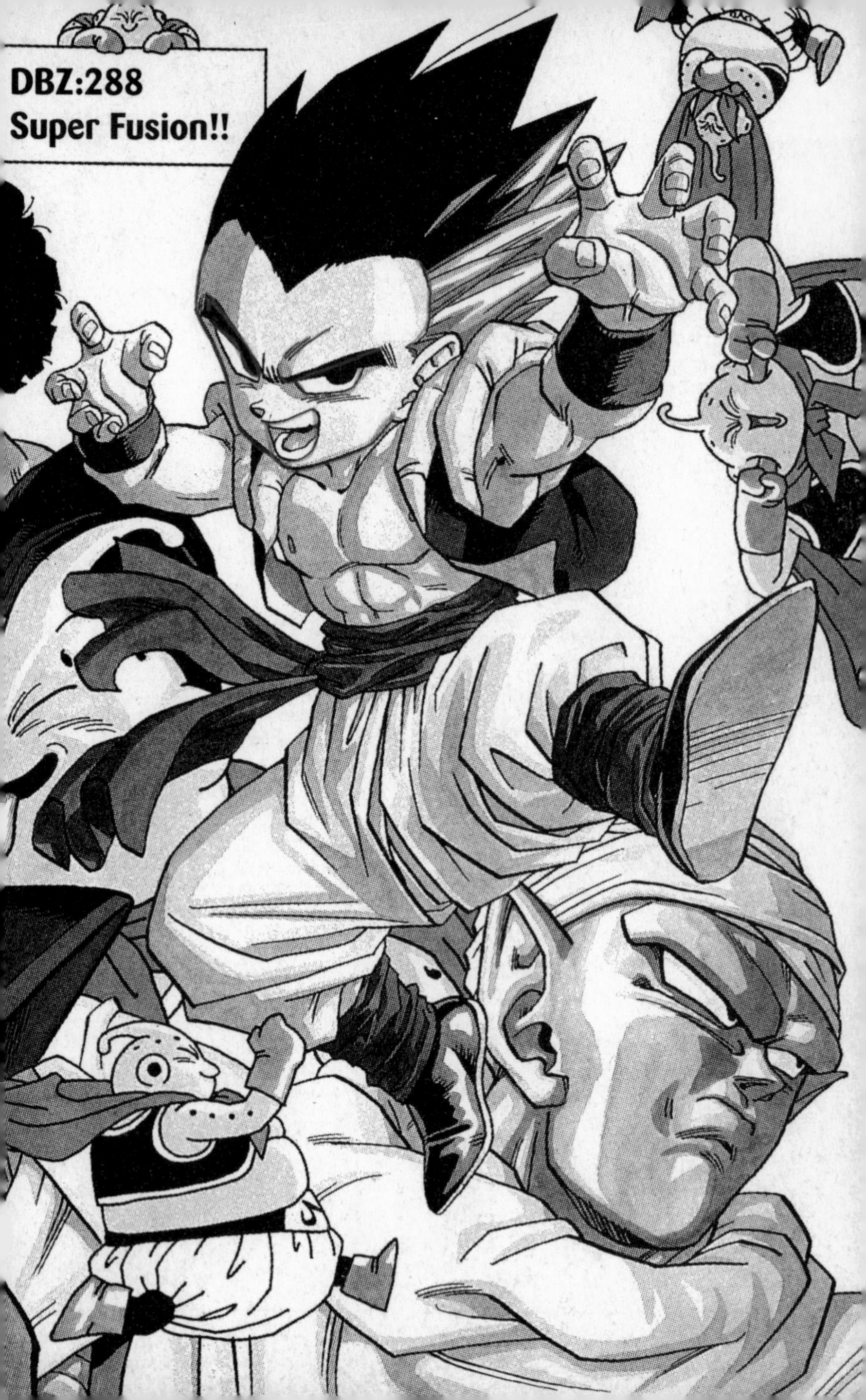

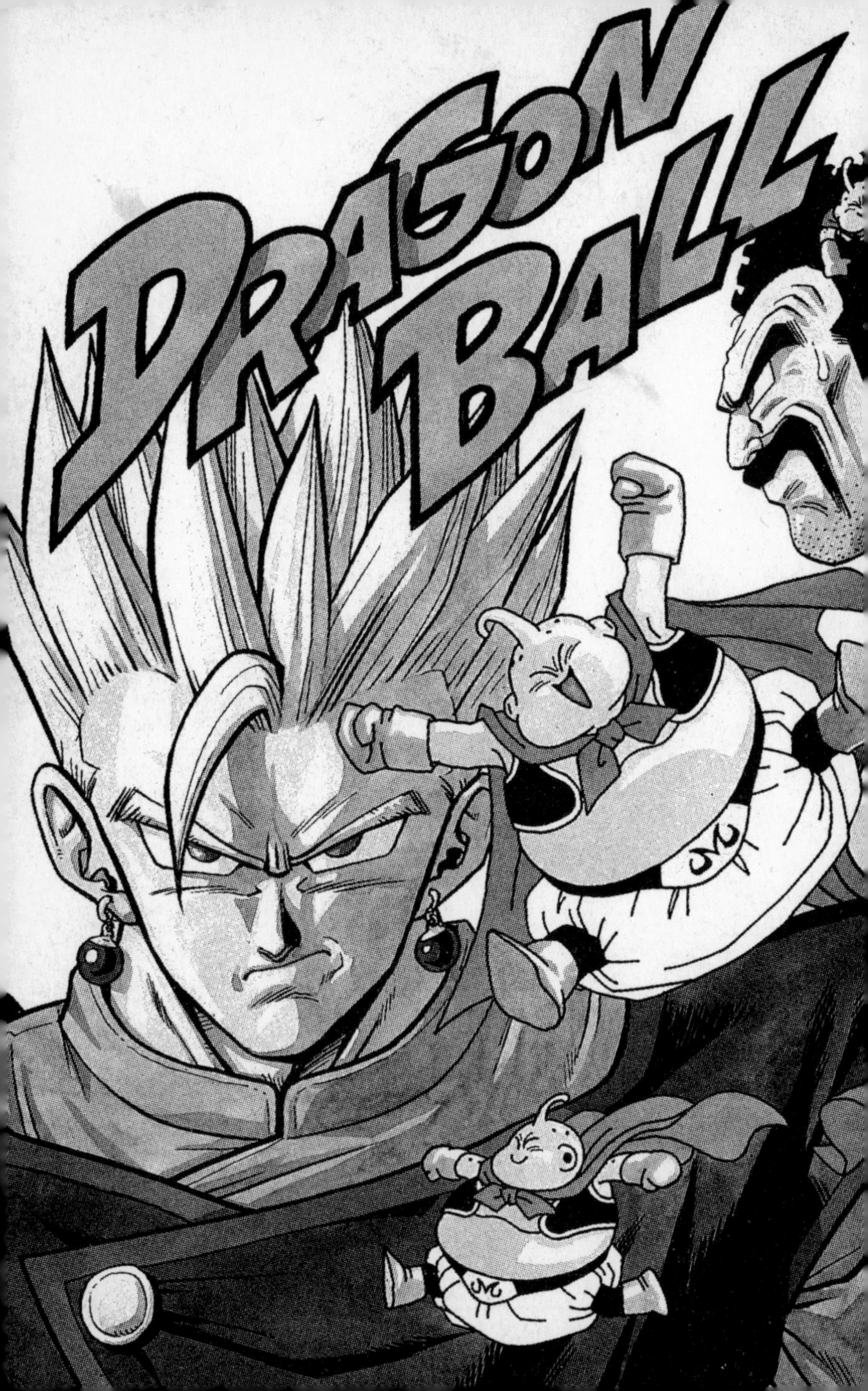
DRAGON BALL

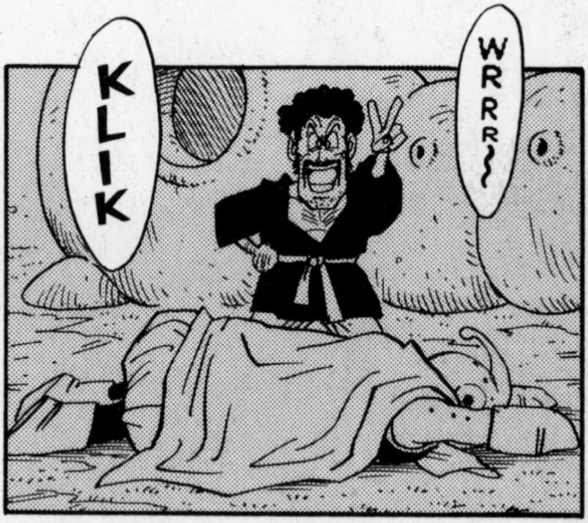
WRRR~
KLIK

READ THIS WAY

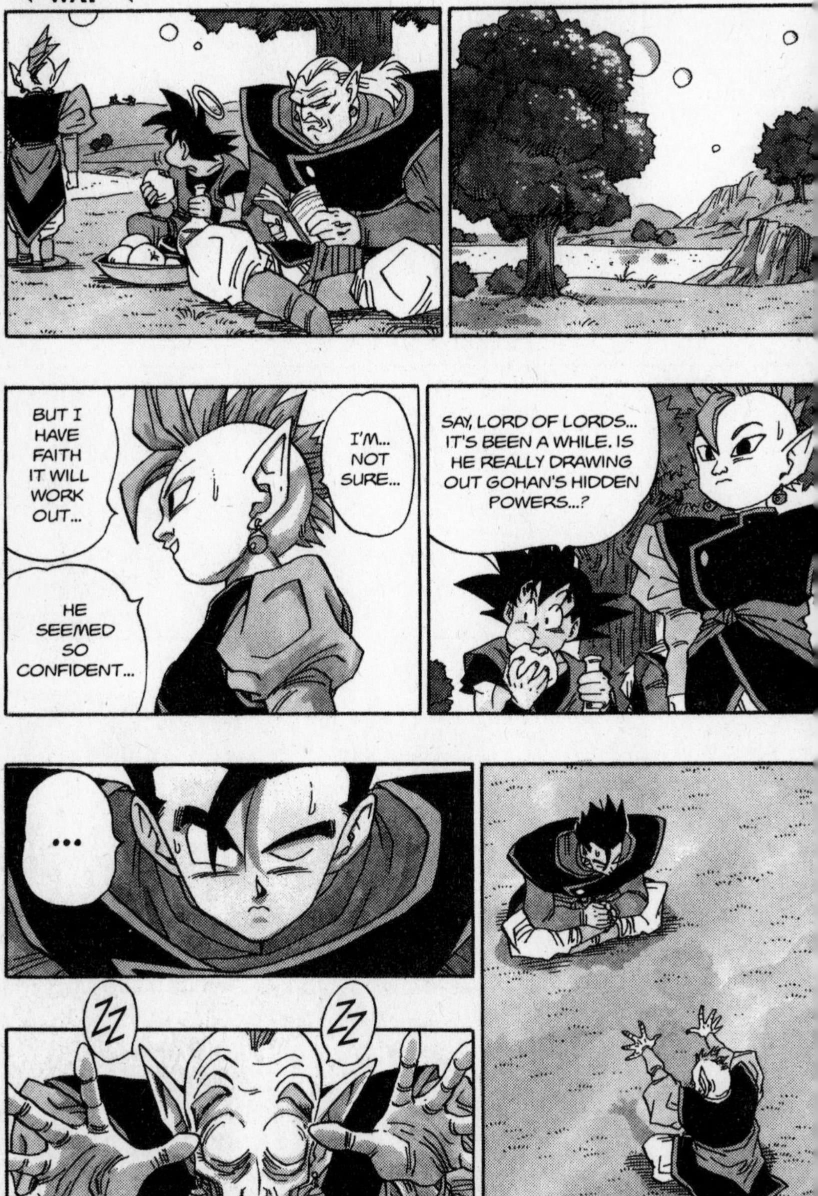
SAY, LORD OF LORDS... IT'S BEEN A WHILE. IS HE REALLY DRAWING OUT GOHAN'S HIDDEN POWERS...?
I'M... NOT SURE...
BUT I HAVE FAITH IT WILL WORK OUT...
HE SEEMED SO CONFIDENT...
...
ZZ
ZZ

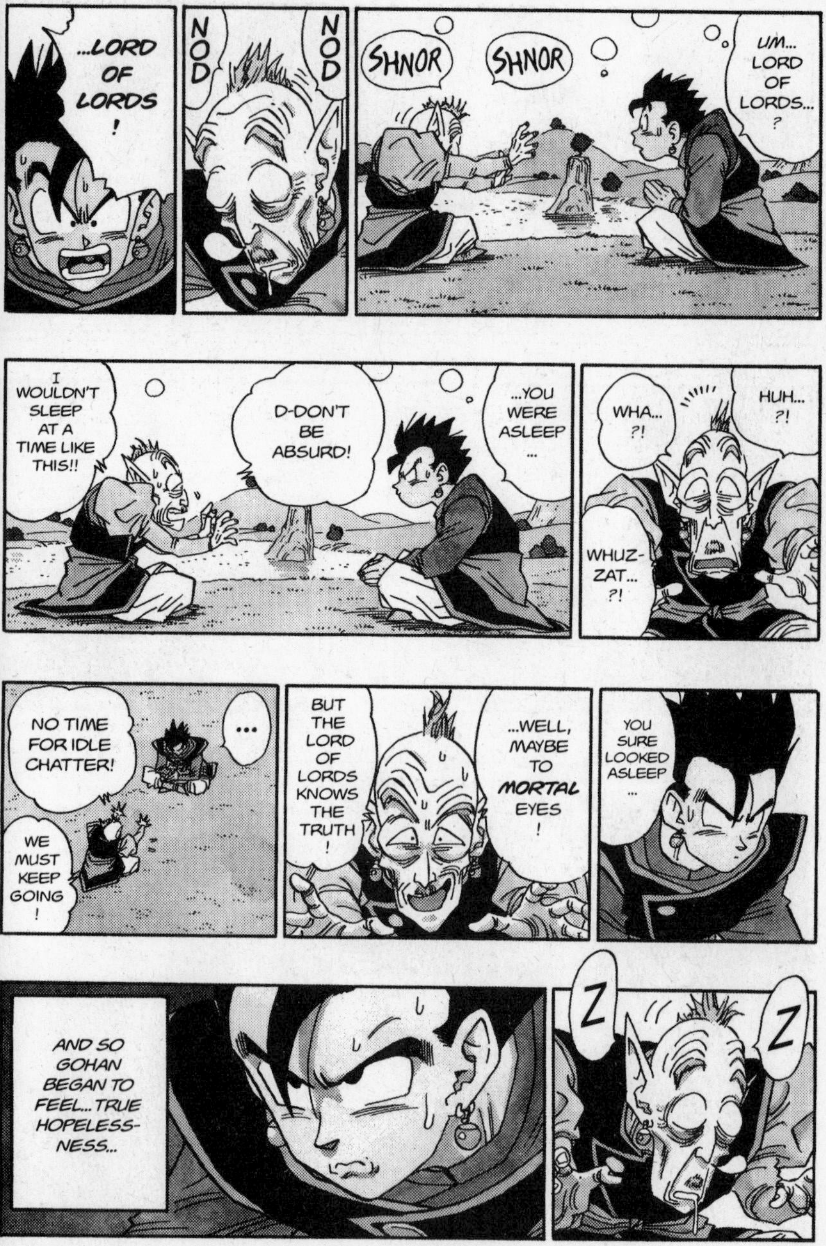
UM... LORD OF LORDS...?
SHNOR
SHNOR
NOD
NOD
...LORD OF LORDS!
HUH...?!
WHA...?!
WHUZ-ZAT...?!
...YOU WERE ASLEEP...
D-DON'T BE ABSURD!
I WOULDN'T SLEEP AT A TIME LIKE THIS!!
YOU SURE LOOKED ASLEEP...
...WELL, MAYBE TO MORTAL EYES!
BUT THE LORD OF LORDS KNOWS THE TRUTH!
...
NO TIME FOR IDLE CHATTER!
WE MUST KEEP GOING!
Z
Z
AND SO GOHAN BEGAN TO FEEL...TRUE HOPELESS-NESS...

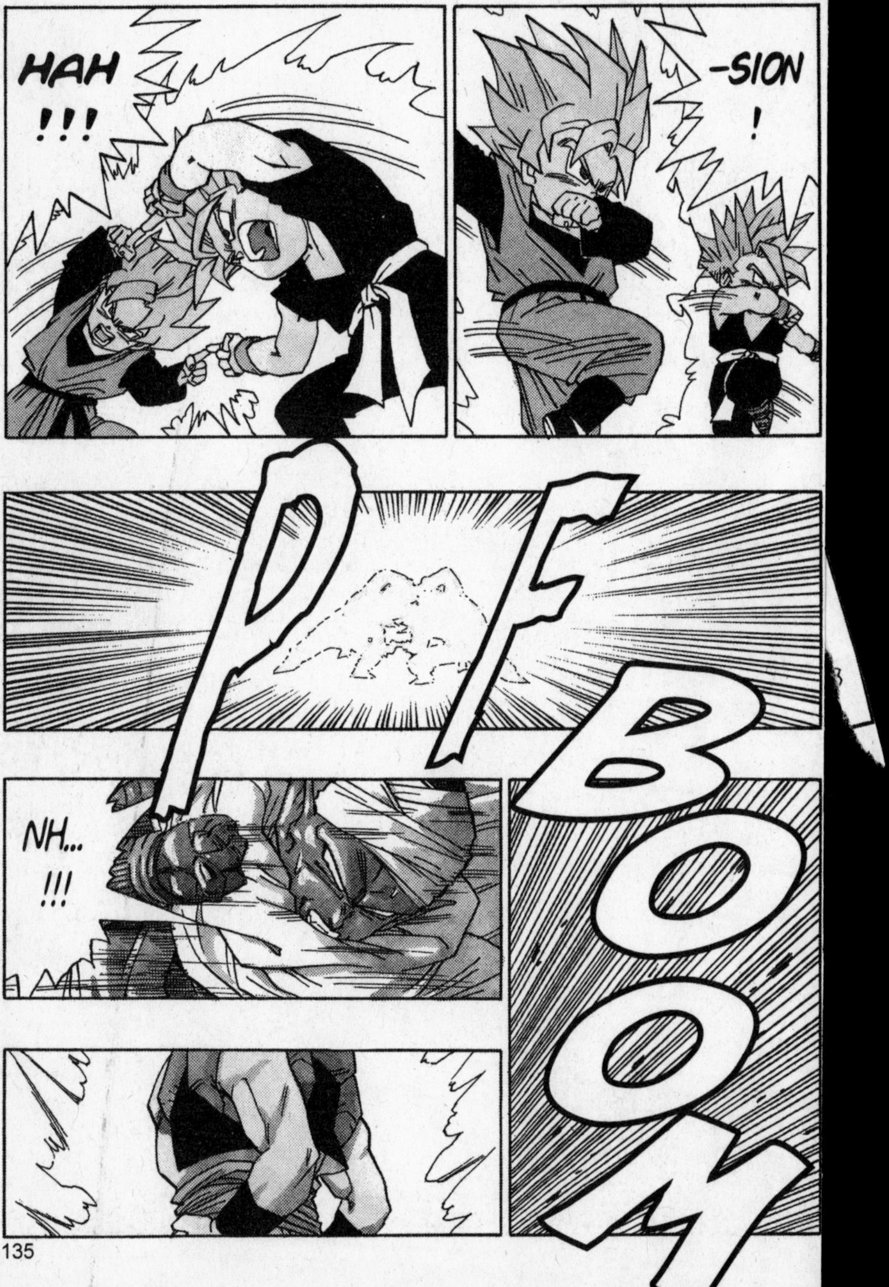
-SION !
HAH !!!
PFBOOM
NH... !!!

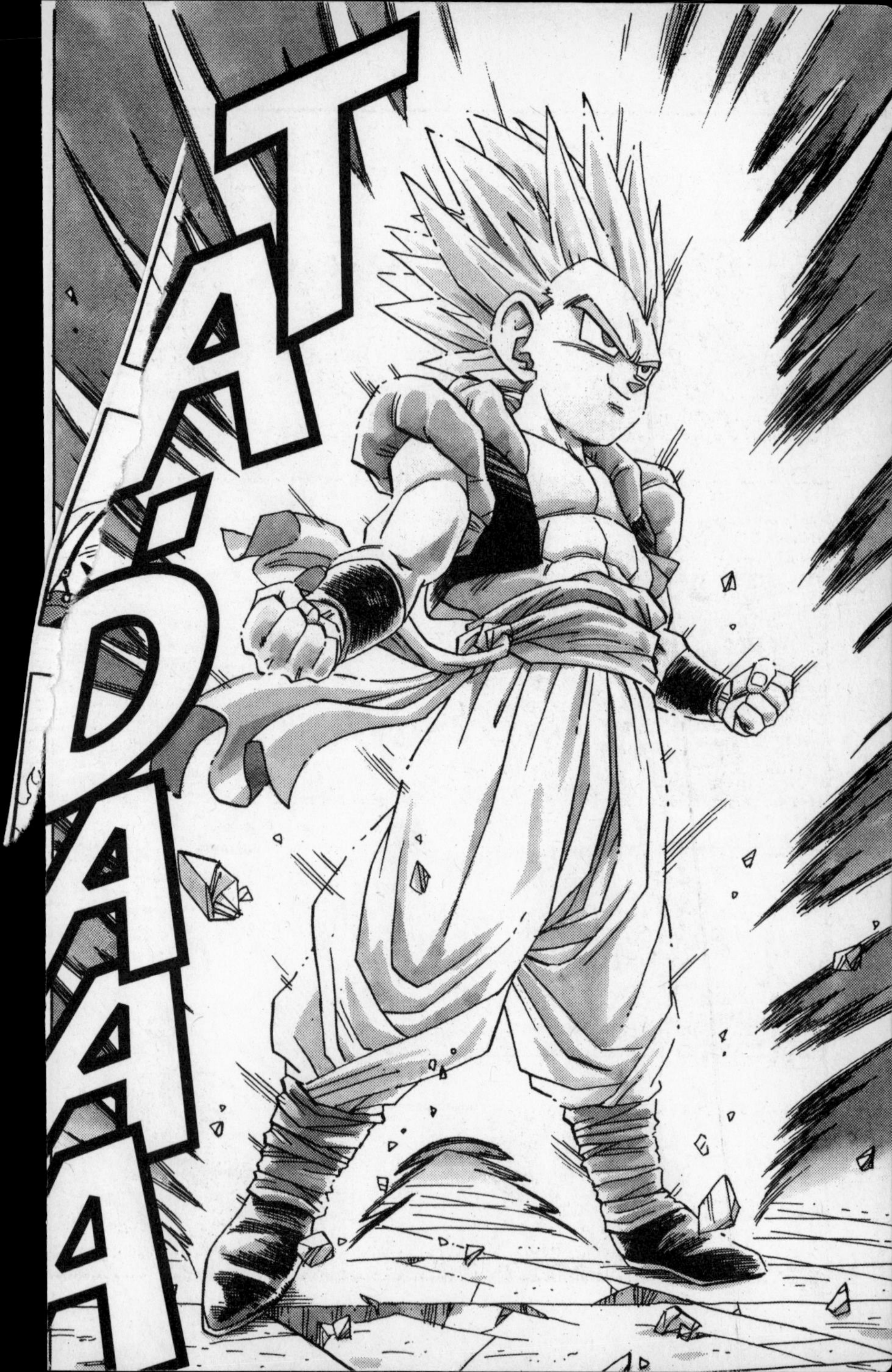
TADAAAA

READ THIS WAY

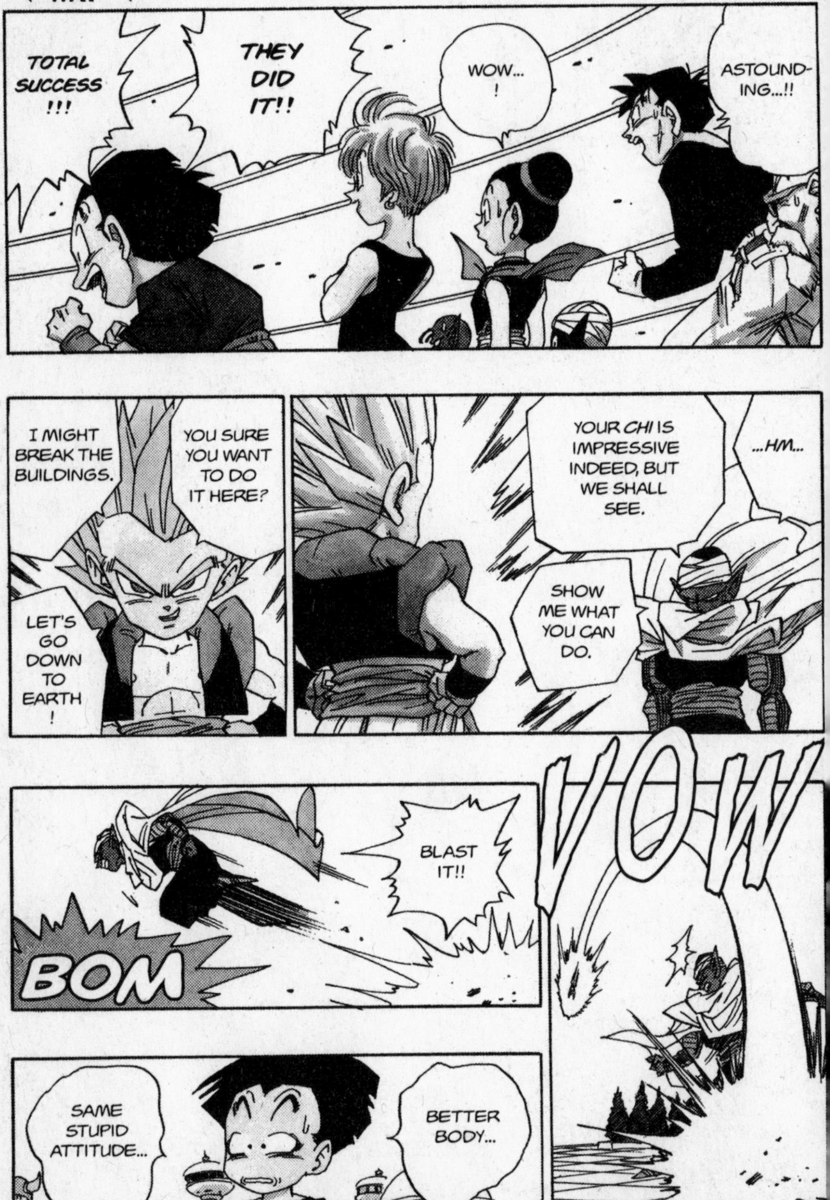

ASTOUNDING...!!
WOW...!
THEY DID IT!!
TOTAL SUCCESS!!!
...HM...
YOUR CHI IS IMPRESSIVE INDEED, BUT WE SHALL SEE.
SHOW ME WHAT YOU CAN DO.
YOU SURE YOU WANT TO DO IT HERE?
I MIGHT BREAK THE BUILDINGS.
LET'S GO DOWN TO EARTH!
VOW
BLAST IT!!
BOM
BETTER BODY...
SAME STUPID ATTITUDE...

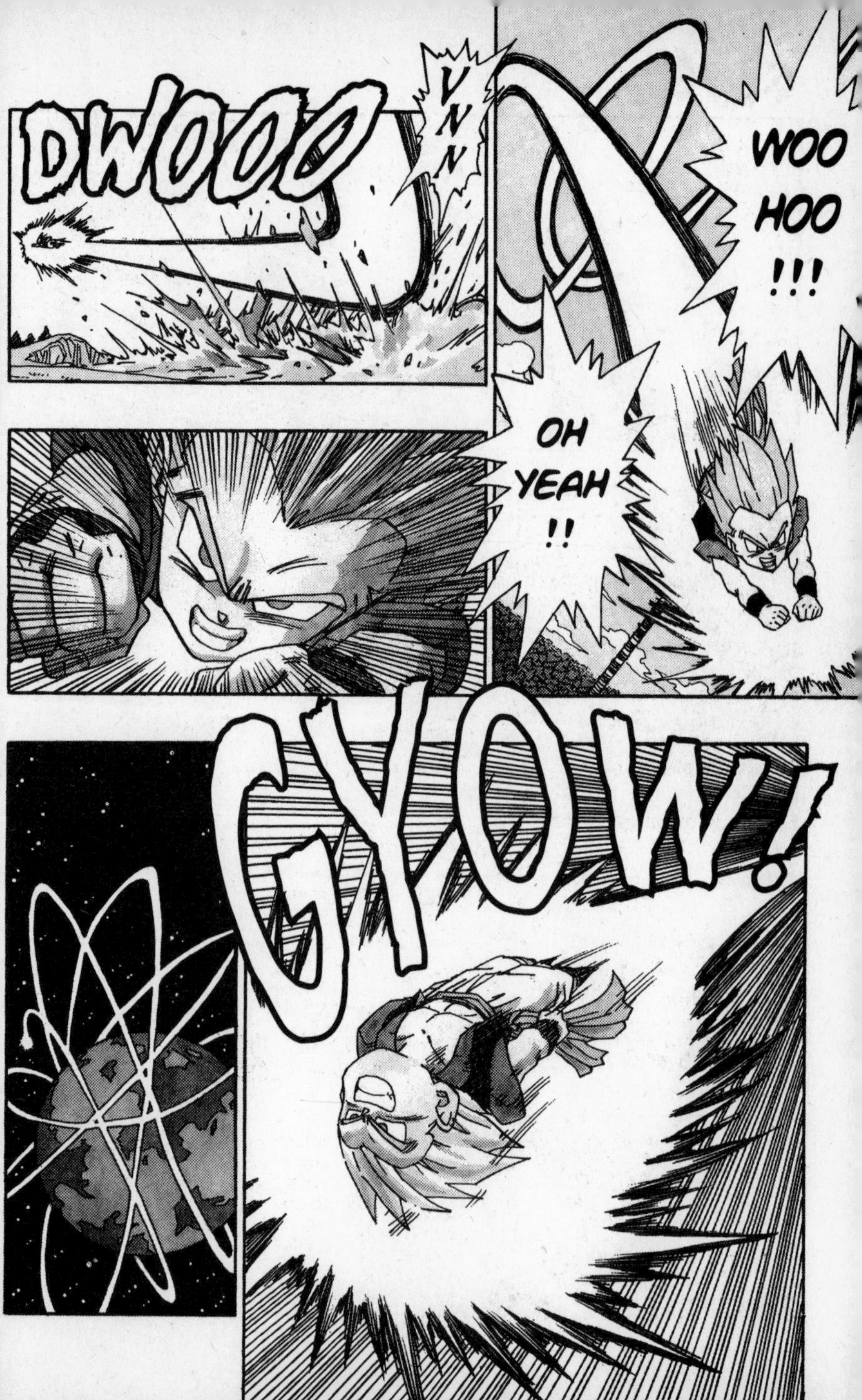
WOO HOO !!!
OH YEAH !!
DWOOO
VNN
GYOW!

READ THIS WAY

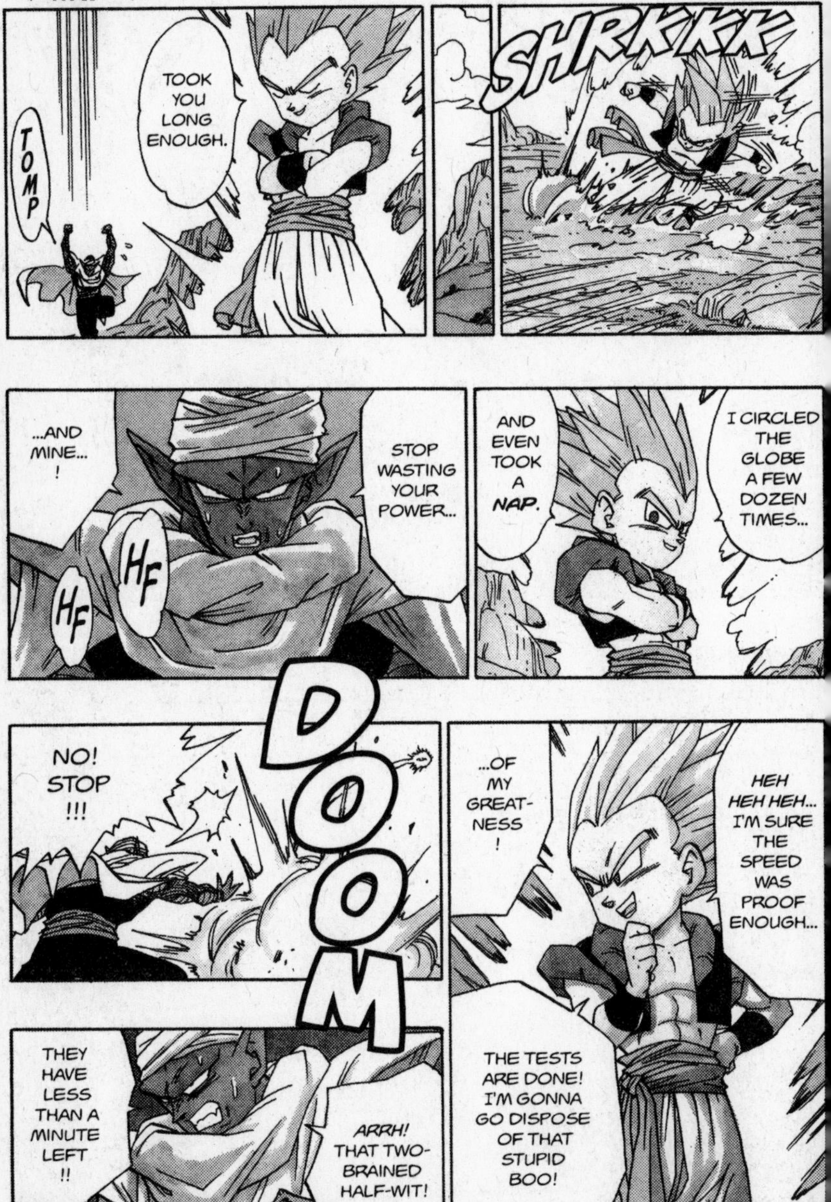
SHRKKK
TOOK YOU LONG ENOUGH.
TOMP
I CIRCLED THE GLOBE A FEW DOZEN TIMES...
AND EVEN TOOK A *NAP*.
STOP WASTING YOUR POWER...
...AND MINE...!
HF
HF
HEH HEH HEH... I'M SURE THE SPEED WAS PROOF ENOUGH...
...OF MY GREAT-NESS!
THE TESTS ARE DONE! I'M GONNA GO DISPOSE OF THAT STUPID BOO!
NO! STOP!!!
DOOM
ARRH! THAT TWO-BRAINED HALF-WIT!
THEY HAVE LESS THAN A MINUTE LEFT!!

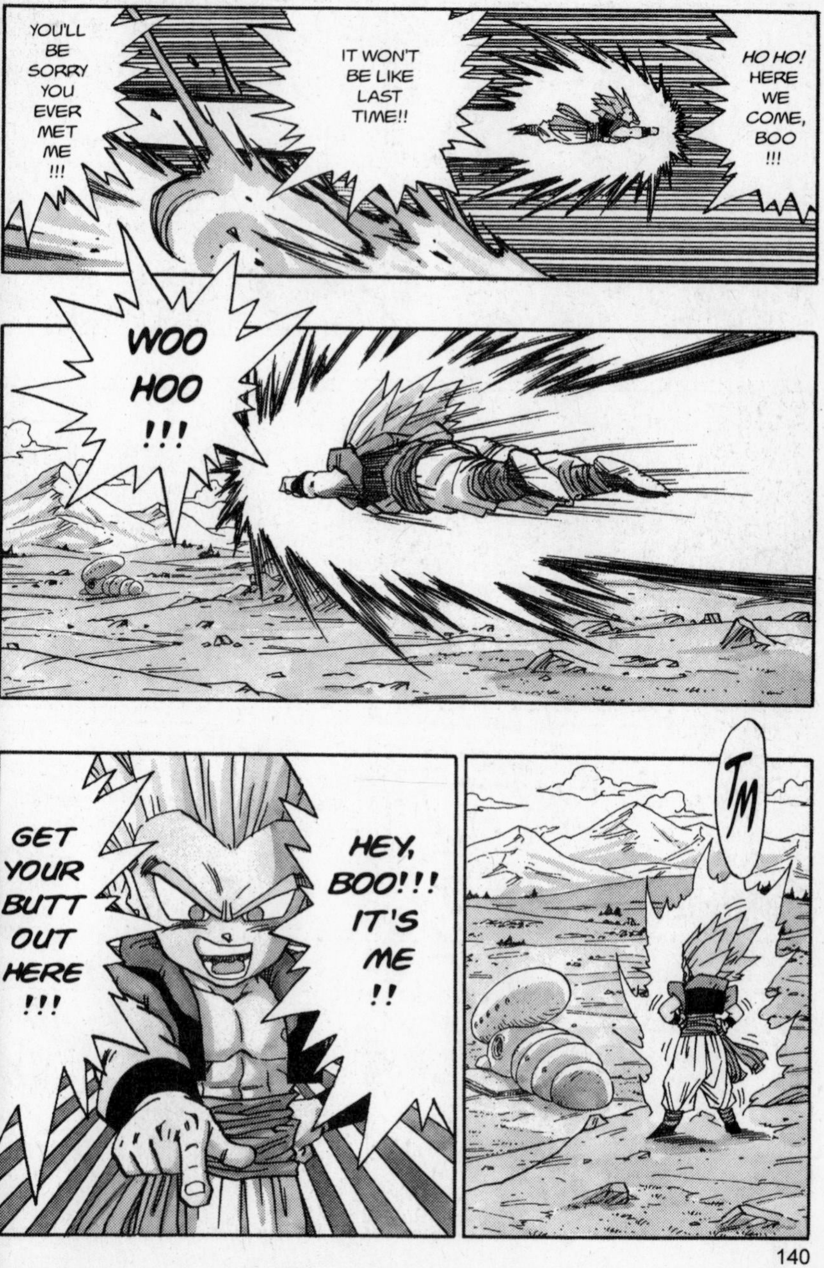
HO HO! HERE WE COME, BOO!!!
IT WON'T BE LIKE LAST TIME!!
YOU'LL BE SORRY YOU EVER MET ME!!!
WOO HOO!!!
TM
HEY, BOO!!! IT'S ME!!
GET YOUR BUTT OUT HERE!!!

READ THIS WAY

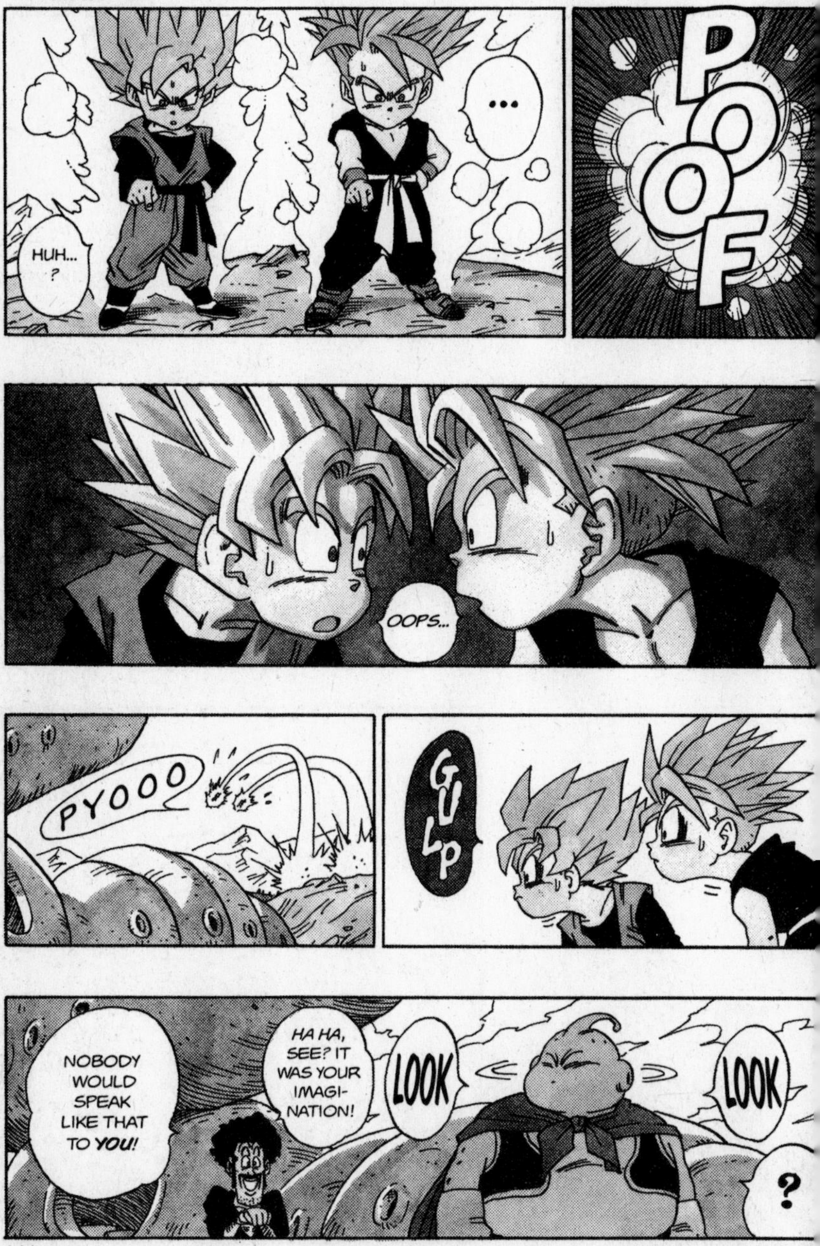
POOF
...
HUH... ?
OOPS...
GULP
PYOOO
?
LOOK
LOOK
HA HA, SEE? IT WAS YOUR IMAGINATION!
NOBODY WOULD SPEAK LIKE THAT TO *YOU*!

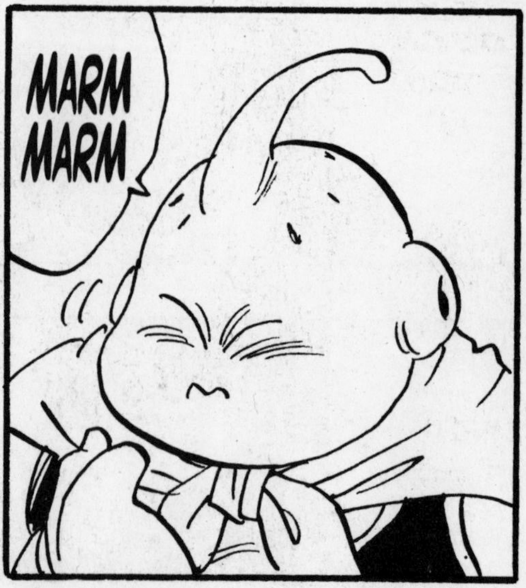
MARM
MARM

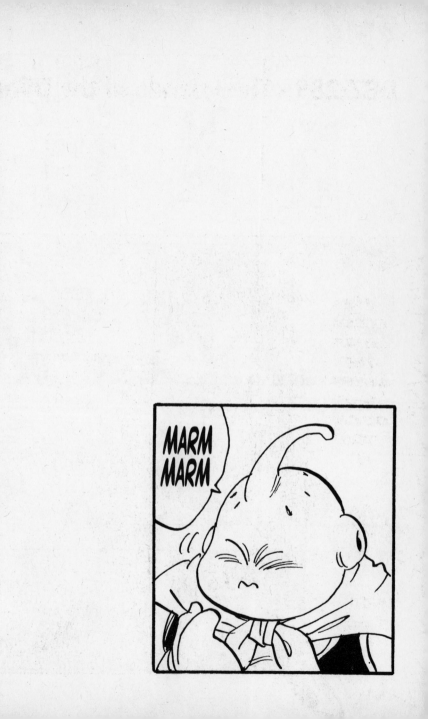

DBZ:289 · The Friends of the Djinn

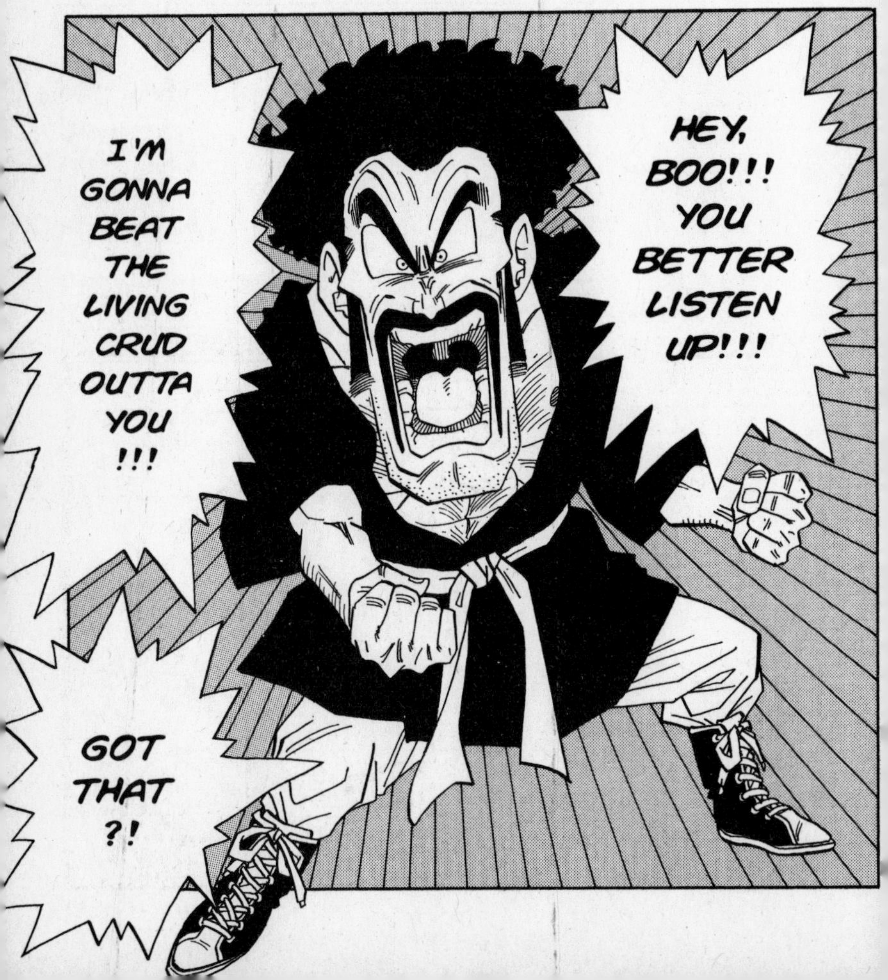
HEY, BOO!!! YOU BETTER LISTEN UP!!!
I'M GONNA BEAT THE LIVING CRUD OUTTA YOU!!!
GOT THAT?!

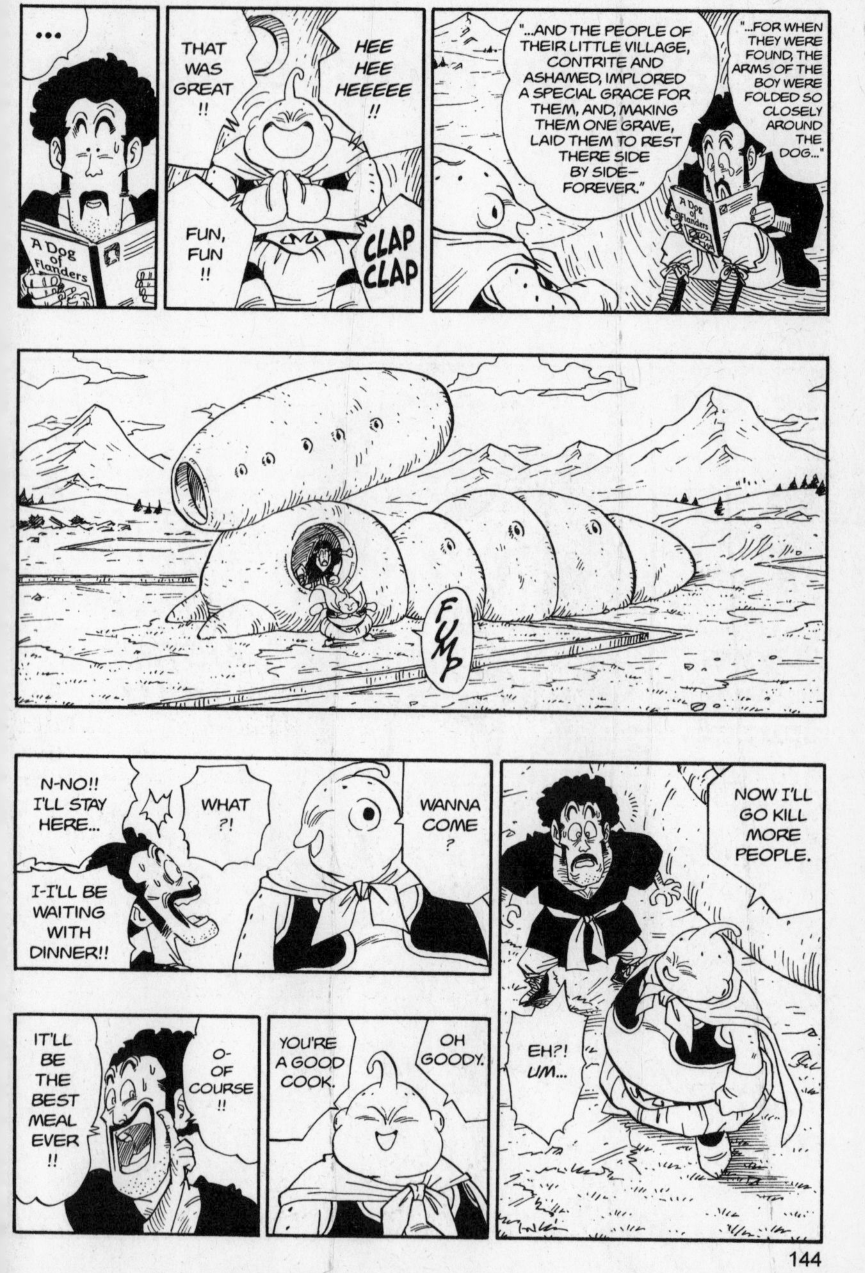
"...FOR WHEN THEY WERE FOUND, THE ARMS OF THE BOY WERE FOLDED SO CLOSELY AROUND THE DOG..."
"...AND THE PEOPLE OF THEIR LITTLE VILLAGE, CONTRITE AND ASHAMED, IMPLORED A SPECIAL GRACE FOR THEM, AND, MAKING THEM ONE GRAVE, LAID THEM TO REST THERE SIDE BY SIDE—FOREVER."
A Dog of Flanders
HEE HEE HEEEEE!!
CLAP CLAP
THAT WAS GREAT!!
FUN, FUN!!
...
A Dog of Flanders
FUMP
NOW I'LL GO KILL MORE PEOPLE.
EH?! UM...
WANNA COME?
WHAT?!
N-NO!! I'LL STAY HERE...
I-I'LL BE WAITING WITH DINNER!!
OH GOODY.
YOU'RE A GOOD COOK.
O-OF COURSE!!
IT'LL BE THE BEST MEAL EVER!!

READ THIS WAY

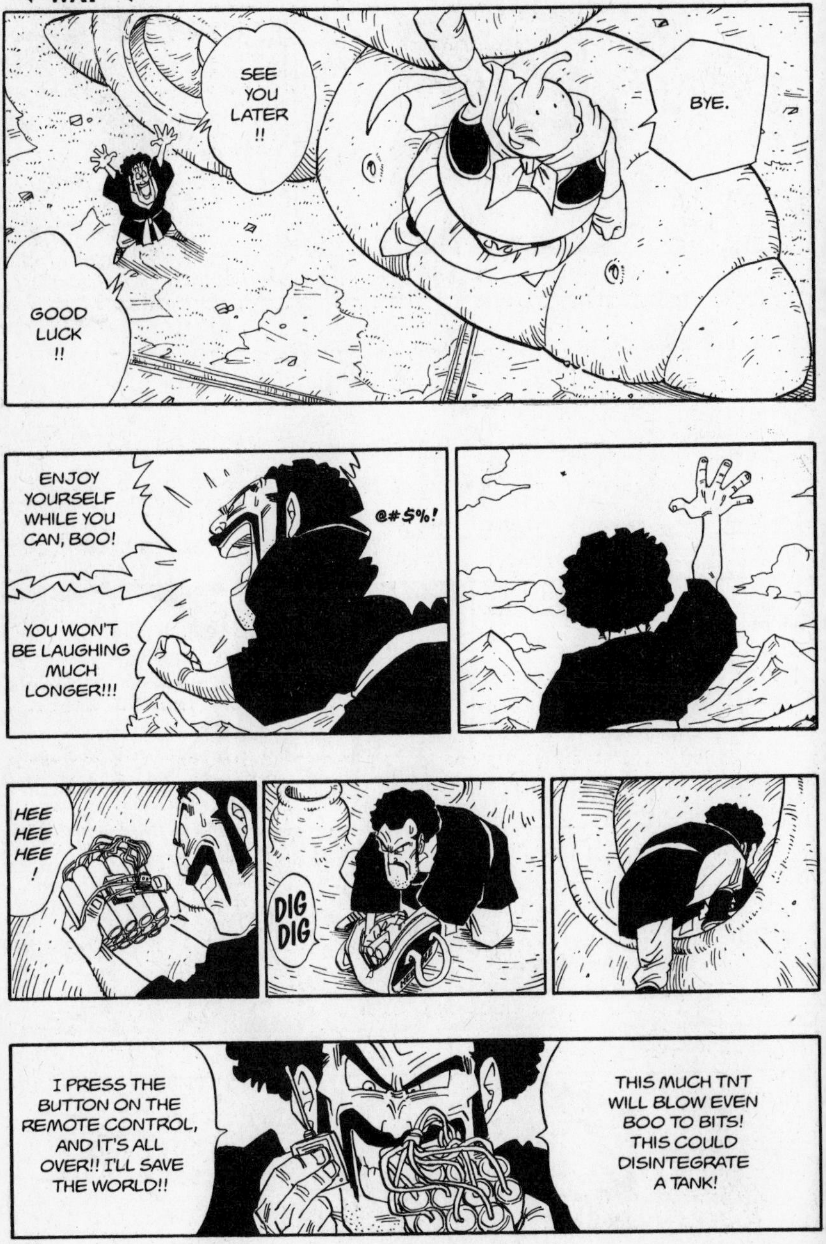
BYE.
SEE YOU LATER !!
GOOD LUCK !!
@#$%!
ENJOY YOURSELF WHILE YOU CAN, BOO!
YOU WON'T BE LAUGHING MUCH LONGER!!!
DIG DIG
HEE HEE HEE !
THIS MUCH TNT WILL BLOW EVEN BOO TO BITS! THIS COULD DISINTEGRATE A TANK!
I PRESS THE BUTTON ON THE REMOTE CONTROL, AND IT'S ALL OVER!! I'LL SAVE THE WORLD!!

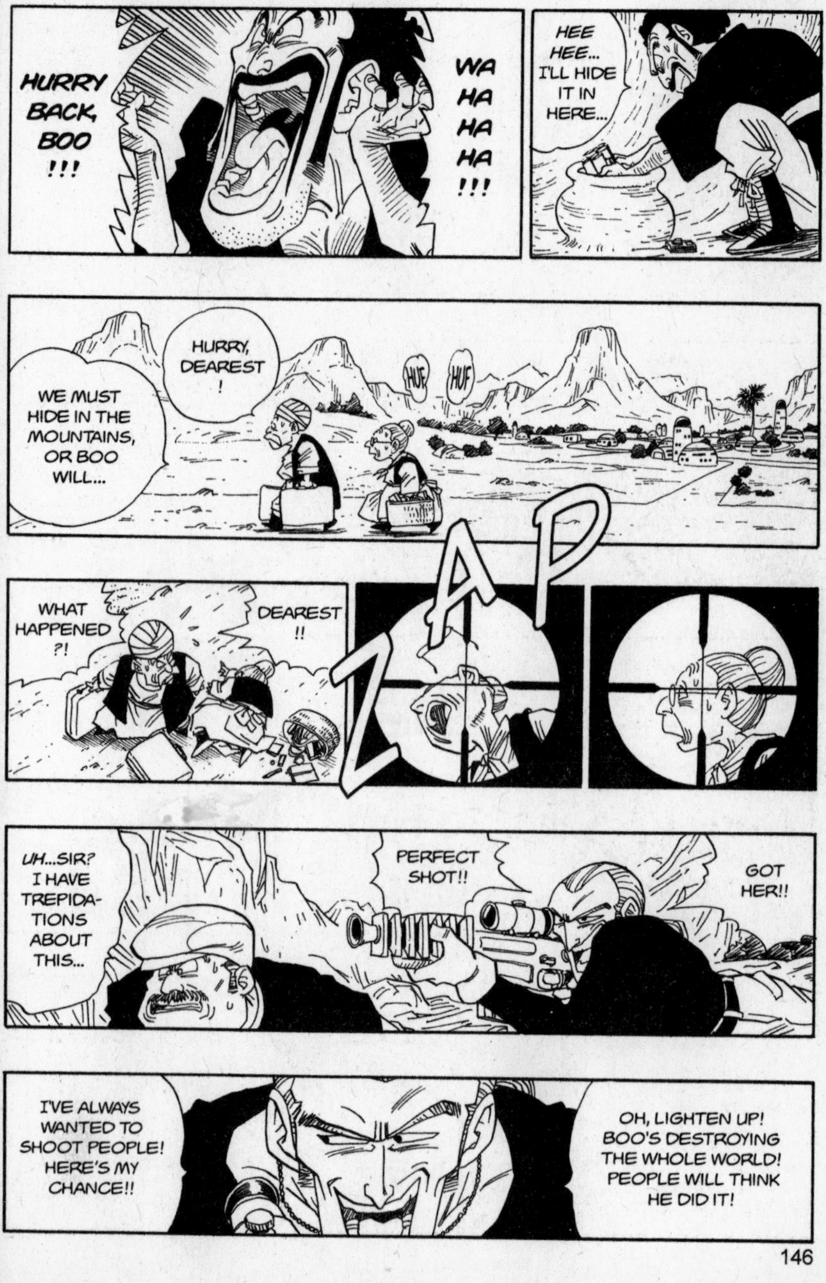
HEE HEE... I'LL HIDE IT IN HERE...
WA HA HA HA!!!
HURRY BACK, BOO!!!
HUF
HUF
HURRY, DEAREST!
WE MUST HIDE IN THE MOUNTAINS, OR BOO WILL...
ZAP
DEAREST!!
WHAT HAPPENED?!
GOT HER!!
PERFECT SHOT!!
UH...SIR? I HAVE TREPIDATIONS ABOUT THIS...
OH, LIGHTEN UP! BOO'S DESTROYING THE WHOLE WORLD! PEOPLE WILL THINK HE DID IT!
I'VE ALWAYS WANTED TO SHOOT PEOPLE! HERE'S MY CHANCE!!

READ THIS WAY

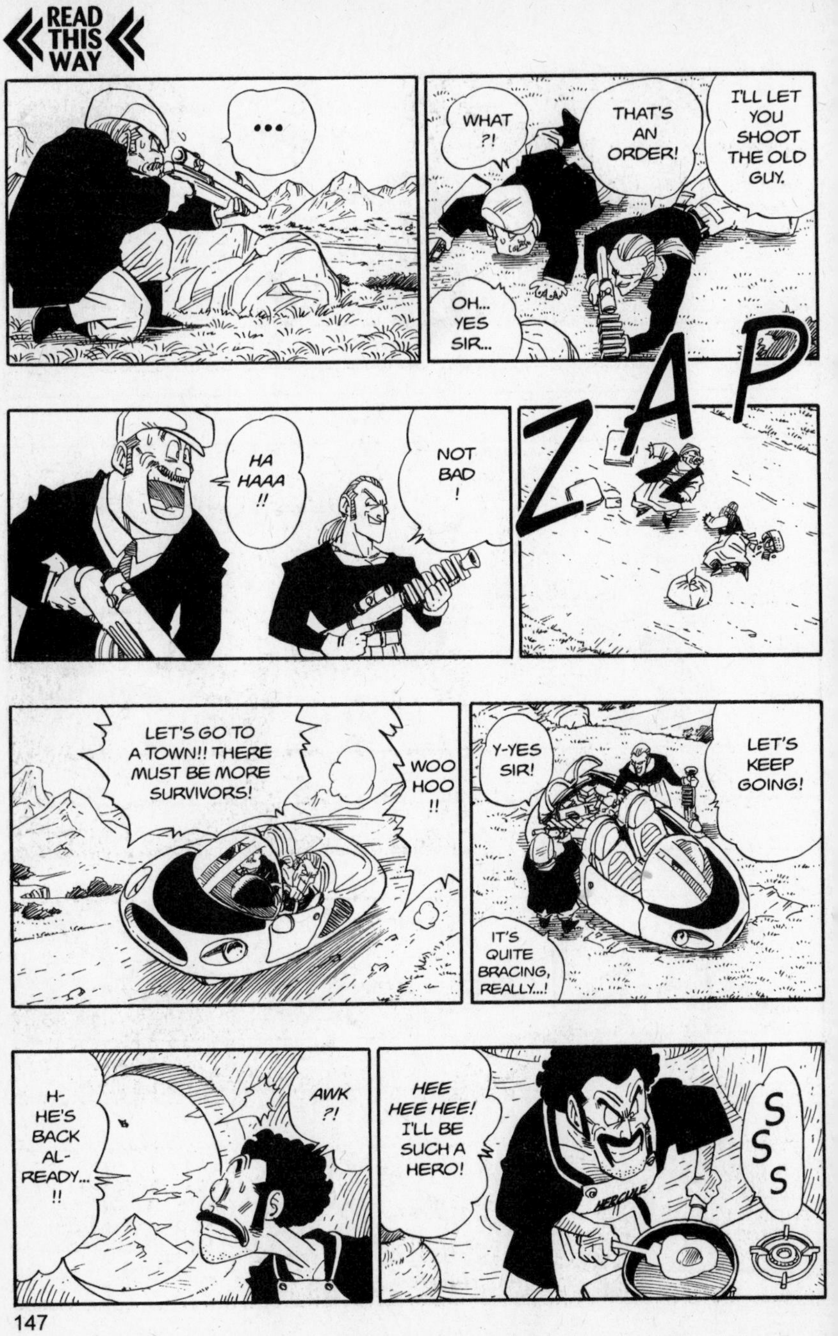

I'LL LET YOU SHOOT THE OLD GUY.
THAT'S AN ORDER!
WHAT ?!
OH... YES SIR...
...
ZAP
NOT BAD!
HA HAAA!!
LET'S KEEP GOING!
Y-YES SIR!
IT'S QUITE BRACING, REALLY...!
WOO HOO!!
LET'S GO TO A TOWN!! THERE MUST BE MORE SURVIVORS!
SSS
HEE HEE HEE! I'LL BE SUCH A HERO!
HERCULE
AWK ?!
H-HE'S BACK AL-READY...!!

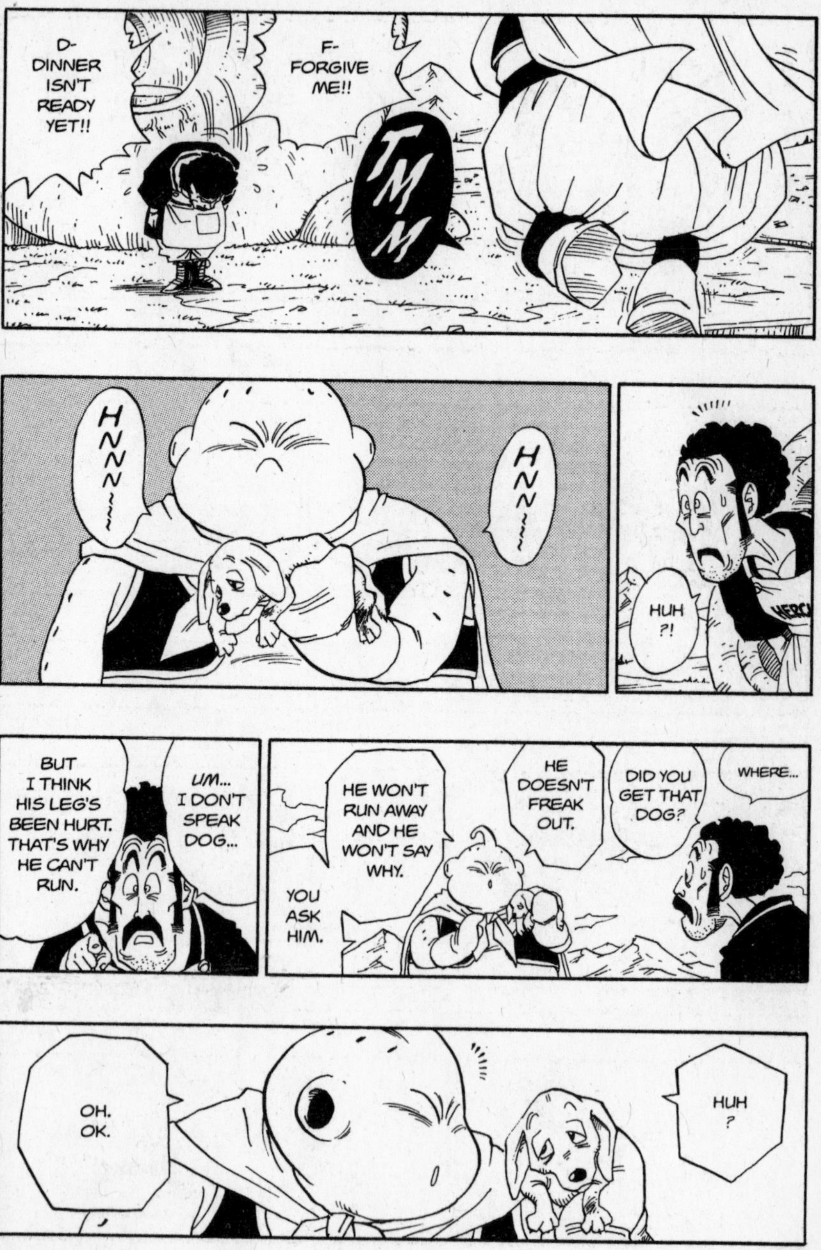
TMM
F- FORGIVE ME!!
D- DINNER ISN'T READY YET!!
HUH ?!
HNN~~
HNN~~
WHERE...
DID YOU GET THAT DOG?
HE DOESN'T FREAK OUT.
HE WON'T RUN AWAY AND HE WON'T SAY WHY.
YOU ASK HIM.
UM... I DON'T SPEAK DOG...
BUT I THINK HIS LEG'S BEEN HURT. THAT'S WHY HE CAN'T RUN.
HUH ?
OH. OK.

READ THIS WAY

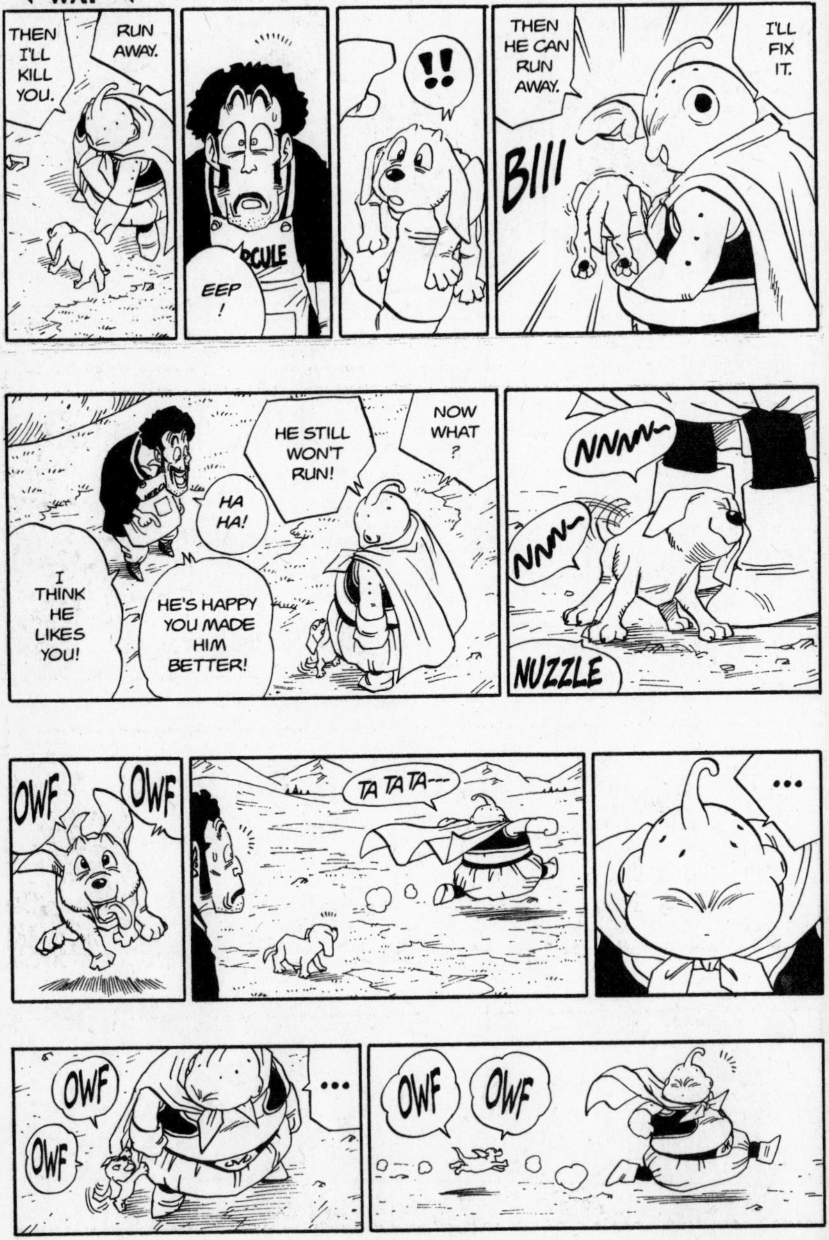
I'LL FIX IT.
THEN HE CAN RUN AWAY.
BIII
!!
EEP!
RUN AWAY.
THEN I'LL KILL YOU.
NNNN-
NNN-
NUZZLE
NOW WHAT?
HE STILL WON'T RUN!
HA HA!
HE'S HAPPY YOU MADE HIM BETTER!
I THINK HE LIKES YOU!
...
TA TA TA---
OWF
OWF
OWF
OWF
...
OWF
OWF

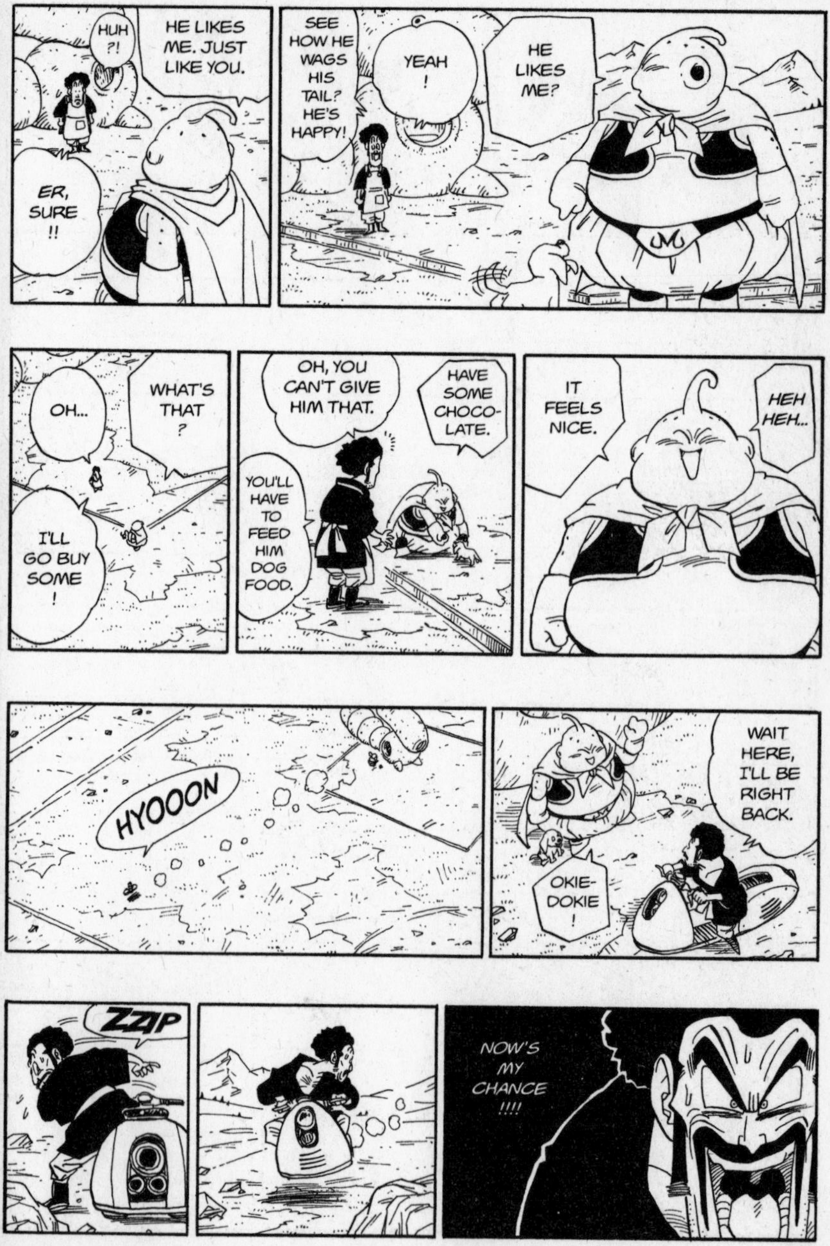
HE LIKES ME?
YEAH !
SEE HOW HE WAGS HIS TAIL? HE'S HAPPY!
HE LIKES ME. JUST LIKE YOU.
HUH ?!
ER, SURE !!
HEH HEH...
IT FEELS NICE.
HAVE SOME CHOCOLATE.
OH, YOU CAN'T GIVE HIM THAT.
YOU'LL HAVE TO FEED HIM DOG FOOD.
WHAT'S THAT ?
OH...
I'LL GO BUY SOME !
WAIT HERE, I'LL BE RIGHT BACK.
OKIE-DOKIE !
HYOOON
NOW'S MY CHANCE !!!!
ZZIP

READ THIS WAY

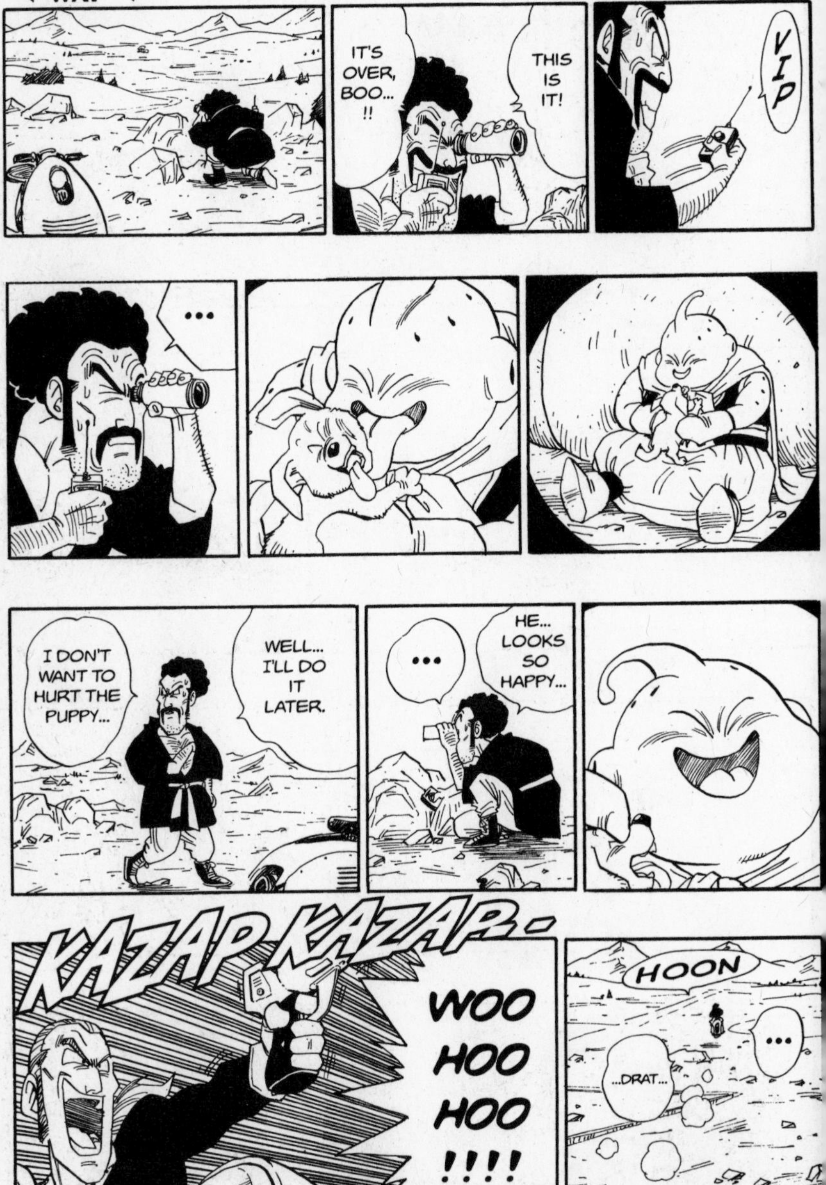

VIP
THIS IS IT!
IT'S OVER, BOO... !!
...
HE... LOOKS SO HAPPY...
...
WELL... I'LL DO IT LATER.
I DON'T WANT TO HURT THE PUPPY...
HOON
...
...DRAT...
KAZAP KAZAP
WOO HOO HOO !!!!

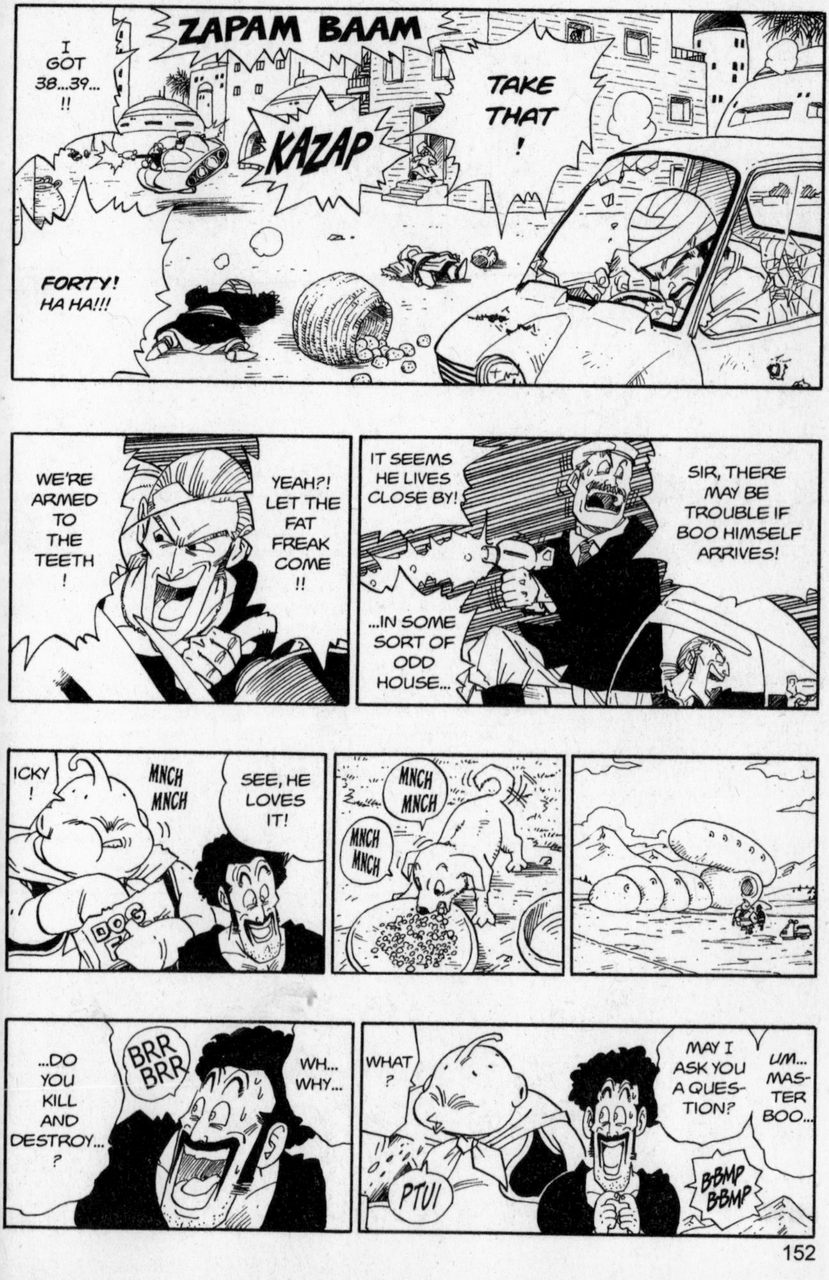
ZAPAM BAAM
TAKE THAT!
KAZAP
I GOT 38...39...!!
FORTY! HA HA!!!
SIR, THERE MAY BE TROUBLE IF BOO HIMSELF ARRIVES!
IT SEEMS HE LIVES CLOSE BY!
...IN SOME SORT OF ODD HOUSE...
YEAH?! LET THE FAT FREAK COME!!
WE'RE ARMED TO THE TEETH!
MNCH MNCH
MNCH MNCH
SEE, HE LOVES IT!
MNCH MNCH
ICKY!
UM... MASTER BOO...
MAY I ASK YOU A QUESTION?
B-BMP B-BMP
WHAT?
PTUI
WH... WHY...
BRR BRR
...DO YOU KILL AND DESTROY...?

READ THIS WAY

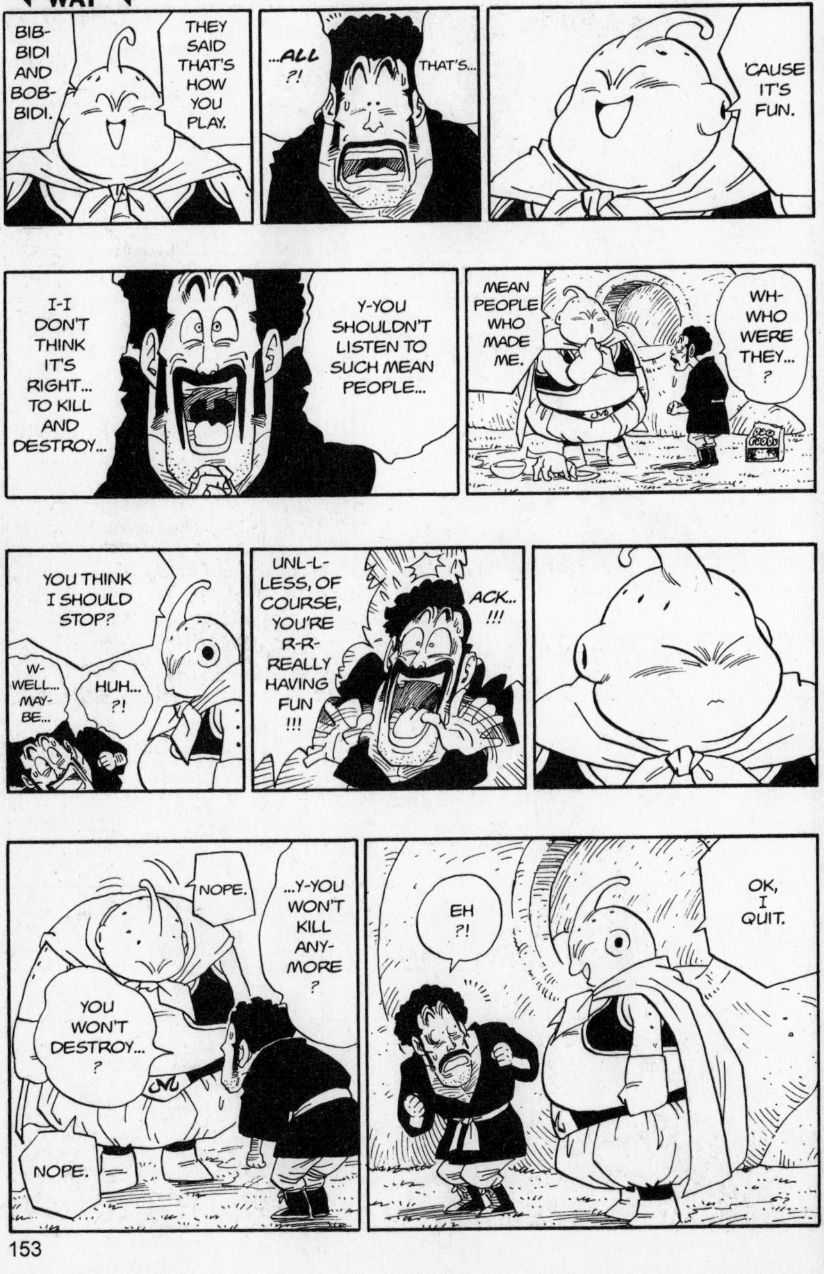
'CAUSE IT'S FUN.
THAT'S...
...ALL ?!
THEY SAID THAT'S HOW YOU PLAY.
BIB-BIDI AND BOB-BIDI.
WH-WHO WERE THEY...?
MEAN PEOPLE WHO MADE ME.
Y-YOU SHOULDN'T LISTEN TO SUCH MEAN PEOPLE...
I-I DON'T THINK IT'S RIGHT... TO KILL AND DESTROY...
ACK...!!!
UNL-L-LESS, OF COURSE, YOU'RE R-R-REALLY HAVING FUN!!!
YOU THINK I SHOULD STOP?
HUH...?!
W-WELL... MAY-BE...
OK, I QUIT.
EH ?!
...Y-YOU WON'T KILL ANYMORE ?
NOPE.
YOU WON'T DESTROY... ?
NOPE.

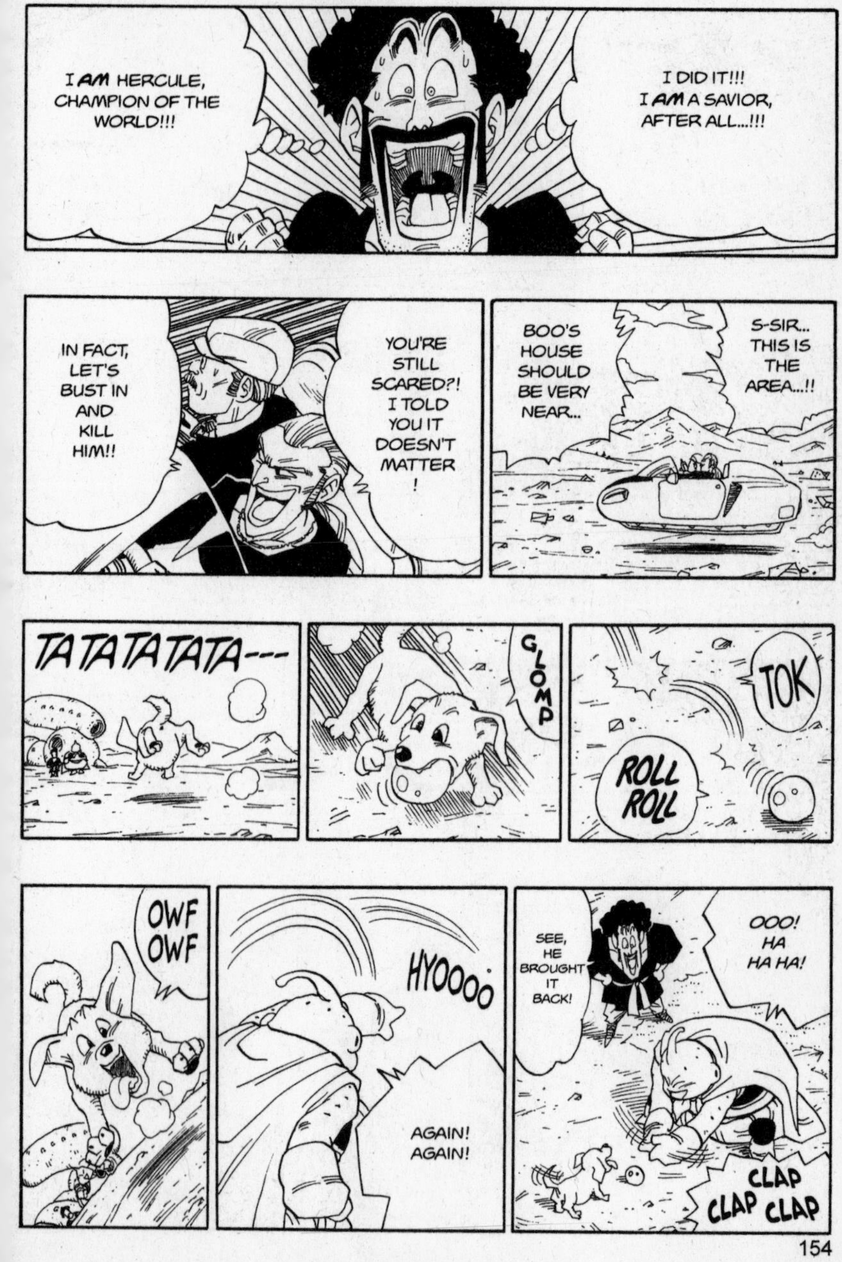
I DID IT!!! I AM A SAVIOR, AFTER ALL...!!!
I AM HERCULE, CHAMPION OF THE WORLD!!!
S-SIR... THIS IS THE AREA...!!
BOO'S HOUSE SHOULD BE VERY NEAR...
YOU'RE STILL SCARED?! I TOLD YOU IT DOESN'T MATTER!
IN FACT, LET'S BUST IN AND KILL HIM!!
TOK
ROLL ROLL
GLOMP
TATATATATA---
OOO! HA HA HA!
SEE, HE BROUGHT IT BACK!
CLAP CLAP CLAP CLAP
HYOOOO
AGAIN! AGAIN!
OWF OWF

READ THIS WAY

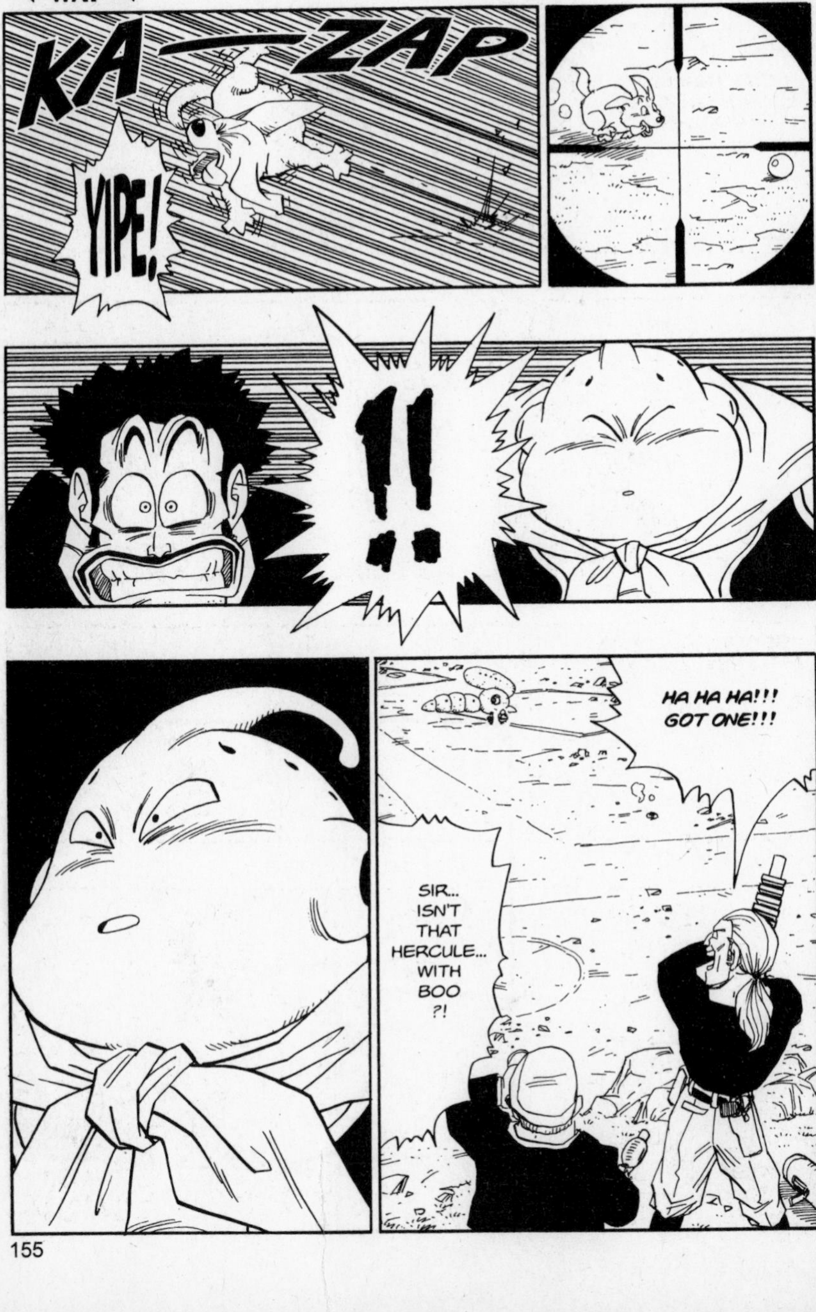
KA—ZAP
YIPE!
!!
HA HA HA!!! GOT ONE!!!
SIR... ISN'T THAT HERCULE... WITH BOO ?!

DBZ:290 • The Creature of Wrath

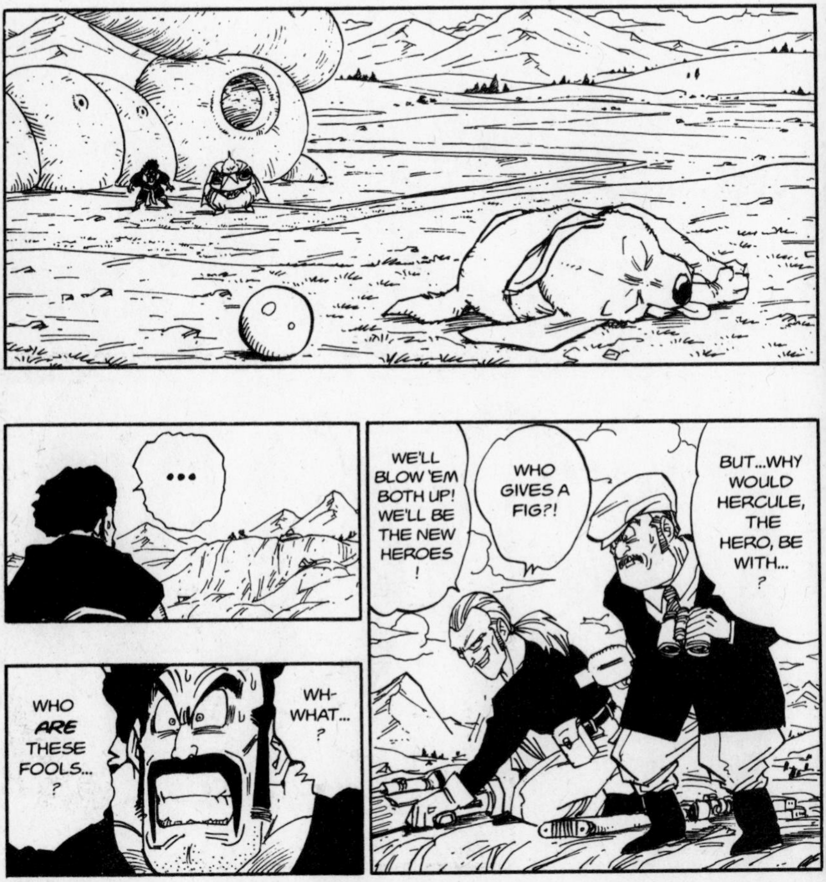

BUT...WHY WOULD HERCULE, THE HERO, BE WITH...?
WHO GIVES A FIG?!
WE'LL BLOW 'EM BOTH UP! WE'LL BE THE NEW HEROES!
...
WH- WHAT...?
WHO ***ARE*** THESE FOOLS...?

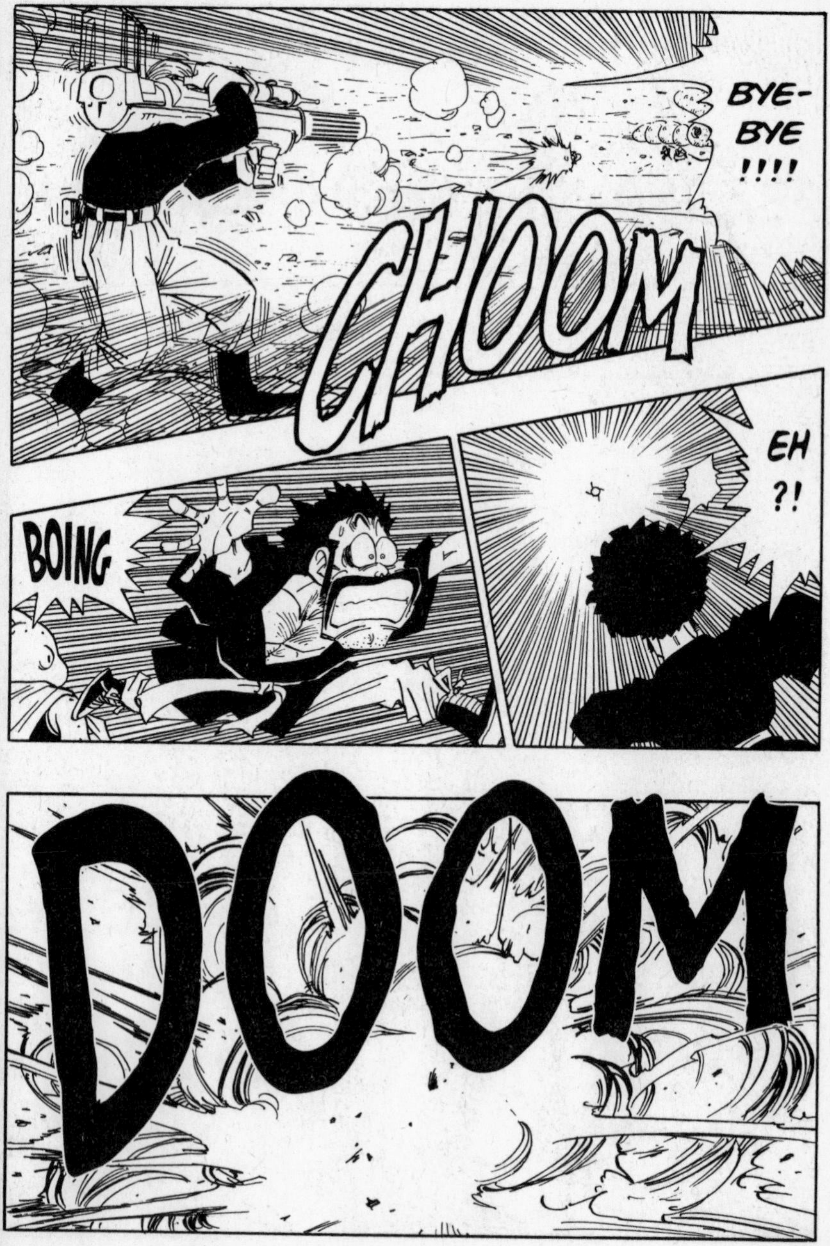
BYE-BYE!!!!
CHOOM
EH?!
BOING
DOOM

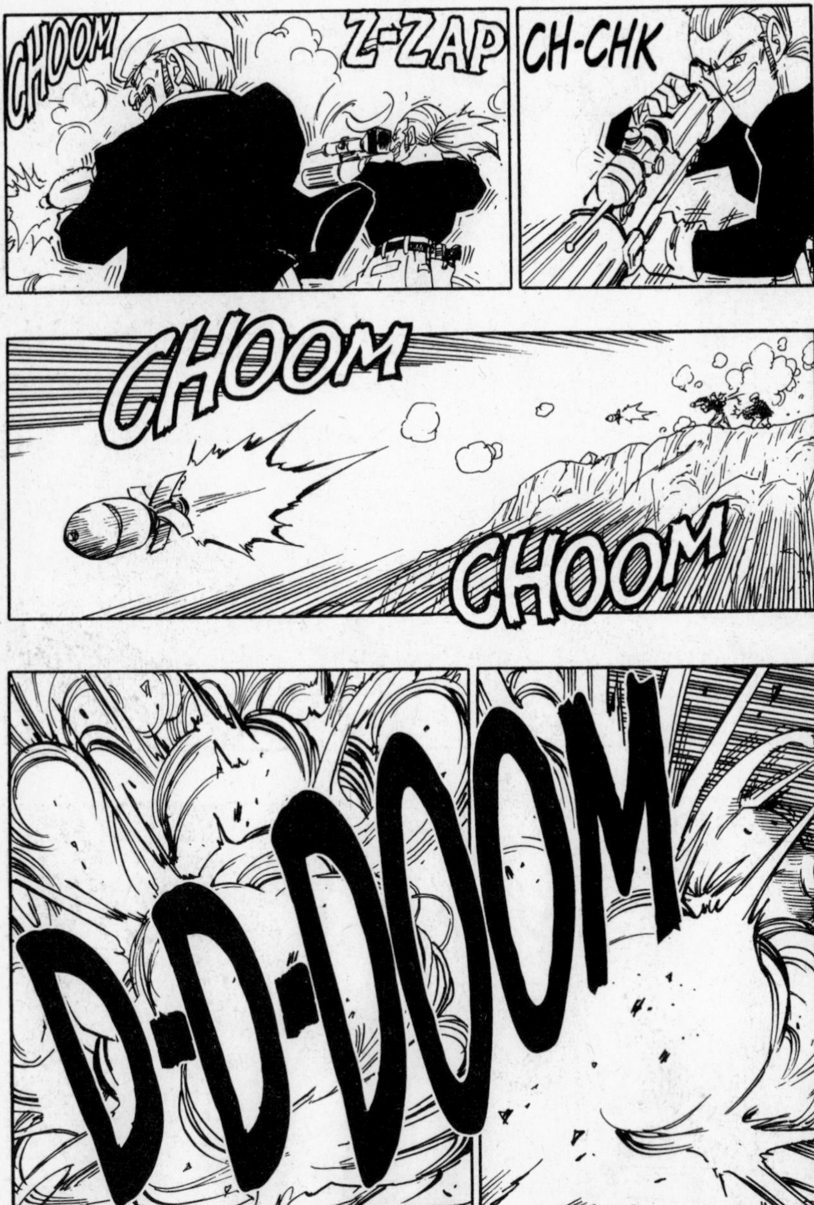
CH-CHK
Z-ZAP
CHOOM
CHOOM
CHOOM
D-D-DOOM

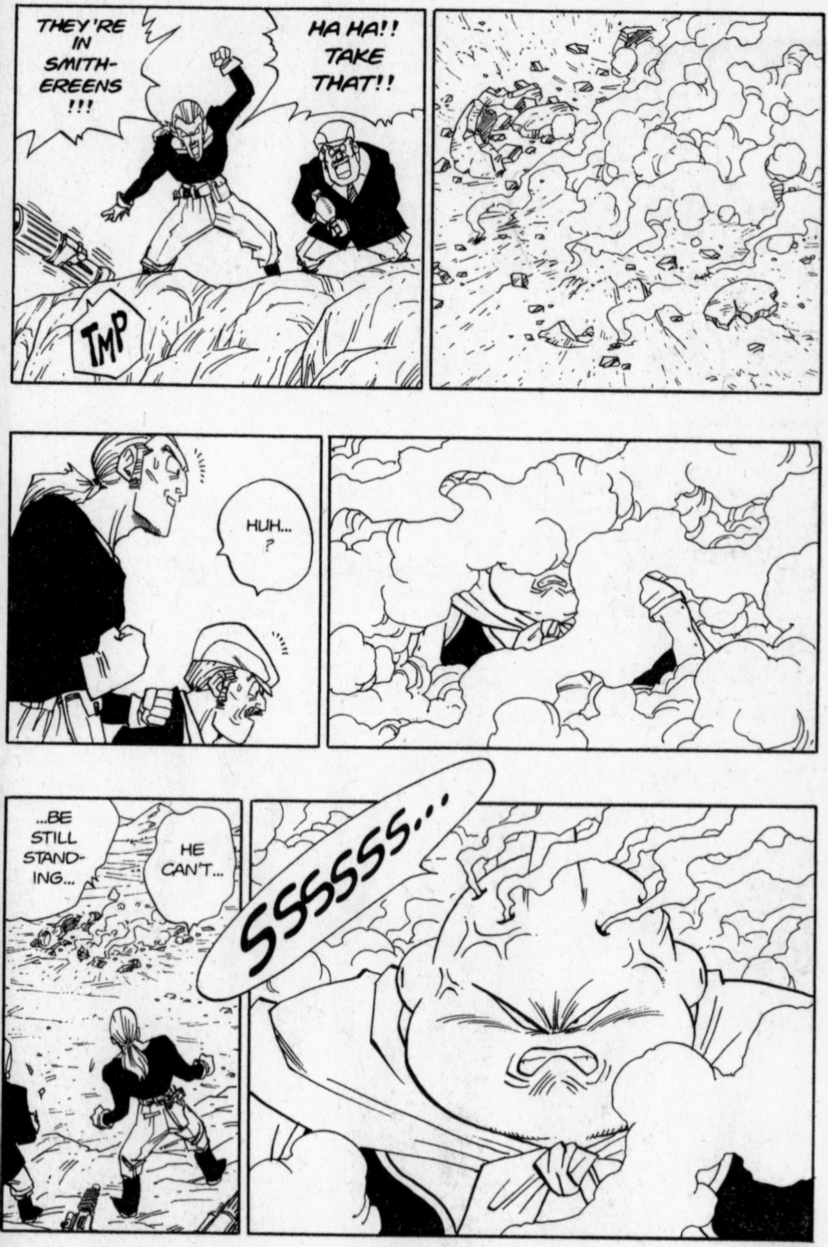
HA HA!! TAKE THAT!!
THEY'RE IN SMITHEREENS!!!
TMP
HUH...?
SSSSSS...
HE CAN'T...
...BE STILL STANDING...

READ THIS WAY

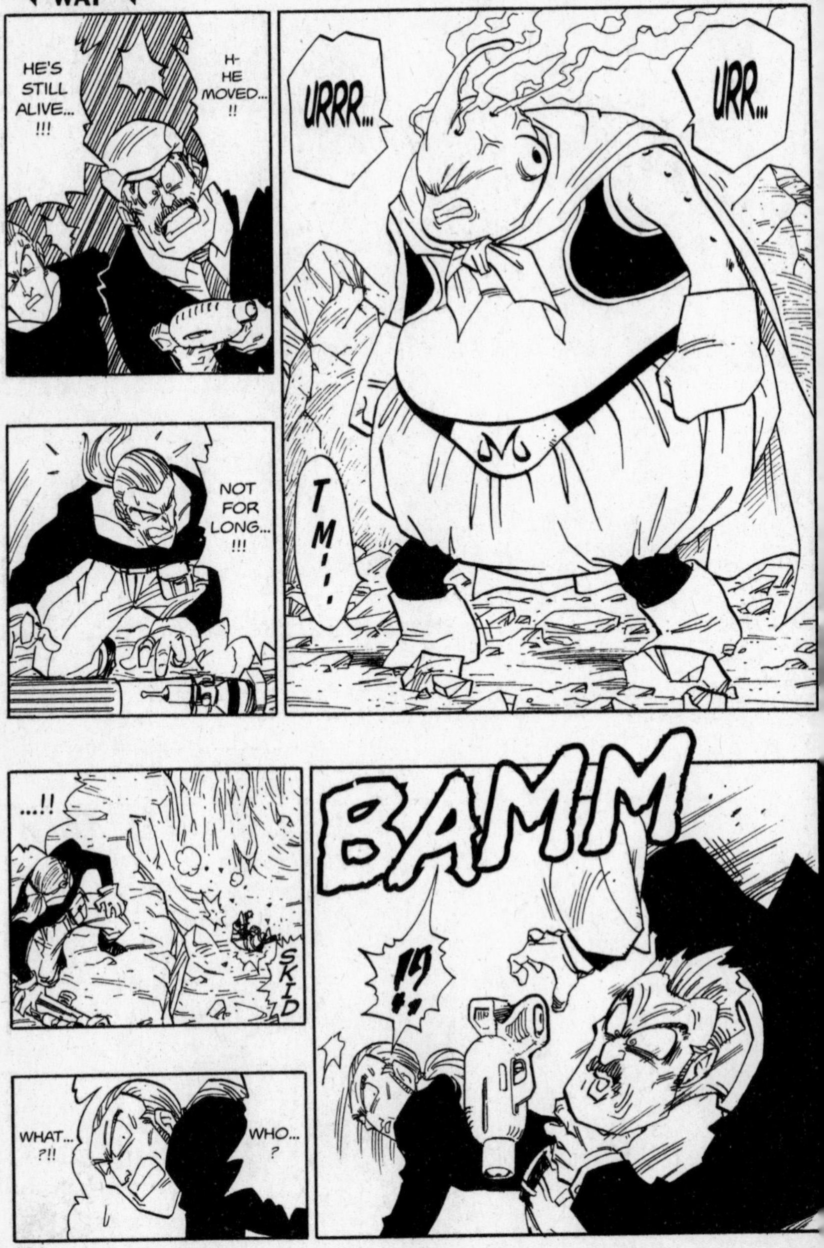

URR...
URRR...
TM!!
H-HE MOVED...!!
HE'S STILL ALIVE...!!!
NOT FOR LONG...!!!
BAMM
!!?
...!!
SKID
WHO...?
WHAT...?!!

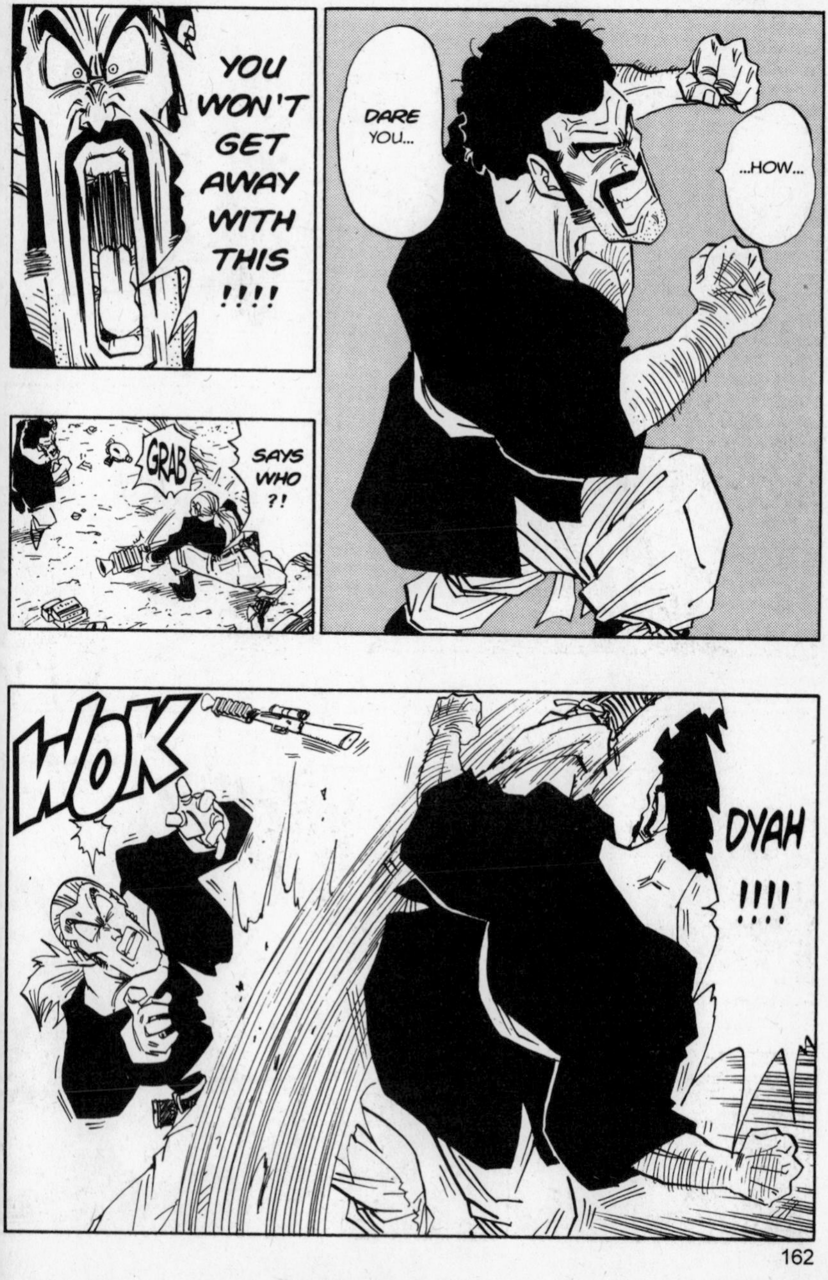
...HOW...
DARE YOU...
YOU WON'T GET AWAY WITH THIS !!!!
SAYS WHO ?!
GRAB
DYAH !!!!
WOK

READ THIS WAY

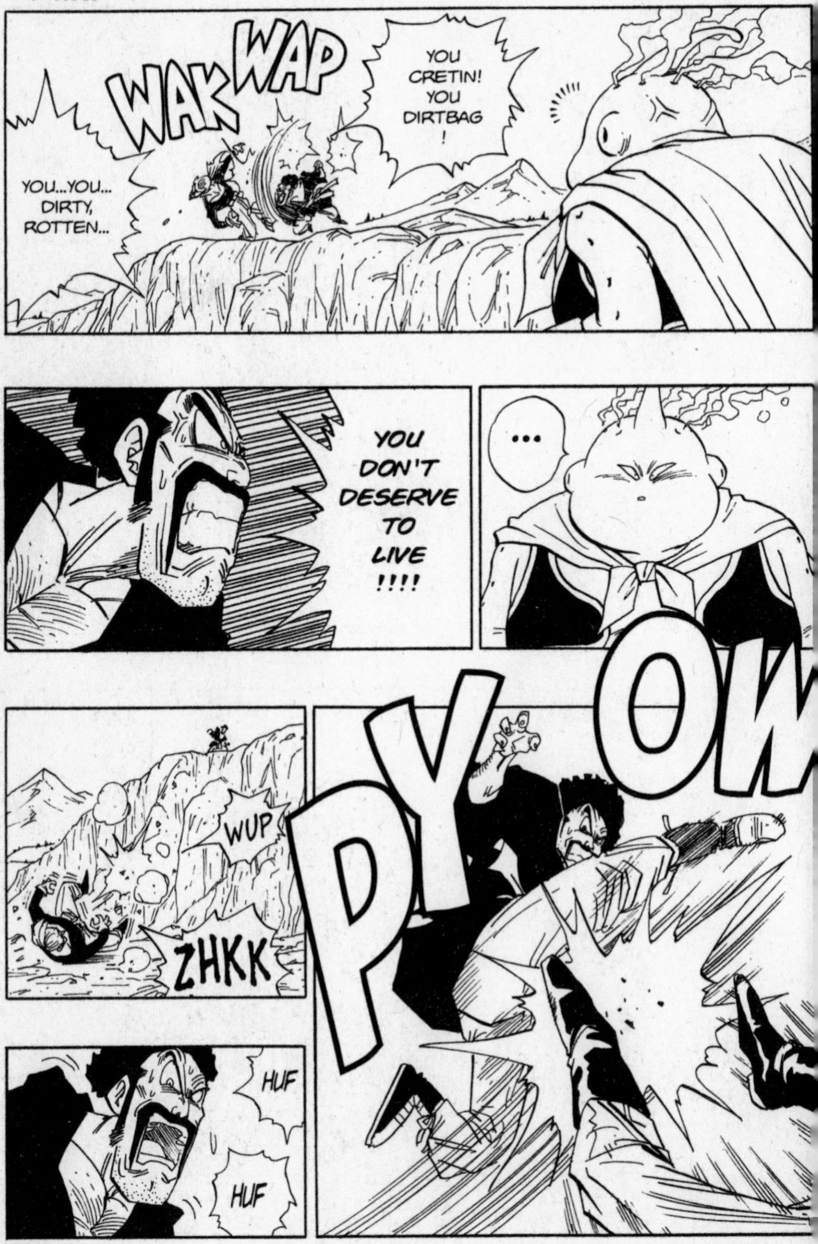
YOU CRETIN! YOU DIRTBAG!
WAP
WAK
YOU...YOU... DIRTY, ROTTEN...
...
YOU DON'T DESERVE TO LIVE!!!!
PYOW
WUP
ZHKK
HUF
HUF

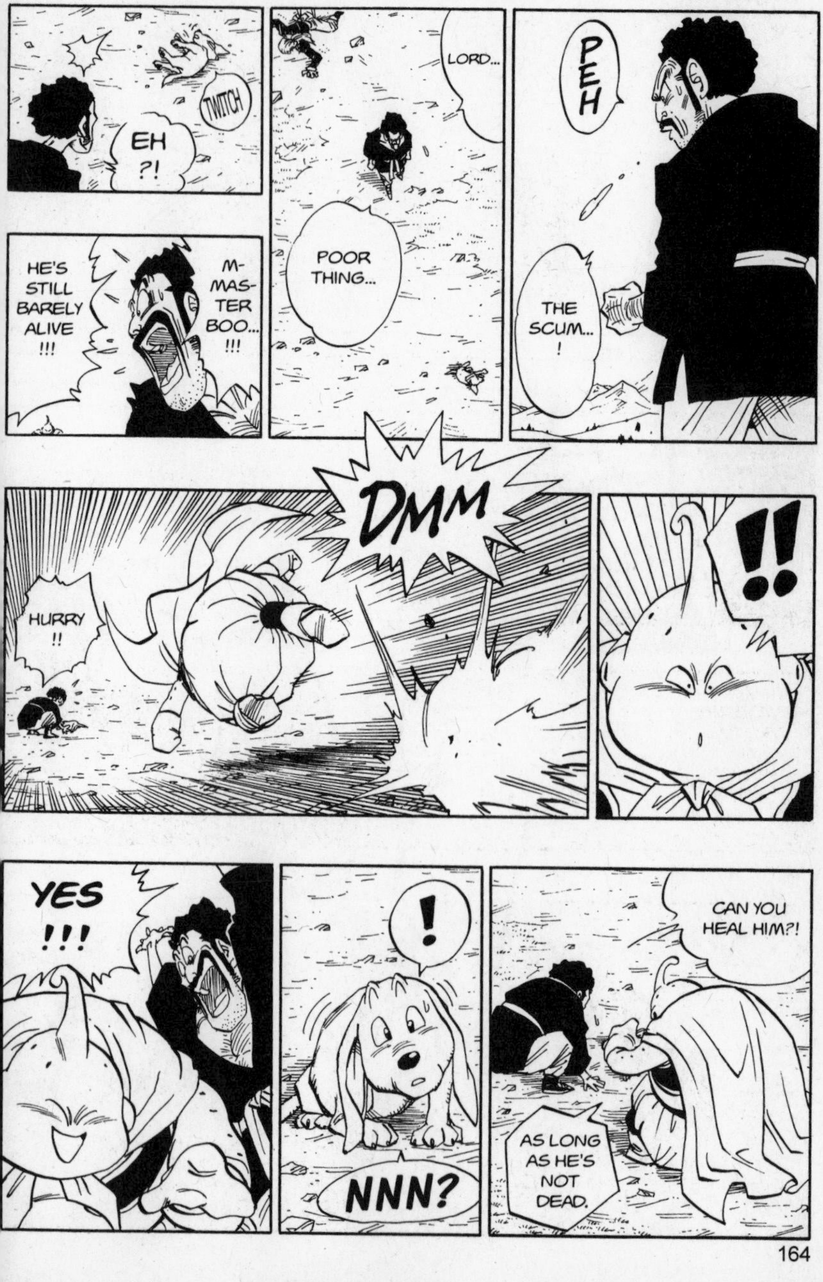
PEH
THE SCUM...!
LORD...
POOR THING...
TWITCH
EH ?!
M-MASTER BOO...!!!
HE'S STILL BARELY ALIVE!!!
!!
DMM
HURRY!!
CAN YOU HEAL HIM?!
AS LONG AS HE'S NOT DEAD.
!
NNN?
YES!!!

READ THIS WAY

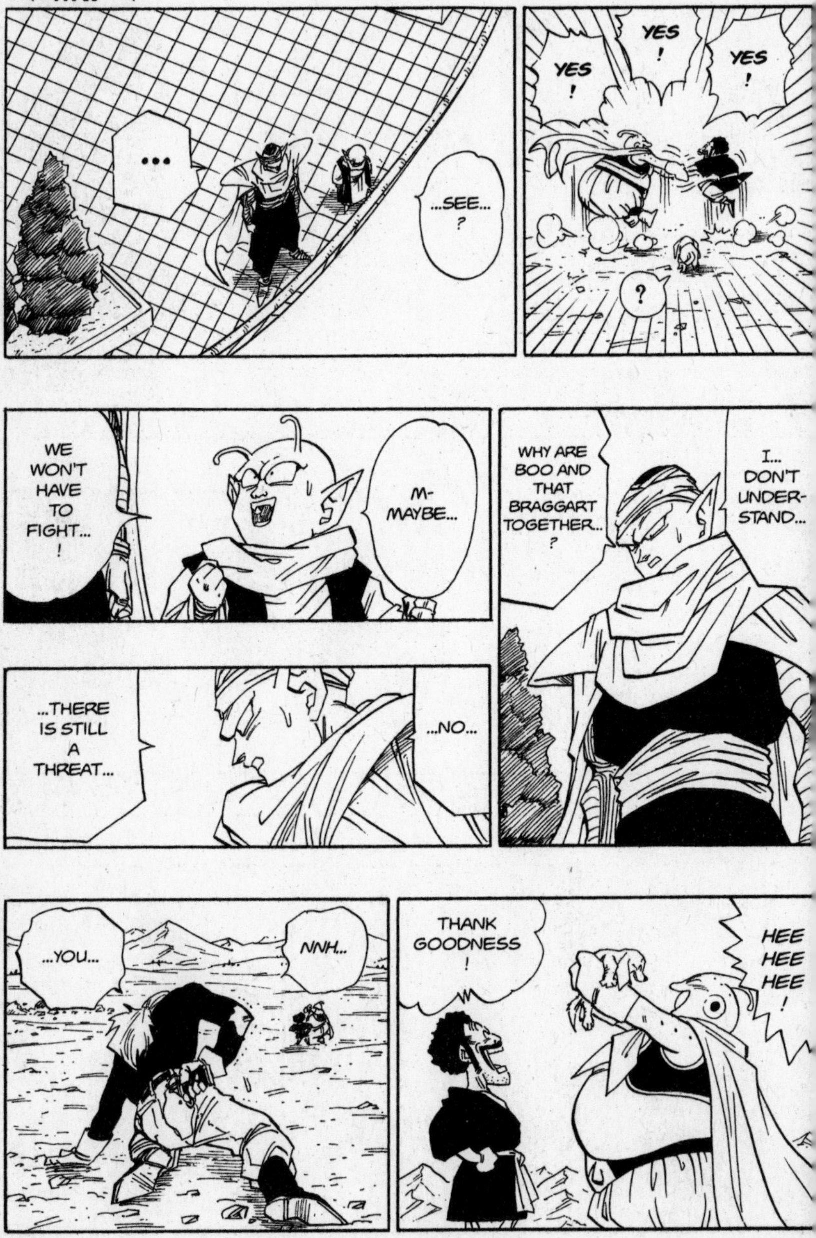
YES!
YES!
YES!
?
...SEE...?
...
I... DON'T UNDERSTAND...
WHY ARE BOO AND THAT BRAGGART TOGETHER...?
M-MAYBE...
WE WON'T HAVE TO FIGHT...!
...NO...
...THERE IS STILL A THREAT...
HEE HEE HEE!
THANK GOODNESS!
NNH...
...YOU...

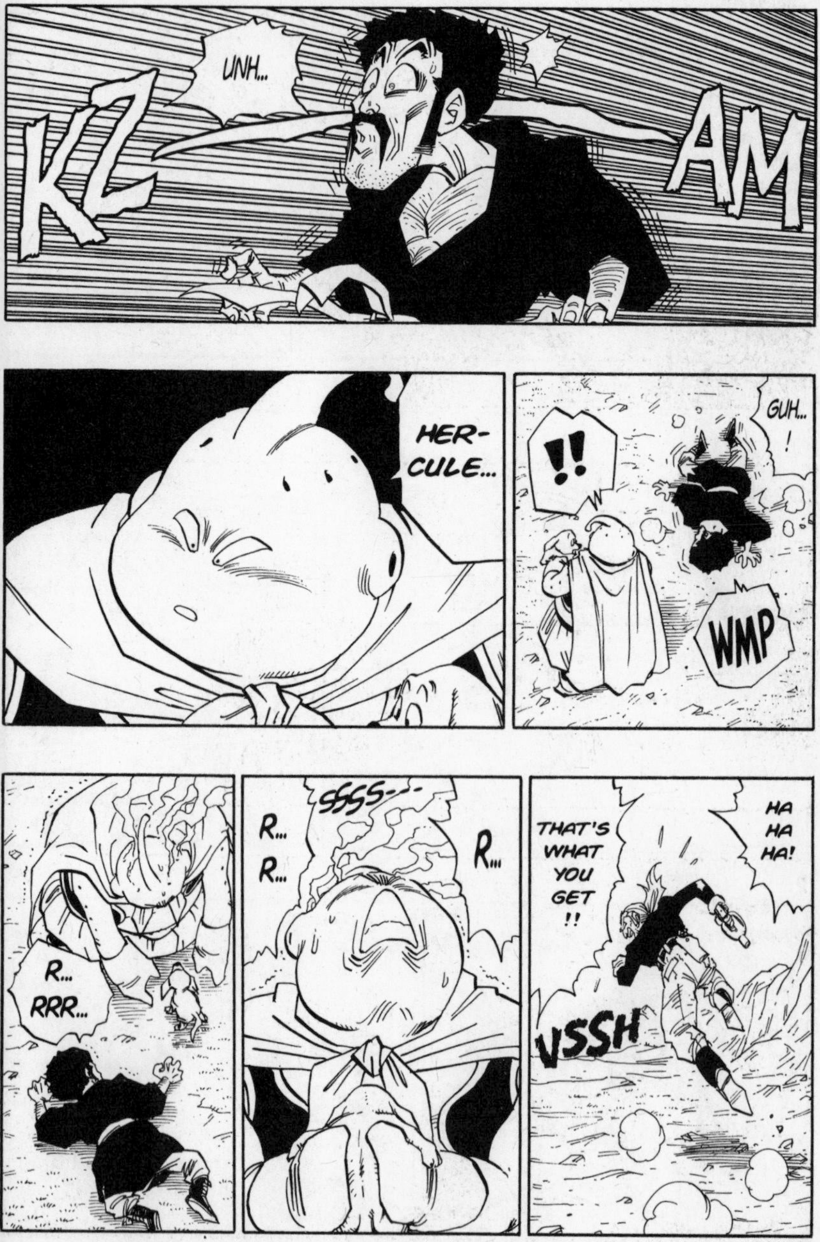
UNH...
KZ
AM
GUH... !
!!
WMP
HER-CULE...
HA HA HA!
THAT'S WHAT YOU GET !!
VSSH
SSSS---
R...
R...
R...
R... RRR...

READ THIS WAY

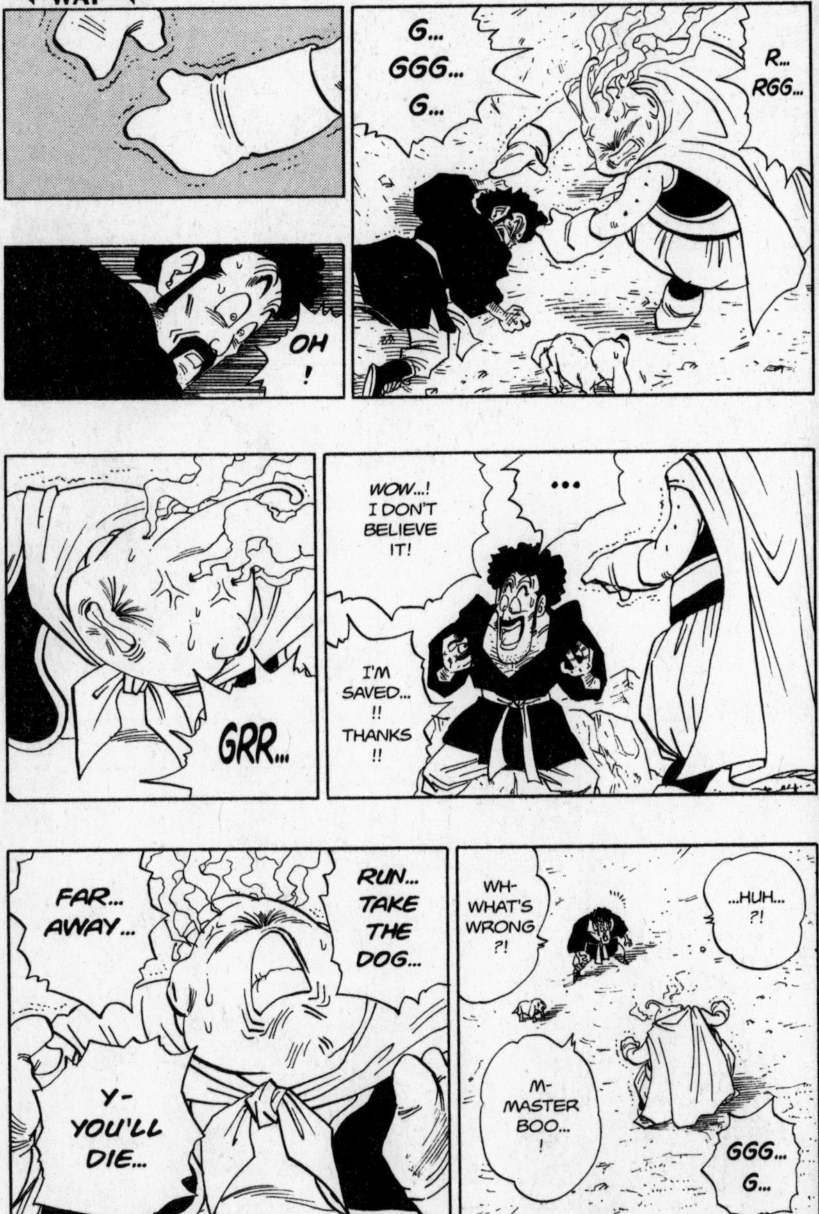
R... RGG...
G... GGG... G...
OH !
...
WOW...! I DON'T BELIEVE IT!
I'M SAVED... !! THANKS !!
GRR...
...HUH... ?!
WH- WHAT'S WRONG ?!
M- MASTER BOO... !
GGG... G...
RUN... TAKE THE DOG...
FAR... AWAY...
Y- YOU'LL DIE...

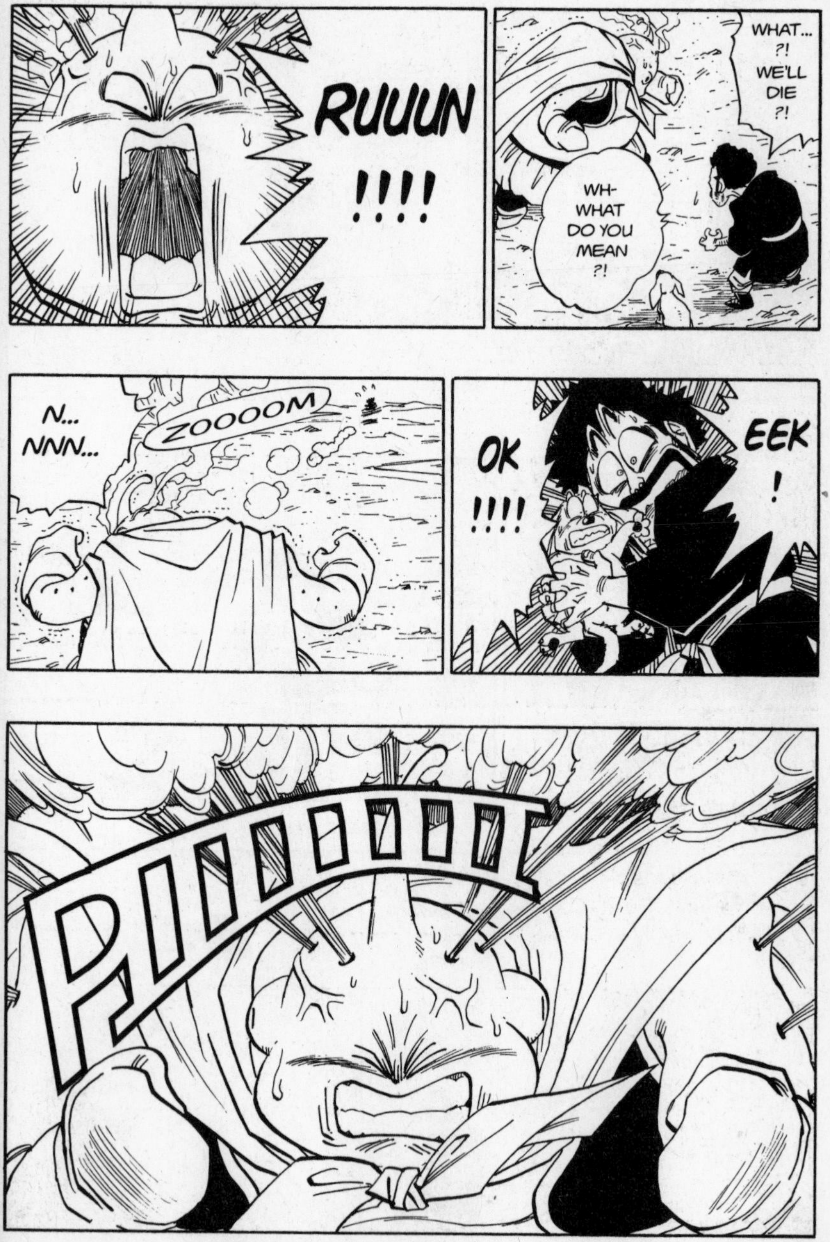
WHAT... ?! WE'LL DIE ?!
WH-WHAT DO YOU MEAN ?!
RUUUN !!!!
EEK !
OK !!!!
ZOOOOM
N... NNN...
PIIIIIIII

READ THIS WAY

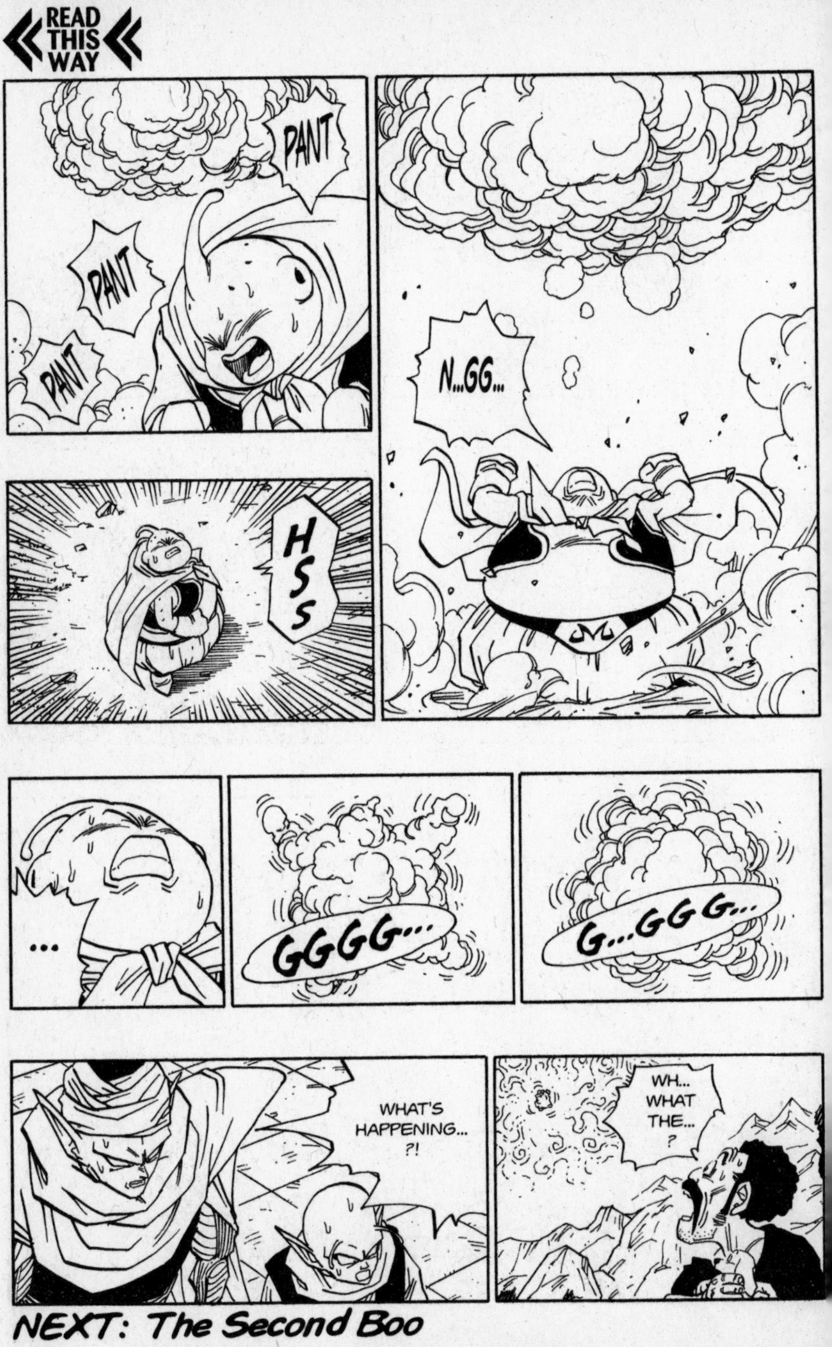
N...GG...
PANT
PANT
PANT
HSS
G...GGG...
GGGG...
...
WH... WHAT THE... ?
WHAT'S HAPPENING... ?!

NEXT: The Second Boo

DBZ:291 • Two Boos?!

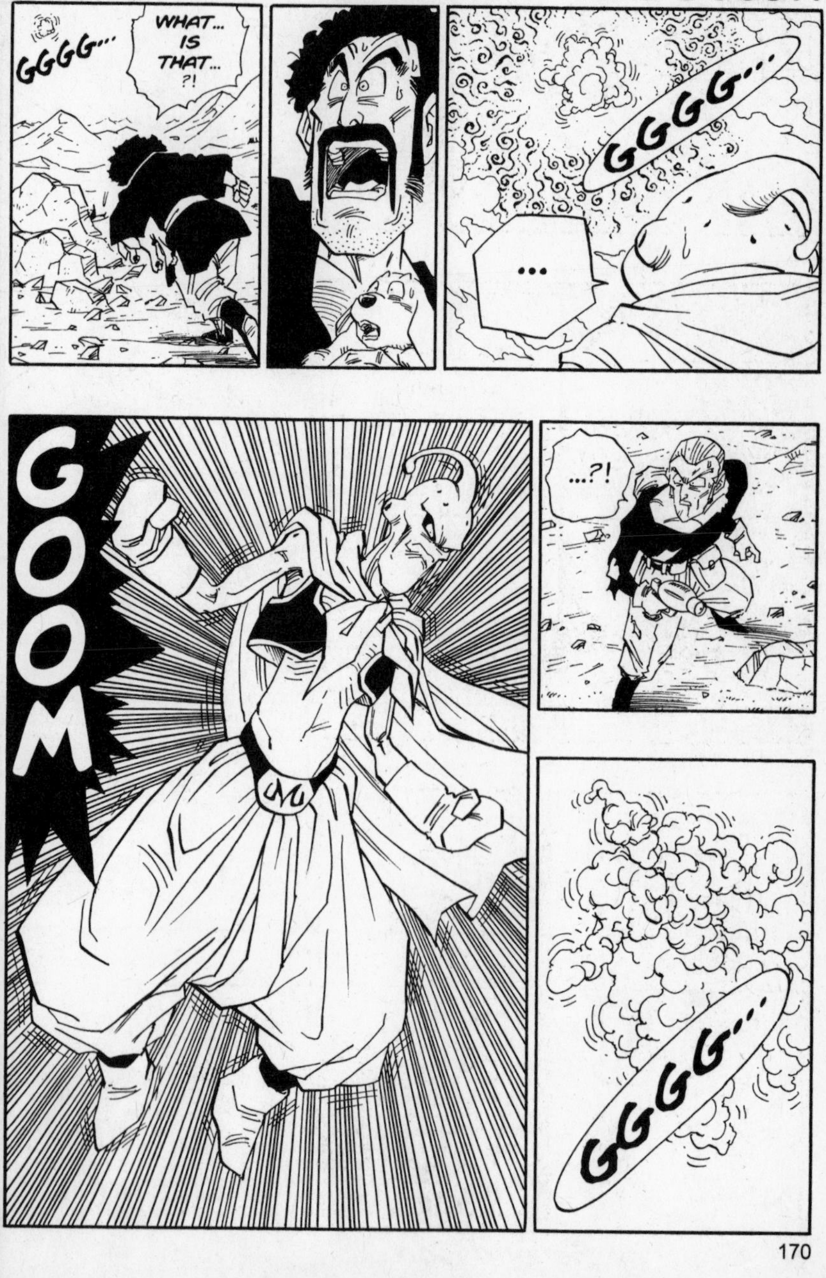
GGGG...
...
WHAT... IS THAT... ?!
GGGG...
...?!
GGGG...
GOOM

READ THIS WAY

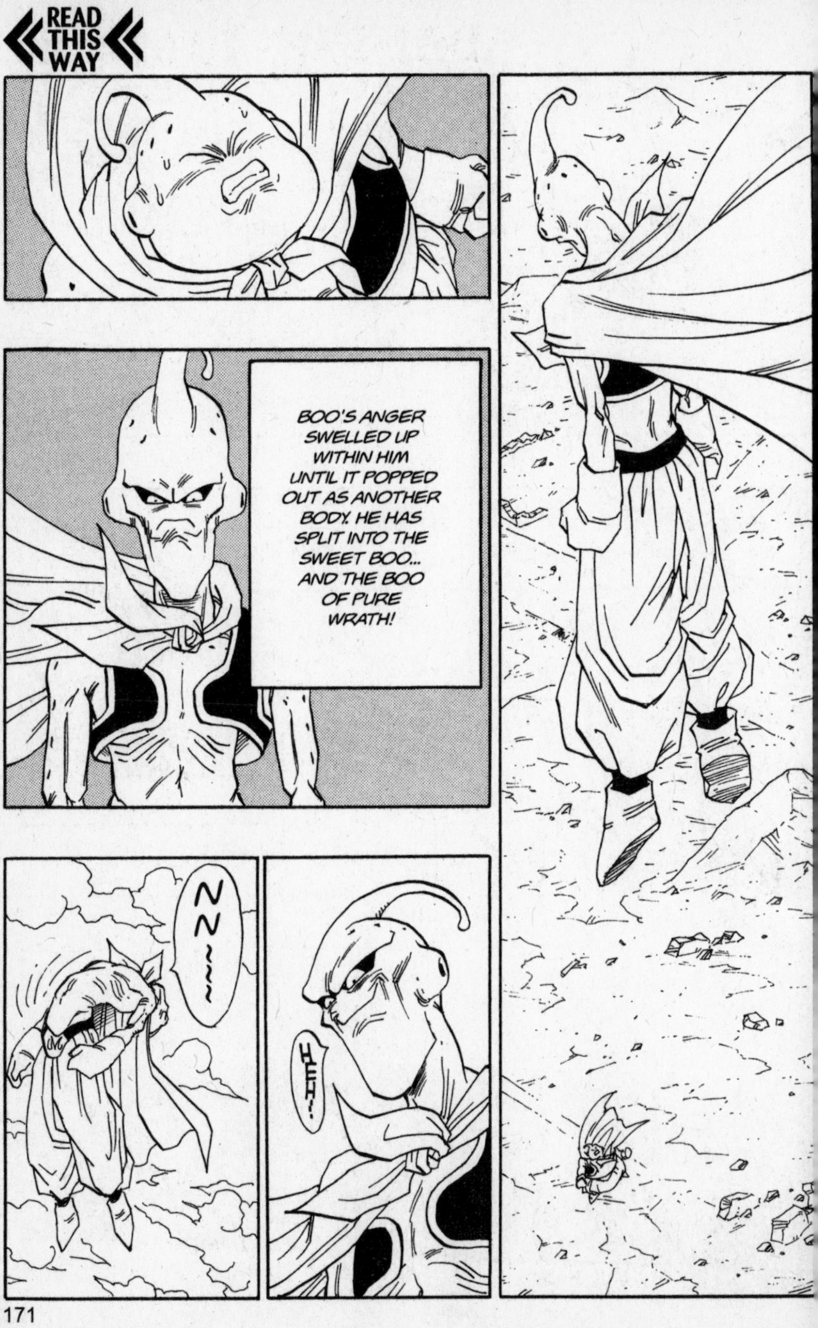
BOO'S ANGER SWELLED UP WITHIN HIM UNTIL IT POPPED OUT AS ANOTHER BODY. HE HAS SPLIT INTO THE SWEET BOO... AND THE BOO OF PURE WRATH!
HEH!!
NN~~~

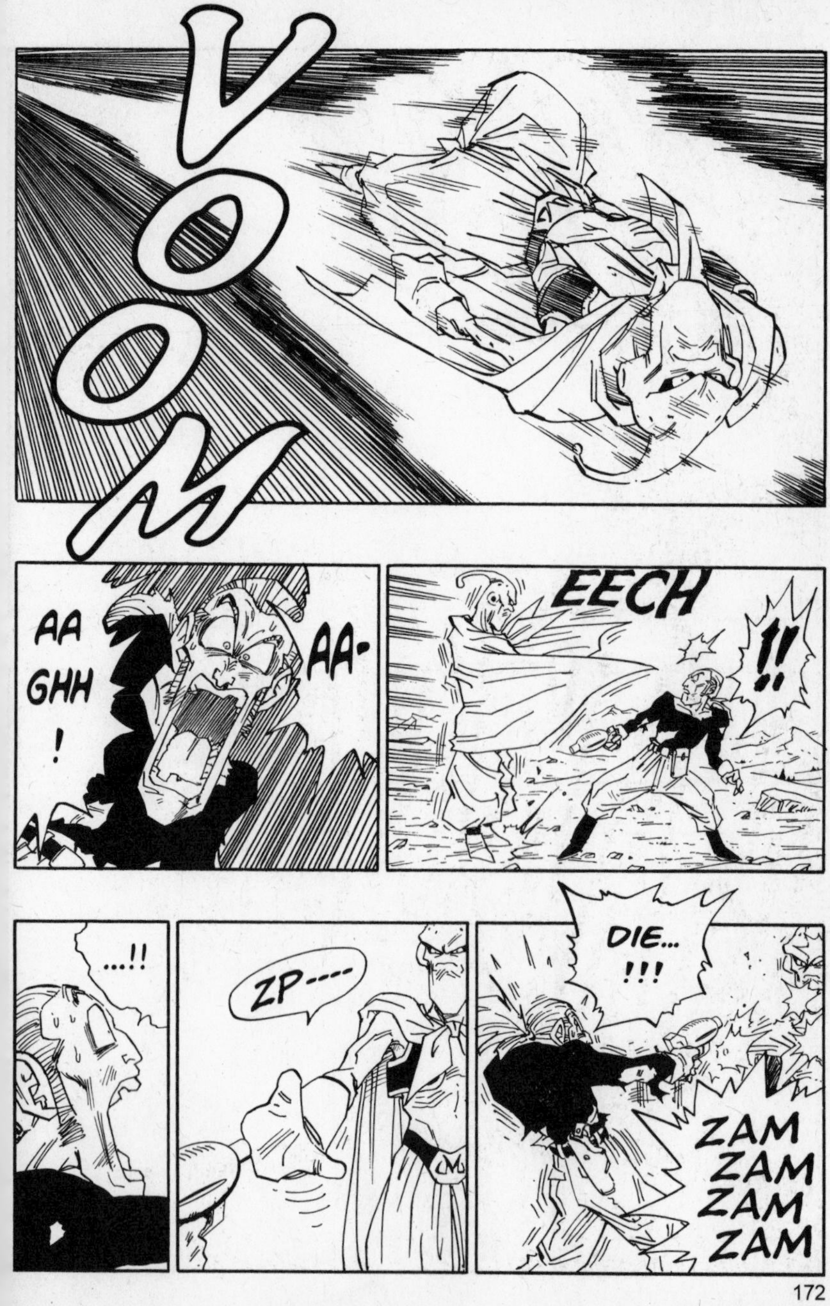
VOOM
EECH
!!
AA-
AA GHH !
DIE... !!!
ZAM ZAM ZAM ZAM
ZP----
...!!

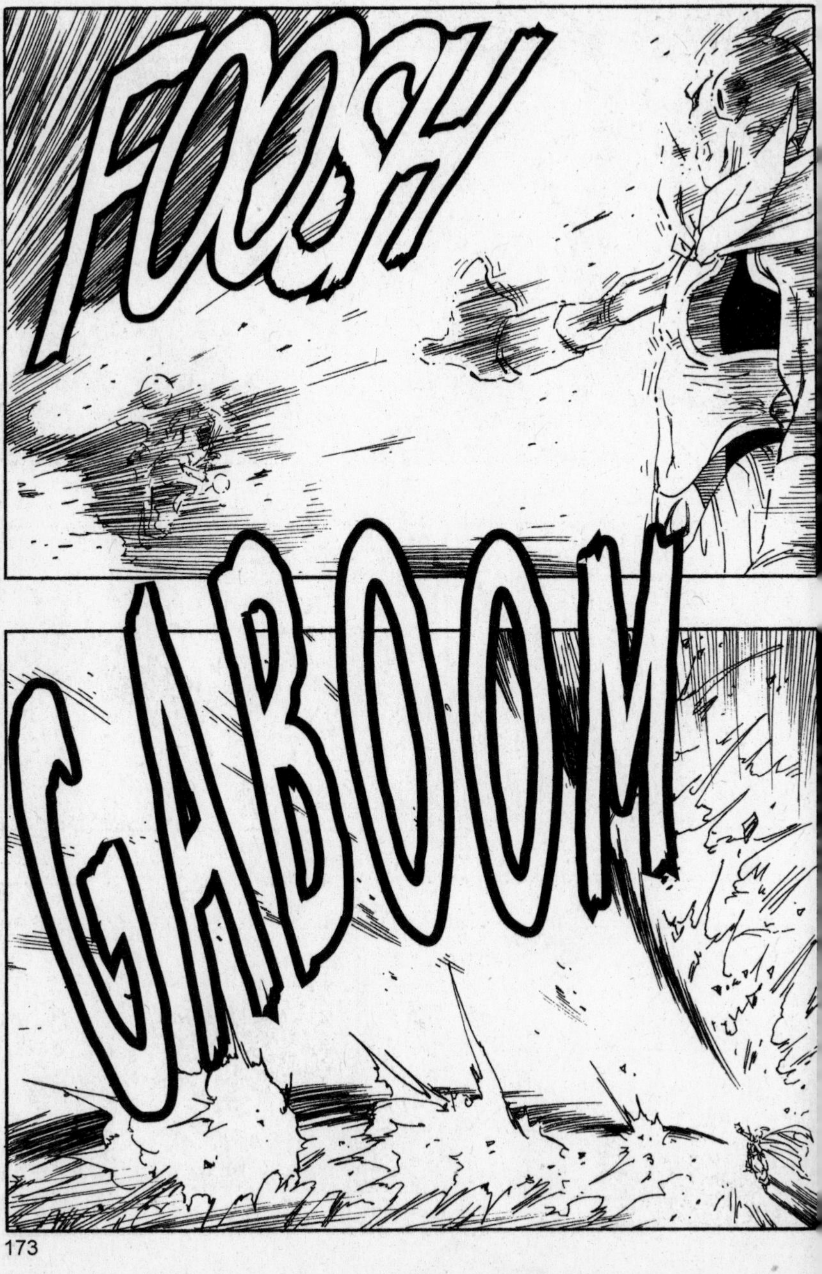
FOOSH
GABOOM

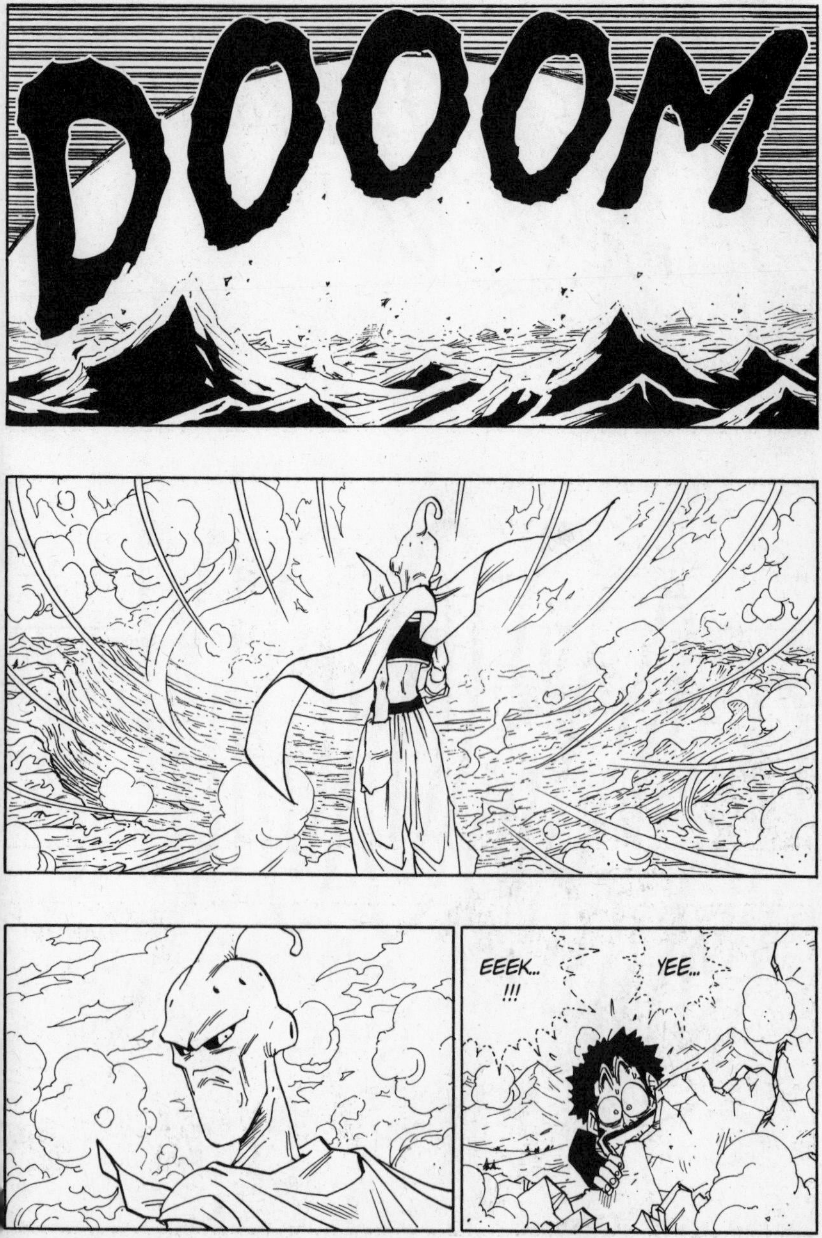
DOOOM
YEE...
EEEK...
!!!

READ THIS WAY

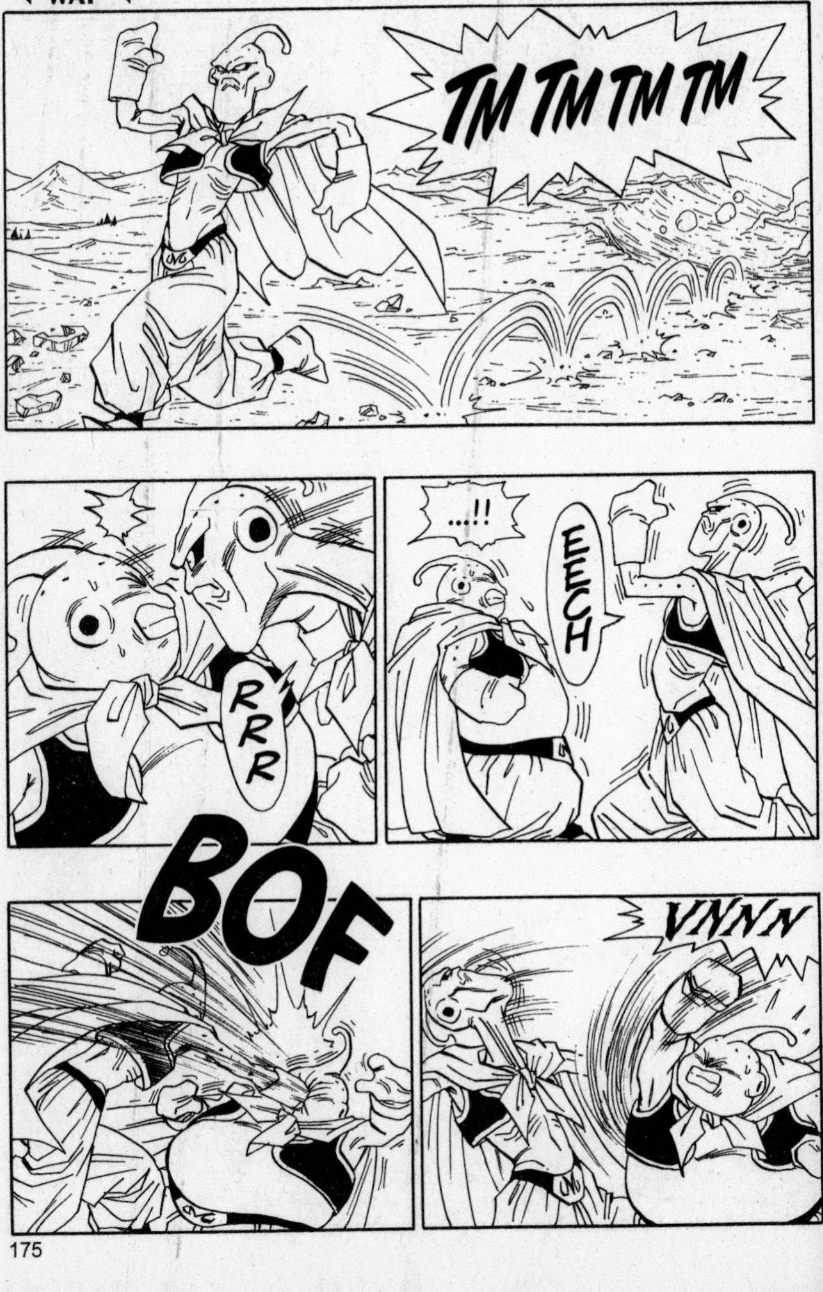
TM TM TM TM
...!!
EECH
RRR
VNNN
BOF

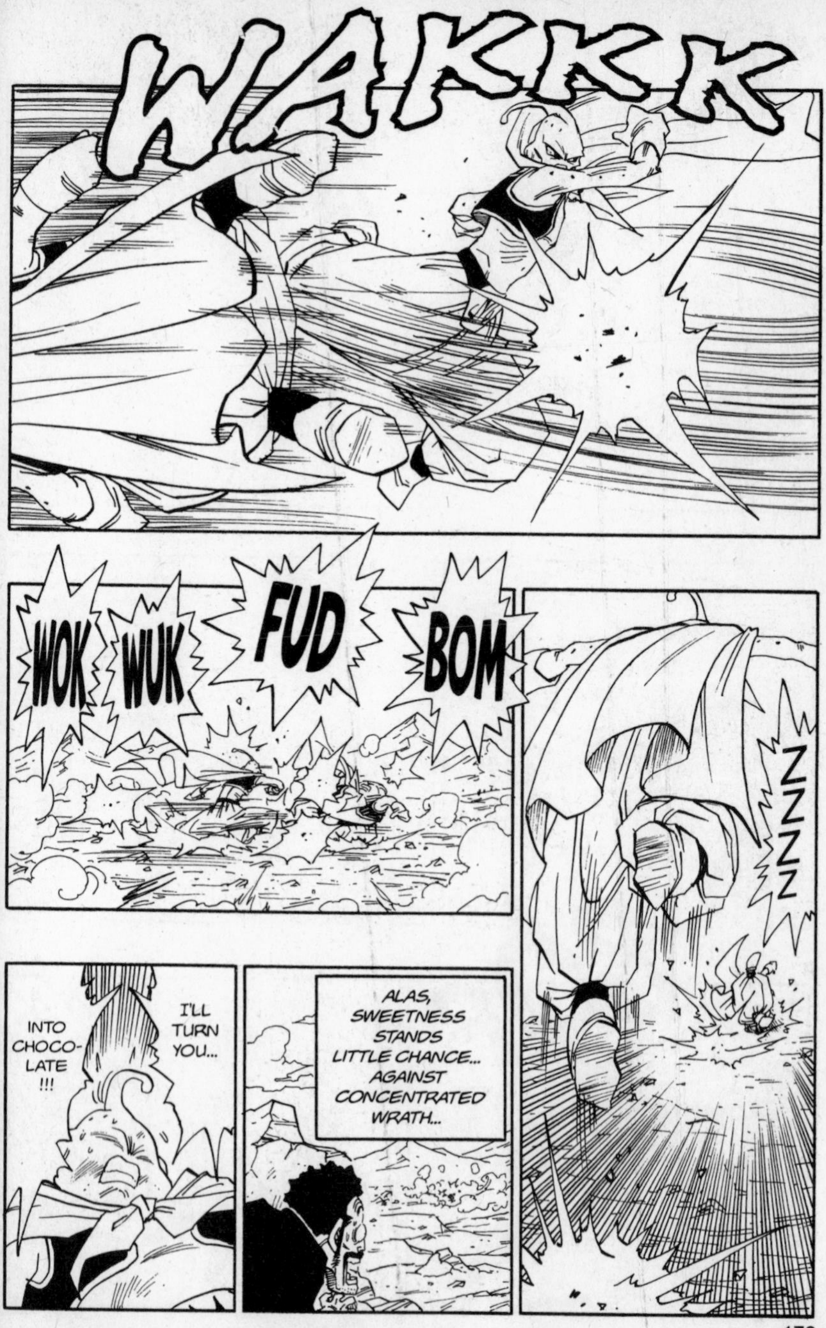
WAKKK
ZZZZ
BOM
FUD
WUK
WOK
ALAS, SWEETNESS STANDS LITTLE CHANCE... AGAINST CONCENTRATED WRATH...
I'LL TURN YOU...
INTO CHOCO-LATE !!!

READ THIS WAY

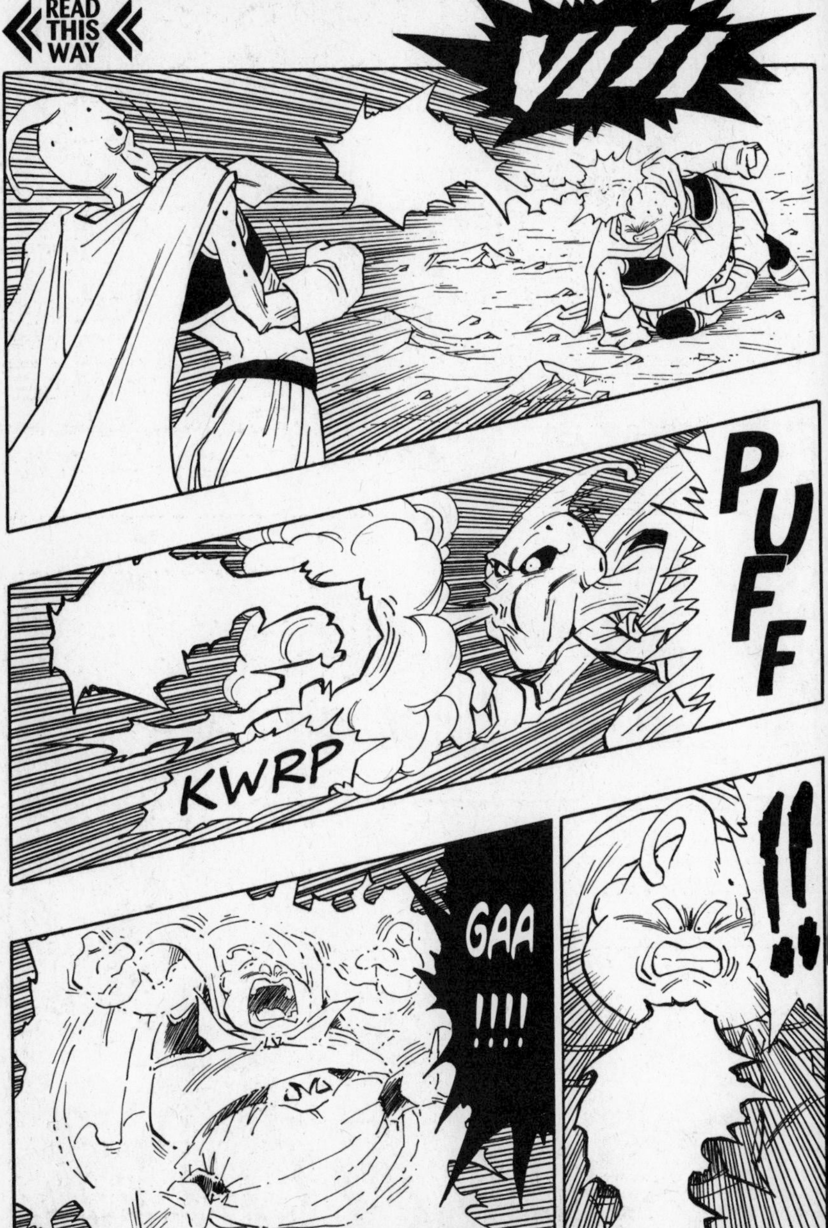
PUFF
KWRP
!!
GAA !!!!!

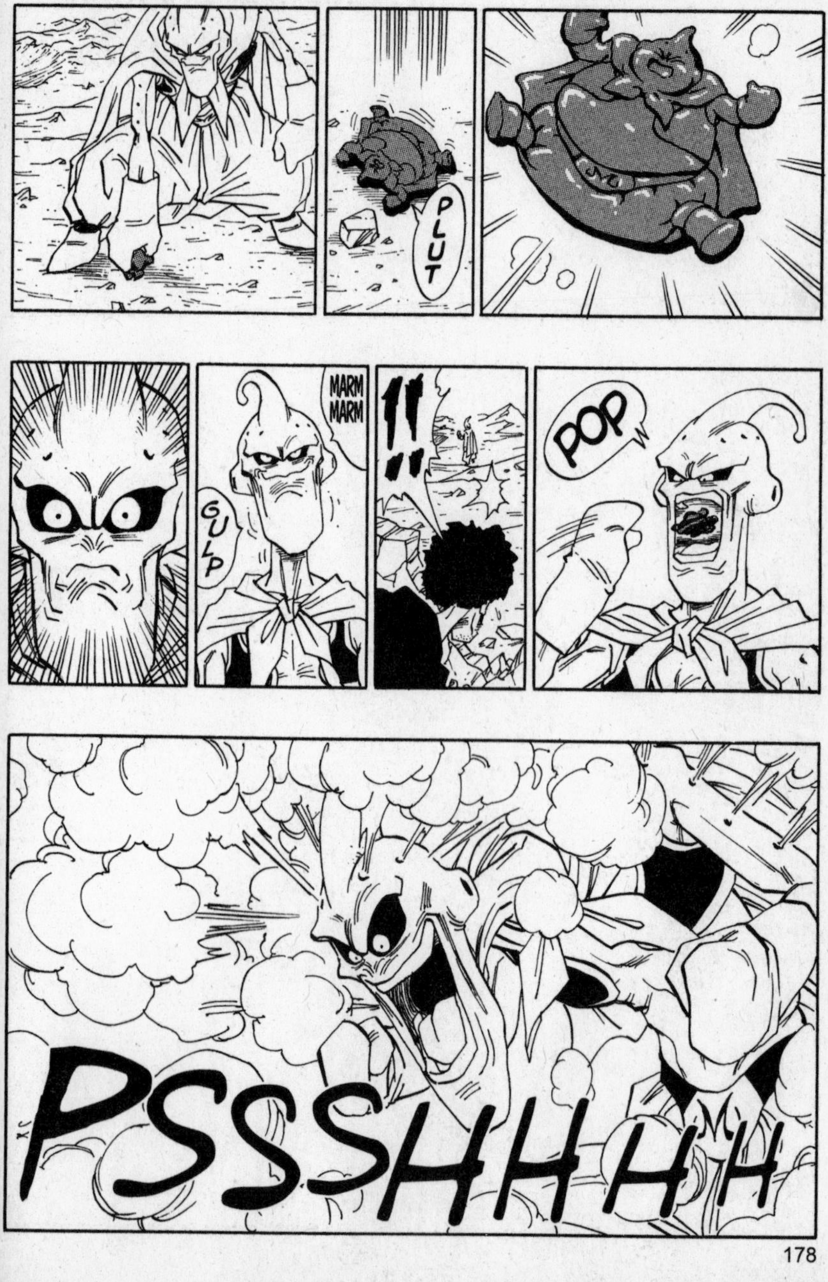
PLUT
POP
!!
!!
MARM MARM
GULP
PSSSHHHHH

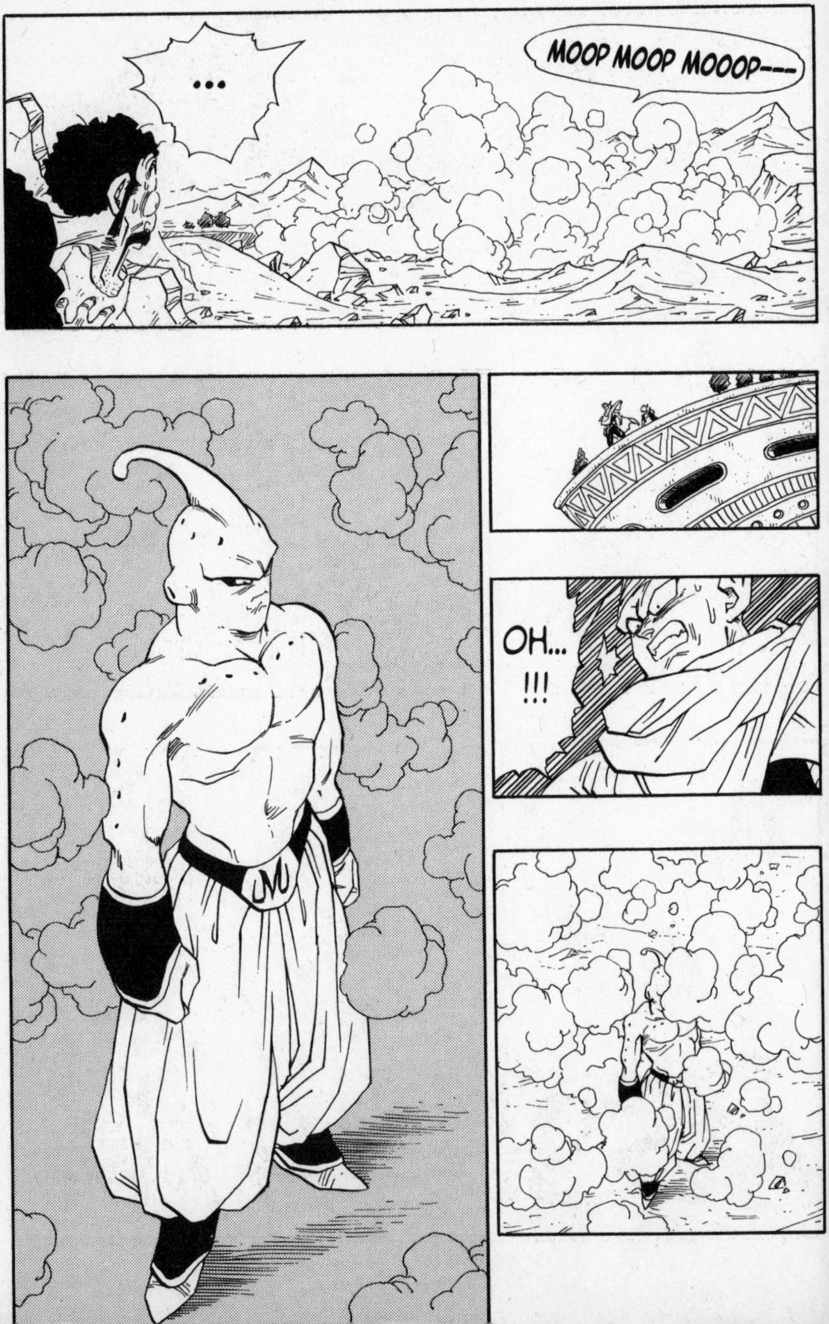
MOOP MOOP MOOOP---
...
OH...
!!!

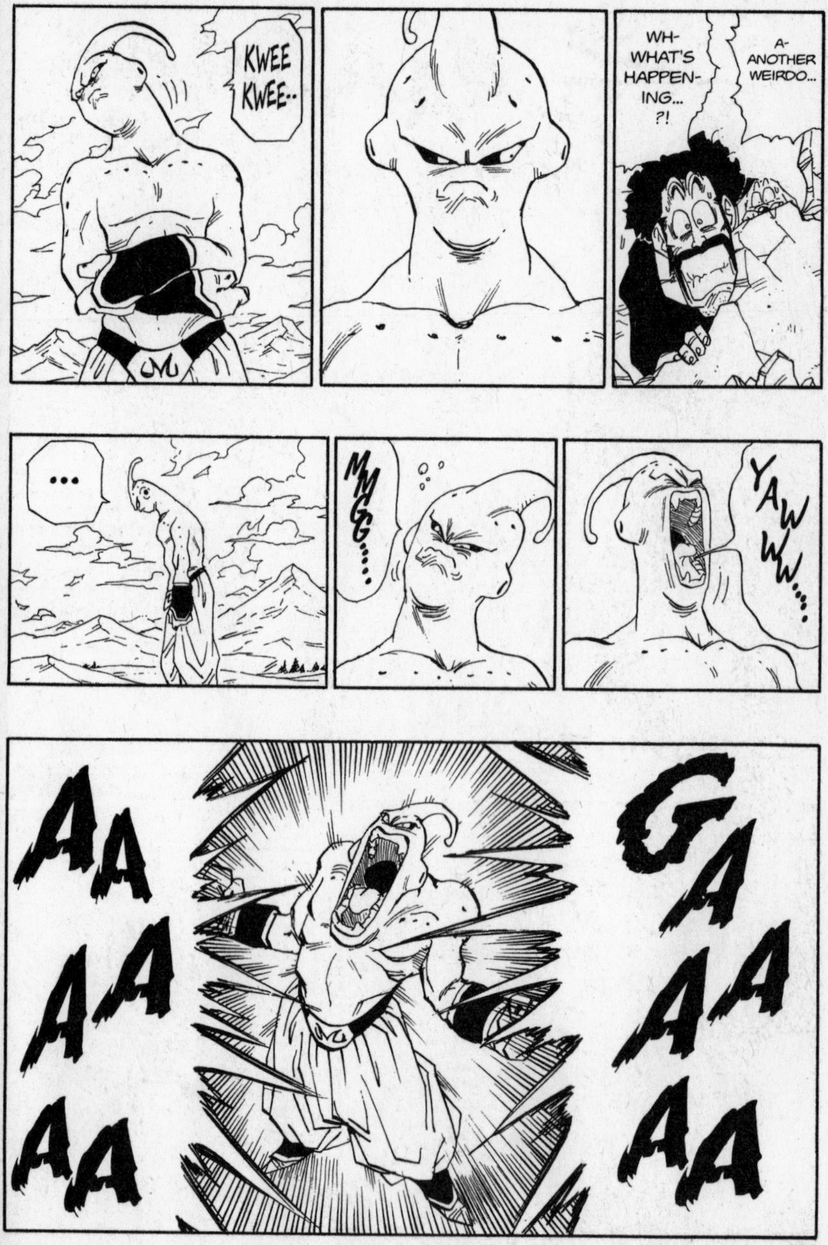
A-ANOTHER WEIRDO...
WH-WHAT'S HAPPENING...?!
KWEE KWEE..
YAWWW....
MMGG....
...
GAAAAA
AAAAAA

«READ THIS WAY«

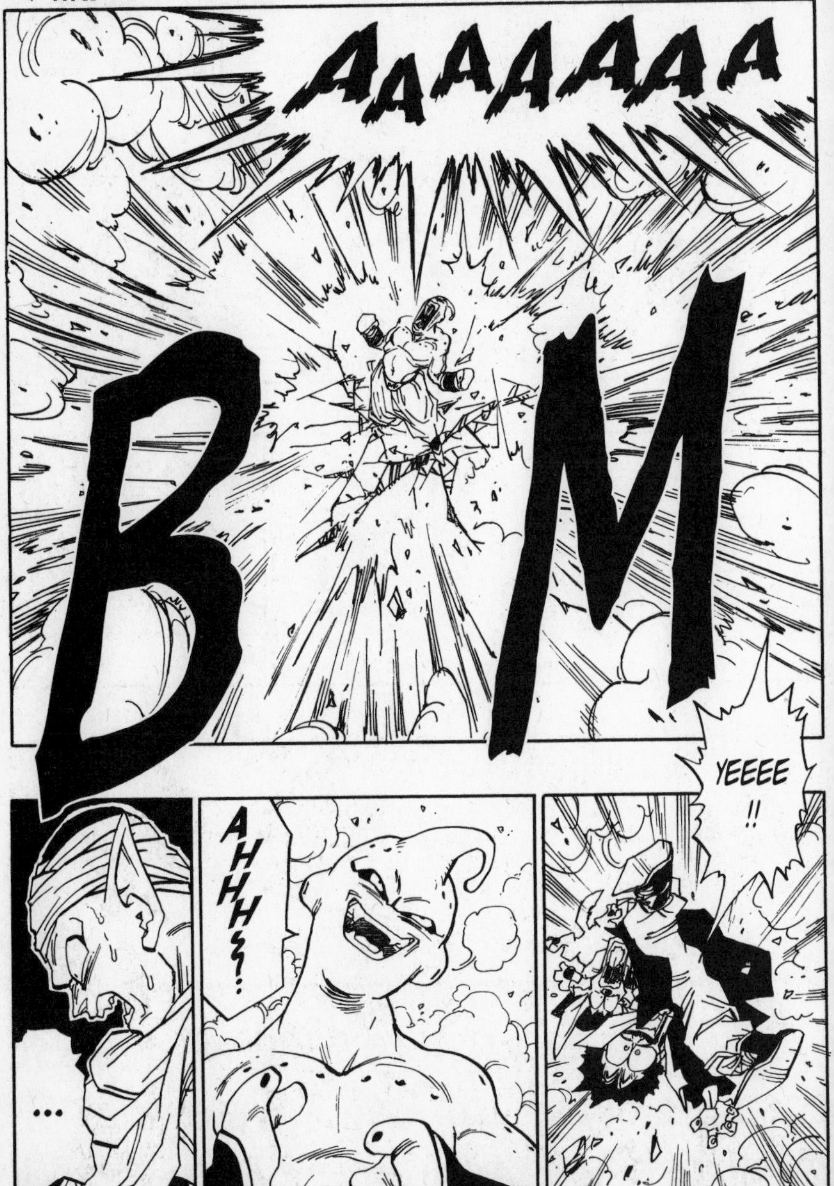
AAAAAA
B M
YEEEE !!
AHHH?!
...

NEXT: The Third Boo!

Title Page Gallery

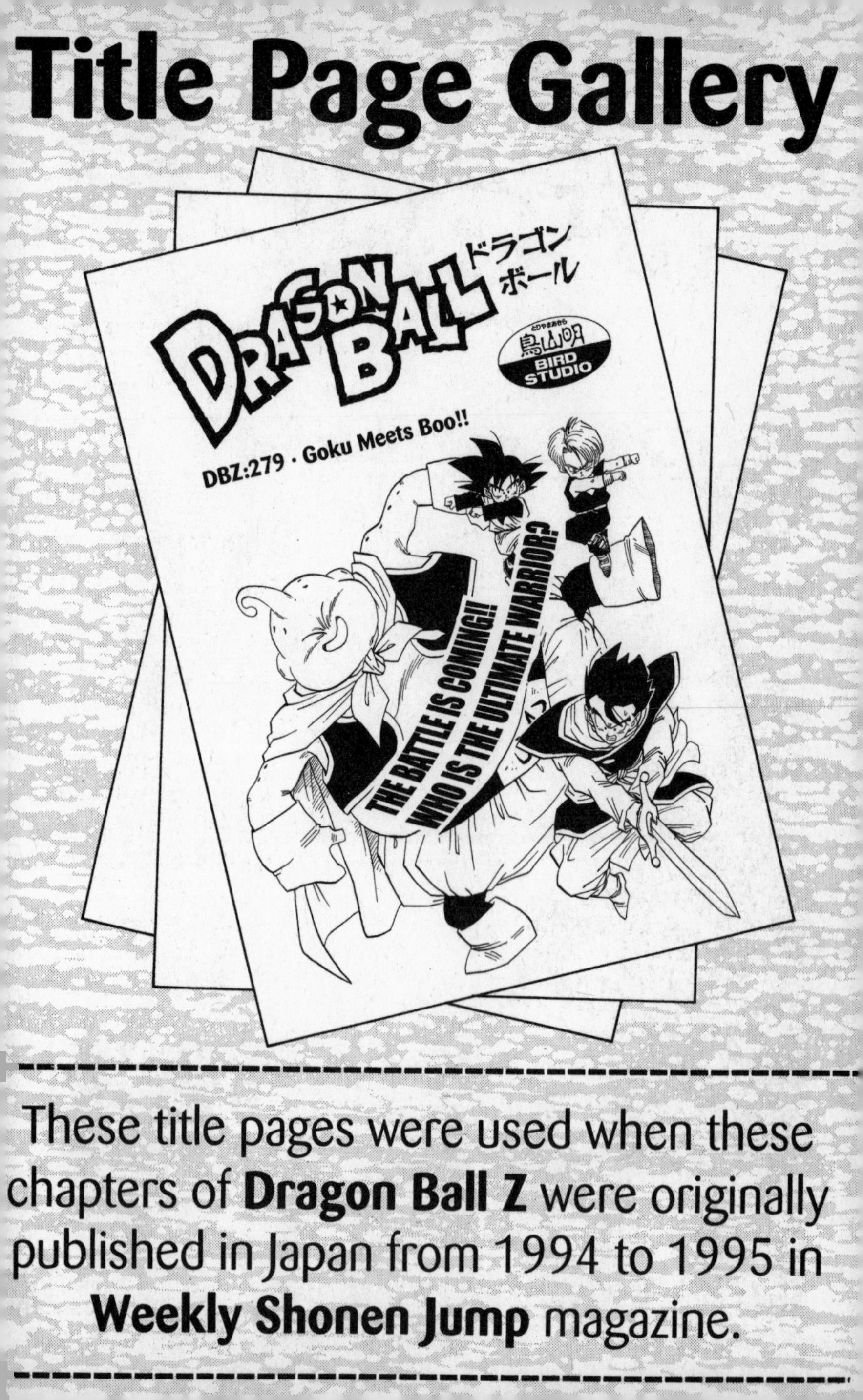
DRAGON BALL
ドラゴンボール
とりやまあきら
鳥山明
BIRD STUDIO
DBZ:279 · Goku Meets Boo!!
THE BATTLE IS COMING!!
WHO IS THE ULTIMATE WARRIOR?

These title pages were used when these chapters of **Dragon Ball Z** were originally published in Japan from 1994 to 1995 in **Weekly Shonen Jump** magazine.

DRAGON BALL ドラゴンボール

とりやまあきら
鳥山明
BIRD STUDIO

DBZ:281 · Boo Unbound

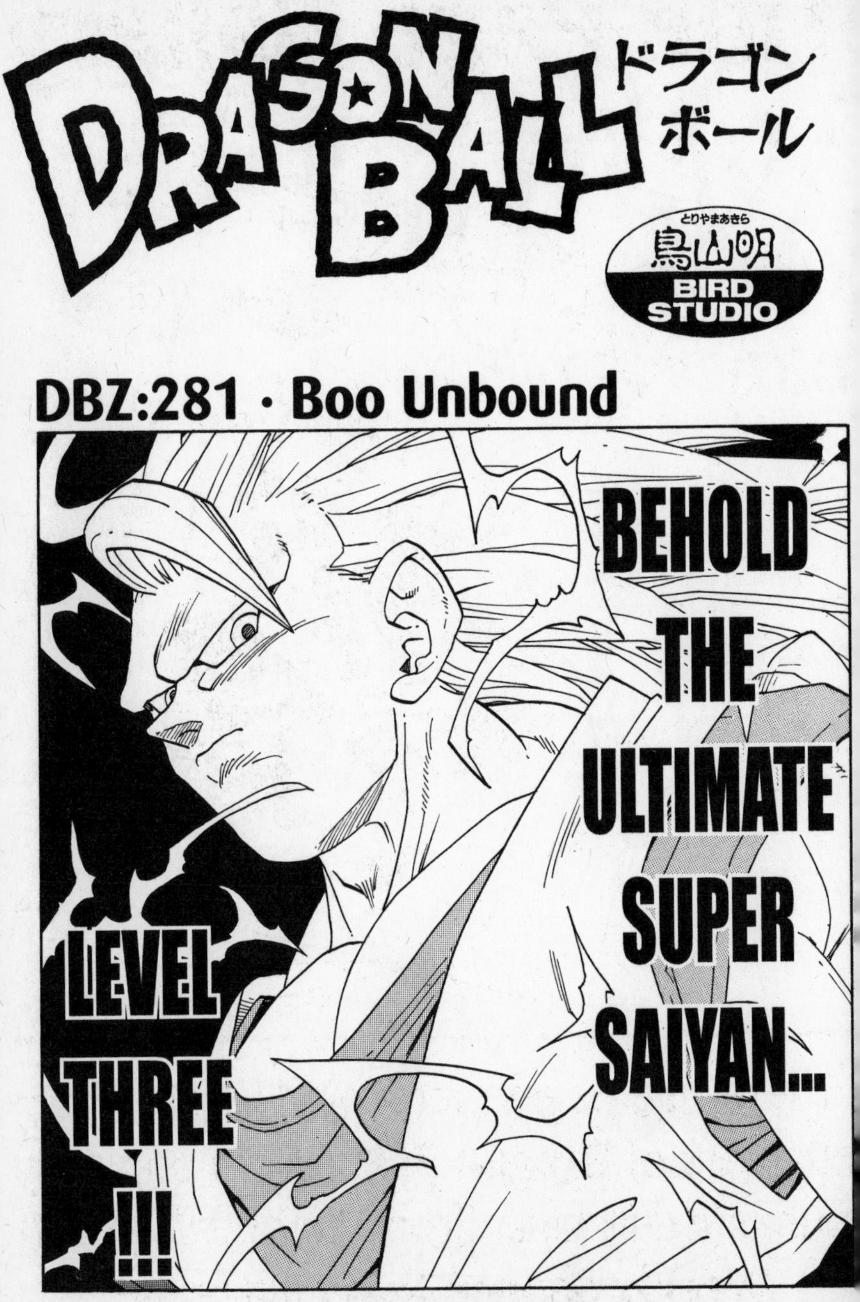
BEHOLD THE ULTIMATE SUPER SAIYAN...
LEVEL THREE !!!

DRAGON BALL ドラゴンボール

とりやまあきら
鳥山明
BIRD STUDIO

DBZ:291 · Two Boos?!

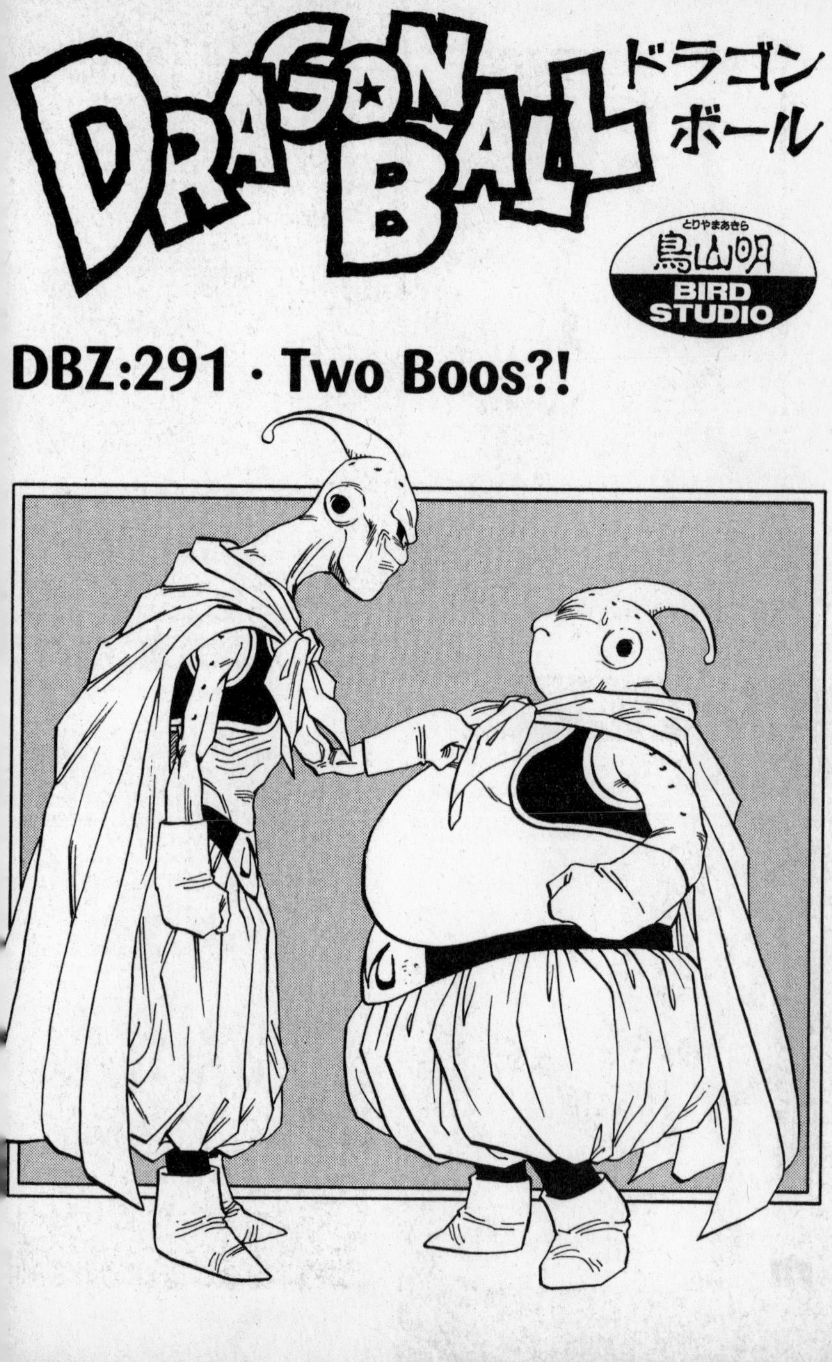

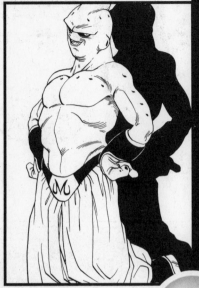

IN THE NEXT VOLUME...

Shorn of his last vestiges of goodness, the djinn Boo is now pure, undiluted evil! Only the heroes in Kami-sama's sky palace are safe from his wrath…but for how long? Inside the palace, Goten and Trunks merge into Super Gotenks, the only being in the world who might match Boo in raw power. But luckily there's more than *one* world. On a faraway planet, Gohan prepares for his turn to fight…to save the devastated earth before the planet itself is blown away!

AVAILABLE NOW!

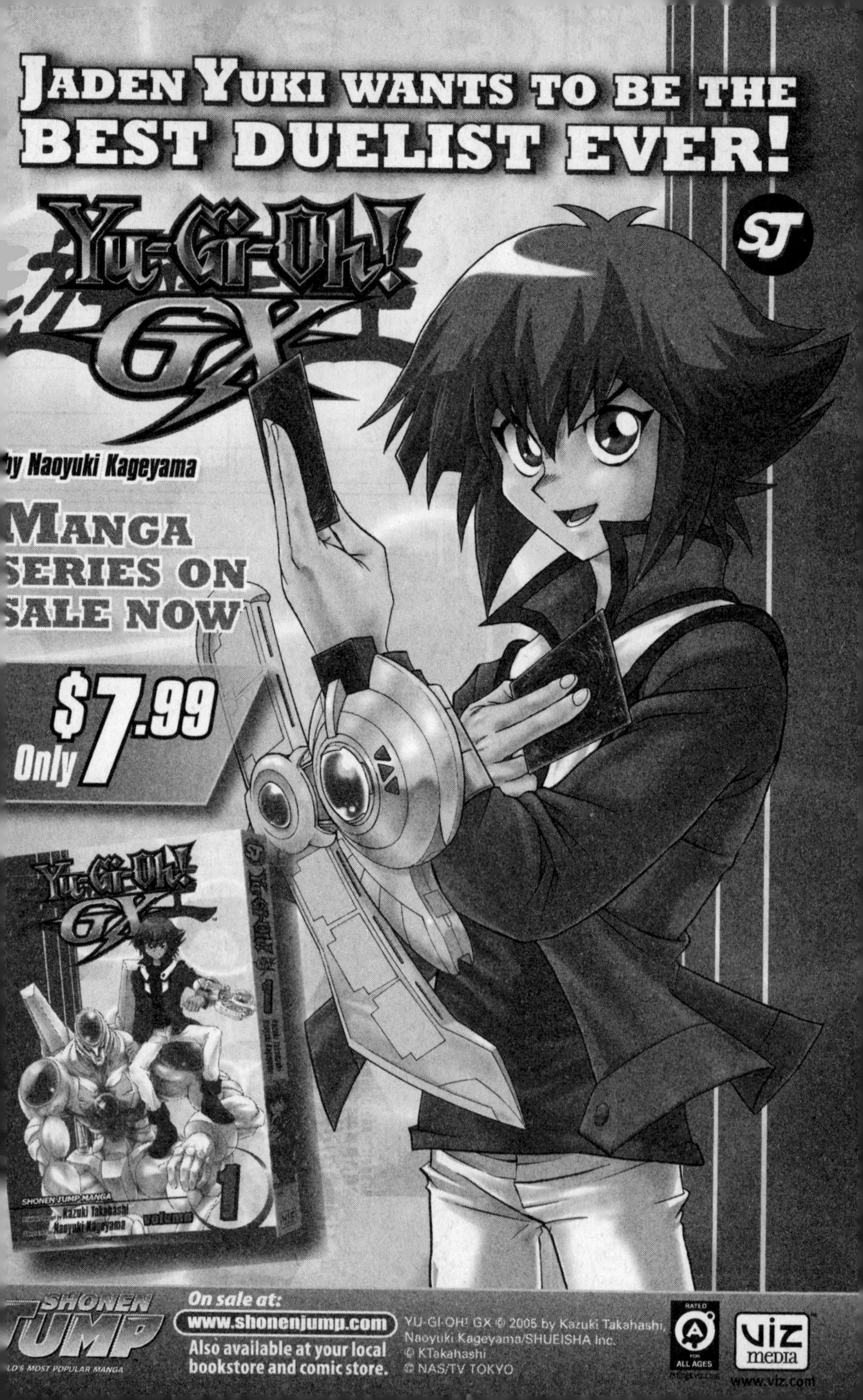
JADEN YUKI WANTS TO BE THE
BEST DUELIST EVER!
SJ
YU-GI-OH! GX
by Naoyuki Kageyama
MANGA
SERIES ON
SALE NOW
Only $7.99
YU-GI-OH! GX
SHONEN JUMP MANGA
Kazuki Takahashi
Naoyuki Kageyama
volume 1
SHONEN JUMP
LD'S MOST POPULAR MANGA
On sale at:
www.shonenjump.com
Also available at your local
bookstore and comic store.
YU-GI-OH! GX © 2005 by Kazuki Takahashi,
Naoyuki Kageyama/SHUEISHA Inc.
© KTakahashi
© NAS/TV TOKYO
RATED A FOR ALL AGES
VIZ media
www.viz.com

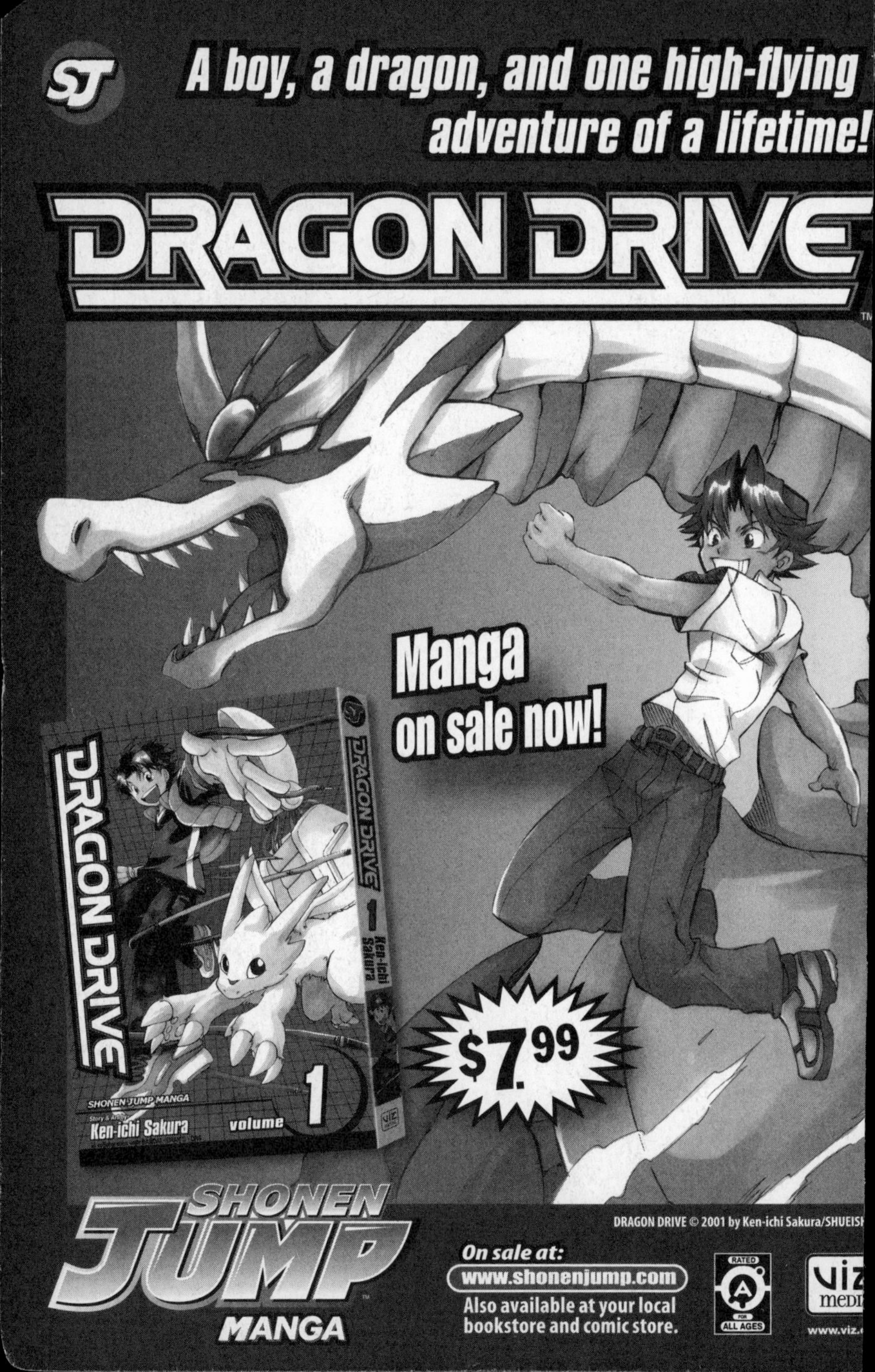
SJ
A boy, a dragon, and one high-flying
adventure of a lifetime!
DRAGON DRIVE
Manga
on sale now!
DRAGON DRIVE
SHONEN JUMP MANGA
Story & Art by
Ken-ichi Sakura
volume 1
DRAGON DRIVE 1 Ken-ichi Sakura
$7.99
SHONEN JUMP MANGA
DRAGON DRIVE © 2001 by Ken-ichi Sakura/SHUEIS
On sale at:
www.shonenjump.com
Also available at your local
bookstore and comic store.
RATED A FOR ALL AGES
viz media
www.viz.

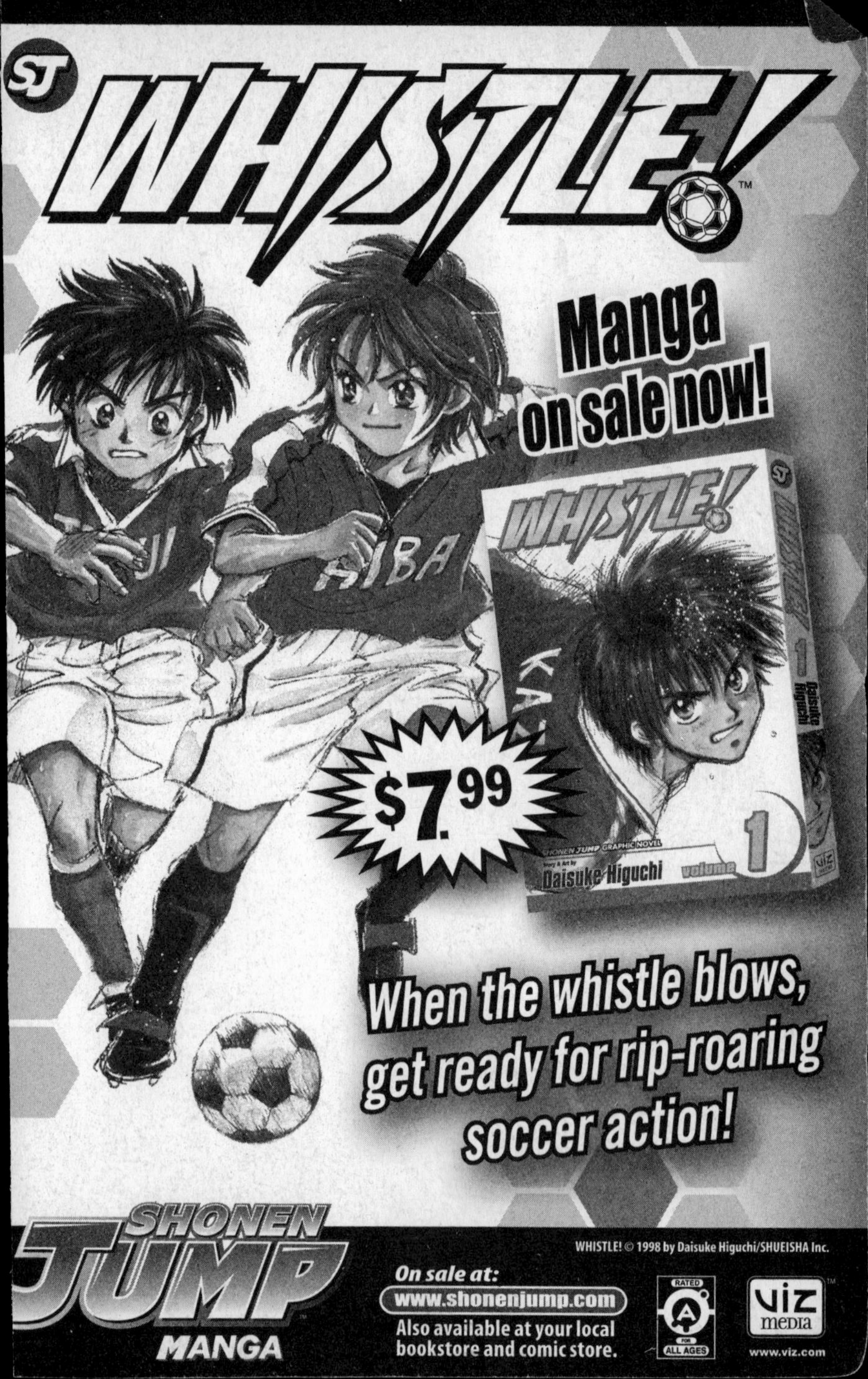
SJ
WHISTLE!™
Manga
on sale now!
WHISTLE!
1
Daisuke Higuchi
SHONEN JUMP GRAPHIC NOVEL
Story & Art by
Daisuke Higuchi
volume 1
$7.99
When the whistle blows,
get ready for rip-roaring
soccer action!
SHONEN
JUMP
MANGA
WHISTLE! © 1998 by Daisuke Higuchi/SHUEISHA Inc.
On sale at:
www.shonenjump.com
Also available at your local
bookstore and comic store.
RATED
A
FOR
ALL AGES
viz media
www.viz.com

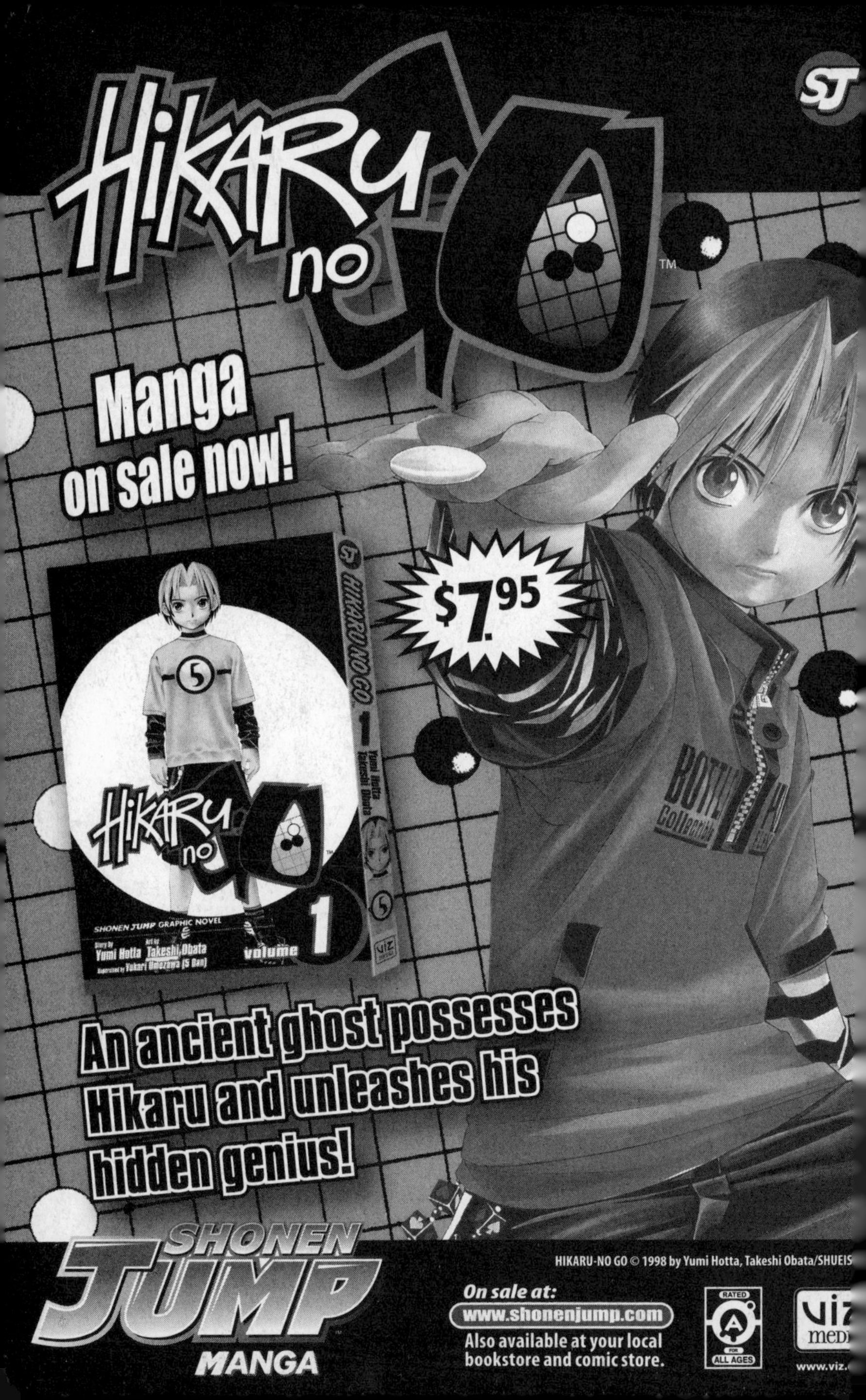
SJ
HIKARU no GO™
Manga on sale now!
$7.95
SJ HIKARU NO GO 1 Yumi Hotta Takeshi Obata
HIKARU no GO™
SHONEN JUMP GRAPHIC NOVEL
Story by Yumi Hotta Art by Takeshi Obata
Supervised by Yukari Umezawa (5 Dan)
volume 1
An ancient ghost possesses Hikaru and unleashes his hidden genius!
SHONEN JUMP MANGA
HIKARU-NO GO © 1998 by Yumi Hotta, Takeshi Obata/SHUEIS
On sale at:
www.shonenjump.com
Also available at your local bookstore and comic store.
RATED A FOR ALL AGES
VIZ MEDI
www.viz.

Tell us what you think about SHONEN JUMP manga!

Our survey is now available online.
Go to: www.SHONENJUMP.com/mangasurvey

Help us make our product offering better!